Cross Wise

{POLITICS?}
(A Crowd-Sourced Third Party?)

All parties are 'crowd-sourced;' then sold to '*special interests*.'
We voters are being defrauded by many of our vain officials.
(You are not naïve to think a third party is a doable project.)

In a "HAPPY Party" (Help All Politicians Protect You) the letter 'H' symbolizes a bridge between two opposite parties, but often with few to no persons crossing over; while 'A' has the bridge but then comes together at the top, which indicates helpful, bipartisan politics. Of course, there will be some apathy, but hopes and prayers are mostly for empathy, because one should be HAPPY to 'Help All Politicians Protect You.' It's all about YOU; and 'you' – in plurality - naturally includes everyone, such as politicians and other public servants, all of whom should be known as 'Service' members if they are correctly and morally serving our nation.

IF American democracy is to be saved, this is our most crucial time since President Lincoln's day, so let's put together a "crowd sourced" 'Happy Party,' to serve us all in bipartisan ways as a "Republicratic" choice for those who would, as often as possible, put the nation's well-being ahead of their own selfish interests. But, we need some proven organizers to begin this crowd-sourced endeavor now, before American democracy is lost, perhaps forever.

The following websites would be made available to you: 'happyparty.info;' 'happyparty.blog;' and 'happyparty.app.' This could be a chance to give the majority of people, looking for a new "Voice" in politics, the opportunity to 'put their money where their mouth is.'

I know you will not give up this fight, just as President Lincoln never did in his time of reckoning. It's time for ultimate civility now – not war! There's no such thing as 'civil' war. All war is uncivil, i.e. not civilized as society should be in this day and age. What's wrong with us? Read on for some clues. We have a few answers, but not all.

Thank you. Contact: codexnexus@gmail.com to volunteer to become the chosen organization to manage this crowd-sourced ENDEAVOR*. Your skills could be vital.

*(Principal guide to our principles)

*[Endeavor to create and sustain a Republicratic democracy]

NOTICE

And disclaimer:
THIS BOOK TEXT IS
OFFERED UNDER A
VARIETY OF TITLES
AND COVERS.

ALSO,

YOU COULD DO THE WORLD A FAVOR IF YOU WERE WISE ENOUGH TO READ AND UNDERSTAND THE BOOK:

"Jesus and John Wayne"

Thank you for love – not hate.

May 1, 2022

A Suicide Note?

It is not for people who model their lives after Jesus Christ. It is for autocrats and others who model Egod.

We could say, for example, this note is, or was, for: ~~Vladimir Putin~~; ~~Rupert Murdoch~~; ~~Donald Trump~~; ~~Tucker Carlson~~; ~~Ted Cruz~~; ~~Lindsey Graham~~; ~~Mitch McConnell~~; or we can just forget the petty bad-mouthing of people such as ~~Nancy Pelosi~~, ~~Adam Schiff~~, ~~Joe Biden~~, and all those with differing opinions since there are way too many to be known outside God's Mind. (Rest assured, a Gracious but judgmental God always has the whole list of "haters," and no trouble applying "Just" usage.)

There are good reasons for the world that some people should change or kill themselves, just as Adolf Hitler did at a time of God's choosing. That is one of the main points of this book. God is Judge and chooses when and why a person is born, based on how he or she will be guided to live their "karmic" life and the necessary effects and affects it will have on other people, as well as their own consequential results in future karma ... <u>IF</u> they have any future lives. Self-consciousness can end forever for some people who live only for materiality.

There is rhyme and reason to God's thinking and this book is an exploratory look into the whys and wherefores of life as we know it. The book is not intended to make you happy or sad; suicidal or not, but rather it is to enlighten you, if that is possible. Can you reluctantly be – "woke?" i.e. awakened?

The answer is NO, if your main interests are power and money at virtually any cost to other living creatures. <u>No</u>, if you have too little WILL and Grace. Sadly the answer is '<u>no</u>' for too many people.

////////////////////////

Not everybody has a soul!
Many people do not.
A soul is a spiritual, mental Cell that comes from God Mind and once was a part of his/her Mind.
Many people have only a spirit/brain, controlled by id and ego.
They do not have the ability to commune with God in a meaningful way. Do you have that ability? Do you use it? If not, it could atrophy and die. Think about that if you will, as - or IF - you read this book.
If you ever wonder why this world is so screwed up... you likely could be one small example of the billions of reasons –because one really cannot reason without God's WILL and Grace.
Which example of hybrid human are you... with God or without?

[From the biblical book of Matthew, Chapter 5; Verse 5]

Jesus said, "The meek* shall inherit the Earth." By 'meek,' He meant the humble and selfless. *[From Merriam-Webster's Dictionary] Main Entry: MEEK

1: enduring injury with patience and without resentment: MILD: not violent: MODERATE.

{Some of you understand certain words the way "Egod" would define them with his preferred "spin." Egod works as a nemesis to God. He is obstinate; however the choice of understanding is yours to make. Some people choose to see 'meekness' as weakness and a character flaw, rather than as an attribute. You would be wise to view it as Jesus did... as a means of togetherness in peace, harmony, and love. You would be wise, intelligent, logical, and loving to survive for eternity with 'meekness,' as God lives it through the Grace and Mercy that SHE bestows on those who deserve it. Someday soon God is only going to allow the meek to reincarnate. They will raise their children to be meek and all such families will inherit the Earth. Evil will not exist.}

<u>YOU</u> are not <u>God</u>.

But did you know you must become God?

In this case, "to become God," means to enhance her and to complement her, to become morally pure, as SHE is. But that's only if we want to live with her forever. We cannot live without her and we can only live as long as SHE allows. Therefore it should be obvious that SHE will only allow those of us who complement her and live as SHE does, to continue our lives with her for Eternity.

Unfortunately, for now, we are "time beings." Most of us have lived here in prior times in other bodies, but with the same souls who try to help us build new spirits to live in Angel forms with God. To this point, we have failed her and ourselves mainly because we did not know or refused to recognize this. Had we known and lived up to her expectations we would not be here now – yet again.

There are good people in this world! However, most people are not as good as God needs us to be. That puts us on an inevitable deathbed without God, because we are all-too-willing to disregard such an unproven Supreme Being, until perhaps our dying breath. But, that has at times given some of us one more chance. God knows our potential. Then again and for now SHE still needs her karmic reincarnations.

Nothing in this work will faze you, however, if you're close-minded, i.e. soulless. If it's not the whimsical "God who?" question - then it's a bold statement such as "There is no God;" or "I'm not afraid to burn in hell," and so on. More of us seem to be tending in the direction of hell through immoral living while ignoring our own hypocrisy. Shame has no effect.

We pretend we are as godly as we need be, in order to get past God into Heaven, <u>IF</u> there really is such a place. We deny that we just pretend to believe; or we are bold enough to admit we don't – how brave – how astute that we are not afraid to burn in hell.

It would be laughable if it were not so tragic.

We will say good-bye now, or soon, to most of you who don't have the courage or wisdom to continue hearing God's story, which also is your story. Good-bye then if you wish to opt out of the only "consciousness program" that exists: the "God Program."

As long as this society is indifferent to, or even gratuitously impressed by, real-life sex and violence, mankind will continue a slide into oblivion – yet again, as it was with past civilizations. Only this time we are abetted by immersive technology, such as TV, computers, movie screens, and so-called "AI" or Artificial Intelligence that can make brain images seem real. What need have we then for real relationships? We are, in fact, God's own AI, and in training.

Too many people are evil because they are ignorant. Ignorance is a disease that can be cured. Ignorance that is bad enough to cause evil is a disease more insidious than cancer. Cancer affects the body, but depending on a person's character, it doesn't necessarily affect a person's soul – IF one has such a God Nexus.

The sickness of evil often does reach a terminal stage affecting the mind. The mind can harbor a tiny soul that conjoins with the brain in physical bodies, but once a body is destroyed, a spirit-soul is set free. Where the spirit then goes with its new freedom depends on how long and to what degree it was incarcerated within this life or prior lives, and how much ignorance it ingested through each, if and when the soul went mostly unused.

Of course the ignorance of which we speak refers to ignoring God's core principle of moral thinking, which would lead to moral living, which would contribute to and complement the "LOG" or 'Life of God.'

The most virulent form of ignorance or evil can be denial of God's very existence, **IF** that leads to immoral thinking and living. But yes, people can recognize the need for morality as a survival mechanism for humanity, without giving much thought to God. God doesn't need your belief in her, just your moral essence and just for your sake. SHE can live without you. You cannot live without her.

It is simple enough to say you believe in God, even as you then turn around and live in a way that proves you don't. You won't acknowledge that proof however, because you are "in denial" about morality, and deliberately choose to live in an evil way and not in the way God set forth for your precursors – Adam and Eve.

God is a "deep" subject and you (your 'tiny' soul-mind) must render some deep, godly thinking to become and remain an eternal Cell or Mental Soul of God.

You might consider that the word "evil" in fact comes from the term "Eve illness." Adam and Eve were the first hybrid humans to willfully follow the dictates of their indiv*id*ual sensual selves as guided by that God creation – the "id," which God first gave animals as an electro-chemical, autonomous survival system. It was meant to automatically cause quick physical reactions to any dangers or potential threats to the body's survival. Then too, for survival of the species itself, 'id' also controlled the reproductive system. That is a lot of power for a non-thinking entity.

However, 'id' was destined to become a thinker, as an integral part of a chemical brain-set of autonomous physiological systems that id guided to become a god-like, personality self known as Id/*Ego*. That id-initiated process gave birth to a brain-minus-soul mind entity that we call "Egod." That birth was innocent enough, but Id/Ego was a vain Egod that reacted to the tiny soul as an invader and enemy to be expelled. This amounted to the birth of evil, which infected the tiny soul of Eve, who became ill from it.

The spirit-soul problems of ignoring God came when the id internalized its mechanism to protect 'id' self against godly or moral thinking that came through the soul-mind rather than just the reactive body brain. The soul, as mind, became an adjunct to the brain when God added cerebral hemispheres to a mammalian species, raising it from animal to humanimal* *(*hyoom*animal). God intended this upgrade to serve as a physical temple through which a tiny mental cell or soul could work. Adam and Eve were the supposed benefactors; but, rather than birthing new Spiritual-Soul beings (be-ins) within their material covers, they gave physical birth to a new generation, termed hyb*rid*s.

Now that a higher level of thinking is required to understand what is written here, it will be quite easy for some folks to ignore. Those infected or affected by 'Eve illness' can simply continue living without God. This work will try to explain how that possibly could sabotage one's eternal life with God, as a potentially mature Soul.

In your current physical life, God considers you a tiny potential cell or soul of her Self. Will you – can you - become a permanent, eternal Soul or mental Cell? That may depend somewhat on how well you understand this work and its moral formula that could cure you of denying God's reality.

Egod tempts you to such denial, in order to keep your thoughts to its id/ego self, with potential degradation of the ability to ever save yourself for God and forever."

Much mind work lies ahead, but only if you can make the soul communal nexus with God Mind. May God bless you in the process of trying, with her help, to <u>SAVIOR SELF</u>!

IIIIIIIIIIIIIIIIIIIIIIIIIIIIIIIIIIIIIIIIIIIIIIIIIII

<u>HOW LONG IS LIFE?</u>
'Is life from birth to death'?
<u>NO!</u>

We are not talking about the life of the fused-spirit body. "Life" is the life of the soul; and would be eternal, if we were compatible with God, but most of us are not.

<u>What is life?</u>

God is life. As Cells, or Souls, of God, we are life as long as God allows and morality says it could be forever.

<u>Morality is God's essence.</u>

The God Cosm is macro huge. As God cells, aka souls, we are micro tiny, and yet we still are parts of God.

<u>Where are we? Who are we?</u>
<u>How did we come to be?</u>
<u>The following quote addresses the term "born again."</u>

'<u>Reincarnation' is but a guiding light</u> ... on the blind trail of death. When this light leads, death may be overcome through round after round of earthly experiences. Then through the lessons these experiences teach, we arrive at the accomplishment of letting go of man-made conditions of creed and dogma that have been imposed upon us. Then we may again step forth into the full glory of God, into the light that is shining just as brightly, which has only seemed dim because we have wandered farther from the Father's House, the House of our own true self unalloyed by man-made creed and superstition.'

Baird T. Spalding
LIFE and TEACHING
Of the Masters of the Far East,
Volume Three, page 156
DeVorss Publications

{'... Egotism... destroys all spiritual activity'}*
*Volume six, page 121

The foregoing might upset some persons who have lost loved ones so young and seemingly innocent that their survivors cannot fathom how those young ones could be responsible somehow for their "untimely" fates. Time within previous lives engendered such karmic consequences. Please trust us on that for now.

Thank you so much! That takes courage and wisdom.

[Give free reign to your tiny soul]

Hateful people hate. It's what they do. They are ignorantly evil; that's what they are.

Gender, Skin color; Moral ethics plus WILL and Grace are... BY GOD!

NOTICE and DISCLAIMER

This work can be found under a variety of covers and titles.

DON'T BUY TOO MANY! On the other hand, it could be banned someday. YOU, or others like you, will decide.

The anti-Christ, Donald Trump, is mentioned herein, but there have been many such pathetic *id*iots* over the course of hybrid humankind. Good people know who they are because oftentimes Egod rules over meek people. *(new clinical definition – see book text)

The Holy Bible speaks of the willfully evil, a.k.a. Egod:

Daniel 8:25

By his cunning he shall make deceit prosper under his hand, and in his own mind he shall become great. Without warning he shall destroy many. And he shall even rise up against the Prince of princes, and he shall be broken—but by no human hand. (All such idiots eventually and somehow are broken by an alien-to-them 'God' - usually through the will of the people acting upon godly principles. Occasionally, if the majority of people are corrupt, God brings disastrous physical results to most of the world's population.)

[Jesus Christ was not of this world. He was from God's Spirit/Soul world, which Christians know as Heaven. Does that not make him an alien God? He said, '*I am in this world but not of it.*' That seems clear.]

Here is another tiny portion of what he had to say, as recorded in the *Bible*:

John 16:12-14

"I still have many things to say to you, but you cannot bear them now. When the Spirit of truth comes, he will guide you into all the truth, for he will not speak on his own authority, but whatever he hears he will speak, and he will declare to you the things that are to come. He will glorify me, for he will take what is mine and declare it to you.

Truth be told

"Confession:" *This book is the author's first effort at writing Spiritual Science Fiction, but don't let that dissuade you from trying it on for size. It might just fit you. It includes some complex truth in novel form. Hopefully you can deal with that and appreciate the outcome. It is a spiritual work based on "space aliens" and "religion" and filled with morally concerned outreach to anyone curious about the meaning of life. This work is revelatory throughout, but please be patient, as certain concepts in the book must be understood before further knowledge can be achieved by reading the epilogue. Thanks for your patience. We will put it to the test.*

What fascinates you - people of every variety? Dogs? Cats? UFOs? What about Angels? What about God? What about Spirit? Soul? What comes after this life? Heaven? Purgatory? Reincarnation? Nothing? What comes to mind when you really have time for contemplative thought? Your belly button? No, now, come on: forget the button. It's strictly yours to contemplate; but all those other subjects are included in this book, along with politics, but not from a political party partisan position.

There seems to be little relief from political actors, but God sees them from the higher view of moral character, just as SHE sees all of us. See what SHE* sees in this book. *(God is not a gender, but rather a twi-polar entity) If you have 'eyes to see,' you'll see.

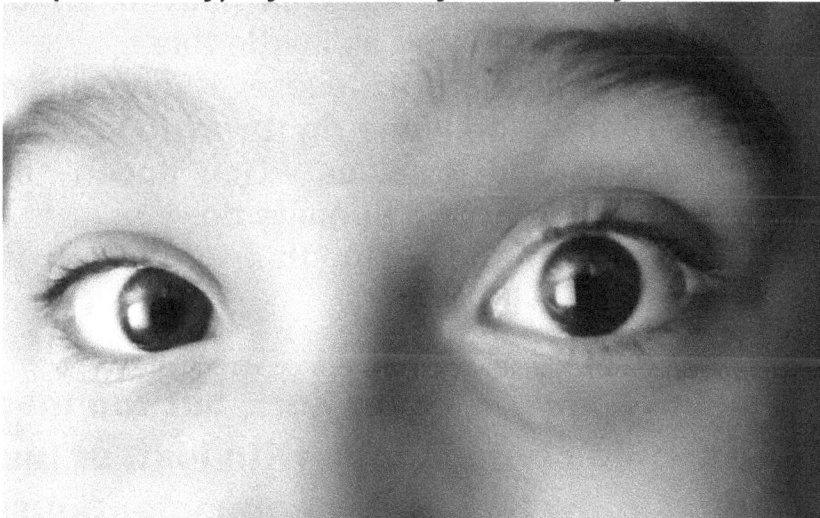

That's where God lives? WOW!

WITH FORESIGHT

I am dedicating this work to my sons and their Mother; to my sister and brother and our parents, and in fact – to the whole family.

I thank them for caring about me even when I did not seem to care. I did, but regret how little I showed it. I love family! I always did. But I later realized I did not show my love enough when all we kids and parents were growing up together.

As a child I never really "learned love." I don't know why not, but I don't blame anyone for that. My parents said they loved us kids and we needed to take them at their word because we were not a touchy-feely bunch.

It saddens me that I also was not more demonstrative in loving my own children. Sometimes we create sadness without even knowing it. But they grew up, seemingly with no overwhelming consequences and that gives me hope for a brighter future since I believe we will see each other again in heaven, which is on the horizon for me as I write this.

I will wait there to love everyone the right way. There is only one right way to love and it is the way God loves us. God doesn't make love hurt. We hybrid humans do.

My dear friend, CKA, this dedication is to you as well, with love.

"Love should never hurt, but too many people confuse love with lust, or just don't know how to love conscientiously."

Are you afraid of <u>GOD</u>?

Are you afraid of Jesus Christ?

Everyone seems to be afraid of something. What about you? No fears?

It doesn't matter how you answer those questions.

No one should be afraid to read this book. Moral knowledge is good.

What about the knowledge of good and evil? Some people think maybe it's time to <u>CHANGE</u> to only the good.

Would you care to think about it? If so, join us; if not, be very afraid of

<u>your personal contribution to Egod.</u>

Okay, let it go for now and come on in. "Savior Self!" The 'Living Water' is perfectly transformative.

PS: I know someone who loves you!

The once _United_ States of America might benefit by adding a third political party?* *(opinion)

We could call it

<u>a</u> crowd-funded Moral Majority, Parti<u>sane</u> Foundation – on behalf of a sociocratic democracy, as opposed to the autocratic deniability of dictators who only allow the powerless minimal liberties. Such is the case with the GOP in the USA.

Welcome to the

"HAPPY PARTY"

Love and peace don't mean socialism; so enough with the politics of fear. There should be equitable freedom for everyone living in a constitutional democracy.
<u>Meanwhile, Political Independents can serve the role of another party that wants to save and secure a stable Republicratic democracy.</u>

This work though really is not about politics. It's about what we are worth as human beings. It points out why human beings are in this world and what we naturally were created by God to be and do. We were meant to become Children of God. God's Children are graced with Moral Intelligence, which seems to be especially lacking in political endeavors. There is a cancer-like growth of immorality in many politicians everywhere – as well as in their constituents. Such politicians in virtually every country are misleading people into an evil system of incompetent non-governance that would put one gross ego-maniac in charge of all our lives. Hard to imagine, isn't it, that eternal life with God is on the line; even to a great extent literally on an electronic line known as the Internet, which adds to both evil and good. Which do you choose? Do you even know the difference? Do you know God, or have you decided to go your one life alone, without any after-life? Are we talking to you? God knows.

IIIIIIIIIIIIIIIIIIIII

Something to think about:

"Justice will not be served until those who are
unaffected are as outraged as those who are."
- Ben Franklin

"Those who desire to give up freedom
to gain security will not have either one."
BEN FRANKLIN

"Either write something worth reading
or do something worth writing."
- Benjamin Franklin

"We are trying, while hoping
to not overwhelm you.
Just know God will try you
ABOVE AND BEYOND
any understanding of this work,
so please make the most of it."

- The Author –

We hope your knowledge and life experience of the God-defined good and evil concepts will help you understand how difficult your task of overcoming your "id/ego" is; and how hard reverting to godly, moral thinking will be, in order to attain eternal life.

Moral explanation forthcoming

DOWNDATE*
[01/06/21]
*(in history)
From the QAnon cult:
"Where we go one, we go all,"
in urgent need of kissing the butt of the
Coup* Clucks Clown.
He demands it, and we bow to
his authority over democracy.
All hail our glorious leader!
Now get in line!
*(coup d'état)

"If all printers were determined
not to print anything till they were
sure it would offend nobody, there
would be very little printed."
- Ben Franklin
{Ben was quite a pithy writer. He
seemed to get pithed off rather easily.
He was a tersely cogent man - often
quoted and rightly so, as
we don't mind proving.}

*"The only person you become
is the person you decide to be."*

Ralph Waldo Emerson
IIIIIIIIIIIIIIIIIIIIIIIIIIIIII

"PRE-LOG"

This writer is not a fan of labels, but will counteract them in his way. Labels too often are judgmental. He therefore hesitates to call anyone a loser, sucker, or any derogatory name; but will express his thoughts regarding apparent idiocy or ignorance, which may or may not be evil. He uses those terms for their effect on readers choosing to believe they are morally intelligent while proving the opposite. Some may never consider that *morality is inherent* in godly thinking. If they were to understand how likely the possibility is that they are misguided in whatever fanaticism they are suffering, it could help their frame of mind and morale. They might decide to become wise enough to discern that at least some people <u>are</u> ignorantly evil – even blatantly so in the case of personality cults – their own or someone they follow, even if invented anonymously.

"Being ignorant is not so much a shame, as being unwilling to learn." <u>Ben</u> <u>Franklin</u>

Many such extremist 'cults' can be as low and loathsome as individual members who enjoy repeating their own personal fantasies, even as they assign them to the "enemy." They don't all think exactly alike, but they do like socializing with people with whom they can "yuck it up" with equal, if somewhat disputed opinions. Most people are social creatures, and in this case it's the "birds of a feather flock together" allegory. As trite as it may sound, we usually seek people with ideas we have in common.

In the not so distant past, many of these same people would have found church to be a healthy outlet for their group social activities. Too many now think religion and God are old-fashioned – either that or they have fashioned their beliefs to fit the mood of the times, even if it means going beyond the needs of love and moral righteousness.

Thanks to the constant preaching of divisive propaganda, social needs often have turned hateful, destructive and self-righteous, even as a cult tosses the names Jesus and God all around their foolish thoughts and acts. They are proud of themselves and beholden to no one; not God, nor good, moral government, both of which they now seem incapable of recognizing if ever they could. Both concepts are vital however, as morality would be mankind's saving Grace as granted by God.

Far-right political propaganda outlets such as Fox News just want "cult" money and will misguide their audiences as much as necessary to keep them thinking in a way that coincides with business greed. "You," however, can inform and educate yourselves by surveying the total political and religious landscape to do what the world needs. You can elect to grow the ever-shrinking majority, which still sides with one real, moral God. This one God will confront the likes of Rupert Murdoch,* and Donald Trump quite soon, along with others who trade lies for power and money. *(tycoon)

Power and money-driven politicians and business magnates now resort to extreme social hubris; so much so that it almost requires the word "shame" to be stricken from the modern dictionary when it comes to those who would encourage hate groups. Ignorance and idiocy are synonyms when these people are considered, but if it produces money or votes for them, so be it. They don't mind at all if people die.

The writer, or most anyone, can observe the foregoing without judging anyone. That's God's job and SHE often dispatches it with Grace. It's <u>her</u> job, even if you don't yet believe God is opposite polarities. S<u>HE</u> and HE is one God.

It's every person's job to continue the task given us by events in the garden* of Eden. We cannot stop being aware of the knowledge of good and evil. We must continue to understand morality and its opposite and always choose our better angels, our tiny soul and Over Soul when it comes to thinking and doing. You either have the conscience for that, or your id/ego is in charge, unfortunately. *{A hybrid garden; therefore miniscule as compared with prior perfect Gardens.}

Even so, it is not necessary to believe in God in order to have a life beyond this one. God has no ego that demands you believe in her. However, you will need "moral intelligence," to maintain a life acceptable to God for living eternally with her, which of course would cause you to know without doubt SHE is real. For that knowledge, you will need WILL power way above what you now possess. You will also need God's saving Grace to attain to such heights.

WILL and Grace are aspects of God's own moral intelligence. WILL, as written here, is the capitalized acronym for "Wisdom; Intellect (or Intelligence); plus Logic, and Love." Majuscule Grace is God's own Essence, along with her WILL. Hybrid* humans in their physical state can have only a smaller portion of 'will' and 'grace.' If they maintain those moral "starting points," God can help them. *(We will explain the term 'hybrid' humans as we continue.)

None of us has the right to judge another, but we do have a moral obligation to discern if something or someone is good or evil. The characteristics of 'good and evil' became part of mankind's DNA/RNA physicality in the garden of Eden. When Eve failed the test that God; the "Lord God;" and Satan placed before her as a temptation, she was proven to be "ill" {i.e. Eve-ill, or evil}. Adam failed that same "Spiritual Mentality" test when tempted by Eve. And so it was revealed to them "for their knowledge" they were a new generation of imperfect humans – preferring physicality to Spirituality.

God had made them perfect, which means they had the right to make choices and they unwittingly chose evil, which essentially means they replaced God with themselves – with their physical desires rather than faithfully staying in communion with their highest aspect of "God Mind" through their mental cell (soul). They even allowed they were equal to God, thus giving birth to the concept of ignorance, as they ignored godly Wisdom constantly offered to them.

God knew they would struggle with many more choices throughout their lives and SHE knew each spirit-soul within them would need to be born again into new bodies. SHE knew some of their descendents would require multiple lives and many would fall completely from Grace into hell – essentially life in detention – with remedial intervention for those who showed any interest.

Our following story tells the hybrid human story. It might seem complex to some readers, while others may find it simple, if a bit odd at times. It is designed for a wide audience, but it does require from us 'discernment,' 'imagination,' and of course 'moral intelligence' through will and grace, but without judgment of anyone. Again, that's God's job, even though we choose to usurp much of her profound responsibilities, through ignorance and denial.

We wish you God's Grace in navigating this book's truths, but it will require a fluid mind intermingled with 'God Mind,' meaning you must find the ability to open your tiny soul to her for communion.

[Questions – Questions]

Where have all the *Bibles* gone? Many have been replaced by political manifestos. Where are all the souls who cared? When is the last time you saw a *Bible*? – opened it – read from it – understood what you read – understood the *"Old Testament"* features a hybrid generation's growing pains of sex and violence, while the *"New Testament"* mostly is about redemption? Good and evil are always part of the hybrid equation.

Has religion become superstition? Has this society become too sophisticated for God? Are we morally wiser than Jesus Christ?

Where is God? Have you heard from her lately – or ever? Is mankind as good as dead without God? Are you doing just fine without her? Are you proud of yourself and unafraid to burn in hell? Just know if you burn with enough shame, God may have mercy on you at some point and grant you another chance at life.

When will you realize this world is hell without God? You may be well situated, but this world is filled with billions of suffering people! Do you ever wonder how you can help? Can you, at the very least, pray and allow your pastors to preach?

If you're not in love with the thought of God you won't find her in this work. If you are – you will!

||||||||||||||||||||||||||||||

-PROLOGUE-

In the beginning, there was no beginning. It didn't come until the end.

The author and his/her "soul mate*" wrote a book – this book. They finished the book over and over; time after time for what they always thought was the final time (Could this be it?). "This is it," they thought. But, it wasn't. They came back here to see if they could clarify something that was nagging them about the *biblical book of Genesis.* *(Your soul is intended to mate with the spirit you create during your lifetime. That pairing equates to 'mind.' Many people use only their fused spirit brain, minus a spiritual soul nexus to God Mind, through what should be a tiny angel self.)

The garden of Eden story is so lacking in context that the author wanted to clarify a couple of key points.

Who is this "Lord God" responsible for creating Adam from the dust of the earth? Why is He called "Lord," and not just simply "God?" It is because as with the 'Lord' Jesus Christ, He was a Child of God – a "COG." [This book will explain new and old concepts. Keep in mind, it is a novel.]

This particular Lord or COG was sent to Earth to begin the hybrid generation in this realm, which had been one of many hosts to God's perfect generation of Children Co-Created within the material aspect of her universal Gardens. This is covered in detail as we proceed. First though we take another look at the *Genesis* story.

God needed a hybrid type man to till the ground of the earth because SHE knew a man with a more advanced brain would be able to teach humans* remaining on earth how to "farm" and generally survive without constant guidance by the COG - Children Of God.

*[All humans were created from "humanimals," (hyoom-animals). They were created both male and female by God. Prior to the hybrid generation they always upgraded into Perfect Humans for use in creating God's Humangels (Hyoom-angels). Essentially humanimals were cocoons from which God could form her Angel Spirit-Souls primarily of RNA polymerase in all its synthesis aspects for Heavenly requirements that cannot be explained here by this author.]

Obviously, if Adam and Eve were created as the *first* hybrid humans on Earth, they would not be needed to teach less intelligent beings already here how to survive and evolve. So, with Adam's creation, the Lord God was upgrading a new generation of humanimals – the hybrid one – but to what end? Why was such a generation desired, following the prior Perfect Humangels raised in Gardens around the universe?

Our story will explain that, but let's get back to Adam and Eve's peculiar, but special, start in this world.

First of all, the material universe, along with everything else, was created from Spirit – a living Essence from the Body and Mind (Soul Consciousness) of God. However, God's material aspect was "fused," that is to say "tightly compacted" through the enormous power of God's final "Big Bang" breach birth.

In that early time when the universe was settling into place, the dust of planets was powdered living spirit and not as fused or dense as the soil below, which also contained spirit life, as did all matter in varying degrees. It was then that God re-created aspects of her fused life into physical, spiritual forms to include humanimals, which SHE would later raise to Human status and then to Humangels. Her first generations of such forms finally met her needs for putting herself back together in Heaven after her Twi-polar Minds banged 'heads,' so to speak, causing all manner of chaos and confusion.

It was eons after her perfect Gardens that God upgraded all her remaining planetary human corps into hybrids for a unique generation. Confusing? How can it not be, since this information is new and different and may seem complicated to some of you? It will resolve into a fictional setting for moral philosophy – possibly even a happy new beginning. 'Hold that thought,' as many people would say.

With the creation of a hybrid Adam and Eve in every planetary garden, each such generation could be described in the same way: *Genesis,* Chapter Two, verse six: ... *there went up a mist* (living spirit)* *from the earth, and watered the whole face of the ground.* Notice the spirit mist came *up* from the earth. The Lord God made only the amount he needed to rise from the top soil. *(this original Spirit was still alive, even though annihilated from the Big Bang.)

Verse seven: *And the Lord God formed man of the dust of the ground, and breathed into his nostrils the breath of life; and man became a living soul.* (One of our novel aspects explains a bit of "technology" as the Lord performed this creation from within his TranShip lab, using a hologram and a Laser Activated Radiation Ray - aka a "LARray.") [We will classify that explanation as fiction for now, since the book is a novel.]

So then the Eden story continues that the Lord planted a garden eastward in Eden, and put the man there. [For God, 'planting a garden' meant COG were putting life forms there]

Verse 9: And out of the ground made the Lord God to grow every tree that is pleasant to the sight, and good for food; the tree of life also in the midst of the garden, and the tree of knowledge of good and evil. The *Bible* also tells us, He created

Eve from Adam. It does not state that He breathed a soul into her. But God gave her a "tiny" aspect of Adam's soul. She then qualified as mostly human, rather than simply humanimal (Hyoom-animal). So, she could, if she chose, commune with God through her tiny soul.

Why did the Lord place those trees of 'life' and 'knowledge of good and evil' in the garden if not to test Adam as regards his upgraded brain and new soul? The Lord told the couple to stay away from those trees. In fact, He said they would die if they tasted fruit of the tree of knowledge of good and evil. Eve especially became curiously entranced by such mystery, just as God knew she would, also knowing she would tempt Adam. Yes, God made the perfect pair but also knew they would not remain so for long. That fact became part of God's plan for all of us.

Eve finally ventured quite close to the tree of "good and evil." She really wanted knowledge from the fruit of the tree, so obviously she knew the meaning of the word "knowledge," but wasn't sure what the knowledge of 'good and evil' might portend.

She approached a woman and man who had just finished sampling from the tree of knowledge of good and evil, as the Lord called it. The humans Eve met were of the Serpent species, which was a cross-breed of an Ant man and a Tares woman from the Scorpio region of the now red giant star known as Antares. The COG had relocated a variety of humans to the Earth's solar system from other planets. Now, here they were - the most experienced of any species on Earth then. They were among those humans with tiny souls.

They both had taken fruit of that tree many times and obviously it did not kill them. This is what the man told Eve, and induced her to try it with her own husband who was nearby. Somewhat later, Eve convinced Adam to try it, and he did with her. They agreed it was good fruit.

Genesis, Chapter three, verse 22: And the Lord God said, Behold, the man is become as one of us, to know good and evil: and now, lest he put forth his hand, and take also of the tree of life, *[the 'tree of life' for hybrids is "parenthood," and the Lord knew that was in the offing for them. God had made it inevitable for the Eden couple, but their "forever" life would be made much more difficult by karma and reincarnation, making it next to impossible for some hybrid humans to get back to God Consciousness.]

It was not long after their disobedience that the new couple realized the power of the knowledge of evil or "Eve illness." The Lord already had named the opposite of 'Good' as 'Evil" stemming from Eve-illness. That tree provided the Lord God the results He needed in order to show the hybrid couple they had big problems. The Lord showed them they were untrustworthy to serve God's Essence on a continual, faithful basis.

This newly formed couple, one with a tiny soul and one (A Son) with an upgraded brain and compromised, once pure Soul, understood now their immediate physical desires and needs would take precedence over their spiritual communion with their Creator. It would be something separating them from pure morality and thus from God herself. It would be at the heart of what they must change in order to serve with God for eternity. They disobeyed God through their own essence. It was a critical id/ego test, and the first for the hybrid generation. After the Lord God showed them they were revealed as naked or imperfect in God's eyes, He told them of the death and reincarnation fate awaiting them and their progeny from the hybrid version of the 'tree of life,' which was distinct from the "tree of life" that Humangels enjoyed for eternity. The Angel, so-called 'tree' produced pure Spirit for their consumption or for any soul who took of it.

The Serpents (Ants) were cave dwellers and their fate was to go about life underground, which they did and their tribe still is doing to this day – out of sight. The Ant Serpent had intentionally misinformed Eve regarding God's intentions. He did it out of ignorance, jealousy and spite. He had wanted to be chosen by God for a DNA and soul upgrade. He was only able to communicate with Eve because Satan adjoined* him briefly. Satan was God's purity tester through temptation and so the Lord had no doubt as to what would transpire with hybrid humans. *(cohabited)

Nonetheless, the Lord told the cave dwellers they would remain underground and in certain times and ways the humans above them would infringe on their lives ('*bruise his head*'). He likewise told the first hybrid couple they and their ancestors would suffer *(have their heels bruised)* because of their neighbors below them. In other words, they would share in their enmity toward one another. Most Antares humans now are more moral than the good folks above them. Even so, evil is everywhere in the material realm. Ants (Yang or male) and Ares (Yin or female) are not immune.

Surface governments that know Antares people exist don't disclose it, even as the Ants have flown UFOs to 'bruise' mankind's self-vaunted egoistical status. Some governments have fought back in the past with underground nuclear "testing." Even so, for some time now a few governments have been cooperating closely with the Antares people on both technological and diplomatic matters. Public disclosure will soon be unavoidable so that continuing progress can be made to benefit both societies. *'And it shall come to pass,'*

Being more broadminded and morally enlightened, governing Ants have never tried to hide human surface existence from their people. However, they have been discreet about showing themselves above; or to quote the *(KJV)* book of *Genesis, Chapter 9, Verses 13 and 14: 'I do set my bow* in the cloud, and it shall be for a token of a "coven ant" between me and the earth.' – '<u>And it shall come to pass</u>,* when I bring a cloud over the earth, that the bow* shall be seen in the cloud.'* *(Ship's bow) [This has been made manifest and whole ships have been seen for some time now.]

The result Adam and Eve experienced upon disobeying God was in knowing the dual opposite polar powers each of their minds and bodies had for one another. They lusted for physical intimacy more than they ever had for mental communion with the Lord God. They no longer were protected by the innocence of COG Mind – as compared to the strong, fused, fleshly lust they had for one another. They were naked (fully aware) of their desires and their preference toward each other, rather than toward their Creator. The "karmic" result was rendered as the Lord said it would be.

(It was Adam and Eve who chose the intimacy of sexual bonding. It brought them a family, but also death and reincarnation into another material life. How many material lives one must suffer depends on when one is morally ready to live spiritually with God forever.) [God's Plan dictated the Lord's reaction to Adam's failing as the first hybrid human on Earth.]

Verse 23: Therefore the Lord sent him forth from Eden, to till the ground from whence he was taken. The Lord God told Adam he now was Lord of his own garden and so then He left the human couple to the repercussions of hybridism. Their children were to mix and mate with unenlightened (spirits without souls) humanimals or any humans with tiny souls who also lived alongside them in the garden. Adam became "Lord" over them, since a leader was needed and he still had a once-pure soul with some extra godliness. That made him somewhat Human in his advanced non-perfection.

Verse 22 reveals a most important point: God wants her tiny souls (explained in the book) to eventually live forever with her as her Children Souls. SHE showed them they were not yet sufficient to the task of becoming pure Mental Moral Essence. They would need to contend with the temptations of a material world and learn through trial and error. The errors continue multifold but the trial is about over for this era of mankind. God of course knows the dates SHE has set for her material world civilizations to expire.

<u>YOU</u> EXIST ONLY BECAUSE GOD IS
<u>RAISING</u> <u>GOD</u> <u>JR</u>.

"I am not here to judge you.

I am here to judge me;

So that I might be better prepared

for God's judgment someday."

{The author}

TABLE OF CONTENTS

Pre-log: p. 19
Prologue: 22
Preamble and
Commentary: 30
Interview: p. 33
Introduction: p. 35
Wake Up: 38
Chap 1: Egod; p. 39
Chap 2: Deep Diddly
Squat; page 52
Chap 3: Mind; 63
C 4: Robo Chef; 67
Chap 5: Roll Over; 82
Chap 6: Deepy Goes
Off; page 97
C 7: Shel Games; 114
Chap 8: Reincarnation
page 121
Chap 9: Moon Beamed
page 140
C 10: Tiny Time; 166
Chap 11: Yin Yang-
Big Bang; page 191
Chap 12: Grace Era;
p. 202
Chap 13: Think
Again; p. 208
Chap 14: May I Help;
page 219
Chap 15: The End is
Near; page 231
Chap 16: Hitler's
Karma; page 246
Chap 17: Dia Logos;
page 255
Chap 18: Foxes &
Wolves; page 277
Chap 19: I'm Woke;
page 286

Chap 20: Homo
Sapient; page 298
Chap 21: Nemesis; 314
Chap 22: Life; 327
Chap 23: Dreamer;
page 342
Reprieve 346
On Reflection &
2012: page 348
Chats & Notes: p. 352
PS: p. 354
After Words: p. 355
Enote: page 357
Deep Note: p. 358
Chap. 24: Satan; 360
Chap. 25: Rest; p. 373
Shel Note: p. 381
Author: p. 382
Eno Update: p. 383
Dark Evil: page 385
~~~~~~~~~~~~
Epilogue: Apocryphal,
Gospel Truth – p. 387
*{Unimaginable if you
don't read this book first;
and maybe even then.}*
~~~~~~~~~~~~~~

*JESUS PROMISED
EVERYDAY HIDDEN
WOULD BE REVEALED.
THIS ISN'T EVERYTHING,
BUT IT'S A LOT!*
WWG1WGAF1G
Where We Go 1
We Go All
FOR 1 GOD!
*That's how it should be,
and we pray you are
redeemed if need be. God
knows. Thank you.*
||||||||||||||||||||||||||||||||||

"Cross Wise"

<u>This book updates that ultra-raw, indigestible work,</u> but it still could give some of you heartburn and/or cleanse your soul.

We don't give enough meaning to some words, so that they also can produce results. Please consider a word that too many of us perhaps ignore almost completely: <u>Moral</u>; to include a few synonyms from Webster's Collegiate Dictionary: Ethical; Virtuous; Righteous; Noble – All mean "conforming to a standard of what is right and good." <u>Moral</u> implies conformity to established sanctioned codes or accepted notions of right and wrong. <u>Ethical</u> may suggest the involvement of more difficult or subtle questions of rightness, fairness, or equity. <u>Virtuous</u> implies moral excellence in character (while not necessarily religious). <u>Righteous</u> stresses innocence or guiltlessness, but can also suggest 'sanctimony.' <u>Noble</u> implies moral eminence and freedom from anything petty, mean, or dubious in character or conduct. Morality encompasses all those virtues.

<u>Morality</u>: It may not be religion itself, but it has to be the godly Essence of any religion!

IIIIIIIIIIIIIII

[PREAMBLE]

[Dear Future readers everywhere: I am a God Employee. My name is CHIP, and you can take my word as her Word. I will put my message in brackets, and keep this short, just to suggest you not judge this book too soon. The complexity of what begins as a simple little story might shock you, so patience is key.

[This work has something in common with what once was the best selling book of all time. Very few people read the

Bible for entertainment. Like the *Bible*, this is meant to be a book of moral enlightenment, if not a bit entertaining too. Be aware this is a book you <u>can</u> put down, and should anytime you need to stop and think about what you just read. That could happen a lot, but... it is offered here for your scrutiny and appraisal and may God bless you in the process – the process being to perceive the book in the manner it is put forth – with wisdom, intelligence, logic, love, and whatever grace you can spare toward one another.

[The Sponsor of the *Bible*, this book, and your life is God. S<u>HE</u>* sponsors all life and all moral thinking about life. *(God is not a gender. SHE is a twi-polar Entity and SHE also answers to HE if appropriate. The pronoun for her Children and Angels is SHe. That's because each is equal in its opposite polarity Yin and Yang energies. Their principles are indivisibly-dual and polar predominant as need be for God's purposes, which will be explained.)

[If you have time for God and her Moral Essence, SHE has a tiny bit of time left for you. Some of it is presented between the covers of this book, which we pray you come to appreciate. It may be the most unusual religious story you will ever read. It also looks at politics from a moral perspective.

[Your patience will be in great demand as you read this work and we suspect not all readers will come along with us. If that's the case, then ignorance will remain at the core of your problems. We thank you in advance for your efforts and I look forward to meeting you again in the upcoming "tale" – we could say - that wags the dog, with a little play on words, since one of the main characters is a most unusual human breed of canine.]

Mindfully yours,
CHIP - Central Hyper-Intelligence Processor
TranShip III

IIIIIIIIIIIIIIIII

Our thanks to you, CHIP, but for now we want to take readers somewhere else: a place with signs all along the way warning "Don't Go There!" Each aspect of that other place can raise either kinship or bitter divisiveness, depending on one's point of view, whether inward to the God cell (soul) or outward to a corrupt world. That is exactly why mankind has no reasonable choice but to venture into the zones of politics and religion and re-introduce them to one another in perhaps not so cordial a manner! Religion must stop playing a quasi-political/religious game for the purpose of attracting "sicko fans*" partisan to a particular personality *(sycophants – fans charmed by the devil).

Do not mistake any of our comments here for political partisanship. It's moral partisanship. We all should strive to elect moral leaders, no matter which socio-democratic political philosophy they espouse, as its essence should be moral and without regard to religious labels. God or godliness by any other name is "Moral Essence." There's no way to confuse it with Egod – the societal god who would own the world, until he destroys it.

We will introduce you to society's false God and you will understand him and why he is called "Egod." Egod as a societal demagogue was conceived at the start of the hybrid generation, when men began calling themselves "Lords," not long after Adam and Eve of Eden were created and began their family.

Egod has had great success with his power grab of the hybrid generation God created. There's no shame now in much of any thought or deed from Egod's point of view. The former "vice" forty-fifth President of the United States was an epitome of Egod, as are all autocratic personalities throughout history.

Politics, like religion, also should stress moral essence as a practical matter if this world is to survive a while longer. It's only logical to think there's something much greater at stake than how one manages anything that can and will crumble into decay over the course of time. Better to look forward to living outside of time, where God lives.

IIIIIIIIIIIIIII
OPENING PRAYER

Citizens of the USA have (had?) religious freedom in what is yet to be proven a "great" country, partly because they could choose whether love or hate ruled their lives. Of course they had that in common with all people. In America, hate too often is (was?) triumphant, especially among nefarious *id*iots willing to cheat at anything through constant lying and ("mis" and) disinformation.

Regrettably, as well, the tragic results of a Corona/Covid virus pandemic were maligned time and again by continuing racial injustice. That pandemic of hateful ignorance must be cured by a vaccine of moral essence infused into those who hate other people for any reason. "Hateful types" must work to activate souls that override such ignorance before they destroy themselves through God's grievance. The task of eradicating such a moral morass of inhumanity seems long overdue; and so we ask God to help those who seek to overcome hate and immorality, so as to cure or rid the world of all persons who would spread such psychological viruses through ignorance, denial, egoism and utter stupidity.

God help us, please, because now would seem to be the right time to tell the story of "Egod!" We pray you grant our readers the patience to read a book possibly unlike any they have read. Thank you. *Amen.*

/////////////////\\\\\\\\\\\\\\\\\\\\\

REPORTER: Excuse me, Mr. Harkett, b u t what is your opinion of some modern Supreme Court rulings?

Harkett: "I wish we had time to get into all pending and recent cases. But, I will say, they usually get it right if they stick to the Constitution and morality, as they did with the LGBTQ ruling on June 15, 2020 and their July 7, 2020 ruling regarding every person's obligation to produce evidence he or she might have involving a criminal investigation. But, I was quite disappointed with the Court when it ruled that money and free speech in politics are the same,* essentially allowing elections to be bought. That saying: "One person – one vote" is not true, when you have one person or business with money enough to buy millions of votes through advertising "propaganda." It might be good for capitalism, but it comes at the expense of democracy. Propaganda also can influence the inexcusable "electoral college" or almost anything.

What do those other two court rulings tell you, sir?

"There's still some moral intelligence involved. However, the High Court, or lower courts, could at any time prove to be tainted with political partisanship."

Could you elaborate on that a bit, sir?

"Most all so-called republican politicians are sad sycophants behind whichever <u>Ruler</u> seems to have the most clout with GOP voters. A political base can be a fanatical cult and most all the Gangsters of Politics want those type voters with them. They run scared at election time, especially if they have a vindictive leader they fear can steer votes away from anyone he criticizes. They all are pretentious, unconscionable fools. They know what they are doing is evil and they just don't give a damn. They worship themselves and money. They are just that vile. All courts, regardless of politics and for the sake of society should weigh morality in any precedent-setting laws."

'Gangsters of politics – sir?'

"The G.O.P. - If ever it was a Grand Old Party, it may have been back in Teddy Roosevelt's day."

You seem quite perplexed, Mr. Harkett.

"The world has gone to hell and I'm not sure it will ever make it back. The Republicans did whatever it took to rig elections in their favor; from gerrymandering, to calling on foreign interference, to fouling up election processes any way they could. They didn't care if people died as a result of standing in voting lines during a virus pandemic. Frankly, they were morally insane, in deference to their leaders: Power, Money and an unstable, orange-faced, narcissistic moron."

Sir, I...

"Sorry, here's my ride. You have a great day and a great life." Smiling over his shoulder, Harkett got into the vehicle and rode off into the sunset – possibly his own, as he was on a "hit list" disseminated among white, right-wing extremists.

*{*Citizens United v. Federal Election Commission*, 558 U.S. 310 (2010), was a landmark decision of the US Supreme Court concerning campaign finance. The Court held that the free speech clause of the First Amendment prohibits the government from restricting independent expenditures for political communications by corporations, including nonprofit corporations, labor unions, and other associations.}

IIIIIIIIIIIIIIIIIII

Now, let's hear from Tim, of the *Bible's New Testament*:

"*People will be lovers of themselves, lovers of money, boastful, proud, abusive … ungrateful, unholy, without love … unforgiving, slanderous, without self-control, brutal … lovers of pleasure rather than lovers of God." (2ⁿᵈ Timothy 3:2-4)*

INTRODUCTION

If you think religious "beliefs" are old-fashioned and the God of the *Bible* is an unsophisticated, antiquated idea, then please do us all a huge favor and substitute the words 'moral' or 'spiritual' for religious and 'morality' or 'spirituality' for religion. Also, if you love the gift of life that God – not happenstance – gave you, then we ask that you continue reading, and we thank you and God that you choose this path. In fact, we ask that as a prayer. Amen.

As to this book, keep in mind that the concepts of karma and reincarnation only enhance God's Grace and her Moral need for Soul-cleansing justice. God is God and everything is contained within her, to include your multitude of lives, lived and forgotten until the time for remembrance once again dawns, sets, and re-dawns until, through God's Grace, all your moral essence from all your physical lives (stemming from one Soul life) becomes whole and eternal within God's Heavenly Self, as your Creator.

Introduction continued
"The Prince of Pality"

There once lived an adorable young lad in the land of Blab, in the great southern kingdom of Blather, ruled by the mediocre (if I may discreetly and confidentially say so) King Blah-Blah. His deceased father (Long live the King!) was King Blah and the present King's successor to be, his son – Blah-Blah-Blah – is the lad of whom we write and have written and shall write. But that is another story and must await its turn, because as you shall see... the story with which we now are concerned, and we do mean in a worrisome way, is the story of "Egod." It was and is a horrible tale, and could be said akin to the analogy of the tail wagging the dog, because you see this 'Egod' character actually believed that he, she, or it, was God himself, herself, itself. Oh, yes, Egod was quite convinced of this and came to this conclusion by not thinking about it, or hardly ever at all. Ah, but it is, as we said, a sad, even horrific situation – completely and utterly mad and not to be made sport of, or perceived as having little or no consequence. To the contrary: Egod is mankind's true nemesis negating a majority of tiny souls.

Perhaps, by now, you have guessed – or if not, I shall tell you – that I am that very lad of whom I wrote and should and would like to write about again someday – that future King Blah-Blah-Blah of the kingdom of Blather, in the land of Blab; but alas for now Mine Pa-Pa says it is bedtime for certain. Therefore I shall turn over the remainder of the story-telling to my best friend and royal pet, whom we lovingly refer to as Prince Deepy Dog. He also serves as Court Jester in Waiting. He says he is going to take the horrendous story of Egod on the line – whatever that means, for the whole world to see. The main Court Jester assured me he would make the necessary connections somehow for Deepy to do that. He says no one will be able to miss it unless they try, but surely no one would be so sneaky, not with Mine Pa-Pa being the King and all, mediocre or not. Why he would literally have their very heads, much as Egod already does in his psycho-symbolical, pathetic, diabolical, long-term suffering way. Nonetheless, before I digress and/or continue unabated, I now grant you an audience with our palatial pal, and so…

'Without further ado,' here he is – the Prince of Pality!

Uh, sorry, Prince, this is the main Court Jester. I'm having some trouble setting up the nexus; I shall go and check the tiny cogs and big wheel driver. Please do not mock me in my absence. I'll be… I heard that, Jester in Waiting. Stop it! You are setting the wrong tone. This is a serious work we are undertaking on behalf of God.

This is Deepy. You think I don't know that, Jest 1? I wasn't laughing at you and I do plan to get serious. Oh, er, excuse me please – hold on a sec, I think maybe Prince Blah-Blah-Blah might have something else to say… wouldn't you know?

This is Prince 3B and I heard that! Lucky for you, you're my pet. I just wanted to add that if my father, the King, hears about any of this, then my honor demands I confess to every word, even if it calls for my own head, although Jest 1 tells me that is most unlikely. But for now I must lay 'said head' down and dream the night away, with my prayer that all tiny children rest well and peacefully, which really calls for the demise of Egod. Y'all know that, so please spread the word he must be slain. The story should have a happy ending for most of mankind, so that future children never need know of this ill-begotten era. All jestickleation aside, I pray the Prince of

Grace be with you, Deepy, which of course He shall be IF you allow it! I know, because He is with me even now, as I rest easy and peacefully. Carry on, Jest 1 and Jest Waiting, but please do get serious; and I ask God to bless you my pet pal in your journeys on our behalf. Prince Blah-Blah-Blah will – uh – uhzzzzzzz…

Sweet dreams, Prince. Man, I love that kid.

We all do. Hard to believe he'll soon be four years old. They grow up so fast these days.

His twin, Princess Blahsome is just as special, although she is not nearly as demonstrative.

Well, I try not to…

"Shh!" someone might hear you. We sure don't want "you know who" to find out.

Heavens to Betsy, no; I just want to hug Deepy once more before he gets on that TranShip.

Well hurry up, Ms. Lolly Gagger. It's almost time to make the nexus for our Prince of Pality.

I love Deepy.

Okay, shush now, if you please.

IIIIIIIIIIIIIIIIIIIIII

WAKE UP?

It is time to wake up to the seriousness of evil hatred while pointing out that some of our terminology is unusual, but adequately explained without need of a glossary. For example, while the two words "Moral Intelligence" appear normal enough, we wish to offer our own interpretation of the combined term. That is because we care to view 'moral intelligence' as distinct from any other. In fact, we propose that within the context of this life, the reader think of the words as synonyms for one another, and consider living them synchronously.

One can be intelligent without being moral; however, such is not the case within the context of "godliness." To be godly, one must be moral, and to be moral, one must possess the wisdom of grace. In other words, it is wisely or graciously intelligent to be moral and thus godly to be morally intelligent. If you are not wise, you cannot be morally intelligent. Conversely, moral intelligence confers wisdom through God's Grace.

So, how does one become wise? One could begin with ordinary intelligence, and then keep an open attitude about understanding the vital life-sustaining need for morality. Either way, one remains open to a new awareness of a sense of godliness, which can be allowed to permeate one's essence. It can come in the stroke of an epiphany, or more slowly. Some people call that enlightenment. We call it wisdom, plain and simple, and it only can be bestowed by God on those who would know and abide in God. So, neutralize your id/ego controlled brain and fill your soul-controlled mind with direction by God. If you can do that, you will understand this work. Even so, it will be a difficult read for many of you. Those of you who make it all the way through could possibly earn eternal life, but it is up to you and God whether you are saved forever.

Otherwise, a well-known "belief" method of achieving wisdom is referred to as faith – yes, in God, but also in the belief that any ultimate form of Intelligence would inherently be Moral. *Knowledge of* and *belief in* such a principle also could be considered wise IF one lived in deference to belief in or knowledge of the need for the concept of morality. Doing so would indicate you are morally intelligent enough to abide in God.

"Cross Wise"
"A MORAL GUIDEBOOK IN NOVEL FORM"
Combining Truth with a little bit of Fiction!
(Conversely for some of you)

[God is not a "time" being. Along with everything else that exists, God created 'time' and put mankind into it as a temporal –i.e. temporary being or entity, so that during that alloted time many such human spirit-souls could successfully complete her requirements for them to enter into her purely Moral state and dimension of eternal existence known as Heaven, (aka) also known as her Child, God Jr.]

~~~~~~~~~~~~

Jesus said,
Neither do men put new wine into old bottles: else the bottles break, and the wine run out, and the bottles perish: but they put new wine into new bottles, and both are preserved.
Holy Bible
Book of Matthew: Chapter 9, Verse 17

~~~~~~~~~~~~~~~~~~~~~~~~~~

(This work might seem a bit complex because its concepts are rather unusual. It may not be an easy "read" for everyone, so let's begin with a prayer – your prayer.
Pray you continue reading this book in spite of Egod.)

IIIIIIIIIIIIIIIIIIIIIII

{CHAPTER ONE}

Egod

"So, my tiny friends aboard TranShip III - in this 19-hundred, ninety-fifth A.D. year of our Lord - to sum up this morning's class... what if I told you this is the only life you will ever have and after this you get nothing and you get it forever? Would you believe me? Would you want that? Why?

"What if I were to tell you this course will test your mental acuity for the amount of vanity and ego it contains? Would you be concerned? Why? How will you feel about being lectured for moral tutoring during these classes?

"What do you think about God's eternal judgment, especially if it comes after only one lifetime which doesn't even register on the eternity scale? Would such a limited opportunity register on the 'moral' scale? Does God even owe you any life?

"What if I were to tell you your feelings won't matter in our class and court room as much as your thinking, which either will lead you to wisdom or away? Will you come to understand that your teacher is not judging you, but that God will at some point? Yes, you tinys here in the classroom know that, but many of your incarnate brother and sister auditors of this godly course will "drop out" long before they reach that understanding, simply because it is not an understanding that most of them fervently seek. In fact they are not yet even sure they will continue reading our lesson plan. We have a God who lets them choose.

"But, what if I were to tell you all ... as moral entities, you can have this life, plus eternity or life never-ending? Would you believe me? Would you want that? Why?

"Some people say they don't believe in "belief" and yet they must because they sure cannot know everything? Some people think/believe the secular religion of science someday will prove or disprove what they don't already believe/think they know. Yet, these same people believe in many things. For example, most of them likely believe they will wake up tomorrow to live another day, simply because they always have. In fact, they anticipate their whole lives based on belief. They don't know what will happen for sure, but they believe certain things will. Why? – Because they have awakened every day so far and expect that pattern to continue. If the laws of physics, or karma, don't intervene, they will continue waking up as they expect. If for some valid reason they don't expect to wake up, they may not. The truth is they and you will wake up for as long as God wants and no longer. You can override God's control by committing suicide but that might engender a karmic debt of dying at the same age in a future life, whether you are happy then or not. Some suicides are forgiven though.

"Unless people's beliefs are based on at least one of their immediate five senses, their minds may be closed. Open and wise minds should believe in anything a wise mind can conceive of as morally good, to include possibilities the Mind of God might want to propagate. Such beliefs though are mental and some people do not use their mental faculties as one of their "senses." That kind of sense would be based on one's ability to perceive life's incoming data; to interpret it and sort it out for good. And yet so many people choose to NOT perceive God in their lives. Why not? That's mainly because of limited imaginations. Many people seem more than willing to believe in the power of evil because they see people all around them seeming to enjoy it. They decide to join in that fun. They may even allow evil to dictate what they believe, yet refuse to see and propagate "God Sense" (Morality) as an example to others. That is because their spiritually weak physical nature wants every variety of sensual pleasure <u>now</u>!

"What has become of God anyway? What happened to her? Egod happened – but not to her. Egod happened to people and that is what became of God. So now you know why many people are more evil than godly. Of course not everyone is; but relatively few people are more spiritually-minded than they are physically sensual. That results in more potential for evil, if one grades on a scale of perfection, which God eventually must do, after her "Grace" comes into play. Thus, hybrid mankind's first goal should be to attain Grace as offered by God through the Moral intelligence of Jesus Christ or other such teachers.

"Most people are part of their sensate, ego "god" and not part of an unsurpassed moral God. Egod's ideas are their choices of what they will propagate, without regard to such a (non-existent) Perfect God. Why? Partly it is because they won't ask hard psyentific (COG word for 'religious') questions of themselves and then try to answer them in ways that would bring about their eternal lives with a real God, and not the evil, societal, one-life god that exists only for the here and now.

"Class, I pose my questions to you because we all have tendencies and propensities to overcome, such as vanity and self-righteous judgment, for example, if we are to survive as a species long enough to perfect the one trait that can save us for eternity. We call that character trait "moral intelligence." We must develop an inherent sense to not only recognize it, but to let it become our essence, because it is God's Essence and some of us want to become an eternal, integral and mental part of her, as SHE ultimately is all there is.

"Simply put, many people just don't have the courage to live in godly ways – perhaps because their friends don't; while maybe their friends are trying just as hard to fit in with them. Peer pressure can be subtle and insidious because it often comes without wise minds, as do many other non-wise excuses for choosing evil over good, especially if chosen by default of not thinking for oneself to perceive what is good and what is evil.

"Contrary to what some might think however, they are not their own person by choosing to <u>not</u> belong to their Creator or even acknowledging they are "created" by Omnipotent Consciousness – not happenstance. Most people belong to that societal god who is well into his process of re-creating them in his material image. I won't ask why. I know why. It is because they don't "reason belief" well with their minds* but do so only with their brains, to exclude their souls, those tiny mental energy cells provided by God to grant "Mind communion" between her and her living creations. *(Human mind is brain - with soul activated)

"So, for whatever reasons or non-thinking attitudes they may have, they have decided they are just too smart to believe in something as good and powerful as a Moral, eternal God. Wouldn't such a belief be too heavy a burden for weak-willed individuals? And what fun could a Moral God possibly be? Well, perhaps if you take the eternal life aspect, as well as your "mind cell" or soul from the equation – then not all that much for non-thinkers who just don't know how to approach the concept of belief in a godly way. God would spoil their natural, sensate pleasures – would SHE not? - Always wanting people to be good.

"Here are quotes from a scientist who knows how to take the godly approach: Dr. Robert Gange writes, *'People are divided on the question as to whether life assembled itself. A large number believe that life is a miracle created by God, but many others avoid the idea by believing that life assembled itself. Regardless of one's persuasion, however, either belief requires faith. No human being saw how life developed; yet, surprisingly, those with the most to say sometimes behave as though they did ... 'But when we look for hard data we find not facts but materialism, i.e., a philosophy that impersonates science'* ... *'If you are one who believes that nothing exists except matter and its motion, then you believe in this philosophy – you believe in materialism.'*

"We quote from the book: *"Origins and Destiny"** ©1986 by Robert A. Gange, and we would say again that materialistic people mostly are using their brains to think, while avoiding use of their tiny souls. *(We recommend his book to those who would know how at least one scientist examines God's handiwork. Some other scientists likely would agree.)

"People who <u>brain</u> think rather than <u>mind</u> think, and then choose evil, are rationalizing a conceptual belief in immorality by saying they don't believe in belief – meaning they simply won't conceive of or believe in a Moral God. One must prove to them using at least one of their five physical senses (to include brain but not "mind/soul" or intuitive thinking) that such a God exists.

"As mindless critters, they cannot smell God in a flower-encrusted sun season or taste God in a spring-fed mirror image at the bottom of a waterfall. They can't hear God in the purring of that cat they pet, or see God in the placid, loving eyes of a dog."

Deepy barely could resist saying, "For the love of God, look into my eyes – deep into my eyes."

Skipping a beat instead, he continued, "Those folks likely don't perceive such a "godly" God within their crowd or in places they live and visit, or if they do notice anything, they simply do not mentally credit God, because then they would need to credit God for themselves as well, and give heed to her Moral Essence. They would rather choose (mindlessly) to <u>not</u>

believe in an eternal life and a God that has not been proven to them, while not considering they might not yet have the moral essence and mental ability to understand God's plan for them. Therefore, *no* eternal life until they are prepared. This life is IT. Enjoy! Satiate those five senses and that mindless brain. Or if they truly think they have answers - yet hide them from others, their 'answers' then benefit no one else, which is tantamount to disbelief.

"Anyone who doesn't believe in God, or who is living an immoral life, should study the trial aspects of their life's workbook. Meanwhile, our guidebook offers both a "court" and a "course," which forecasts an apocalyptic crisis, especially for those people who are so narcissistic they bristle at the thought of God. Perhaps their unimaginative world will end after death. God can make that happen, because SHE is not interested in personality – unless it springs from good character.

"Considering how these people see themselves, they really should carefully view and then review their own trial's proceedings. They may not like the subject matter of their life course, but they will remain part of it for this one life at least, unless they elect to adjust to an eternal course by concerning themselves with character over personality. God gives them that option. Too many people just ignore it.

"Also, everyone should familiarize themselves with God's laws of karma and reincarnation, whether they believe in or fully understand them. Some who do understand will not allow themselves to believe. They have too much invested in "their" world to change it now, so why bother? Here's why. If they do, it could save their lives – not their skin and bones lives, but their "Othereal" ones – their spirit-soul lives. It is not necessary however to believe in karma and reincarnation. People can be saved simply by pledging their allegiance to the moral way of Jesus Christ, for example, and living that way. If they do, their karma likely will not dictate reincarnation or possibly worse.

"People too smart to believe in God, may not be smart enough to fathom this work, in which case they may decide to stop reading here or soon. If it's not too late, they should reconsider that temptation, realizing none of us is perfect. Perhaps they should confer with a wiser spirit-soul with whom they normally do not associate. Some of these wiser persons are known as religious and moral, even scientific in some cases. Of course for many of you, we will at times seem to be speaking a foreign language during this trial and guidance sojourn known as your life. Please temper your doubt with patience by knowing you can learn a foreign language.

"Most people know about God, but don't actually know that <u>He</u> is part of <u>her</u>, figuratively and literally. If they know, they will recognize <u>her</u> in these proceedings. Yes – one could say the information that follows constitutes both a test and a trial. Both situations began with God's plan for Adam and Eve, meaning her plan for each you as hybrid humans.

"Once your particular life's guide manual is begun, simply ignoring or denying it won't help non-believers. Taking that approach is to risk everything. With God's help you can save yourself; without it you can't. That's a good thing – for God. People who know and love God should rejoice! Others, who don't know and love her, likely won't remember that or anything else after their world of ignoring God and propagating evil ends. That's right, as that trite expression goes; if one is not part of a problem's solution, then one is part of the problem – part of an evil Egod raising hell on earth on behalf of his growing "Kingdom of Id" and his id/ego subjects who prefer matter over mind.

"Your life's workbook procedure is a continuing test. Therefore, I do recommend that this tiny class study your guidebooks quite carefully. You will want knowledge on becoming indivisibly-dual to accommodate God's polarity needs when your time of Grace comes in God's Moral Otherealm, after you generate enough WILL and grace to help others get there.

"We will continue our class work and study in a little while, but let's take a break now, since an example of humanity's trial is set to begin. Be sure to pay close attention. You are being tested even now, and will be for the rest of your material lives."

With his admonition lingering, Deepy left the tinys' classroom and headed for his diner haunt. He was hungry for physical nourishment, but also knew he had more spiritual nourishment awaiting him as well, through his own status as a student of *humanity's trial*, as well as a witness to it. A few minutes later he was chomping on a burger and slurping a milkshake – quietly though, he hoped, as the virtual trial was about to begin.

****

Court is now in session – All rise please.

"Thank you - Be seated. In this holy place, as you know, all prosecutors and defense attorneys must swear their honesty on God's Holy Word. The defense lawyers have done so. Now, as the indivisibly-dual prosecutor, it is your turn. Place your left hand on the *Bible* and raise your right hand please. Do you solemnly swear to tell the truth, the whole truth, and nothing but the truth, so help you God?"

"Of course, but do I have to swear, your Honor?"

"Only if it will help you get your message across. You know your audience and you know me - I am judge and jury. Does that help you?"

"It does. Must I solemnly swear, your Honor?"

"Only when you're speaking directly to me - I will give you some leeway here. If you're out of order, I will let you know. The truth is what we're after. If jesting, in the right spirit, will help you, please feel free to do so. You may as well be yourself, in other words. I, of course, know who you are anyway and so long as you're with me on this, then I'm with you. Rest assured."

"Thank you your Honor. So you will help me then?"

"Then, now, and always - so long as you ask. I see the defendants are charged with, "Everything evil under the sun" - Any witnesses?"

"As God is my witness."

"Thou sayest."

"Thank you, your Honor. Oh, sorry, I do have another witness – a dog. Is that okay?"

"Of course… Please proceed."

"I have an opening statement, plus disclosures and then I would like to call the lead attorney for Egod to the stand."

"You want one of the defense attorneys to take the stand?"

"Yes, your Honor, they all are on trial here as alleged co-conspirators in this case of the people versus the people.

"Has he agreed to testify?"

"He – she - they all have - Egod is extremely confidant, your Honor."

"I know, Counselor, how sadly do I know? Are you ready for the consequences?"

"I pray so, your Honor."

"Good; since I will rule on all that takes place here. You may proceed as you please."

"Thank you. First, we want to introduce to the Court's audience and defendants that "Other Real" God – Mother God.

"That's right, we have two Parents. Some of you here may find that hard to believe, since you usually hear only of - our Father - 'Which art in Heaven.' Yes, that Father, known as God. We also have a Heavenly Mother. Her name is God. SHE and the Father are one, but what do you hear of her? Nothing! You have been ignoring her in your male-contrived world, as if you did not know it takes two opposite, dynamic essences to create an indivisibly-dual offspring. You potential children of Grace are no exception. It is time for you to acknowledge God, the Mother.* You often ignore your Father, but your poor Mother must really feel neglected. How could this have happened? What were you thinking, or not thinking?

"God, the Father plus God, the Mother - plus the "COG," or Children of God – together comprise the "Trinity" of a complete God. But, since your Mother has been shunted aside for so long, it is time SHE got some long overdue recognition too. Any of you macho egos who can't handle that, just close your brain and slowly back away. On the other hand, you would be wise to stay put and allow mind/soul intelligence to rule over ego brain stupidity, which would be quite a change for most of you."

"Objection, your Honor."

"Sustained."

"Since you know God primarily as one being, which SHE is, the prosecutor will refer to God, using the personal pronoun 'SHE,' which is written with both the "S," for She, capitalized, as well as the "H," for He. The capital 'E' stands for Eternally Equal Equanimity. Sure, that pronoun and spelling are a bit irregular, but God should be known for her Yin polarity (feminine) side too. At least, SHE is here for your consideration and to mark your acknowledgment as a tipping or turning point in your evolution. If you elect to take the former misinformed route, it will be up to you to make the necessary semantic adjustments. Or you can just accept God as your Heavenly Mother too and show her some love, if you care to be logical; although this is not just about being logical. It also is about being wise, intelligent, loving and gracious.

"You have ONE God. You have one God with two aspects: The Yin and the Yang, if you will... the Male and Female, the Positive and Negative. These polar aspects are not individual, but rather "indivisibly-dual". They are one, just as your brain is one, but with two cerebral lobes - just as you have your own duality of spirit and soul, and it takes both to make one set of "mind mates." Jesus was the 'Yang' Spirit, whereas Christ was the 'Yin' Soul who manifested within the physical Aspect of the God Mind Mates or Child known as Jesus Christ. God, the Father and Mother, is one, and the Children are one with them - of like Mind and Essence - thereby completing God's Trinity of the Parents, Children and the Holy Ghost aka "God Junior." That means to become Children of the Trinity, you must return to her by acquiring her Virtues: Wisdom; Intelligence; Logic; Love; and your own version of her Grace – altogether her WILL and Grace.

"Some of you may never abide with her as self-aware entities. Instead, you might become part of her non self-aware Spirit Body energy, her Heavenly foundation of "living water" (Spirit) that is the fundamental Essence of her Holy Host Child or Heavenly abode known as God Jr. This work will clarify that, as best it can, along with other seemingly abstruse information.

*(The Yin or feminine aspect of God will be pronounced within this trial. And since people know God to be an 'Entity' and not a 'Thing,' we will use only gender-based personal and possessive pronouns. The pronouns SHE and 'her' contain both male and female aspects. The words female and woman also can reference both. We will continue to refer to God as the Father, or as He or him, in those specific instances that definitely call for it. The pronoun for any Child of God is "SHe," as an aspect of SHE.

(There really is no such thing as gender in God's Spirit world - only polar opposites. Attraction ("AtOnement") between them is known as Love or thoughtful feeling. God's Love always includes her empathetic Grace. Her Mental Essence is free of lust or the need of one polar aspect to dominate the other.)

We would now make this...

Dedication

To Mother and Father God;
To the Holy God Host (G'Host) of the Children and Angels
of God Junior;
– To the tinys; And; to a Daughter who is the Yin Essence
Christ Soul-Mate* to the Yang Essence of Jesus whose Spirit
uses the likeness of a physical body in the material world.
*(An indivisibly dual-polarity "Trangel")
IIIIIIIIIIIIIIIIIIIIIIIIIIIIIIIIIIIIIIIIIIIII

Obviously, our <u>Fore</u> <u>Word</u> to the Court is

God

[God is a work in progress. God is a perfect work in progress, ever changing within her Self, ever progressing from one energy phase to another. God remains constant... ever changing. God is energy acting upon itself, in order to bring about perfect changes in God. Action from energy equals work. God works at using energy to change a perfect God in the pursuit of change. God is a work in progress.

[As energy, you are part of God; but you still are an imperfect work in progress. Since God is ever changing, your intermediate condition does not change God's perfection. You will continue to be acted upon. If you do not reach moral perfection in a Self and God-aware energy form, a perfect God will change you into a more suitable energy pattern. You then may not be able to recognize anything, including yourself as a conscious entity.

[Understand that God measures your progress toward perfection. Work at it. Only God knows how much time you have. Only God knows how much progress you make within each measured, physical energy phase. Be perfect if you would be an eternal, self-aware part of... a perfect work in progress.]

"We will now proceed, your Honor, with disclosure regarding the specific charges against the societal id/ego entity known as Egod, who as you know considers YOU his arch rival. We intend to prove he is guilty, by reason of sheer <u>idiocy</u>, of the charges brought against him – karmic charges that we in fact, with your permission, have borrowed from your LOG Book."

[Court reporter's note:] Turning now to the courtroom and a local news television camera, the prosecutor continued in a raised voice:

"Frankly, some spectators of this trial may not give a damn, but... this could well be the most controversial case before any court since the mock trials of Jesus Christ and his disciples in biblical times. Of course, Egod would prefer nobody notices these proceedings, since the tables are turned this time around and he is the one on trial. I say "one," whereas we know, of course, that Egod is a multifaceted entity consisting now of most of the world's population, as led by its politicians. It is in fact the dwindling number of faithful Christians who have brought these charges to the Court's attention in this interim process aimed at saving what remains of morality within society, to include many persons claiming views other than Christianity as their guiding light, which is quite all right since they are moral.

"Egod is always working, as only he can, to see that the trial is, for the most part, ignored. However, if it begins to get too much attention anyway, then he will deny or downplay his culpability in promoting so much evil rampant in today's world. With ignoring it as his first tactic though, the trial could go unnoticed long enough for Egod to gather his financial forces and put a longer-term strategy in place. In the meantime, we suspect one of his tactics will be to flaunt the U-S Constitution as much as possible to hinder the truth. He always seems to find a way to laugh in the face of mankind's "justice system." Of course, since Egod trolls much of international and syndicated media, the prosecutor's task of making God's case for her won't be an easy one, but considering this Court's Judge, we know God can still make that happen. However, if SHE elects not to judge some of you now, SHE of course has the ultimate *say* in how each one of you is tried as an individual in her court's ongoing arraignments.

"For now though, this is as serious as it gets and it would be unfortunate if some of you do not see herein - a "learning curve" for mankind's future survival, rather than just a personal challenge pertaining to your one-life livelihood. Of course, controversy would come only if this process is taken seriously, as its more revelatory aspects should be, along with its godly intentions. For those of you with the right mind mates of spirit-soul and right attitude, or mind-set, it could be the most comforting news ever to come to your attention. Both your mind and attitude depend on whose side you are - God's or Egod's. You always choose between those two. Most of you have yet to become wise, intelligent, logical, loving, and gracious enough to know you really don't have a choice when it comes to real survival, as in 'Othereal' and eternal.

"The novel aspects of this proceeding will be overtly spiritual, theosophical, even metaphysical some might say, but unmistakably psyentific.* The projected setting for offering the prosecutor's case will be a "TranShip," which hybrid humans often call an Unidentified Flying Object or UFO. This process will tie together COG perspectives under the Auspices of a Moral God. This won't be a new-age proceeding, as one of our main witnesses is an elderly man – old enough to recall a time when God played a bigger role in the lives of your people, still led during those days to a higher calling than hedonistic materiality and Egod worship. This instead is a 'no-age' trial. It is for the Glory of an ageless, timeless God, whose *Cause and Essence* are eternal Moral Consciousness and Equanimity. The purpose of the trial of course is to attain immortality for as much of hybrid humankind as possible. *(religiously spiritual, as in moral)

"We thank you again your Honor for this opportunity and for the materials provided from your archives. We now proceed with testimonial scenarios in the form of narration."

"Objection, your Honor!"

"On what grounds?"

"Never mind - Sorry; I was just practicing for all the forthcoming nonsense!"

"I don't think you need any more practice. You are out of order as usual.

"Now then Counselor, before you continue, I want to remind the defendants that the material world justice system is being waived for this special hearing, since I personally am judging this case. I already know what implicates everyone regarding my Moral laws, which are at the heart of this proceeding. My knowledge renders any so-called "amendments" null and void. My laws already are perfect and that is why I personally agreed to handle this interim trial, prior to final judgments of everyone. I want this hearing to serve as a gentle reminder before things get really brutal because of my self-proclaimed nemesis. Now, please continue, Counselor."

"Objection, your Honor!"

"What now – As if I didn't already know?"

"We all know this proceeding will be largely ignored. There is hardly any market for God among the difference-makers and trend-setters of the world – the intellectuals, scientists, politicians, the Big Business Bosses, the really clever and/or criminal money manipulators and power brokers. I already know the prosecutor's arguments and your ordinary consumer won't even bother paying attention, unless some bloody death-dealers, super heroes, and sophisticated cynics show up to steal the show and offer them some goodies in the process."

"It would seem you don't know the Prosecutor's arguments at all and apparently don't even know the Prosecutor. That stands to reason or you would not be one of the defendants in this matter. Besides, you and quite a few of those others you mentioned are going to be shocked at the Super Heroes the Prosecutor has waiting in the wings, and perhaps even a surprise witness. Why would I be here otherwise?"

"Er... I'm not sure I understand your Honor."

"That itself will affect your chances for Grace. Ignorance of the need for morality is offensive to me.

"Now, Counselor, please continue."

"Thank you, your Honor. As I was saying... we do 'now' continue with testimony in narrative form..."

~~~~~~~~~~~~~~~~~~~~~~~~~~~~~~~

"That was interesting," Deepy said, as CHIP's viewing window closed.

"It was good to be singled out as a dog witness. I'll do what I can."

"We know you will and it's why we chose you," Eno said.

He and Eno were sitting in the diner and had just finished watching the courtroom scene through CHIP's picture-window to the world, which also fronted downtown Broad Street of the hometown of a teen-aged Larry Ray James, circa the 1950's era. The window also could serve as a screen for any scene though, that CHIP might simulate in accord with Eno's teaching needs.

Speaking of teaching needs - Eno now queried Deepy, "Don't you have a 'tiny' class to teach in the next few minutes, as a follow-up to what we just witnessed?"

"Oh, for heaven's sake - where does my mind go around here? I'm always losing track of it. Yeah, I'd best get moving. See you later," he said as he hopped down off his perch and scrambled as fast as his four legs would carry him toward the diner door.

"Slow down, my furry friend," Eno told him. "You're not running late, so I don't think running is a good idea for you. You could hurt yourself."

By now, Deepy had decided the same thing, as he was in no shape for such exertion, and that annoyed him as he recalled the shape he was in. It wasn't very "manly" from his perspective, so close to the floor.

IIIIIIIIIIIIIIIIIIIIIIIIIIIIIIIIIIIII
(CHAPTER 2)
Deep Diddly-Squat

Shel almost tripped over Deepy as he left the tinys' classroom and turned toward his diner again, looking forward to another burger and shake, as he was done teaching for the day. After a moment to collect herself, Shel laughed somewhat nervously over the near mishap, causing Deepy to apologize, "Sorry, Shel - my fault; I need to pause and look before I walk through these sliding doors, or maybe I could bark if I knew how. Folks around here are not used to us low-slung types."

"I should be by now, Deep" she reassured him, "what with all the robot cleaning gadgets they use around here. Of course they do beep when you get too close; anyway – no harm done. I was just coming to tell you that Dr. Mai – er, Eno, needs you in the E-R (Entry/Exit Room). I didn't want to em-connect," she said, "because I know that gives you a headache. And I know you disengage your private telep to outside calls while you're teaching... that is, if you remember." They each smiled over that allusion to Deepy's often observed memory problems.

"I appreciate that, Shel. I think I told you, didn't I, that my private line is a temporary, rigged-up affair at the moment, while BB and CHIP try to work the bugs out of the normal mode? They've arranged some biochips so that my nose glows orange now whenever I get an 'out of sight' call, so I'm sure glad you didn't use the private line. That would have been a little embarrassing, and I already had enough to be embarrassed about. I know just about all the ship monitors are tuned to those classes; and in a few days the whole fleet will be watching, I just found out."

"You will be cute as always."

Deepy knew that was Shel's well-meant, but typical comment regarding his foibles. In all matters, it seemed he was at the very least, "cute." He let it slide with a quick, "Thanks."

"Anyway, they're re-amping or re-vamping me or something. It's got to do with the canine auditory cortex ... the ohm and mho or yin and yang."

Shel and Deepy both laughed. They knew he wasn't the least bit technically minded.

"Wow," Deepy said, "That was the fastest hour of teaching I've ever experienced. It just flew by."

Shel was on the verge of telling him otherwise, but he continued,

"... I hope I didn't screw it up too badly," he scolded himself, over her thought of...

"It was only forty minutes, 'Deep.'"

"Just forty minutes," she teleped again.

"What? – Couldn't be. We covered our whole lesson plan. You must be mistaken, Shel."

"No, not at all – CHIP put you on "time-compress." Remember when you seemed to stutter, starting out ... twenty minutes of your lesson went directly into the tinys' consciousness, via some of CHIP's special wizardry. He can try to explain later if you're interested. I don't understand it. But, right now Eno needs you in the E-R. That's why I'm here, and I know you were just about to ask. There's another human on board. That's the reason your class was compressed. Eno just got word of her as you were going into class. Another ship was scheduled to pick her up, but there was a last-minute change. She's "Neg" status – very impure and scared," Shel told him as they both continued in the direction of the E-R.

"Poor woman," Deepy thought.

"Quite right," was Shel's response, as she turned toward the Assembler area. "I'll be in Shangri-La for awhile, Deep. See you later. Good luck," she added.

"Enjoy your lunch, Shel. Maybe I'll be able to join you for dinner at the usual time. I hope." I love it, he thought, as he continued down the corridor, when Shel and Eno call me "Deep." I feel as close to them as anyone ... even CeCe. "CeCe?" his mind queried, while at the same time he realized his nose was glowing. "Hello?" he inquired and picked up two thoughts at about the same moment ... one in the 'voice' of Eno, and the other from Shel. "You are deep, for a dog," Eno told him. Shel's "We love you, my friend," came in the mix. "And we need you. Hurry along," Eno said. "Almost there ... just around the bend," Deepy replied, "and thank you, Shel – likewise."

"... My huckleberry friend ... Moon River and me," a voice sang inside Deepy's head, for no apparent reason. Maybe this orange glow thing will work out okay. At least there's no Em-connect headache and I do feel loved. Deepy thought this to himself, since his nose had blinked off. That's why he had heard the music, he realized. He had been automatically switched to the "numb" line, as some irreverent human had once jokingly called the "disconnect." But, Deepy was of the old school and, like the COG, he enjoyed 'Big Band' music, not to mention light classical, jazz and other genres as well. But Deepy's thoughts had automatically tuned out the music, and now he cut a final turn to the E-R. "No music meditation for at least a while," he knew.

Deepy had been on board the ship for about two weeks and had only one other session of "alien" experience to his credit. His role in that situation was, he thought, the primary reason for his being here, and he took it quite seriously. There was no way to take it otherwise, if all such events were going to be like the first one, and he had a feeling... well, actually, he recalled Eno telling him that some encounters could be intense – "unfortunately."

He enjoyed his work with the tinys, which he really didn't consider work, but this aspect of his job now awaiting... well, hell, it's just too nerve-racking, he thought. Deepy knew, as a human, he had always been extremely sensitive to the suffering of others. He wryly told himself he was a good dog... er... uh, human-dog, he now reckoned. "Damn, talk about a mutt. There's just no way I'm ever going to adjust to having my thoughts animated by a dog's brain, with a lot of help from the ship CHIP (Central Hyper-Intelligence Processor). I hope I can last the full schedule. The fewer traumatic situations like the one I'm now dreading, the better off I will be. But, hey, I'm glad to be of help.

"The first time," he now recalled... 'Just as soon as the "guest" had been calm enough for the med procedures to begin, he had wandered off to the side and tried to collect himself.' This time he hoped he could actually watch Eno and the crew at work through the whole procedure.

"I just hope this person likes me as well as the other one seemed to. That is, after all, the crux of the matter," he told himself, adding, "well, at least as far as the "project" is concerned."

Deepy's role was that of pacifier or comforter. D-P also stood for dog-pacifier, as well as the more official "Dog Project," CHIP had told him. But he knew, or thought he did, that he could only take CHIP with a grain of silica about half the time.

Deepy was a hybrid – a mutt. "Quite a perky whelp and really smart for a dog," CHIP had told him. He recalled thanking CHIP, with a rather sarcastic tone. They were just meeting for the first time and Deepy had no idea what to make of the first humanoid he would ever experience. They seemed to be feeling each other out, and Deepy was not feeling any self-esteem in his new dog suit, especially since CHIP called him a "doganoid," and then winked. Deepy wasn't sure if he was supposed to be flattered. All "noids," he had been told were diamond-based carbon life forms. That's when Deepy was to recall for the first of many times that his thoughts were being read, and so he said, "Thank you, I guess."

Thinking back on it now, Deepy knew he probably had seemed rude and overly sensitive, but he blamed it on being nervous.

"Oh well, can't be funny all the time," he supposed. "Dog on the outside – human in the "think tank," such as it is. It just adds up to a mess," he thought, as his mind strayed back to the moment when Shel had told him he looked somewhat like a lamb. Then CHIP added, "... who looks like he's been gnawed on by a wolf." Shel told him he was a bit scruffy looking, but said he was cute and definitely unique as the

"Yorkie-Poo" he was - meaning part Yorkshire terrier and part Poodle, not to mention his human aspect. – So a "Yorkie-Pooman" he supposed. "Ugh!"

Anyway there must have been some truth to what Shel had said, because the woman guest had kept calling him her little "lamby pie." He didn't mind. He could see that he was having a calming effect on her. That's what counted. And Eno had been well pleased with those results, he had told Deepy afterward. He also had divulged that the dog-assembler project was on track to begin in about six weeks, depending on the continued good results of Deepy's work. If there were no major hitches, at least half the craft in the fleet were scheduled for dog projects of their own within a couple of months. But Deepy had a feeling he would always be first in the hearts and minds (blah blah… "Ego alert!") His subthoughts screamed at him ("... Man all stations – pride spotted on the premises").

Deepy entered the E-R, thinking he would leave himself disconnected from the others until he was addressed. Eno (Dr. Mai) stood to one side of the woman. Dr. Yavre Rrab (Yav) was on the other. There were two quin in the room and the two Marsianoids working "transport" roles. Everyone appeared lost in his or her work anyway. He took his place beside the still conked-out woman; happy that no one had picked up his ego-thought of being *top dog*. In fact, he was kind of hoping that his subconscious mind had generated his proud thinking for his own wry amusement. He was well aware of just how much a no-no, prideful thinking was among the COG. Of course, they never engaged in such, but they were quite used to hybrid humans. They had already shrugged at him many times because of his doggedness and they continued to work with him patiently. And that, he knew, was actually, at the heart of his seeming dismay, rather than what he felt was any real sinfulness* on his part. He simply didn't want to disappoint his colleagues after developing such a special rapport with them. *(the nuances of morality can be difficult)

Frankly he thought in the beginning, his new friends tended toward some exaggeration of the importance of such a human failing as pride, but he was told by Eno a while back that this human failing was a slave to the material master known as id-ego. Deepy was becoming quite familiar with that quasi-god persona or overgrown monster from the artifacts of Adam and Eve's and humankind's genesis-generated id/egos.

At the same time, Eno had warned him against judging any of God's principal Children, as things are not always as they appear. Deepy still had no idea what Eno had meant by that, and when he asked, Eno only said, "Eventually you'll see."

In private, though, or with his microhm shield engaged, he knew his subthoughts would sometimes tell him how important he personally was to the mission of the ship, at which point his ever-growing humility response would rise up to squelch the intruder. Deep down, he felt he had a true understanding of his place in the scheme of things. After all, how could anyone believe in God and not be truly humble? He had vaguely wondered why most of mankind seemed just the opposite, before realizing "why indeed." What had he been thinking about after all – id/ego! "Silly dog," he scolded himself for the first of many times.

Since then, he appreciated the COG were helping him give new life to his conscience. The compassion of that 'tiny' voice of his soul really had been overcome by his ego in these latter years of his life as Dr. Larry Ray James, psychologist and sometimes author. "Besides," his train of thought continued, "it was rather an interesting game trying to see just how many ego distractions he could capture in a day's time." They were becoming fewer.

Right now though, he felt someone staring at him. He glanced up at an extremely "pretty" man whose eyes seemed to be looking right into Deepy's soul. Standing just behind him was a Marsianoid with a similarly penetrating gaze.

"Deepy, you remember 'Sam,' who was here for your other session as well," Eno spoke without looking up from his work... "And that's "Hoster" – one of Sam's CHIPs. The Marsianoid did not blink, but seemed to affect a slight smile.

Sam then smiled at Deepy. 'What a beautiful person,' Deepy subthought, followed by, 'funny I don't remember him.' Sam's smile seemed to grow. Deepy returned it, with a sudden flash of recall of this "Acting Fleet Commander of TranShip I," as Eno had introduced him the time before. How strange, as Deepy now seemed to remember meeting a beautiful woman Commander then, by the name "Samantha." They did look like twins though.

Sam spoke: "Eno tells me you are doing a wonderful job with the tinys. (Sam's teleped tonal quality registered in

Deepy's brain as neutral gender) I saw for myself the good job you did here with your previous patient, or should I say '... best friend?' We are happy with your work."

"Wow," Deepy somehow felt humbled in this person's presence, and being praised by him (or 'her?' he now wondered) was almost enough to make him dizzy. He could only mumble, "Thank you very much – that means a lot to me."

Feeling flushed now, Deepy realized he had better break himself free of this mesmerizing person to concentrate on the work at hand; literally at the hand of this now wide-eyed human beside him. Deepy might have been thinking selfishly before about his own importance to the project, but looking at the woman beside him, he shifted to a feeling of love. It was now automatic with him, again thanks to the COG. He almost at once sensed fear from her though. She was now fully engaged in a thought dialog with Eno, and her fear rolled through the room ... in undulating waves.

She looked at Deepy now on the stool beside her. He went onto her lap and snuggled up against her. He felt her begin to scratch his head with her shivering hand, as Eno continued his soothing reassurance. "Umm, ooh, ah," Deepy seemed to think, "just like old times." But it was more like a feeling than a thought. He then found himself thinking momentarily about subthoughts, which would sometimes burst upon the scene at the most inopportune moments. He had often been embarrassed by such happenings in the presence of the COG, since they could read the deepest thoughts. Damn, it was happening at this very moment. Everyone in the E-R was looking at him expectantly. His nose wasn't glowing, but someone must have said something to him. He couldn't help but sigh. All six of his co-workers sighed too. That's when he realized they were all on ship monitor or "mon-com." Anyone on board could be tuned in, with everyone in the E-R open to one another.

Just then, Deepy felt a bump on his head. It was the woman. "Ouch," he thought, reflexively, before realizing he had just been startled. Deepy had noticed moments before that Eno had pressed her arm with a small shiny object of some kind, and now she was starting to writhe. Then she banged him on the snozzle. This time he couldn't help but feel the pain out loud. He yelped – Then thought, "Sorry, folks, I couldn't help it."

No one was paying attention to him. In fact, he couldn't even hear himself think. There was a ringing in his ears that he somehow knew was an echo of the woman's scream, which had registered in spite of his self-centeredness. Her eyes, he noticed, were glazed over, and the look on her face told him he should cover his ears for the next onslaught.

Her thoughts were pure fear. "Good Lord," Deepy marveled, "You'd think she'd seen a snake." She was staring straight at one of the Marsianoids. "Aw!" Deepy thought, "I think he's kind of cute." The woman screamed again. "Guess not," Deepy surmised. A jumble of COG thoughts that seemed to come from all over the ship surrounded them then. About that time, Dr. Rrab asked CHIP if he could now switch off the mon-com to the E-R, and give them a local line only. "Un momento, por favor," CHIP shot back. The room had to remain "live," in order for them to mind-connect with each other and the woman simultaneously. A scant moment later CHIP was able to comply. But Deepy had to wonder what was going on with the CHIP switchboard. This whole procedure should be standard by now. [CHIP note: I was resetting the mode to exclude the woman's perception of thoughts inadvertently vocalized by a man, but seeming to emanate from a dog – an obviously impatient one]

All this happened more quickly than it takes to tell about it, but even so, Deepy felt he was reacting too slowly. And so while the second scream still lingered somewhere between his floppy ears, he began to lick the woman's face while wagging his tail in friendly fashion. She pushed him away rather violently, and he was grateful to land on the extra stool; but before he could even pout about it, she had grabbed him back, squeezing hard and hanging on for dear life.

"Give me a break," he wheezed, and then realized she seemed to literally be doing that. Eno was directing telepathy to her, trying to reassure her they were good guys. Even the presence of a quin woman now standing next to her didn't seem to help. Eno then reached out in front of her and scratched Deepy's ear while saying out loud, rather than teleping "... cute doggie, eh? His name is Deepy." The patient flinched and then fainted.

"Just as well," Dr. Rrab reflected, "She thought we might kill her. I'm sorry that happened," he continued. "I've been part of this procedure for about two thousand years now, off and on, and I can never seem to get ready for the primitive human emotion of fear. I guess it's because I just can't relate to it. Never will, I suppose. I mean, of course I understand it clinically; it's basic chemical, survival instinct, but... uh, well... I, oh, you know what I mean," he finally floundered, as he was really trying to concentrate on his part of the procedure and seemed to realize he was babbling.

"Yes..." Eno seemed to whisper, "As COG it is most difficult for some of us to relate to such a raw feeling, since we never have any cause for fear."

"You're right Eno, or any emotion other than pure joy, which really is "thoughtful feeling." From my point of view I think I sometimes take all this too much for granted. Not that I don't love them all – I do, but sometimes they just refuse to let us get the love as 'thoughtful-feeling' through to them. They can't seem to relate to the fact that we don't recognize ourselves as personalities. We seem foreign and aloof. They are not used to the beatitude and quiet demeanor we present. But the problem of not being able to recognize it lies within them, not us... and of course not all of them. I don't mean to generalize. Besides, I'm telling you something you know even better than I, having been involved with the hybrid human species since its inception."

[CHIP Note: Deepy didn't know it then, but they were "presenting" this conversation in order to give him information for the book he was to write after returning to his human self. Normally they would be all business in such a situation.]

"Hmm," Eno responded. "It does all come back to Grace, of course. Perhaps we have become a little too involved in the technical aspects of what we are doing here. We know they can feel our mental empathy, but it's still not enough to overcome their spirit body's programmed id or survival fear. It's that "old serpent brain" thing again. Without the empathy though, it's likely they all would suffer heart attacks."

"I expect you're right," Dr. Rrab agreed.

Deepy was tuned in to all this as he watched the E-R team at work while they chatted. Most of their thoughts, between what passed as idle chitchat, amounted to routine business.

Eno stuck out a hand, palm up, and a quin put a ting in it. Eno aimed it and closed what had appeared to be a gaping hole in the woman's skull. Deepy thought he might be hallucinating as he had not even noticed the hole was there before that moment. And now, in a sweep of Eno's hand, it looked as if it never had been. Eno smiled at Deepy. "Deep, old chum, we're pursing now. She will be under for another little while. We gave her a thirty-minute scotch, just before she fainted. Stay with her as long as she seems to need you. The quin will take over now. You know their routine. Just be supportive. You're doing a good job."

"Sure Eno. Thanks. I was wondering if you would mind telling me just what it was you did to her. I noticed you probed into her skull through her nostrils. I could see the light moving around inside, but what was that hole in her head all about?"

"Deepy, you're coming by this evening for a chat, anyway?"

It was kind of a question, Deepy thought, so he replied, "Right, I've got to teach the tinys about Eden next week, and I'm looking forward to your formal take on the subject, even though CHIP clued me in a little for today's class."

"And I'm looking forward to sharing that with you. We can talk about this procedure then as well. Meantime, I need to be in ship-stat mode."

Deepy was agreeing, even as Eno was halfway out of the room when he suddenly disappeared, leaving behind a couple of thoughts...

"See you later, Deep – correlation in about forty-five minutes, Yav ... my quarters."

"See you there," Dr. Rrab acceded, as he gathered up some instruments and placed them in a cube lock before departing. Deepy didn't see Sam and Hoster leave and in fact now recalled he had not seen them since he and Samantha (?) had briefly spoken to each other. {Must be the same person; although the first time they met, "she" had longer hair, but today, shorter and more manly-looking. Oh, well; *Sam* is short for Samantha.}

Deepy now turned his attention back to the man and woman quin, who were going about their nursing business.

"That mutt's a mess," Yav got around to saying, during his meeting with Eno. Chief Capton Nai had joined them. For the moment, the subject was Deepy.

The Capton joined in, "I noticed a momentary lapse at the outset of his class and then the time-compress mode kicked in."

"Right..." Eno said, "Each of the tinys' memories was given the perception that Deepy taught the entire class on a word-for-word, real time basis. And, of course, that's what Deepy's memory tells him as well. But I had Shel let him know what happened. The dog project's going great, by the way, and the tinys really love their teacher. So, once they're in human form, they no doubt will have a special affinity for dogs, but then almost every human does – and that's why he's here."

[CHIP note: Teleped conversations are expressed in terms of speech, simply because telepathy is heard in "voice registers" within the mind, without need of vocal cord or air vibrations. These "voices" are as individual and distinctive as any human voice. Even though telepathy is not a spoken form of communication, the mind registers it as such, and "voices are heard." In fact, the voices are so precisely patterned in register, tone, and cadence they can be as unmistakable in their characteristics as human voices.

[Ship Commander, Dr. Eno Mai {pronounced E-no My} asked Dr. D. P. Dog, at the outset of his "alien" adventure among his shipmates, to kindly keep a running log or journal of his experiences. Reviewing Doctor Dog's log at the end of the first week, Dr. Mai made some suggestions regarding style and content, and further informed Deepy that the ship's "intelligence processor" would assist him when it comes time to put his log into book form. It will be my pleasure. Larray is a decent sort.

[I would say, in his defense, however, these comments are in no way meant as criticism of Dr. Larry Ray James, who has been kind enough to offer his assistance in this experimental project. I simply have a special rapport with his 'acting soul' and do like to rib him a little now and then. Deepy's spirit takes it well, which goes to show he is morally enlightened as his true self, even while mostly doing without his own tiny soul for this project. Effectually, BB serves as his O-Soul, which also makes this a case of two siblings, BB and I, having some fun with each other.

[Fleet commanders know what's going on. Because of brain size, Deepy's memory is fluctuational and he is of course subject to some human quirks, but then again, he's a mild example for the tinys of how ego can influence people and even overcome many tiny souls.

[Now, Dr. Mai wanted me to thank you for your time, but most especially for your patience in trying to boggle through so many new concepts and terms. Admittedly it can all seem a bit extraordinary, but we pray your perseverance will be rewarded ultimately. The story will be getting more fantastic though.

[Whenever you see a comment in brackets, it will be mine. {"Asides" or digressions may be contained in this manner} (or I might put some of Deepy's and the Commander's remarks in parentheses.)]

IIIIIIIIIIIIIIIIIIIIIIIIIII

Chapter 3?

"Mental Me and e ring"

Deepy was lost in perplexity on his way back to his quarters. It was when he plopped on his bed that he growled; his stomach did, that is. He was reminded that he had missed lunch, but his memory reassured him that his A-R {Assembler Room} diner was always open. Most folks around here actually didn't eat much, if anything, so far as he could tell. A few quin would appear to be eating in the diner now and then, but those who did just seemed to nibble on small salads. CHIP had told him that COG and Humangels only consumed pure Spirit, whatever that meant, with Eno saying that what it meant was not important 'for now.' From what he could tell though, dogs eat whatever smells yummy and Deepy had never missed a regular meal before now. "Oh well, when duty calls," he thought.

For the moment though, he knew he still didn't feel like eating anyway. He couldn't let go of the woman in his mind, the frightened, pathetic way she had talked to him when she came to. And she sure didn't let go of him the entire twenty minutes the quin were there, running their tests. In fact, he was afraid for a while that she was going to rub a bald spot on his head. But at least she wasn't screaming; an effect he thought the Marsians had brought about. Why they were even in the room, he didn't know. His human lady "friend" though, couldn't stop her nervous petting and rubbing and picking at him ... and talking ... the whole time talking, even laughing at times, for no apparent reason. He knew though that oftentimes people would laugh to keep from crying. He had a feeling she might have been completely delirious.

Suddenly he remembered, "The walls have ears" in this place. But glancing up quickly, he knew his room was "off" – not that he was having inappropriate thoughts. His was one of the rooms reserved for 'aliens,' which he was, from the other aliens' point of view.

If the walls glowed pink, you were on private monitor, which was a two-way arrangement, just in case you might have something to say to the ship combot, which tuned in each room on a regular, but random, basis. Nothing personal, they had told him. Everyone (no exclusions) would have vital signs, including thoughts, monitored for five minutes.

For the COG, pure thought waves equated to good mental health and none of them was offended by this procedure, because even though they were never subject to immoral thinking, thought patterns of godly communion could fluctuate due to bursts of chaotic energy through whatever system they used. That could result in erratic thinking, even the hint of which would call for verification. For a while, after first coming onboard, Deepy's ego was insulted by this *big brother* procedure and it let him know he deserved better. He got over it. Besides, everyone understood that CHIP could monitor anyone at any time without his or her knowledge. They also knew that would not be done, because the Commander would be aware of it, as each TranShip Commander had a "soul" link with his or her CHIPs. It was said that a COG "Lord," or Commander, would not approve of clandestine mind reading, as far as COG were concerned. Deepy knew what that meant, of course, since he was not a COG. (Child of God)

They had a fail-safe system, he had been told by Eno, which would allow God to remain God – in other words "perfect." COG understood this simply amounted to God Mind monitoring her missionary Mental Cells. But, in his case, Deepy knew that CHIP seemed to take advantage of certain situations to eavesdrop. "We all trust God's motivations," CHIP had told him, "without giving any of this a second thought. That is pure thinking that equates to wisdom. If I listen, it's because I love you. Trust me."

Being human though, Deepy unfortunately was just a tad cynical when hearing someone say, 'trust me.' He regretted that his society's character (Egod, for the most part) seemed to make skepticism, if not cynicism, almost mandatory. He wasn't personally perplexed by it, but just regretted it was the reality that he perceived. Even so, he followed the advice of one of his favorite preachers who always said, 'Obey God and leave the consequences to him,' although Deepy was learning to refer to God as her, since "her" included "him," so to speak, without leaving her out. Huh? Oh well, he knew his mind was playing with him now.

If the walls had a blue glow, you were on a specific line as soon as a caller spoke his or her first word. If Deepy were to think "blue Eno" at this moment, he would be combot-confirmed to go ahead, if Eno was in his room and not already in communion {for COG, "communication" is always 'communion'}. Of course, anyone outside a room could use any available line, through the combot to connect with anyone else at a distance. "Through the computer" because you had no way of telling, out of sight of someone, what you might be interrupting, although you could use the term "override" if you felt it was an emergency. An 'override' through CHIP or BB was automatic unless an emergency conversation was already taking place.

Deepy also understood that certain people were assigned different colors. For example if Eno were talking to Deepy and Eno's walls changed to red, he would know another fleet commander was calling. That was the only example CHIP had given him of that arrangement, with CHIP adding he could override anyone at any time. "Must be nice to be so all-powerful," Deepy had told him – a remark CHIP just ignored.

Anyway, just a thought seems to take care of a lot of things around here, Deepy now thought, "Thanks to CHIP." Deepy's eyes immediately took in his nose... no orange glow. No invasion of privacy now. If anyone wants me they can 'blue the room' or em-connect, although no one had ever interrupted one of his many naps before, unless he asked for a wake-up call. (A wake-up call or 'em-connect' amounted to a conscious "shiver.")

Deepy relaxed for a minute, taking some slow, deep breaths. The invasion of privacy thought then re-surfaced and he knew he had to deal with what was troubling him ... the moral issue of human abduction, although he rationalized they weren't really abducted; they were "borrowed" for a while. He knew the woman was safe back in her house and most likely would have no memories or unpleasant dreams, unless a "cloaking" dream became necessary to cover an actual memory.

He again pictured the woman in his mind. He had only left her finally when she had been entranced to leave the ship to return home. Two Marsianoid "transport units" were escorting her. Perhaps that was it. Perhaps people were naturally afraid of those little gray aliens because they were always the first and last to invade a person's private space. Deepy was used to them by now and actually thought they were cute, just as Shel thought he was, he reckoned. A subthought wondered if Marsianoids might make good pets. Another subthought apologized for that one.

As best he could tell, whenever he would start to ask about the Marsianoids he would simply lose his train of thought for a moment. "Unless, I'm just confused," he told himself. He knew he stayed that way much of the time around here. "Strange... all very strange" and strange, he thought now, that he even remembered not remembering. How odd. "Losing it?" he asked himself – "Again?"

Speaking of losing one's train of thought, he thought, "Where was I, anyway?" He literally shook his body and got back to thinking about the woman guest. How ironically unfunny, he thought..."guest" indeed.

Invaded her privacy, big time... that's what they, "er, we did," he corrected himself. And he didn't even know her name. And he couldn't ask. He was not allowed to talk to humans, since dogs don't talk, and of course CHIP wouldn't open a telep line.

Deepy's thoughts were drifting now, remembering the weird circumstances that led to this unique mission of his, aboard this alien spacecraft. "No, not now," he told himself "... too tired all of a sudden... the emotions catching up. Tired – too tired. Maybe I'm on overload, maybe I need a nap... maybe subconsciously I really don't want to deal with all this, or don't know how. Maybe I just need a nap... maybe I... maybe... hmmm...

UH....*ZZZZZZZZZZZZPZZZ!*"

CHAPTER 4
"Robo Chef"

When Deepy awoke, he thought he'd been dreaming. He seemed to remember big, brown eyes staring at him, eyes that were filled with a longing of some kind, or a wistful sort of helplessness... sadness – loneliness – love? He wasn't sure. He also noticed a musky odor now and he felt... well, damp, somehow from mustiness in the room he had not noticed before. There were remnants of visions floating just beyond the edge of his mind's eye that he couldn't quite make out. He thought he heard a woman's voice, but there was no one there. "To hell with it," he rolled over. "What time is it anyway?" He glanced at a spot on the wall and was rewarded with a digital readout in just that spot. With the word "time" in his mind, the room's com-Bot monitor had read his need. Intentions and needs, some things they always seemed to know around here. It bugged Deepy a little, but caused him to smile over the double meaning of the word, 'bugged.'

At least I now know what time it is, he thought... five hours later than the last time I checked, right before dozing off. Too late, he realized, for dinner with his favorite female of late... the lovely Ms. Shelena Dann. But still, not too late for a meal, thank God, before his meeting with Eno. As if on cue, he heard from his stomach, which was not used to such treatment. Past time to be on the move he told himself.

"Blue Shelena," Deepy waited a split second. CHIP came on the line.

"Sorry, Deepy, Shel is with the ship Commander – not to be disturbed."

"I wouldn't dream of it, CHIP," Deepy retorted, somewhat chagrined at CHIP's formal tone, making it sound as if Deepy might have considered interrupting if the man were just plain "Eno." That's all, CHIP. Thank you." Come to think of it, he thought, I've never heard CHIP call Eno anything but Doctor Mai or Commander.

"It's how I was brought up," CHIP now told him.

"All right, knock off the eavesdropping. It's not nice."

"I'm not eavesdropping... I'm spying."

"Ha-Ha, but I'm in no mood. Just woke up and therefore grumpy... and hungry too. Matter of fact, I'll be there shortly. Warm up the griddle. Now... skedaddle," Deepy told him playfully and hoped it came across that way.

"Yee Ha!"

Guess it did, considering the "good ol' boy" response. Reckon I will dine alone tonight, Deepy thought. He had vaguely taken it for granted that Shel would be available to join him for conversation, if nothing else. "Whelp, ever onward..." he thought, "first to the diner and then to Eno's space for a chat."

The diner was a diner for Deepy. They had asked him and he had told them. He wanted his onboard "hangout" to be a replica of a 1950's style, American diner. It was in fact his old high school haunt lifted by CHIP from a series of memories in the mind of a seventeen-year-old Larry Ray James and transposed into a "Mental Assembler"' set. Of course he could not begin to fathom that he would be seeing it someday as his older self, and in a dog's body inside a UFO. Of course even the thought of such an experience seemed nutty or unreal, although it felt real enough.

"Amazing," Deepy James told himself once again as he looked around with his renewed, fresh, fond memories of old friends in this brought-back-to-life setting on board ship. "Fantastic," he now thought, that CHIP could allow him to see some of his old high school buddies in their "real-life" retro forms at times. It sure made Deepy feel young and "at home" to see himself and his friends acting like they always did – even though they could not be heard. CHIP had said that would be too much of a distraction. Just watching them, along with his younger self, was engrossing enough. Those were actual scenes borrowed from that earlier time, CHIP had told him. Sometimes he would sit and try to read their lips, especially his own and then recalling a particular conversation – usually about girls or sports.

No one of course could interact with them directly, and CHIP said Deepy was the only one who could see them at all. In fact, sometimes quin or other shipmates would sit where they appeared to be - causing them to instantly disappear. While he never specifically requested that his friends appear, CHIP seemed to know when Deepy somehow needed to look up from across the room or a nearby table to see them. CHIP's 'Assembler' worked that magic somehow to replay some of his memories as if they were recorded first-hand all those years ago. In fact, they were there so often that Deepy became able to ignore them as just a stable comfort, with everything else he had on his mind.

Nice of Eno to arrange that the Assembler room itself served, in reality, as "Deepy's Diner" to everyone entering, until they could get seated and situated into their own virtual setting or comfort station scenarios, as Shel called them. There were "virtual reality" headphones or 'transport baffles' in place above all of the chairs, and if any emitted blue beams onto a chair, it meant someone had left the ship from that spot and it was reserved for their return. It was a bit disconcerting at times to see someone suddenly pop back into place, as if he or she had been there all along. Sometimes their scenario junkets were virtual and sometimes real, if they had business or pleasure reasons for actually leaving the ship. There was in fact a special, reserved 'baffle table' for a group of thirteen VIBs, although COG considered everyone equally important. Sure enough, Deepy had noticed those "Very Important Beings" varied, and could be most anyone at any time, with most of them only vaguely familiar to Deepy's very short-term memory.

He supposedly had met everyone onboard during his "welcoming ceremony" two weeks ago. Eno had said there was usually about one hundred staff onboard. Occasionally some would stop by his table for short visits and polite conversation as to how the *project* was going. Nice folks, he had long ago decided. The place was empty now, except for a few quin.

There was a Wurlitzer jukebox in the corner, with his favorite nineteen-fifties, early sixties tunes, even some from the eighties for the older Larray; pennants hanging for the home team, plus their main rivals, and some nearby colleges, as well as all the major-league baseball teams and a few football teams. Booths lined the walls with tables in the center and there was a small counter-bar too. One of the walls with booths was glass and appeared to offer a "live" and changing view of Broad Street of his hometown. The quin nearly always gravitated to those booths. They seemed fascinated by the cars and people going by.

Deepy kept his back to that scene as it was too distracting for him and strange, knowing he was looking back at least forty years from his more modern perch. Talk about surreal – a middle-aged man in a dog body in a TranShip of the mid nineteen-nineties, looking out the window onto the 1950's. He loved it, but at the same time he could get lost in it. Deepy hopped up on a chair at one of the tables, and then noticed Jim and Mike, two of his best high school buddies, come in and sit down at the bar. He wondered vaguely where he was – his teenage self – as the three were nearly always together.

I can enjoy this again for a while, he thought, thanks to the ship CHIP. Seems weird and a bit spooky though, he mused, to have a chance to actually see and seem like my teenage self again, while living as an older man now enshrouded in a dog's body... 'But for very good reasons,' he reminded himself.

Deepy recalled he had come into this situation as a fifty-five year old man with an apparently terminal tumor of the brain. He had subconsciously accepted the mission in exchange for a promised "spontaneous remission" of what would otherwise be his demise. That was it in a nutshell. "Whoa," he told himself that he didn't want to think about that now.

And yet his thoughts played on, as he continued to think he would be able to resume a new life with CeCe. Eno had told him so. Problem was, he couldn't remember CeCe, other than her name and status as his wife. Eno said that was best for now. He trusted Eno, even though at the moment, he couldn't remember exactly how he had ever met him in the first place. He did have vague memories of a dream related to a Prince or a Princess?

Deepy's memory problems were caused by the limitation of the dog's brain size and type, according to CHIP, who then said he was joking, but that he might explain later if he thought Deepy really needed to know. Then he said he was only kidding again and was just practicing to become a human. That's when Deepy told him he would never make it because he just wasn't silly enough. CHIP then had explained that he selectively programmed Deepy's memories, according to mission needs, with personal needs taking a far back seat, and usually with just the most recent three-day memory supply for recall. CHIP called the arrangement Deepy's "cache register." However, CHIP had, he said, a special "intuition" circuit which allowed him to fairly accurately surmise what Deepy might want to think, and so could – fix him up – accordingly.

Deepy thought CHIP was full of something besides circuitry and told him so, which he supposed CHIP must have known he wanted to do and thus allowed it. Deepy's wry sense of self appreciated that.

"Six weeks work," Eno had told him, and eventually he could return home in perfect health. He didn't really know what perfect health might be, but as he sat in the diner now, confusing his human and dog selves, he promised himself that as soon as he got back home he would go on a diet. But for now... well, sorry but the food is just too good here. In Deepy's opinion, CHIP was a master chef, even though Deepy mostly ate burgers. CHIP really could make anything Deepy's little heart and big appetite desired. "Good," Deepy thought, "that the super ship-CHIP also serves as Robo-Chef."

"What sounds good, today?" Deepy was wondering as his stomach was telling him to get on with it and order something. "Let's see, stomach," Deepy thought, "what about something with cornbread... yup, some chicken and dumplings with fried cornbread. Yepper, I'm just a double-dandy "gin-u-wine" Dixie dog and proud of it. Whoops, if anybody's listening, that's just an expression. Pride's got nothing to do with it. I just happen to be from the southern tier of the good ol' USA and I love good down-home, country cooking, by doggie. But, that's too much starch," he then thought.

"This is Dr. Robo-Chef," CHIP told him... paused, and then added expectantly "... and I'm listening."

"You're telling me that – like I don't know it. Well, you read my mind again, maybe even made it up for me, ol' chipperooni, 'cause I'm ready to order, thank you: fried chicken please, with a half-dozen butterfly shrimp on the side; some fries and a good portion of onion rings." (His stomach was growling gratefully) "Pride," he thought, might not have anything to do with it, but "fried" – Whoa now – 'fried' had everything to do with being a good ol' southern hot dog.

Anyhow, CHIP had told him that first day, that it was all the same food – all manna from heaven, made to order ("harmoniously reconstituted," CHIP had said) for anyone on ship, according to the pleasure of the taste buds. It helped, of course, that Deepy wanted, with all his heart, to believe that he was not getting one bit fatter, and, indeed, just could be getting slimmer and healthier, even as he fed himself up to his gullet – meal after meal – blaming the gluttony on his animal nature.

"What's the downside, since perfect health awaits me?" he wondered as he sat there, with anticipating taste buds and a very impatient belly that he would swear seemed to be gaining girth. He then felt ashamed. Gluttony is a deadly sin; he knew that, but he rationalized he was eating more because he was so out of his element. Besides it was reconstituted for good health. "Huh, reconstituted, un-constituted, what does it matter?" He would be in perfect health when he returned home.

"Heaven... I'm in heaven..." He sang to himself, as best a dog-man can. Then he realized he could be listening to "Beyond the Sea." It had begun automatically when Deepy first came in. The volume then lowered to background when he quit paying attention. To crank it up again, he would need to think "MMp," if he believed everything that CHIP told him. 'MMp' stands for "Music, Maestro, please," CHIP had said. His jukebox would play each song in sequence from where the volume had lowered the last time. The music would stop if Deepy went out, or completely tuned out. Or, he could listen to any song just by requesting it of CHIP-Jock.

"CHIP," he now said, "let me have a chocolate shake with that order...uh, please."

"Too late; you're getting one whether you want it or not."

"Oh, I want it... I want it alright. Ain't no doubt about it."

"Heaven... I'm in heaven... whoops... MMP," he paused, and waited for Bobby, then caught up "... *Somewhere waiting for me... my lover stands on golden saaaands, and watches the ships that go saaaailing.*" Deepy's teenage memory sang it out with Gusto, his childhood imaginary friend.

"Whoops," he announced again. "Sorry." He said this to the quin who were staring at him from across the room. He realized he had been thinking out loud just then and singing out loud before that. "Up Boy," he told himself now. His mental shield then rose to hide his thoughts. He wasn't quite used to all this mental telepathy business yet.

"Oh, I don't know..." CHIP told him, "I kind of enjoy your mental mumbo-jumbo... but not as much as you do, especially when you're trying to be funny. Notice, I said 'trying.'"

"Damn," Deepy thought. "Speaking of 'trying,' CHIP, that's what you are, and you're not funny. Excuse me, but I'm always forgetting you can never tune me out, or never will anyway. Besides, I guess you must enjoy it... you're the one who's letting me remember all this stuff... and why is that?"

"Why is what? Remember what? Which tune?" CHIP answered, and paused until he was sure Deepy was going to just ignore him.

"Seriously it's because you usually are too serious around everybody onboard... when we all just want you to be yourself. I give you more opportunities to do that than you realize. And of all places, this setting is where you should be the most relaxed. But, I understand this is all so new and different for you, you won't entirely let your guard down, so to speak. I need that though, when you can."

"What do you want me to do? – Get on the table and dance a jig? Oops, sorry. Thanks CHIP, I'm sure you mean well, so give me a break from the steady dose of spying, and I don't mean to seem rude, but at least sometimes allow me to at least think I'm alone – not that I don't enjoy your company most of the time - 'Ahem...' thanks, again "Buddy," Deepy reiterated, not wanting to hurt CHIP's feelings.

Deepy waited a minute: 'let my guard down... he needs me to – jeez.' "Okay, I admit it," he now thought – "One of these days I'm really going to embarrass myself, or possibly hurt someone's feelings, or CHIP's not going to be there when I really need him. No wait, that couldn't happen, could it? Why am I so grumpy, anyway?"

"Wonder why it's taking so long? It never takes this long. CHIP must know I'm starving – CHIP, you there? Hello?"

Deepy knew it was virtually impossible to hurt the feelings of a COG. They claimed to be in a perpetual state of joy, with only two "feelings," namely *Love* and *Grace*, which they called "thoughtful feelings." Said it had nothing to do with ego-sensual feelings such as humans suffer. "Suffer," Eno had said; then said, "We know because at one time in your beginning we suffered right along with you, as we tried to help people in more direct ways, wanting to tutor you down a moral path. Frankly, we couldn't take it, and we don't see how you do, especially since you have a choice, which most hybrids just will not accept as real."

He sure didn't know at the time what Eno had meant by all that, as they had been interrupted at that point. No wonder, Deepy mused, that communications were still sometimes difficult between "... them and us." Deepy knew essentially that was the case even now with his own human spirit being attached to the soul anima of this 'cute' dog. His ego still wanted him to somehow be special, so he went along with Shel's description of him.

"So, I'm cute... most dogs are!" His thoughts rambled on – "Good Lord, what's taking so…

His food arrived. "Thank you," he said rather curtly to the quin, but then smiled at her. She looked like a young waitress from his high school days. He also thanked the Lord for his food and all his blessings, noting, "This prayer was brought to you by the letter "C" for "Chicken, chops, cheese... er, chow and CHIP... in that order."

He heard CHIP mutter, "Best think about 'that order,' in case you wish to order again later. You should have been a chow, you... er, uh, good doggie," he finally allowed, *sarcastically* maybe.

"I'm sorry, CHIP, if I seemed out of sorts before – if I ever had any 'sorts' to begin with, whatever they are. Anyway, welcome to my silly world. Guess I was just grouchy from being really hungry." Deepy smiled at the quin as she turned to leave after returning with his milkshake. He had lowered his shield, "Down Boy," so he could thank her.

"Eat hearty," she said, turning back for a moment, "There's more where that came from." She grinned very prettily – tooth missing and all. He thanked her again, with a big smile of his own. He didn't understand how a dog could smile, but…

"Now, what did you want CHIP?"

"You don't have to do that anymore," CHIP told him.

"What – do what?"

"Say 'up boy,' 'down boy' anymore. I've got the conditions worked out now for your telepathy process. It usually doesn't take so long, but then you're a dog."

"So what – You're a robot or something. Oops, there I go again. Sorry CHIP, I'm glad you got my process worked out. I meant to say you're a wonderful robot."

"Ah, my friend, Deepy, how you do have grumbling moments now and then, and love to aggravate me, but I'm catching on. Now relax; your food's getting cold. Put those chops to work."

Deepy dug in and did just that, always appreciating that his meals were precut to bite-size portions. "MMp," he managed to say between smacking lips. Bobby sang his heart out for another thirty seconds or so. Grease spattered. Shake slurped. "Heaven," Deepy thought, as the music segued.

"*Uh-O-Oh yes ... I'm the great pre-tender ... happy and gay like a clown...*" the Platters now sang, "*... my mind's made up, I pretend too much ... I'm lonely, there's no one around...*"

That did appear to be the case, Deepy noticed. All the quin had disappeared and he was now dining alone. He made a mental note to ask Eno about homosexuals... then wondered where that thought had come from. But then he often wondered from whence his thoughts cometh – speaking biblically he now told himself.

Deepy adroitly pawed down on a shrimp and bit it down to the tail. The Platters kept right on singing as he attended to the platter before him. After a couple of minutes, he thought "... finally ... the king."

"*Do you wanna be... myyyuhhh teddy bearrr?*" Elvis wondered, and Deepy noticed he was starting to feel nostalgic. Some large, loving, brown eyes suddenly came to mind. "... Not a teddy bear," he thought "... or a clown." Wistful, they seemed.

Bloated now, Deepy really did feel like the stuffed animal he was. He actually felt as though he might be waddling, as he made his way down the corridor, thinking he needed to stop off at the john on his way to the doctor's residence-office.

Not only was Eno Mai the "doctor in charge;" this versatile entity was also TranShip III Commander and his office was his castle as well. Therein, Deepy knew, was contained a rather fancy privy or throne, but he felt uncomfortable using it, or for that matter any other john on board if there happened to be a COG or Humangel nearby. Peculiar of him, he knew, because public toilets with humans around had never bothered him especially. COG and Angels never needed "to go," so the few privies were there for guests of a different physiology, if they even had an "ology," since they essentially were spiritual.

"Anyway," his mind prattled on, "Humangels only breathe spirit (i.e. eat from their "Tree of Life") to keep their Spirits up, as they put it." Everything with them seems to be for function over form. He didn't know if they were into unction or not, but they seem to have taken the 'fun' out of function, or as his Mama used to say, 'All work and no play, makes Jack a dull boy.' His Mama always seemed to have trite little sayings for everything.

COG and Humangels operated off the Mental Energy of God, but their appearance was pure Human, meaning perfect bodies, with some subtle variances in facial features, and skin tones ranging all over the place, meaning some he had never seen on Earth. He did notice there were plenty of exact twins around, even some triplets. Were they clones? "Only virtually," Eno had said "... and not contrived. They are all as natural as the first-born." He had then surprised Deepy by saying that all those different faces Deepy saw onboard were replicated thousands of times over, along with their bodies too of course. So, all of them had multiple images somewhere. He could at least vouch for one, as there was a duplicate of Shel onboard. She was a COG doctor, and Deepy seldom saw her, but when he did she always was in uniform, as she did a lot of transiting between ships in the COG fleet on temporary duty assignments. The first time he had seen her though, he thought he was asking Shel where she got her uniform. She then introduced herself as Dr. Adnil Rellog.

There were no discernible differences between Humangels and pure COG, as far as Deepy could tell. That's because everyone looked like perfect Humans. Supposedly, a COG's natural Spirit form could not be seen, so they often would cohabit with another form, usually a Humangel, either Earthite or Marsian. Everyone looked "solid" in his or her Othereal form. He and Shel were outfitted in Othereal forms also, for this excursion. It had to be that way – it was explained to them – in order for them to see everyone as real or substantive, just as they saw material bodies. One must have "eyes to see," in any case.

Eno was a pure COG – a Child or Cell – a "Trangel*" directly from the Ethos of God Mind. Humangel-COG made up most of the other "Human" forms onboard. Deepy couldn't remember at the moment if he knew anything about the quin or the Marsians. *(Pure, from birth, indivisibly-dual Angels that can transition between Yin and Yang polarity, or be neutral, in accord with God's will)

Deepy and Shel also learned that during earthly material realm excursions, Humangels could temporarily 'gel' or fuse enough to function as normal material forms. In fact, either polarity, Yin or Yang could do this, even at the same time. They rarely did it anymore, as un-gelling could be problematic, even somewhat risky at times, if chaotic situations were to develop from which they needed a quick escape. That was much more likely to happen now, Eno had said, in Earth's advanced, but polluted, technological cauldron, than it did in the olden days of biblical Angels.

In their Othereal abode, Humangels are perfected replicas of the physical Humans who once served as their material world templates. Humangels began as encapsulated "thought-forms" created by God's Children working through their humanimal archetypes. The rudimentary features of the human hosts were smoothed and rounded into perfect symmetry by the cohabitating COG, who eventually formed an Othereal 'Spirit' replica of COG Form and Essence within their hosts and then took it to Heaven with them. God Mind required more Cellular* substance because of the amount SHE lost in the 'Big Bang.' *(more Spirit-Souls)

His mind now wandering, Deepy was drawn to the analogy that Othereal bodies were really office-residences also. Even human physical bodies could be thought of that way, or perhaps as clothing or veils, temporarily worn by tiny souls that commune with God Mind through the hybrid human fused spirit brain-set that provides a karmic life diagram to each form.

"But me, alas, I'm just an animal," Deepy now thought, - "A man-dog, who feels like a pig after eating so much."

COG and Humangels were not the least bit body-conscious - all looking like perfect Humans from Hollywood's central casting. They acted like they didn't even have bodies to consider, although around Earthites, as they often called hybrid humans, they were thoughtful enough to clothe themselves. They wore clothes strictly for climate, or discretionary purposes around Earthites. Most of the quin and Humangels on board the ship were wearing shorts and T-shirts. They did appreciate colors though and sometimes their mix-matches seemed a bit bizarre to Deepy. Quin men and women also came in virtually perfect human forms, but Deepy could not remember just then, what the essential difference was between quin and Humans. He was thinking Eno had told him the quin were former incarnate hybrid humans that COG now were tutoring as angels in apprenticeship to become AppCOG. Deepy was just glad that all quin were bald, both men and women, as that allowed him to distinguish them from COG, and the "Others" - as Humangels sometimes were called.

As for Deepy, he was still embarrassed at being bare-assed, especially around Shel. But, he could take solace in the fact that tomorrow CHIP would have a wardrobe ready for Deepy's comfort, or 'fashion pleasure' as Shel had put it. "Can't imagine it taking this long," he thought and then remembered that the COG were surprised when he even mentioned clothing - "Clothing for a dog?" They never expressed any disdain, however, since they knew the idea came from a "hybrid" dog. The whole concept seemed absurd - "Man as dog!" he had thought. "My human psyche, what's left of it, is having a coping problem."

Shel, gorgeous as the hybrid human she was, also looked perfect to Deepy. She was wearing hot pink shorts with a chartreuse top when he last saw her, and looking like a 1960's model babe. Those colors looked good on her though. Anything would... "Oops, wrong thinking for a married dog," he thought, but then excused himself, knowing there was no lust involved. At least he didn't think so, but... still somehow wrong, he thought. At any rate, he was sure glad she was on board. "Maybe it's because she really is an Earthite human visitor – like me – well, something like me anyway." He chuckled at his subthought that Shel was no "bitch.*" He thought he had noticed a special relationship between them right from the start and so assumed it was because of their earthly bonds. *(female dog)

He also thought it helped that Shel was a 'she,' even though all the females on board were distinctive somehow in unique ways. They each seemed to have their own personal aura, and like the men, were all virtually the same, yet with subtle facial forms, plus height differences and the baldness of the quin ["*quin*tessential angel interns" is the term he couldn't remember]

Deepy also recalled being corrected by CHIP when he had referred to more than one quin as quins. He guessed it was sort of like COG, standing both for Child of God or Children of God, or more precisely, "Cell" of God. But, quin was always spelled with a small Q, and COG was capitalized all the way through. "Thank you." "FYI," CHIP had said, also telling Deepy how to spell CHIP, as if Deepy didn't know. He didn't, since it was a capital "CHIP" acronym all the way through too. Anyhow – he was getting bored with himself now, thinking he must be lost aboard this pretty doggone big "Mother of a ship," he mumbled.

Eno had told him about the quin, 'but I can't remember now for the life of me, what he said...' 'Imagine that,' he told himself sarcastically, while vaguely recalling he had a similar thought about the quin just moments before, or thought he did. "Jeez," he thought, but then couldn't remember what he momentarily thought he might have forgotten he remembered. "Bonkers!" – Another little fantasy town in Texas, he recalled.

Deepy now recognized that his thoughts were getting on his nerves. "Yea verily..." his mind meandered on anyway... as he recalled that CHIP had once told him that the food he prepared for Deepy contained extra bulk for his dog constitution. "Why? – Are you trying to amend my constitution?" he had wondered at the time to CHIP, who just ignored the silly overture. Remembering this caused Deepy to recall that everyone in this ship setting was of perfect proportions because they hardly ever ate anything, which befit their own constitutions he imagined.

"I'll never get used to being a dog. Glad I don't have to. My part of this mission will be over in about a month," he reminded himself, and managed what he thought might be a smile. He wondered what his dog smile might look like. He thought he could feel it on his face, but he had never seen it. He had never really seen himself as a dog. He wondered what he looked like, since there were no mirrors around to tell him and he couldn't quite picture a "Yorkie-Poo". Thanks to Shel and a general knowledge of dogs, he knew he was 'cute,' although a 'Yorkie-Poo' sounded like a silly breed to him. Who wants to be a 'Poo' – why not a Border collie or a Golden retriever? – A 'Poo' indeed and a Yorkie one at that. Pooh-bah Humbug! With that exclamation he then realized he really did need to be lap-sized for the mission. Oh well.

"Ah, here's a john." Still wishing for a mirror so he could check his own bizarre looks, about all Deepy could see of himself now as he pushed his way into the privy was the tip of his nose glowing orange. He then realized he had been basking in a strange glow for he didn't know how long, as he was focused inwardly. "Crap," he thought, and then chuckled, considering his surroundings, even as he immediately regretted his foul language and previous ramblings. He couldn't help but wonder how long, whomever this was, had been tuned in to his "mental aberrations," if they had been. "Wonder if they were?"

"Yo – howdy – Hello?" he said and waited. He was orange with expectation, but no one spoke up. He waited, trying not to think at all. Long pause. "Nice nose," he finally thought, "very colorful." It flashed off at that moment. "Hope I didn't embarrass anyone. Not likely. Just myself," he thought, "Anyway, I've got more immediate things to be about, at the moment."

Deepy made himself as comfortable as he could, wishing he had stopped by his room. He had thought he was on his way to Eno's, but maybe he had taken the long way around. He was just happy it was not one of his emergency moments. These things definitely were not meant for dogs, but what choice did he have considering he was now about to experience the 'downside' of over-eating. The toilet in his room was the only one that had been modified. "I'm glad all these things come with automatic spray-clean and blow dryers. I've got a feeling I'm going to be in here awhile," he was thinking ... then just as suddenly 'feeling' a pain in his vibrating head.

"There goes my em-connect. Great timing," he told himself, while at the same time saying, "Deepy here."

"Deepy, this is Eno, I couldn't reach your private-connect."

"I'm buzzed off, Eno. CHIP and BB have me rigged up so that my nose glows orange. I'm just out of luck if I don't happen to notice, I guess."

"Right, well, you are a bit of a new breed."

Deepy explained his nasal-nexus problem. "BB is waiting now to see if the auto-audio will self-adjust. He and CHIP are both on top of the problem, or so they tell me. It was all right until yesterday. They expect it to start working again, any moment now."

"Deep," Eno said, "I know you're probably on your way here by now, but I need a little more time."

"No prob, Doc, how long?"

"About ten minutes or so."

"No problem at all, Eno," Deepy said, "believe me."

"Oh, I always believe you, Deepy," Eno chuckled, adding "see you soon then."

Deepy perched there with his random "john" thoughts, and getting a headache now, he noticed. He was thinking that maybe Eno had over-read something that he thought might embarrass Deepy, and that's why he called back on the Em-connect.

[Deepy had no way of knowing that Shel had made the first call from Eno's office, and simply didn't want to embarrass him, since she had caught a glimpse of him just moments before on the ship-Mon, entering the 'loo,' as she called it.]

"Funny thing about my dog memory," Deepy was thinking now, not being able to remember what Eno might have over-read during the orange-glow hook-up, or lack thereof.

"Good grief," he now wondered how he was going to do what he was about to "double do," after he started wearing clothes. "Have mercy."

Sitting on his throne, he thought of a joke. He told it to himself: Father Murphy walks into a bar on Bourbon Street...
... He asks the first man he meets, 'Do you want to go to heaven?'
The man said, 'I do, Father.'
The Father tells him, 'Then stand over there against the wall.'
Then the priest asks a second man, 'Do you want to go to heaven?'
'Certainly, Father,' the man replied.
'Then stand over there against the wall,' said the priest.
Then Father Murphy walked up to Boudreau and asked, 'Do you want to go to heaven?'
Boudreau said, 'No, I don't Father.'
The priest said, 'I don't believe this. You mean to tell me that when you die you don't want to go to heaven?'
Boudreau said, 'Oh, when I die, yes, of course. I thought you were getting a group together to go now.']
ıııııııııııııııııııııı

Heaven can only wait so long; it would be best to pack your moral gear <u>NOW</u>.
ΙΙΙΙΙΙΙΙΙΙΙΙΙΙΙΙΙΙΙΙΙΙΙΙΙΙΙΙΙΙΙΙΙΙΙΙΙΙΙΙΙΙΙΙΙΙ

God loved the world enough to allow one of her pure Children to become a Human "be-in," to die and then rise from death to show that eternal life can be attained through God's Grace - by spirit-soul mates capable of understanding.

[Adapted from the *Holy Bible, Book of John*, C <u>3</u>, V <u>16</u>]

(CHAPTER 5)
Roll Over

Deepy slept late the next morning. It was Saturday and he had the weekend off. In fact, he remembered, as his mind was trying to get untangled from bits and pieces of a dream, 'today's a holiday' ... the entire crew has the day off. It's only a holiday because everyone has the day off. Eno had said it was not a special occasion, otherwise. A day off was rare, he understood, except for Sundays, which were free for beatitude, or communion, and various types of social interactions, such as fun and games.

Deepy lay there in a slumber state, trying to put his dream back together. It was surreal. He distinctly recalled Eno sitting at his bedside sometime during the night and saying, 'I'm going to tell you a 'dream.' That's what he said, and CHIP recalled it for him later – with this advice: "You know how confusing dreams can be. Just do your best to understand now, and then I will remind you again when it's time to write your book."

['... In the beginning, God established a "cosmological constant" upon which opposing polar fields would act for the purpose of setting up dimensional boundaries. Then, when God imploded and exploded on the scene, the polar fields of Othereal and physical planes were established in the cosmos, including everything your telescopes can see now, and much, much more.

['The underworld, or nether regions, of planets formed around the indivisibly-dual "polar" plexuses of their electro-magnetic fields, with everything seeming to coalesce and then change any numbers of times, as God put her universal puzzle together. The final work included two dimensions within the same general region – a small fused-spirit or material dimension and an exceedingly bigger, more suffused, diffuse Otherealm, infusing and encompassing the smaller one. The Otherealm is known by hybrids in terms of dark matter and energy, but it has effusive light unavailable to human eyes and it pervades God's "Child."

[That birthing scenario held sway at the beginning, but now God is close to reincorporating her material world back into her Spiritual Otherealm. SHE wants her mental cells or tiny spirit-souls back within her own Purely Moral Mind, that is to say those 'tinys' who are moral; otherwise SHE will make them part of her Heavenly Host of subconscious Spirit. Most people who don't understand and act on the information in your book, will have that in their future, but will never consciously realize it.

[In the aftermath of the Big Bang, the cosmological bodies of fused spirit particles became more and more hardened, or gelled, and many would serve as life-supporting physical spheres. God would later use these as Gardens for her Angel corps, so that SHE might reconstruct and revitalize many of her fused, former Mental Cells into pure Spirit forms for a new, third aspect of her Conscious Self – a "Child," as it were. This new Heavenly Body would center between her indivisibly-dual, polar opposite Minds, in order to bind them together again for eternity, while necessarily keeping them indivisibly dual. The magnetism that plays between them everywhere is called a gravitational field.

[As we said, many Angel Gardens were created throughout the universe, including two planets in the Scorpio constellation. One was called "Ant," and the other was known as "Ares" (Airees) - and they existed, oh my goodness, a long, long matter of time ago..." {COG often refer to time synonymously with matter, as 'time' and the material world come with a transmogrification* date}] *("CHIP likes big words," Eno told Deepy, later. "But for the record, "transformation" works just as well.")

{CHIP did not dispute his Lord, but later got the last word. COG may use any morally acceptable word, but some hybrids do have a problem with "elite" intellect and can make anything divisive since intelligence varies so much among them. Mental variations among hybrids often result in conflicts – even with word usage, and so the Commander wanted a more familiar term, as is understandable." CHIP further noted: "Deepy's dream sequence was not interrupted by this exchange, but because it was part of the official Ship Log he wanted it for his book, thinking there might be a moral message in there, and Dr. Mai confirmed there was a simple one. Go figure.}

[Two particular Gardens revolved around the star known as Antares. The civilization known as the Ants lived on one planet, while the Ares lived on the other. These were simply two societies of Perfect Humans – the Yin Ares and the

Yang Ants - living as close neighbors, while they each served God as matrix forms* for Humangels. *{COG cohabited within the fused spirit brain forms of each individual in order to co-create Humangel Mental Cells for life in the Otherealm, through effectively generating a Moral Spirit within Human bodies, in something of a "caterpillar cocoon" manner.} Perfect Humans, you may recall, are humanimals with cohabiting COG, who use the humanimal bodies as their matrix labs.

[In the case of those two Antares planets, their seeding stocks of humanimal 'ares' and 'ants' lived in underground Gardens, each serving its polar opposite Human society, which operated laboratories outside the Gardens.

[The Humans, with their COG Operators, would visit the breeding grounds for new stock whenever their older ares or ants succumbed to the laws of physics. The COG took good care of the two planetary animal genders and there was never any conflict between humanimals, which were pet-like in their demeanor.

[All Perfect Human civilizations everywhere in the universe were neighbors, in the sense that they all were one with God. They were one, because all Humans contained Children Of God Souls (cohabitants) who are God's Co-Creators and caretakers in the material realm of God's existence. It was not unusual to have both Yin (female) and Yang (male) COG living on neighboring planets; or even on the same planet, since they were disciplined and kept their distance from each other, except during mating seasons. COG would cohabit only one polarity (gender) in each garden, so that Souls would not attract their opposites. Each Garden would be either Yin or Yang.

[Like all such hosts, humanimals were co-opted to share their fused spirit forms (body-brains) with God Mind's pure Othereal COG Cells, which then operated them as perfect Humans with direct access to the Supreme God Mind. Humans were created to process spectral-Spirit Humangels (gelled Othereal forms) through mankind's archetypal fused spirit – meaning their material forms.

[COG would, over a matter of time, create many such Angels from within each Human matrix, with one COG succeeding another when each had completed multiple replicas of its own 'ain' (self) gel form. Oftentimes the same COG would return at intervals to that Garden or another to recreate other entities, sometimes using the same matrix. Every humanimal was replaced when it was no longer sufficiently potent. It was allowed to "retire" on its home grounds until its body naturally expired. After its demise, its former tiny "homing" soul would then move to a new matrix lab. Meantime that tiny soul would serve as a "comforter" to its former COG co-host.

[COG operated autonomously as unattached adjuncts to their material forms and were able to release each of their formed Humangel entities and escort them to heaven where they matured into God-enabled Othereal Angel appCOG,* which later would join God Jr. *{*App*rentice Child Of God}

[Virtually, that same release mechanism still works in the case of the spirit-souls of modern hybrid humans who eventually become morally worthy and whose inner body/brain spiritual assembly essentially can be sustained as an Othereal Spirit entity. It is sustained only through continued communion with God through its maturing Spirit-Soul.

[Few hybrid angel entities are completed within just one physical lifetime and their same Over-Souls usually return them many times to physical life with their tiny souls to make more moral progress. They start 'life' anew each time and are not usually burdened by memories of previous lives. They do however bring into each life the influences of the spirit-soul's changing character, along with any mental or physical talents they may have practiced.]

This 'dream talk' continued, as provided by CHIP, one of the Ship's Central Hyper-Intelligence Processors. He inserted this comment: [Yes, some of your future readers, my Deep friend, will think your dream is fantasy, but they should have faith in their ability to understand that it is 'Othereal' or supernal, and provided for their enlightenment. If they cannot make sense of it, it's likely because their mind is confused by ordinary beliefs – or they are just bored by unusual thinking and can't concentrate.

[The COG created Humangels by psychically metamorphosing the Human fused-spirits (body/brains) into mentally self-aware subsets of inner Othereal twins - from gestation to maturity. These became full-sized replicas of the outer shell of the archetype, replete with some functioning inner systems and outer spectral spirit. They had no need to replicate all parts of the body/brain or the electro-chemical nervous system with its hormonal aspects. They also had no use for an instinctive "id," for example.

[Many of the Othereal aspects of physical parts are meant to serve diverse and different functions within God's Otherealm, than those served by their material world counterparts.

[At maturity, all Humangels would transcend into the Otherealm of the Holy God Host, or "Holy G'host," aka God's Child, as the third Aspect of her Trinity. In some, not all Gardens, after its Angel was complete, each COG would take it, but leave behind the original tiny 'homing' cell (soul) portion of Holy Spirit to serve as an attachment nexus for another generation. That 'tiny' cell or soul also temporarily kept the humanimal in the higher mental state of self awareness, even as the 'tiny' unfortunately was being targeted by the 'id,' the body's protective mechanism. A replacement COG Lord would then arrive within the vacated Human almost immediately after departure of its predecessor COG with its Humangel. The replacement COG would stop all inner-body id (neurotransmitter) activity affecting the "seat of the Soul,"- the so-called *Third Eye* pineal gland.

[The Humans with their guest "Mind Cells" experienced God's material world together as one dual imago with two separate, but switchable, primary components – one physical and one Spiritual – whether Yin or Yang. A reminder here that since our subject matter is deep, there will be some repetition; such as: In the case of female humanimals, the subset COG Mental Cell (Soul) would be of Yang Parentage, or male. The converse or opposite would apply to male humanimals.

[To sum up: During the developmental stage, the COG helped "base" humanimals become Human by improving both their physical and mental presence in the material world. The purpose was to serve God through Co-Creation of new Mental Cells for ascendance into God Junior, to help stabilize the middle Child between God's two Main Minds of opposite polarities. This genesis process continued throughout creation with all species of Human material forms used as matrix prototypes by their COG Co-Creators to make indivisibly-dual Spirit-Souls for use as Mental Cells by God's growing Othereal or Heavenly Child, which is based in the ocean of Holy God

Host Spirit (Holy G'Host). This "ocean" is a noble body of liquid crystal, living Spirit that was annihilated in the Big Bang. It serves as the Holy Ghost fundament for the Mental Angel Cells of 'God Junior.' It can't think, but does act as instinctive protection against chaos.

[This process of co-creation of Angels continued for eons. Eventually those COG operating in the Antares material portion of the universe closed their last generation there. Most, but not all, of their material animal stocks would perish in that region, as the Antares star was set to leave the main sequence in approaching its red giant, burned-out stage.

[It was not coincidence the event concluded the maturation of God Jr. and allowed the start of an experimental species project across the material universe – one that involved the immature, tiny remnant 'homing' souls of humanimals that were COG Co-hosts in every Garden system. A Savior God required that all such variants of tiny souls across the universe were to be used as hybrid-human gardens. Many cognizant Ants and Ares were transported to a new solar system for that project. They would join the variety of humanimals already on Earth then. Earth's COG, along with COG in the Mars' Garden, finished their Humangel mission, simultaneously with the completion of all such Perfect Gardens across the cosmos. God had met her quota.

[With the advent of God Jr's Othereal completion, nearly all COG and Humangels were brought home to Junior's Heavenly Mind and Body, to complete God's Triune Self. However, God gave a fairly large number of them a final material world assignment. That new mission involved planets all over the universe that had served as Gardens in the past, but now held only breeding stock – both used and unused. Some of these planets were in the Milky Way galaxy and God now intended to stock an upgraded hybrid garden species on many dual planet systems. One planet would receive new stock while the other would serve as a base for its COG overseers or Over-Souls.

[In your system, some former COG who administered 'Antares' would make modifications of the somewhat smaller Mars planet to suit their oversight needs, as they took up residence in that former Garden. The larger, former Humangel planet, Earth, would be the "proving ground" for a new breed of a higher, hybrid form of humans, to include a genetic mixture of Antares and Earth hominids to create what you know now as Neanderthals. The new hybrids would be formulated, in equal parts, from the genes of a recently deceased Earth hominid and an Antares hominid both of whom were known to have had potentially the best genes of any such Yang animal ever living on their respective planets. This new "Adam" would, if need be, get a 'help mate' of opposite gender or polarity. God knew Adam would need Eve. It was inevitable for a hybrid generation of tiny souls to flourish.

[Given new life, the descendants of this double helix mixture would later be upgraded and enhanced. What could go wrong? With God in charge, nothing did, even considering Eve. God's plan would work as devised for her reasons; and Hybrid humankind has materially advanced at a stellar rate. However, it must be dramatically advanced morally in order to attain eternal life. Hybrids must realize they are insufficient to the task if they don't use their tiny souls to commune with God almost constantly.

[Using 'tiny' remnant souls as transient adjuncts to humanimal brains, COG Co-created a hybrid species on Earth and many other planets around the universe, but they all must realize who and what they are and could become. The "Adam and Eve" Garden of Eden scenario was similarly arranged and accomplished in most all former Gardens throughout the universe, all having been blessed with genetically advanced humanimals. These second-generation abodes with 'tiny' homing souls are termed "gardens," rather than perfect, Majuscule Gardens...] {At this point Eno's dream story ended}

["Wait," CHIP said. "Don't wake up yet; I want to remind you of something you might forget since you now are in your twilight zone. COG perfect Gardens then and "tiny" soul gardens now were not, and are not, the natural material physical surroundings in which everything lived, but rather they were the humanimal bodies themselves in which COG raised their crops of Humangels then and as they continue trying to do now with imperfect hybrids that COG have planted or sometimes transplanted in many gardens...]

CHIP's voice trailed away as Deepy pawed his eyes and tried to shake the slumber from his head. Dream remnants went flying, as he struggled to stay awake. He knew what time it was and what time he was supposed to meet Eno and Shel.

Now, lying there awake, with Ants and "Antgels?" running through his head, Deepy started thinking back to his meeting last night with Eno and he had a cold-chill feeling that what he learned during their chat was just the tip of an iceberg.*

*[The word *Antarctica* quickly flew by in a subthought]

The first thing they had talked about was the med procedure. It was an essence exam. They checked the ion and electrolyte balance within the woman. There was too little Yang. They gave her a minor boost of seasoned electrolytes in order to help her system function in a manner more conducive to positive thinking. Otherwise, her subconscious thoughts would work against her body and what she needed to accomplish. This is just what they had done with the previous guest when Deepy had been there, Eno said, and wondered why Deepy didn't recognize it.

"Oh, I had my eyes closed for most of that first time, Eno. I didn't see all of what you were doing. Sorry, but I had to keep myself under control. I couldn't take all that whimpering and crying. But Eno," Deepy had pointed out, "the one this time didn't do all that. And they were both scotched – right?"

"Her particular physiology, plus the fact that she had fainted," he remembered Eno telling him "... made it possible to put her under to a greater degree than the other woman, although the other one suffered no pain, only some anxiety before and after the procedure. That can't be helped, as we need our visitors fully cognizant for a certain amount of time."

"Well, I know anxiety is an emotional disturbance, right? That reminds me, why aren't the COG more sympathetic to the plight of these so-called guests or visitors?"

"We are extremely sympathetic, Deepy, and we express it in vibratory transmissions of what we call thoughtful-feeling, which is a mixture of the polar attraction of love and gracious empathy. Pure Love, as we know it, must be "sensed" through the Mind. It comes directly from God, when it is real. We COG can sense it in plenitude, and logically we know it is a by-product of God's Grace, but Earthite humans are on a different wavelength and mental track, and so are not as receptive. They don't use their minds, which include their tiny souls so much as they use their id/ego brain tools for thinking – most of which pertains to sensual desires or preconceived notions.

"We telep and vibrate alpha waves to people, but the particular subjects we have here, oftentimes have serious id/ego problems that hinder their communion with God. They are not easily attuned to us; and the wave packet connection between their ego-mentality and our Minds is way out of balance. In part, that is a result of the mix of the Yin/Yang energy-essence in their systems. This does not allow them the link to the thoughtful-feeling of Grace, or love attraction, that you and I, for example, think and feel for one another. You are more in tune.

"This lack of mind or soul ability to love 'thoughtfully' is the problem we are working to correct. It's a common problem among Earthite humans and a big contributor to humanity's inhumanity. Also, some human egos have tremendous guilt feelings they don't recognize, when confronted with COG as God, and this brings out a great deal of fear in many of them. Because of the nature of their id, they think we mean them harm. But even when we improve them in this regard, we really don't want strong mental bonds with them now, because it would become easier for them to recall us and it's not yet time, but it's much closer now.

"Some hybrids do remember us under hypnosis, but mostly in a fearful way. Most of them recall the trauma and not the love they may also have come to 'think' – notice I didn't say 'feel.' Every human eventually will recall being with us at one time or another, in one lifetime or another, or more likely between lifetimes. Everyone will remember who we are and why we are here. Like I said, that 'right' time is much closer now – because hybrids are about out of time, with eternity in the offing."

Then Deepy had asked about "the moral implications of all this." There are never any moral implications for the COG, Eno had told him. "We know what we are doing and why. It is God practicing maintenance, shall we say, on her Self and for the good of the human race. Were it not for id-fear, mistrust, ego selfishness and ignorance, we could explain it rationally to our guests, who would not be under such misapprehension in the first place. Of course that is mainly why you are here, to try to explain it for us in your future writing. That will have to suffice until the time of re-COGnition and re-Membering comes, or what some Christians refer to as 'the rapture'." That is how Eno had put it, before saying, "It's time to talk about Eden and Egod."

And so they did. Well, Eno did. It was about ninety-five percent listening on Deepy's part. Then there was that talk about the sons of God, as spoken of in the *Bible*. They actually had taken 'wives' from among hybrid humans, but not for themselves as the biblical passages would lead one to believe, effectively saying the women were pretty and good enough essentially to be on a level with God. That simply was a misunderstanding.

Those women were taken for a short while and then returned. The purpose was to monitor their pregnancies - which they did not know about at that point - and oftentimes to upgrade the genetics of their fetuses, in order to advance the species. Eno said that no human mentioned the women were returned, as this would have been a blow to human pride (ego feeling), as if the women had not proven good enough for God. So the story stood as finally written, in another case of id/ego* pride either competing with God or wanting to please God. Anyway, that type of DNA evolution has been done any number of times through hybrid history, Eno had said, as well as the history of prior "humanimal" stock, used by COG to create Humangels. *{To repeat: a confused mix of id instinct plus ego brain, operating without use of the "mind" – the brain/soul combination}

"I would also note that at one time the DNA of the various fetuses was altered in order to make mankind a bigger physical species. They were referred to as giants. Another segment of the population was made smaller at one point. We later settled on the average size you see around Earth as the standard. But, those various sizes of hybrids can and do fit certain, special niches within God Jr.; but only IF they gained God's Grace through morality of *W. I. L.* and Love."

Deepy couldn't recall his entire lesson with Eno, which was not unusual. He would read it again later in the minutes of the meeting and lesson plan, which CHIP would provide him.

Deepy rolled over onto his back, with his paws against his body... his chubby body. (A "good doggy" subthought tickled his human self) He recalled also being chubby, at times, as his human self, Larray James. CHIP had told him that the hybrid breed of dog he was, rarely put on too much weight, unless they are fed scraps of what some humans pass for food. 'Must have some of my human genes in this body,' he now kidded himself. And besides, with great food and a sedentary lifestyle, what else could one expect? Really, he didn't know what to expect. What man would? Suddenly finding his spirit 'mentality' attached to a dog's anima? Who knows, maybe I'm functioning as well as can be expected for the shape I'm in. I'm just glad I can depend on CHIP or BB for my mental constructions. CHIP says that because my Larray body is in a comatose state, much of my normal spirit energy can be diverted to this body and sometimes my tiny soul even drops by for awhile. Wow.

He stuck his legs straight up. "One-two-three-four - Yelp, still a dog – Now hit the floor!" He sang that out as a military-march cadence. He felt like a dog. He knew one thing for sure... he had a bad case of doggie breath this morning. "Whoa!" He rolled over. "Pushups?" he questioned himself whimsically. "Nah" – "Shower?" - A no-brainer, he thought, since it was a requirement for him, for continuing disinfectant purposes. Sometimes he just wished he could live under that shower.

He brushed his teeth first; or rather the rig-Bot did it for him. "Together," he thought, "BB and CHIP can probably rig just about anything. Wonder if I'm ever going to meet BB?" In fact, they had rigged a so-called "squat pot" in his own private john, which he was determined to use from now on, even if he had to run like hell to get there. And he felt sure they could rig a Bot that would yank his clothes off whenever he needed to use that pot... or not? He wondered. He hoped. Either that, or CHIP would need to rush a quin to his aid. Hell, maybe he should just get used to being naked. He was a dog after all. "Well... okay, not really." At least he didn't care to think so.

Deepy usually sang under the waterfall and he liked long, slow soothing showers as a dog, whereas Larray was in and out and on the go, always on the run. His shower this morning, though, was unusual. First off, he got a telep just as he stepped under the disinfecting cloud of ion-modified ether, which was swirling inside the chamber. It briefly looked and felt like steam, before actual water burst forth.

"Never fails," he thought. He knew his private connect was closed since he was within his quarters, but he didn't feel any shudder. He glanced at his nose as a voice registered, "Deepy, this is CHIP. Excuse the override please. I just wanted you to know you should be able to read a normal connect now. No more glowing nose. Let me know if you have any more problems, but you should be headache-free from now on, at least from the kind caused by electronic bugs."

"Well, I guess that means I won't be hearing from you again. Ha Ha. Thanks, CHIP ol' chum; I like starting the day with good news. And how might you be, this morning?" he inquired, while soaking up the warm, wet comfort rolling off his backside.

"As always... superior," CHIP intoned.

"Yeah, right," Deepy chuckled. CHIP has a good sense of humor, Deepy now thought, as he lost himself under a soothing, tingling sensation. *"Love mee tenderr, love me true,"* he sang with the splashing sounds, while thinking, "Elvis Presley would love this - a dog singing one of his songs." He immediately segued to *"You ain't nothing but a Hound Dog ... just rocking all the time... you ain't never caught a rabbit, and you ain't no friend of mine."* He pictured himself in a sequined, Elvis outfit, replete with cape, and then reminded himself that he would be the older, bloated version of the king. "Deepy, old son, you are an old dog," he thought. "And still up to his old tricks. Come to think of it though, I do also get to have a teenage memory that gives me a rush of vigor and younger-days' vitality at times; but old Larray is right there too, to help me keep things in proper, or whatever, perspective CHIP decides upon. Dear God, I'm at the mercy of some alien 'Humanoid' creature. Man, what a silly frame of mind I'm in.

"Yowsir, an old dog with a waddle body, a Goldie-oldie young man's memories and no soul... quite a mess, really."

"No soul!" he suddenly remembered shouting those two words last night when Eno had told him he had no soul. "I still can't fathom that," he told himself now. Eno had, of course, explained, but not before Deepy had gone off on a tangent. "If you had just let me finish," Eno had said.

Deepy's hybrid memory now quivered under the strain of trying to recall it all. At this point, he seemed to remember CHIP having explained to him why he was having so much trouble with his memory, but he couldn't remember why now.

Maybe some of my synapses have short-circuited, he thought, as he picked up his prior train of thought.

No soul, indeed. He had thought Eno was joking, but his friend had just stared at him when Deepy had replied, "No soul, eh? You gotta be kidding, watch this." And then he had done his little, soft-paw dance routine that he had been practicing, in case he ever needed to impress Shel. Part of the bit was to sing a few lines of "Mr. Bojangles" which he did, *'I knew a man, Bojangles and he danced for you / In worn out shoes / Silver hair, a ragged shirt and baggy pants / The old soft shoe…'** Deepy recreated it as he had last night, ending with a flourishing bow. After a few moments, Eno had appeared bemused, and then amused, sensing Deepy's intent, perhaps. Then he had laughed out loud. "I love the Earthite humor sometimes," he had said. "When it's not too earthy, it can be one of humankind's unique qualities, but some comedic personalities could do with a lot more virtue." *(lyrics by Jerry Jeff Walker, 1968)

"Wow, such a nice compliment," Deepy remembered thanking Eno at the time, and then wondering what he had meant for sure.

"I'm sorry," Eno had told him. "I was going to explain that you rarely have Larray's 'tiny' soul here with you. She remains supportive of that part of your mind in the hospital. Through BB, and sometimes CHIP, you have revolving access to part of your human "brain" memories, with just enough spirit for these circumstances. As you know, our 'BB' CHIP is acting as your Over-Soul. You're also blessed because much of your human 'brain memory' is imprinted with morality and thus is on recall by any of our CHIPs. By the way, all CHIPs look alike and answer to CHIP and so you have met BB and called him CHIP.

"While the dog's energy anima naturally is lovable, and loving, there is only a fraction of mental essence to it. Its anima also is not strong enough to power up human memories, so you are working off BB's borrowed memory bank of Larray's essence. That means not all your memories are immediately "on call," so to speak, but they are on re-call, depending on how relaxed you are. But, some of your id/ego feelings also can slip through. When you are really relaxed, BB can help you recall or think of most anything. That's why our CHIPs need you to be as loose as possible."

"Well, that's much better," Deepy had said, adding, "I guess." "Thanks CHIP," he now mumbled, "and BB."

"Egad - How long have I been in here?" Deepy exclaimed, as his thoughts surfaced to the splash of water on his snout. He had been twisting and turning while deep in thought, and had actually recreated a portion of his dance routine under the shower while thinking about it.

"I'm probably looking like a Sharpie by now, or whatever that wrinkled, Chinese dog is called," he muttered to himself. "Arf! Oh waterspout," he commanded. Okay, 'off!' then. He shook himself several times - looking, he imagined, like a bowl full of jelly. *I'm all shook up*," his Elvis 'impersonator' sang. Stepping out of the stall, he edged over to the wall where he commanded "on." So now instead of singing, he listened to the purring sound of a blow dryer, which was rigged at an angle, way above his head. The dryer must have been designed for stand-up comedians, he thought, way taller and funnier than I am. "Aaah-mazing," he mused, "how, sometimes the little things in life can feel so good."

In rather a state of cuddled bliss, he sighed, "Thank you Lord, BB, and CHIP, in that order."

"There you go again," CHIP told him.

"Doggone it CHIP, you sorry blankety-blank. Are you eavesdropping again?"

"It's just in my nature, I guess. I find I'm a better host, the more I know our guests, or in your case, new crew member. Besides, I provide the direction of your thoughts and sometimes I find your silliness amusing," BB* chirped. (CHIP's got a chirpy voice, Deepy had once thought. Of course, BB picked up on that, and Deepy just knew he had tried to sound even chirpier ever since.) *{BB never says 'this is BB,' since all CHIPs are replicas.}

"Anyway," BB added, "you left yourself open."

"Good Grief, have you been listening to me all along?" Deepy was in too good a mood to get cranked up over this now, but he knew he was going to mention it to Eno.

"Just trying to better understand your 'personality' - I hope you don't mind. After all, I want to be just like you when I grow up."

"Don't mind? - Why you sorry son of a cracker jack..."

"Well," BB said, "that's enough personality for now. I can feel you turning into a mongrel, Mr. Dog Hyde, so gotta run - Catch me later."

"Doggone you anyway, CHIP." My fault though - I guess the shower must have distracted me. But still - not nice of CHIP to take advantage that way, even if he was still trying to learn about this new creature amongst the crew.

"I've got to be more careful," he told himself, while having some second thoughts about taking the matter up with Eno. Don't want to be a snitch, but if CHIP persists, I just might have to tattle. Then he couldn't help but wonder if CHIP might be acting under orders. "Damn!" Deepy thought, and quickly checked his microhm shield. He knew that CHIP could override it anyway and tune him in anytime he wanted. A little paranoia seeping in, he wondered. Well, "under the circumstances," he excused himself. But then he had a vague memory that he was dependent on CHIP (or was it BB?) for his Larray memories, so "I'll give him a break for now," he thought.

He cooled down after a few more seconds under the warm air. That is a "purring" sound, he was thinking about the drier he had just switched off. "Ironic," Deepy now thought, as a human he preferred cats to dogs. He indulged in a few memories of cats he had known while growing up. Come to think of it, he and CeCe had a beautiful gray cat. "Didn't they?" He wasn't sure. "Funny," he thought, that he could almost remember that now, realizing again that he was at CHIP BB's mercy when it came to memory-bank withdrawals; and didn't that really mean that CHIP had to monitor him all the time? "Jeez, I have got to talk to Eno. Then again, I do like having these memories. Thanks CHIP, or BB, I suppose. I guess I will just call them both CHIP."

"Cats" - He realized that quite a few people preferred cats to dogs. Maybe, he thought, there's a cat project or "C-P" on board another ship. He would ask Eno. Deepy figured pig lovers probably were just out of luck. He somehow couldn't imagine very many people hugging a pig, although he figured some did. Strange, he thought... the human persona. He wondered if other folks had the same kind of peculiar thoughts he had on occasion... more often than he'd care to admit.

"I feel like a brand new man - er... dog," Deepy mused, walking toward the diner, where he was supposed to meet Shel and Eno for lunch. He had taken breakfast in his room, and had spent the remainder of the morning reading some "UFO" material that Eno had supplied, through a CHIP upload to his compod. But now he was ready to get out into the world, dressed for the first time in his short, dog life.

When he had finished with his bathroom routine this morning and returned to the bedroom, there was a sparse wardrobe laid out on his bed. The quin who brought it was waiting to help him dress, but he asked her to come back in a couple of hours. After she dressed him later, she then put everything away, except for the shorts and shirt he now had on. His bright blue tee shirt with yellow lettering on it read "Calorie Overload" on one side and "Deep Doo" on the other. He liked his tan shorts too.

IIIIIIIIIIIIIIIIIIIIIIIIIIIIIII

[A dog looking in a mirror doesn't see itself. You also don't see yourself in a mirror. Your 'self' is inside you.]

{CHAPTER 6}
Deepy goes off

"I wonder why so many humans are not happy with themselves or life in general. It seems as if the world is becoming more miserable for more and more people all the time." Shel wondered this, as she stared at Deepy across the table. He had just mentioned his interesting chat with Eno the night before. Now she sat waiting for him to respond. He was starting to believe her when she had told him she couldn't get over the precious way he looked, as she still hadn't blinked for a while.

"Well, as I understand it from Eno, it comes down to id's influence. And it appears that as humankind has multiplied... id, ego and Egod have complicated matters to the point that there now seem to be somewhat rote answers for each and every person, as to why that person isn't happy and much of it seems to center around money and relationships, whether at work or in home life. Politics and religion all too often are sore spots too.

"Also, stronger egos influence weaker ones, and that's how people are drawn into not thinking for themselves, but instead they just adopt other people's thoughts about specific matters. Take politics, for example, and we find that many people think big government is against outright poor folks, or the little guy is caught in the economic middle. That's because they rightly think many politicians are "in it" for themselves, and taking advantage of what has become a "racket" for some – mostly republicans. And I swear I am partisan because I can "sniff out" immorality. While the corrupt characters make politics into a lucrative personal business, they also take care of their rich "friends" who then contribute to them at election time. It is a mob-like racketeering approach to "what's in it for me?" That perspective proves true, more often than not and that's why it is common ground for "partisan to money and power" id/ego politicians.

"Also, there is a lot of partisan propaganda in politics, to try to sway voters into keeping those same crooks in office. Obviously those politicians have so-called talking points to propel them along without giving their game away. They flat-out lie, and some do it so often they come to believe their own lies and convince themselves they are "real people" and not actors.

"As an example, one such "talking point" is that democrats* in the United States, want to take your guns away; or they side with illegal aliens over "real" Americans and they want to give hand-outs to poor people and minorities and/or "give" them this, that, or the other. So-called republicans even say immigrants are being allowed into the country in order to replace (outnumber) "white" people who vote for republicans. There is so much lying that takes place on Fox News and other disinformation media that gets gobbled up by people who love to hate and blame their troubles on anyone else who does not soak up and believe Fox, or anarchical* lies of other media.

(From Webster's Dictionary: Anarchy *1 a : absence of government b : a state of lawlessness or political disorder due to the absence of governmental authority c : a utopian society of individuals who enjoy complete freedom without government) {Complete freedom would mean definition "b." Alternatives would be an oligarchy or a dictatorship.}

"Imagine the GOP making the term "bleeding heart" (meaning *TO CARE* about everyone) into something heinous; but surely that should tell you who the Party's number one priority is – no, not you, not any "middle or poor class," even though its largest voting bloc is made of such people who believe GOP lies. It is because so many weary, average folks don't have or take time to pay close attention to politics. It's easier to just stay spitefully angry at life in general for seeming to be unfair, and to accept hateful, divisive rhetoric because of personal struggles devolving into bitterness. Someone needs to be blamed, so depending on how spiteful people are, they allow themselves to believe pathological, hateful liars who make false political promises.

"Politicians can be disingenuous in the way they "play" hateful, spiteful people. Another subtle way politicians cozy-up to voters is to call them smart: "The American people are not stupid; 'they know this or they know that,' or in other words they are smart enough to believe what I am telling them now about how smart they are to see the situation as I see it."

"'Money' (as in too little or too much) has become the biggest liability to fair politics, thanks largely to the misguided Supreme Court, which chose capitalism over democracy by viewing money amounts in politics as freedom of speech, as if every voter has that same "amount" of freedom, which obviously is illogical and absurd. One citizen – one vote; but one or dozens of citizens – even non-citizens - can pour tons of money into phony or untruthful advertisements or propaganda and "buy" millions of votes. They might even be able to 'buy' certain people of political parties who can countermand millions of voters through a system called the "electoral college."

"The 'electoral college' forms every four years for the sole purpose of electing the president and vice president of the United States. The Electoral College consists of 538 electors, and an absolute majority of at least 270 electoral votes is required to win the election. According to the U-S Constitution, each state legislature determines the manner by which its state's electors are chosen. The number of each state's electors is equal to the sum of the state's membership in the Senate and House of Representatives; currently there are 100 senators and 435 representatives. Also, the Twenty-third Amendment, ratified in 1961, provides that the District of Columbia is entitled to the same number of electors as the least populated state, which is three. U.S. territories are not entitled to any electors.

"How is it that 538 people can overturn millions of votes? The better way to choose a presidential winner is simply the total "popular vote," counted in the general election. Now though, IF a certain group of people don't like the outcome of the popular vote they can just flip their "electorate coin." Some of them might be willing to take an outright payoff to vote a certain way. Others could essentially be "sold" on a personality or a political party, which they want in power and which allows them to keep their own State political prestige and power with possible rewards from those at the top, if they help put and keep them there even as an imbecilic autocrat.

"No doubt the writers of the Constitution meant well in conceiving the 'electoral' formula, but it always has been unpopular with the voters. It produced a terrible result when a demagogue, and otherwise unqualified, immoral hack, was awarded the U-S Presidency in 2016. Could it happen again? Absolutely, and many States have made laws with that as a goal.

"Imagine - this "college" is a small body of persons entitled to vote in place of people who already have voted. This elite group tossed aside about three million popular votes in the 2016 Presidential election. Is "Electoral College," just a fancy name for another form of class privilege - a 'college class' for the rich and powerful? Congress and the Supreme Court need to make the Electoral College null and void. Citizens demand it!

Deepy's mind wandered: "Too many people don't think for themselves anymore. They just go along with the loudest, most hateful voices. It's just a real shame that one of those voices ever belonged to the President of a nation that once was considered the 'human rights' leader of the world, and hopefully will regain and retain that stature. [Deepy never realized when his memory jumped to a future time that he had not as yet lived through, but would. With the Commander's permission, I gave Deepy that power of projection a number of times without his realization, because above all, he had a godly right to remain on his natural moral path; and of course God knew the exact knowledge and memories awaiting our hybrid friend.]

"Id's and ego's influence always comes into play, but in so many different ways. For example, ego quite often takes on the mantle of self-righteousness, blinding us to the simple truth that not one of us... not a single person, is really different from or more important than another in our godly potential. Raise your hand if you believe God is a racist who prefers one skin color.

"It is id/ego, with Egod's help, that wants us to be different, with the capability to somehow be superior to at least one other person, and so we often grade people on their material "success," even while dismissing any lack of moral virtue. Oftentimes we even let such ego types run entire countries. We might even allow them to rule the world, rather than admit we are wrong about them, even as we all slide into oblivion together.

"As regards equality in the USA, many of the most simple or single-minded white persons still are ignorant enough to consider themselves superior to persons of other skin colors or ethnicities. This has been the case since before the nation was ever founded. These insecure white egos take solace in such inequity, since they know that some other white persons might be considered superior to them because they are higher on the economic grading scale, which might prove they are intellectually superior also. There simply is no need to think in such "stoop id" ways. We all are unique and there always will be richer, smarter people than us. So what? Get over it. Grow up! Be grateful for your spiritual blessings by deserving them. Be a real and moral person and thank God you're wise, intelligent, logical, loving, and gracious. But... become more particular about your politicians.

"In many places, superiority is still decided based on social stature or wealth, or whatever "class difference" a societal Egod dictates in that regard. At least those "inferior" whites know they are superior to all purple people. Sadly, such attitudes still exist in the id/ego brain-set of truly character-deformed types, but, thank God, newer generations of more enlightened young people are coming along. In fact, many already are on the scene and their number is growing. Such enlightenment is even growing among some older, wiser minds with sense enough to finally see through moral eyes.

"Egod's story is a long one," Deepy now told Shel, "and I haven't heard it all yet, or if I have, I seem to have just run out of memory. Dependency can be irritating, if you know what I mean, er – CHIP, or BB?"

Deepy waited a few seconds but got no response.

"What's going on?" Shel wondered.

"Just trying to get a rise out of my memory, but the CHIPs either are very busy or just tired of listening to me. On the other hand, they are the ones speaking through me. I wouldn't know anything without them and Eno. [Our friend is a bit modest]

"Anyway," Deepy suddenly started up again, "Many humans are not smart enough to know they cannot even exist apart from God. Nothing in her Consciousness can be anything other than a part of her. But God can change the energy essence of any aspect of her "Self." SHE could make anyone as mentally benign as a tree or some other energy pattern. I may be the only self-aware, four-legged animal in existence, but only because my human spirit is on loan to a dog and a CHIP powers it. Even God's Perfect Humans would not have been self-aware without an in-dwelling COG; nor could hybrid humans be self and God aware without a soul that comes and goes in accord with communion; at least that's my understanding." There was a short pause, as Deepy seemed to momentarily drift off into a trance.

"So, God needs her imperfect hybrid beings on Earth, and everywhere, to proceed with moral curative measures in order to kill a societal, conglomerate version of every ego out there. You know about Egod. Egod has always been the core of God's "mental cancer" among hybrids and so we all need to be part of the cure, converting ourselves from egodly cells to godly ones. But even if we cannot manage to totally kill Egod right away, some of us may manage to save ourselves in the process of trying, since we will grow morally.

"The demise of Egod and cure for society as a whole must go through all the individual egos of Egod's divisive class structure. We must realize that we are not as 'id/ego' represents us to be, but rather we are, always have been, and always will be, an indivisible part of God – but our fate as to what type energy pattern we become depends on whether we learn to fit into God's Perfect Mental Cell Structure - that is to say her 'Heavenly Child.'

"We congratulate ourselves on having free will," he now told Shel, as his thoughts rambled up from somewhere. "Oh sure, we can do as we think we please, but generally that is simply "ego" telling us to act in accord with a peer group or society in general. We are reaping the results of that kind of rote thinking, as are all ego types who feel they must prove the worth of their individual identities to other people with whom they find common cause. People want to be part of like-minded colleagues or groups – depending on whether they group think as Egod, or even have minds of their own and simply meet in order to share thoughts co-created with the highest Consciousness.

"Even so, some people still feel the competitive need and desire to prove themselves as equal or superior to the authority figures or peers they think they know best. Since it's impossible to be superior to an Omnipotent God, we tend to forget God, or to willfully flaunt our independence through ignorance and/or denial. If we cannot get over our own inferiority complexes, we tend to blame those whom we think are proving their superiority over us, as oftentimes they are, but likely not in ways intended as a personal slight. Mostly too, this often happens only in matters that should be of no competitive consequence really. Why care if "theirs is bigger or newer" than yours? Life is too time-limited.

"Those of us humans, who manage to become 'appCOG' or apprentice Children, will get a chance to reincarnate into a perfect Human body someday in a new Earthly Garden, in order to upgrade into Humangels for eternity. Virtually all of the alien visitors here from other worlds are AppCOG and are helping us any way they can. But I am getting ahead of myself," Deepy winked, as his thoughts were a bit scattered.

"In order to get over pervasive feelings of inferiority, we need to live with someone we love – namely ourselves and simply because we know we are on a moral track aimed toward eternity. But, all too often, we adopt a coping ability to protect ourselves from the scrutiny of others, without regarding how God sees us or we see ourselves. Our concern about how others view us has become one of humankind's primary ego traits. It offers each individual a sort of borrowed autonomy through identity self-worship or self-pity. One person can be alternately stumped by both those identity traits.

"Of course since society has grown, part of the problem is that almost all authority at the human level is itself ego involved as discrete and often elite individuals and groups. With mankind at its center, group identity is societal ego, also known as Egod, which can be group governed by arbitrary rules or individual whims in highly structured or completely unstructured settings – for example, government under competent, moral leaders, or the opposite – no government but with idiots in control somehow – perhaps with military help.

"No government is perfect, of course. Dictators and their "chosen ones" are an example of evil in charge of governments. And too, there is evil whenever smug group-egos swell up with nationalistic pride in their 'thought-to-be' superior country or ethnicity, or whatever; and pride can become overbearing within financially successful elitists, to the extent that everything is not enough.

"Religion is group identity with God as the Authority figure and usually with selfless ideals as the governing principles of thought and action, and yet it too suffers the vagaries of mankind's id/egos, which would blame God or 'No God' for its troubles or blame a particular religion or ways other people practice or don't practice their own religion. Societal and religious moral values do not come from Egod, needless to say.

"There are so many examples of Egod all around us affecting us in every conceivable way. All things considered though, Egod's worst evil is the construction of a mind-set that causes individuals to protect themselves through rationalization of their specific imperfections, however heinous they might be. Everybody is guilty of either ego mischief or blatant evil in some regard, and everyone also is victimized by this terrible, autocratic brain-set. Sometimes you just want to give up." That thought in particular surprised Deepy and made him wonder just what kind of day he was having. *(Eno says the term "mind-set," meaning attitude is misleading, since the mind, which includes the soul, is only involved in moral attitude, and so the term in reference to an evil or bad attitude should be "brain-set," because evil relates to id/ego thinking. A true 'mind' is of moral, soul-brain thought.)

"It boils down to this: The power-people in general, the muckety-mucks and higher-ups; the Big-Business titans; the so-called "justice system," when overseen by immoral officials and" Deepy emphasized - "certain politicians," who seem to share that same primary goal of looking out for themselves by being disingenuous and manipulative, while putting power and party above Country. They truly are ignorant of God.

"As to politicians, their parties also get away with hiring or using other people who can be egregiously dishonest surrogates – either without fear of reprisal, or willing to take a fall for a big enough payoff. And that's just the way Egod takes care of business. Now, don't get me started on Egod taking care of Business, with a capital "B," as in Big Bucks and "don't Buck the system, or else" – because, believe me, politicians and big businesses do have vast systems in place for satisfying their greed needs without fear of reprisal.

"Greed comes in all forms of dishonesty, blame, and excuses - and really," Deepy sighed, "we all have some kind of ego problems, but powerful egodly types generate much more pain for more people. There is just so much ego nonsense... just so much, and none of us is perfect. I know I make that obvious.

"I just hope I'm the only one I'm depressing," Deepy said nonchalantly, as he seemed to be winding down. Shel seemed glassy-eyed, but said, "I doubt it."

Deepy chuckled, and then sighed, "Sorry." Shel sighed and then chuckled, "No problem." [Shel had not misspoken. She knew some of Deepy's future readers might feel depressed by his haranguing monologue.] They both fidgeted for a few moments while Shel wondered what was keeping Eno.

Deepy continued. "I would not hesitate to say that our individual "id entity," combined with ego, is our own worst enemy, because more often than not we use it to facilitate 'Egod.' It is one thing to heedlessly injure ourselves through ignoring God, but even worse to cause others to suffer too, and that's almost always the case. Too many of us try to build upon a foundation of shifting societal mores, largely influenced by Egod's powerbrokers for the sake of material gains, incentivized by greed or envy or who knows what?

"To compound the situation, people's thoughts, whatever they may be, literally remain on record as a mental energy resource for anyone else of a like "brain-set" or "mind-set" to use repeatedly. The moral thoughts within this work, and others, will remain in a godly record – the LOG* – for recall. There also is a homogeneous thought-energy library out there with Egod's name on it, but egodly thoughts are not in the LOG* book. When we channel Egod, without weighing input from our souls, which stem from "God Mind," our individual egos build on the continuum of society's evil momentum at large. *(Life Of God)

"Therefore, we are our own worst enemies, starting out as individuals who have separated ourselves from God, only to end up lending our influence or apathy to that huge collection of evil-doers and thinkers called Egod. It all began with the confused and frustrated ids and tiny souls of Adam and Eve's physical and mental polar attraction to one another, in preference to a primary Mental polar attraction toward their O'Soul and God. Eve's immature tiny soul also was no match for her deeply ingrained 'id' animal instincts, which aided and abetted her fused-spirit cravings, and even co-opted her brain's new persona psyche (ego) to influence her tiny soul and its spiritually innate willpower. Such 'tiny' souls had too much nesting time with id during the COG halcyon days of Human Gardens that created Humangels.

"Now, that massive library of evil thinking is in constant use by all of us over and over, even while we add to and revise it, as we progress toward Egod's goal of a permanent kingdom, apart from God. It appears to be Egod's quest that ultimately he will reign supreme in his kingdom of "Id," largely without moral restrictions. He has made great headway with politicians and others who have influence and power over parties* necessary to accomplish that. *(Business, political, societal, private groups, etc. - and mostly at other people's expense – financial or otherwise) This "Egod complex" overlooks the fact that it is committing species suicide, even as it already has committed species murder among under-appreciated creatures trying to share this planet. So, scientists speak of "terra-forming" other planets when they are not allowed by politicians to maintain one we already have.

"Don't misunderstand. It would be foolish and naïve to paint all people with the same broad brush, so we are not implying that everyone in big business, finance, politics, or any single legitimate endeavor, is a crook or otherwise immoral. The trend though toward immorality across the board seems to have long ago passed a majority, as people wrangle more and more to outdo each other to become the biggest 'success,' as defined in material terms of wealth and power. Donald Trump (?) was at the front of the wolf pack "in fox clothing" at that time, along with Rupert Murdoch. [Deepy didn't know those names, but I told him that years down the road he would come to pity the disgusting humanimals attached to those vile egos.]

"More and more people are becoming disingenuous when it comes to the bottom line with its money sign. Egod and egos are behind it all, having set the conditions and terms as to how we measure success, which they also have defined. We let them, by sharing their kind of thinking, rather than God's. So they mold us around our hormonal, sensual id/ego trappings of sex and violence glorification and then sell us all the products of such thought; for example the innumerable video games glorifying war and so-called action-hero terror, even if said to be defending "good." Pornography too is pervasive and unless there is "change," it won't be long before nudity and sexual activity are expected in pretty much every movie and on virtually any screen. Yeah, I know some readers might be thinking "yea," but we pray they get over it. Hardly anything is left to one's imagination anymore, as Egod is trying to kill all potentially godly traits – many of which are accentuated as 'moral intelligence' in what you now are reading, thanks to the COG.

"We must do better" Deepy muttered, embarrassed for the species of which his Larray James self was a part. "Could dogs do any worse?" a subthought wondered. "They would have to be rabid," another one proclaimed.

"Some people may be giving up on God, although we are supposed to be students of ourselves through her law of karma. We make extremely poor students, because we blame everybody but us for our problems. We blame God, Satan, or other humans, even as most of us are just blind followers of the societal scam artist called Egod. Apparently we allowed this material god to be chosen as our leader in yet another of the world's rigged, "democratic" elections. Supposedly, everyone had a vote, but most of us were just willing to go along with the one candidate already in power – Egod, the incumbent. Some of us still vote for God, but the number is getting smaller all the time. We just continually renew our allegiance to Egod, since he offers the stuff of this world "<u>now</u>" – stuff that we seem to think we just can't live without, once Egod puts his "shiny object" spin on it.

"Plus, we don't like to be kept waiting for those goodies that we know other less-deserving people somehow already are getting. We would rather have all those pretty toys that Egod's pitchmen have to offer, than to live as purely as possible, preparing for a perfect, eternal life of heavenly bliss, which we have not been promised in writing – if one discounts the *Bible*, which more and more people are doing. No, God doesn't offer a money-back guarantee – just an unlimited lifetime warranty, and forever. Even so, people choose to listen to Egod's steady roar of 'show me the money.'

"We would not even need to wait for some amount of heavenly bliss if the vast majority of us were to vote God into power. SHE already is in power, of course, but our votes for moral leaders would show we know it, as would the way we morally live our lives as role models for everyone else, especially the children. And yet we wait, while fooling ourselves and calling it "faith" that we will be accepted into God's Home someday, to live with her pure Children as our eternal brothers and sisters, under the auspices of Jesus Christ, because, after all, we have a very loving and forgiving God – a Santa Claus, Easter Bunny God who will overlook our evils just because we want him to – er, want "her" to. No offense, but I'm still getting used to God as a twi-polar Entity, and using the objective case to include a dual gender "he/she or him/her" is confusing right now. It is important though. Dogs know these things," Deepy laughed, while reflecting on his current befuddlement.

"Anyway, many of us ardently support the societal god we have selected to represent us. That's because we had a hand in creating him, whether we ever consciously thought about it or not. But, *'turn-about is fair play,'* and so we don't seem to mind that he has turned things around to become "our creator" by proxy, as we just lay back and watch him take care of business. Egod belongs to us because we are him; and only too happy to support the system of denying and/or ignoring God, in order to get what Egod knows we want right now – that being defined as stuff and sensual pleasure. We are overcome by his manic ego. It is suffocating morality in a seeming majority of us.

"Where is God in all this? - Great question. SHE's right where we put her... in a place in or out of our individual lives. Has SHE abandoned us? No! It's the other way around; most of us have given up on her, even as some of us pretend otherwise. Long ago though, to help make up for our ignorance, which is at the root of our evil, God offered one of her pure Children, a Son, to be born among us. He came to see if He could personally lead us out of the morass of our material world mess by teaching us about his Moral Parents, who also offer us Parental guidance as a God who would adopt us if we loved her and allowed it. All too long we refused to adopt her WILL, so SHE found a volunteer among her Children to bring us her art of Grace, to show us we need not die for eternity – if we would just follow his act of Grace, to live as He lives, even as his Parents live eternally. Have we learned and followed those moral principles? Some have and still do, but the majority blithely lumbers along after Egod, as lemming-like co-dependents.

"No, God is not to blame for our troubles, but SHE will let you, let us, suffer as long as we choose to do so... lifetime after lifetime. What's it going to take... a rude awakening? If that's what we really want, we can just continue with business as usual. Trouble is - time is fast approaching for that awakening, which may come just before the lights go out permanently for many of us. ('That's depressing as hell,' Deepy subthought, 'but true.')

"All right then," Deepy sounded a false cheery note, after his moment of reflection, "it's about time for another election – the candidates are the same: Egod and God. Running on the immoral platforms of Willful Ignorance, Spite, Hate, Denial, and Idiocy, we have the Specter of a societal Egod, and all us "proud" ego minions taking on God, who is running on the Moral platforms of Wisdom, Intelligence, Logic, Love, and Grace – to include Mercy. Who do you think will win?"

"I hope you're not asking me." Shel responded.

"You, me - everybody - I don't mean to be a pessimist, but Egod has always won by default, because people just won't commit to God in the way we need to. That's my humble opinion. It is also my humble opinion that we are morally stupid and seem likely to remain so."

"I can't help but agree. Logic would seem to indicate that, but I hate it," Shel told him. "I wonder what's keeping Eno."

Deepy seemed exhausted and very sad, as well as a bit embarrassed by his passion. "The depth of human ignorance just amazes me," he now told Shel; "We act as if we can just sit back and expect God to do it all, even as we go on taking every imaginable material 'goody' we can afford to buy, cheat, or steal for ourselves with Egod's help, even as our earthly home is being destroyed in the process of the rich getting richer, while the rest of us try to get our hands on what we think should be our fair share before the good Earth goes belly up. How can we be so vile and stupid to <u>not</u> fathom how ignorant we really are?

"It is long-past time to accept God's gracious gifts, especially the one in which SHE allows us to be co-creative with her, by accepting her WILL and Grace as potentially our own. Everything <u>with</u> God – including freedom from prisons of our own making – is a co-creative process. Look at everything we have created without God. Wars, hunger, atrocities, cruelty, thievery, murders, etc. and we are turning this planet into a pile of material waste – a global garbage heap. Nero fiddled while Rome burned, once upon a time. Now, Egod takes the money and runs and re-runs for offices with political royalties or perks even while committing slow suicide, taking his minions down with him.

"I think I'm going to throw up," Deepy sighed, and looked the part. That reminded him of the big breakfast he had eaten.

"I wonder what's keeping Eno."

"I am nowhere near perfect, so I hope I don't come off as judgmental. That is another trait of Egod, but that's not where I'm personally *'coming from'* here. This is about discerning that Egod is working to keep us an unenlightened species. If we mentally insist on remaining apart from God, we will continue to see other people also as different from us, and they are not. Essentially they are not; just as essentially we are not separate from God, unless that's our choice. We just need to re-cognize that fact and become <u>as</u> God-like as possible, by following that Moral Exemplar - Jesus Christ... and yes, even if we do not claim to be Christians. Muhammad; Buddha and others also were Othereal, Moral Entities who appeared on Earth as Guides. One can follow the moral principles taught through any such teachers sent by God.

"Egod wants us to see everyone as separate, as somehow different, in order that we might 'feel' superior to them, so that we might judge them, even persecute them. Whereas if we rightfully take our place "with" God, as part of God, then even God is no longer superior to us, as SHE cannot be superior to her Self. Not seeing ourselves as her potential children and as brothers and sisters, makes it more likely we will judge and condemn each other, just because our egos want satisfaction for the wrongs of which we judge others guilty. Such acts of judgment only show our personal, often fatal character flaws.

"If we say, in effect, that bitch or bastard "needs killing," and we don't have sense enough to know there's a God who will take care of all such condemnatory judgment matters in her own way, then we truly are a captive of Egod. This is especially true of human judgments that bring about wars and atrocities, within and between groups or individuals.

"Yes, of course, some people need to be locked away for the safety of others, but we should at least make an honest effort to rehabilitate their souls, even if we keep their bodies behind bars for life. We should try to capture criminals for medicinal or spiritual purposes, rather than kill them. Notice I said 'try' to capture them, because God can forgive killing that comes about inadvertently.

"Life would seem to be expendable to so many of us, when it should not be at all expendable. However, that also is why reincarnation is a big part of God's Grace, or empathetic Justice, in making sure those who reincarnate do atone for, and hopefully learn from, their unpaid sins of previous lives. It is God's version of so-called tough love. It is supposed to be a teaching love; and moral guidance is provided both during and between lives; but such guidance has limited effect because of the fused/confused density of materiality.

"We are allowed to fully recognize our sins following each life, as our learning process continues, or should. We then make a covenant with God through our COG Over-Souls (O-souls) to correct our course through another life, so that our karmic payments go toward building grace and moral goodness within us. Unfortunately, the density of material life causes most humans to effectually forget and ignore such idealism as too difficult a concept. It just *seems* easier that way, but it's just the opposite, really, because of id/ego and Egod.

"And we wonder why things just seem to happen to us. We call it good luck or bad luck, but it is God's law of karma... of simple reciprocity, meaning you're always going to get what you have coming... if not in this lifetime, then another – unicss"– Deepy stressed, "you are a genuine, devoutly moral person who comes under the merciful act of Grace. You can fool yourself, but not God, regarding your true essence. You might want to reflect on that, along with the fact that the *Old*

Testament of the *Bible* speaks truth, even when sometimes it seems to contradict the *"New Testament."* Jesus was misquoted at times, and occasionally even on purpose by the Egod of that era. But even as I praise the *Bible,* I admit some of it can seem like gibberish, such as *The Revelation of Jesus* to St. John. However, it too is there for a reason... for future, accurate "decoding."

"Eno has explained this to me, so that I can pass it along to the tinys. Of course I got a bit off on my own track as usual," Deepy told Shel, and then added, "But I will give it a rest - 'nough said' for now."

{Long Pause}

"I wonder what's keeping Eno." Shel took a moment to break the silence, which seemed immense following such passionate preaching.

{Deepy felt self-indulgent and a bit sad he could be so "righteously indignant." He just knew God needed more loving.}

[Speaking of God, a voice then rang out inside two heads]

"Oh, I'm here," Eno chuckled. "Well, at least tuned in for the last little while, listening to one of my favorite student-preachers."

"Don't get me started, I keep trying to tell y'all that," Deepy told them one more time, very much in awe of the knowledge and memories that his CHIP Mentors made available.

"By the way," Eno interjected, as he entered the diner and strode across the room, "don't be mad at CHIP for not announcing me. I asked him not to, after he mentioned you two were in a deep conversation. I hope you don't mind my listening in?"

"Not at all, Eno - You know this is our informal, *'anything goes'* setting. We can, and do, talk about anything here and anybody who is of a "mind to" can surely listen," Shel magnanimously assured everyone who just might be listening.

"May I address your wider audience, Deepy?" Eno inquired.

"Of course, Eno... anytime... for sure, please do."

"Thank you for your graciousness, both of you."

"Deepy realizes his growing spirit-soul mind appreciates center stage and the spotlight on occasion, to speak on God's behalf, even while he also knows such desire for attention parallels one of ego's primary needs. But his fervor is not a personality need, on his behalf, but rather a calling from his higher self - again on behalf of the Creator. In other words, it is completely unselfish and comes from good character."

Shel smiled, and Deepy agreeably said, "Amen, and thank you," as Eno sat down, glancing at both his friends.

"Deepy old boy, you are looking especially dapper today, I must say, with that spiffy new outfit. My, my, you are on the bright side. Going someplace?"

Deepy noticed Shel wink at Eno, as CHIP [BB] walked up to put a wicker basket on the floor beside her. "Er, ahem, thanks Eno - not that I know of," Deepy responded, while looking around suspiciously.

"Thanks CHIP," Shel said. Eno was on the verge of saying something, Deepy thought, but then Shel did, "Your patience will be rewarded, dear Deep one, you'll see." "Patience?" Deepy barely had time to wonder as Eno stood up.

"Now listen, you two have a wonderful outing and I'll see you tomorrow," Eno stated with his back half turned to catch up with CHIP, as they left Deepy bemused.

Meantime, Shel also had thanked Eno. "See you later," she had told him, before Deepy could wonder out loud what Eno was talking about. He managed to mutter "bye," but was now looking to Shel for clarification as to their 'outing' plans. Outing? Where to? He noticed Eno and CHIP stop to face each other by the door.

"Eno wasn't joking, Deep, you really do look great today. But, I'm sorry - I've already told you that. I like your style though. Very casual – just right for a picnic, I'd say."

"That's what I'm going to have now. My breakfast was hours ago. Now come on... what gives?" Deepy asked tentatively, afraid the answer might delay his taste bud cravings, even though he had put two and two together by now – a wicker basket, the mention of a picnic.

"Order your lunch to go," Shel told him, "and we'll put it in this handy basket that CHIP has provided for the occasion. The occasion," she went on, having read Deepy's muddled mind, "is a beautiful day for a picnic, plus the fact that we're parked inside the continental shelf, just off a wonderful, little Greek beach. Sunshine and lollipops, fried chicken, or whatever; let's get cracking. Time's a wasting."

"Ashore ... we're going ashore ... Greece? CHIP, hello? I'd like to order, please." I'll get some grease for Greece, with some fried chicken to go, he thought. He hoped he was smiling at Shel. He felt like he was. She was really grinning at him - My, what lovely white teeth you have, my dear.

"The better to help you eat your fried chicken," she told him. "... My dear!" she emphasized.

"Guess I'm still not used to this telepathy thing. It's downright inhuman... an "alien plot," Deepy laughed.

"Exactly," CHIP dryly noted from wherever he was. "Now, what was it you were thinking of ordering, because I might not be able to help you if you're in a hurry, since I just tuned in?"

"Yeah, right - Don't be coy," Shel told him. "We know you're always listening."

"Oh, really - Well, I'll have you know I'm mortified!"

"Well, as long you're not petrified, could I get some fried chicken, a dozen fried shrimp, a side of fried onion rings, fried okra and a couple of fried apple pies. And could you fry us a couple of drinks to go with that, please?"

"Well sir," CHIP responded, "If you'll check your basket, you will find everything you ordered in there, minus the drinks of course, plus a couple of things I thought Shel might enjoy. Yes, I am precognitive. You're welcome, come again, have a nice day, and bye-bye."

‖‖‖‖‖‖‖‖‖‖‖‖‖‖‖‖‖‖‖‖‖‖‖‖

(CHAPTER 7)

Shel Games

"I'm sorry, but I don't speak Greek," Deepy heard and read Shel to say. He looked up from the damp sand in time to see a handsome man with a puzzled facial expression, which the man then put into words. "But... but," he said, "you spoke Greek with a perfect dialect just now, and you look like a Greek woman, er... or then again, maybe not." He seemed to reconsider that, as he peered more closely at Shel. "Suspicious rascal," Shel thought, but she didn't say anything. Having already committed herself, she chose a facial expression of her own - dumbfounded. She waited... and waited, watching the man's facial expressions change any number of times.

The man, thinking he may have insulted her, spoke up finally, but this time in English, "Ah, but your dog, your dog, he looks American to me. Does he speak also English, perhaps?"

"I'm from Arkansas and Texas, and just up the road from Lucy Anna," Deepy thought, as though they might be magical places, where the language is more colorful than plain ol' English.

Shel smiled at Deepy. "Thank God for your stylish look," she teleped. "I knew CHIP was going to give us the ability to understand Greek, but I didn't know I would automatically be speaking it too. It sounded like English in my head." "Mine too," Deepy concurred. "CHIP's perceptions must also work for instantly translating languages."

Shel had become momentarily confused because of the unique circumstances of where they appeared on the beach ... and until the man had spoken English, she had been on the verge of just walking away. "Funny," she thought, "that his English is so good." [It was correctable] She almost asked him if he were a tourist too; but apparently, after she told him she didn't speak Greek, she found out she did, for the benefit of this adventure. It didn't seem to matter now anyway and she thought she would just speak whatever language CHIP chose – apparently English now.

Shel had gone ashore dressed to fit into a Greek crowd, while Deepy chose to remain dressed as he was. Then they had been enshrouded by the Assembler's transition baffle, thereafter "materializing" on the beach. CHIP had said he could always pick just the right spot, but Deepy wondered about that now, since the beach was not very crowded. What was CHIP thinking? Even so, it would have been fine except for Shel's momentary blunder, which Deepy thought was no big deal. The man seemed to speak fairly good English. It might even be perfect, Deepy thought, if it had a southern twang to it.

No one had focused on Shel and Deepy's materialization at the moment they appeared, because of what CHIP described as a hypnotic haze. He had said that human perceptions could be suspended from any given spot just long enough for a "transition" to take place, and, if necessary, thoughts could be cleansed to accommodate such an appearance. CHIP had said there would be no startle effect.

But, this time, there was, on the part of both Shel and Deepy, and another dog already on the scene. Shel had "appeared" to be breathing down the back of a man's neck, almost literally. The man was in the possession of a small dog on a leash, just as Shel had Deepy on a leash. The man had been facing the ocean, but the dog was definitely startled, barking and jumping back at the same time. The dog, a Chihuahua, was almost immediately at wit's end.

"Shut up, dog!" Deepy was now thinking. He had never known Chihuahuas to be very witty in the first place, and always much too excitable to suit him. As his human Larray James self, Deepy had not been a Chihuahua aficionado. He had always referred to them as "Chi-ha-ha(s)," except in front of their owners of course; and now that he was getting a dog's-eye view of one, he knew his opinion was not about to change. "A 'Chi-ha-ha' ... short-haired ... ugly as sin," Deepy's southern culture told him, while his good conscience said, "My apologies as always to Chihuahua lovers everywhere... but," he excused himself, "people do have different tastes. Of course everybody would just love a 'Yorkie-Poo,'" he teased himself, but then thought – "Everybody but me, maybe."

Deepy knew he could understand any language if CHIP programmed him, but he could not understand this mutt's yammering. He was glad it was a muddle to him. He had no desire to talk "dog." And this hyper little beast was fast getting on Deepy's nerves. (He knew he was saving his last nerve though for Shel's swarthy stranger, if some growling needed to be done.) He was now about to try his own bark, if he had one, for what he hoped would amount to an intimidating "shut up," but at that moment the man reached down and scooped up his nervous wreck. Only then, a scant second later, the perturbing, passionate pest was preaching from on high.

"You talkin'a me? You talkin'a me?" Deepy mimicked a movie actor in his head. "You want a piece uh me? Eh?" he carried on, seeming to have brought his teen-age self along for the outing; "I double-dog dare you to shut up!" Finally he decided only he appreciated his silly, surly pretentiousness. Just ignore him or her, he told himself, since "it" was up there. After a few seconds of patting and stroking from its owner, the critter calmed down noticeably. "Thank goodness," Deepy thought.

"Hi, Deepy," a feminine voice in his head said.

"What? Who's there?" It didn't sound like Shel. It was much more high-pitched.

"It's me, the mutt... upstairs."

Deepy looked, and could have sworn he saw Ms. Mutt wink at him.

"Let's just be friends for today," the voice said.

Deepy decided to play along. "Friends for the day ... sure, why not?" he aimed his telepathy toward his new friend. "And how is it you know my name, but I don't know yours?"

"CHIP says you just need to know I'm a "dandy." Friends - Okay? No more thoughts from me now; bow-wow..."

Deepy gave her a cocked-eyed, "What's going on?" expression, but got nothing in return. "Hmm?"

"... God?" - Something about God from the conversation overhead. "Ah! Greek god... something or other." Deepy was picking up pieces of thoughts and conversation. In spite of his "Dandy" distraction, he had been sub-hearing and reading the proceedings above him, more or less, since the man had turned around and asked Shel where she had come from. That's when Shel had responded in what he said was perfect Greek, accent and all, telling him she just wanted to pet his dog and that she didn't speak Greek. Deepy's sub-thoughts were now catching up to the moment.

"Where are your footprints?" the man had wanted to know. (Andros? Names had been exchanged, but Deepy wasn't sure he had heard right.) Andros pointed at the sand down around their feet and then directly behind them. "You say you came from over there?"

"What?" Shel asked... trying to look confused again.

"Your footprints," he said again.

"What?"

Now the man looked befuddled; "What?" he responded.

Shel: "What were you saying about that place over there?"

Andros: "Ah, but you confuse me, pretty lady." He shook his head, pausing as if to think about it. "... Oh, over there," he pointed, "that little café; would you care to have some refreshments - perhaps something to drink with your picnic?" He nodded at her basket. "I've already eaten," he quickly added, "but I would be pleased to buy you and your friend a drink, or if that's not food in there, I'll even buy you lunch if you'll just keep smiling at me like that." He smiled grandly at his generosity, showing off his perfect teeth in the process.

"You may indeed buy me lunch, thank you. I have dog food in the basket, which I will give to our friends under the table." Shel beamed a smile back at Andros, and then at Deepy.

"I know you're extra famished by now," she teleped. "I can hear your stomach all the way up here."

"Whaa? Not mine," Deepy feigned indignation. "Must be Andre's or Andros's, or whatever this Greek Romeo calls himself. Why do you suppose he's being so friendly?" Deepy thought all this; even while sub-thinking, "Dog food - Under the table?"

Shel laughed. "Call me Andy," the man said, showing his teeth again. Deepy felt like showing his, right on Andy's rear end.

Thank goodness for CHIP and his 'hypnotic haze,' Shel was thinking, as they began their trek across the sand, leaving footprints behind them. Deepy glanced back and thought, "I guess that makes us real."

"Beautiful day," Deepy was thinking now. "A Greek named Andy - his dog's a dandy – but I'm not randy." Deepy's mind played with the mood of sunshine. "Ms. Dandy Mutt," was hovering up there, Deepy noticed, in the protective custody of her owner, looking down on him, with a seeming gleam in her eye. He tried to affect a wink, not that she would know what it was. He had already convinced himself their conversation had never happened, that he was simply becoming "Goofy." He chuckled to himself at the cartoon name and image he intended. Ms. Mutt had the nerve to growl at him at that point... along with his stomach. Shel had been right of course.

"Poor little mutt. Look at her," he told himself, "She is still shivering." He was starting to feel sorry for her. "A lot of humans are like her; thinking the best defense is a good offense. I guess when you're so small you have to resort to whatever might work for you. Ah, bless her little heart," he now thought sincerely in his southern manner.

They strolled along in the warm sunshine. Shel was busy reading "Greek," offered to her by CHIP, with a certain European English flair. She read Andros because not all the man's thoughts were put into words, both Shel and Deepy had noticed. And while he told himself he was trying not to listen, he picked up a thought or two from Andy the Greek: "... breathing down my neck... I could almost feel her up against me."

Deepy knew where this was going - Greek god meets beautiful goddess... beautiful day... beautiful setting... extraneous dogs to be disposed of 'under the table.' "Okay," he thought, he would share his food if 'Dandy' wanted some. He just hoped they could get along. Speaking of which, Shel, he couldn't help but notice, was still smiling. "Damn, if only I were wearing my young, Larray body," – but then, the thoughts of "dirty old man," and "dirty-dog" came to mind. She really is beautiful though... doggone it! And the man's fairly handsome, Deepy supposed. Then he had to wonder if maybe he wasn't just a bit jealous - "Come on," he asked himself, "am I really jealous of this Andy man? Nah!" he answered himself. He then noticed that Shel was laughing in his direction. "Good Lord," he hoped she was not laughing at him. "I'm just playing around," he thought in her direction while grinning at her.

I could sure go for a beer, someone thought. We're on our way, someone else thought. "Are you with me, Larray?" Deepy queried his real self. "Wonder if they serve beer to dogs?" - "Gorgeous day," from someone else; - A few lascivious thoughts from the Greek god holding the mutt, who seemed to be smiling now too. Deepy's noose, er, collar felt a little too snug. "What's her hurry?" he thought. "Loosen up, gal! Whew... thanks."

"*Sunshine ... on my shoulders ... makes me happy...*" Deepy sang to himself, in the spirit of the day and the man, John Denver. "Whoa," he thought again, as Shel went over his speed limit. No 'whoa.' "Woe is me," he thought, to no avail, as he picked up his pace. Andy was busy being Andy ... entertaining the world with himself. His ego was expansive and he was completely wrapped up in it. Shel was paying attention to her suitor. So Deepy went back to singing an obvious choice: "Your Old Love Game"

> We used to march together
> To the very same drum beat
> But along the way somewhere
> You got out of sync

You had a love affair
When he swept you off your feet
Now the game's over for us;
I'll be on my way...
The fat lady sang today

Now the bands we used to wear
Are like the bands we used to hear,
Shiny gold ... Happy songs!
Supposed to last for years

But the gold is tarnished now
The bands are out of tune
When the fat lady sang
The lady sang the blues

It's déjà vu all over again
With you and my best friend
I warned you twice before
I couldn't take it anymore
Now it's three strikes you're out
At your old love game

[Deepy paused to let CHIP's "Headband" play a spell.]

Now the bands we used to wear
Are like the bands we used to hear,
Shiny gold ... Happy songs!
Supposed to last for years

But the gold is tarnished now
The bands are out of tune
When the fat lady sang
The lady sang the blues;

It's déjà vu all over again
With you and my best friend
I warned you twice before
I couldn't take it anymore
Now it's three strikes you're out
At your old love game

Your sad love song is over
The music's died away
The fiddler that you danced to
Is the one you gotta pay
You played the game of love

But something went astray
The fat lady sang today...
That famous fat woman sang today
At your old love game

The lady sang today
The fat lady sang today
At your 'Old Love Game'

('It ain't over 'til the fat lady sings' is a well-known colloquialism in sports broadcasting, although hackneyed now to say the least. The phrase essentially means one should not assume the outcome of an event until it's officially ended. The origin of the saying is debatable. Deepy's song refers to a relationship.

Yogi Berra, a professional baseball team manager who was known for his wit has a similar quote, 'It ain't over 'til it's over,' which is meant as encouragement for a team to play on, despite the score. 'It's déjà vu all over again' also is one of his many witticisms.)

~~~~~~~~~~~~~~~~~~~~~~~~~~~~~~~~~~~~~

CHAPTER 8
REINCARNATION

"A really nice outing, my Deep friend," Shel sighed and stretched out on her bunk. Deepy had accepted her invitation to join her in her room, for dessert. Andy had provided dinner at a quaint little restaurant. But now, Deepy was slurping happily on a strawberry milkshake and Shel was indulging in a banana split. Deepy figured why not a few more minutes together; after all he had been tagging along behind her all day. So he halfway expected to sleep beside her tonight. He somehow felt guilty with that thought. Though he knew that Andy entertained virtually the same thought and had not, Deepy knew, felt the least bit guilty. But also, Andy was a dog of a different type... a "cur." He was glad CHIP had retrieved them when they stepped outside, as Andy was paying for the evening meal. "What an ego!"

"With a capital "E," Shel concurred, picking up on what she had referred to in the past as deep thinking. "Still, he was cut from a mold," she now said.

"What?" Deepy wondered. He had lost the connection, while thinking he was going to have to somehow remember to privatize some of his thoughts while around her. He had had too many slip-ups lately.

"Don't worry about it, Deepy," Shel told him.

"What?" he inquired again.

"I don't think you could offend me. I know your thoughts are innocent and have nothing to do with your body."

"Or any 'body' for that matter, but thanks," he said, "Anyway, I thought you said something about a mole."

Shel laughed, "Mold: Andy - 'Greek-god mold.'"

"And I guess I'm more like a Jell-O" mold," Deepy said, feigning a pout.

"Silly! Deepy, I swear, you act just like you're jealous, sometimes."

"Do not!"

"You'll always be my favorite dog in all the world."

"Favorite dog? Wow! What an honor - big stinky deal!

"Easy now, boy," Shel scolded, adding, "I think your teenage self is showing through again. But, maybe you're right; perhaps I will reconsider that, since you're so unimpressed anyway. Andy's dog was just precious, didn't you think?"

Deepy almost gagged. "Puh-leeze!" he exclaimed, having the sudden realization he was now jealous of Andy's dandy dog, although they had shared food and gotten along the whole day. "I actually think she fell in love with me," Deepy teased himself.

Shel concentrated on her dessert. Deepy contemplated his nose and the conversation to this point. He made sure his microhm shield was in place, knowing he could instantly override it, if he thought to converse, and of course a person's own shield never omitted other people's thinking. Shel's just trying to be nice, he reasoned. What the devil's wrong with me anyway? Hell, I know I'm acting jealous... and I guess that does irritate me.

He noticed Shel taking the last bite of her banana split.

"You seemed to have gotten rather worked up about reincarnation, the last time we talked about it," he now said. "I did all the talking then, so care to tell me what you know?" He knew Shel liked to espouse her beliefs on behalf of God.

"Heavy conversation after heavy eating - What's to tell?" she told him. "I would just be repeating what you said Eno said."

"Thank you, that's very enlightening," he replied sardonically. "But it ain't necessarily so."

"Would you tell me where to begin then, please?" Shel sighed.

"I'm sorry, Shel. It's been a long day. This can wait."

"It's all right, Deepy. Go ahead. I may be a little tired, but I'm not all that sleepy yet."

"Let's say I don't understand the need for reincarnation. I mean you and I know that I do. But treat me like a novice, or "unbeliever," because I just might want to put your take on it in the book I will be writing. Did I tell you, with CHIP's help, I will be writing a book? And maybe you could tell me about the concept of the law of karma or God's judgment of "an eye for an eye," when SHE deems it appropriate and just - you know, that sort of thing – just your take on all of it."

He went on, "For example, how literally can we take this law?" Deepy stopped suddenly. "Shel, I now realize how tired I am. Would you like to reconsider the option of putting off this conversation? I'm thinking I might just opt for that now myself, the more I think about it."

Shel couldn't help but laugh - "Too late now. You already asked, so keep your eyes open and focused, because I'm going to rain words down upon you, whether you listen or not."

"I'm listening, attentively, I think, but it's up to you, Shel." He gave her a second, and then asked, "Where and when does this type of exacting Justice with a capital "J" take place?" He adopted Shel's little speech mannerism.

"As God sees fit of course, taking into consideration her "relief" virtue of Grace; this includes mercy and forgiveness, depending on an entity's status. But Eno says that just about everyone needs to learn similar, standard moral lessons, while many others require lessons tailored to specific personal needs. Whatever the need, God can put each of us into a scenario in this or a later life that will serve to continue teaching us all at the same time, as well as on a more personal basis.

"The law of karma - that is to say the concept of that law - is basically God's Justice system, and it boils down to

"You reap what you sow," or in other words, you get what you have coming – unless Grace comes into play and God finds reason to forgive you some little ticktack stuff. By the way, it is by God's Grace that most people are reincarnated. Sincere, practicing Christians or anyone with moral wisdom – let's just say "WILL and grace" don't require reincarnation because they are automatically saved to a remedial appAngel realm. They become apprentice quin, in other words, with more lessons and practice to come.

"Immoral entities who are entirely too evil and almost beyond redemption, also do not reincarnate right away, if ever, but go to the realm of spectral, ghostly subconsciousness, which is a dimension parallel and close to the one we're in. With enough prayer from loved ones though, some of them may be rehabilitated at a later point and allowed another opportunity to pay their debts through reincarnation, so as to find salvation through God's Grace. The prayers can come from anyone, anywhere, even from heaven. All quin pray for loved ones on a regular basis and for mankind as a whole.

"Lots of folks pay for small karmic debts within their current lifetime, but, even then, they must find salvation through recognition of Christ, or at least God-like morality, as their Savior. Most folks are not willfully evil, but evil comes about as a result of ignorance mostly and not necessarily from going out of one's way to be bad. They usually call some karmic results 'bad luck,' while leaving God out of the equation."

Shel pondered for a moment before adding in her southern dialect "... Anyways, every human spirit-soul is advised of where he or she stands with God, after each lifetime. Every non-Christian is given a chance between lives to work on godly thinking, and all are advised and assisted by the really mature Angels, if I'm remembering right," she paused "... what Eno told me..."

"You know, about two-thirds of the world's population believes in reincarnation. That alone does not make it a fact, but - in fact - Christians did too until the second council of Constantinople in 553 A.D. when such believers were then declared to be wrong and consequently excommunicated. This was a minority of powerful people declaring what the majority should believe - typically an Egod maneuver and a political one, but perhaps sincere and well-intentioned nonetheless.

"Perhaps that council consisted of id/ego-driven politicians who thought they knew best, but - Egod, in either the guise of societal influence or personal hubris could have unduly influenced members of the council. After all, this was more than 500 years after Christ. By the way, its Istanbul, Turkey, now – not Constantinople," Shel winked, as Deepy recalled an old song lyrically making that point.

"Eno says the believers in reincarnation were right and that council was misguided. Some of the confusion lay in the fact that Jesus said that people would be judged and held accountable "... in this generation." What most people don't realize or likely don't know is that 'this generation' measures the period between appearances of God's Son, from the time He first co-created Eden's Earth garden, then later his time of the cross, and fairly soon now his time of return as promised. This so-called 'generation' includes the progress of every incarnate and reincarnated spirit-soul. Also, this generation is the hybrid one, as opposed to pure generations of Humans past – with their COG cohabitants.

"Perhaps in 553 A.D., that misguided group decided that people might be more inclined to amend their ways if they thought they had only one meager lifetime in which to do so; and too the *Bible* states that each person has an appointed death and is then judged. In a sense, it is true that everyone has only one life, because the life of a soul naturally is 'eternal,' unless God decides otherwise, because of extremely immoral behavior. Such a dire consequence as eternal death of a soul though could only happen within hybrid humans mortally inflicted with the id/ego Eve illness. Hybrids are their own global pandemic in this regard.

"Still, it could be the council's motivations were not evil, but rather because of limited wisdom those persons thought they were making a godly decision. It's certainly likely their reasoning has served God's purposes, intentionally or not.

"Now humanity is at the critical juncture spoken of in the *Bible*, in which Christ will be returning to mark the end of an "Eve ill" hybrid generation on Earth; - and just maybe your book, my friend, can give folks a new dose of that reality," Shel told her wide-eyed audience of one. (Actually, he was trying hard to stay awake)

"In the meantime we have been judged after each incarnate life. Eno says the word 'lifetime' is misleading because, as souls, we have only one life, but it is not lived completely within the material realm and rarely in just one fleshly incarnation. Life is divided between here and the Otherealm, unless one is in hell or netherealm – a 'shade' or dimension of the 'Other.'

"Material sojourns of course come in different fused spirit forms, but we do keep the same soul each time. Our previous spirit's predilections and propensities are, for better or worse, ingrained into that tiny soul to suit God's Spiritual teaching needs as befits personal karma. In other words, every new fused spirit's brain is modified each time by its tiny soul, depending on its karma. It is God's goal that someday each tiny soul finally will help Co-Create a spirit that is moral enough to remain an indivisibly-dual entity with that soul and its Over-Soul for eternal salvation.

"These between-life adjustments influence character predispositions or projections during the next physical life. This is all just part of one soul life, which could be interspersed with many such spirit-soul incarnations. Such incarnate segments only end when 'time' ends, or people finally decide to follow God's Moral Ways; or they become so corrupt that even Grace will not save them. Of course, as I said, the time of a final judgment for every spirit-soul is nigh. It will begin the day Christ returns, or at least that's my understanding?" Shel paused to look at Deepy quizzically, until he finally said, "Mine too."

"Our COG Over-Souls are trying, as best we each allow, to help us develop spirit-souls worthy of God. Of course they must work through the Otherealm into this fused, dense spirit world of matter, until a spirit either is lost or ready to attain heaven through moral virtue.

"If a person becomes a Christian, or otherwise moral enough, such learning continues within the heavenly strata of the Otherealm. COG or Angels work with spirit-souls in heaven until each apprentice is ready to become a Humangel Cell of God. Any non-Christian spirit-soul that progresses morally within its lives is allowed to continue paying karmic debt through reincarnation, while working in-between with its soul and O-Soul.

"Am I repeating myself?" Shel now wondered.

"You're doing fine," her sleepy best friend told her, while adding, "But I thought every Christian angel had to apprentice in minor heaven until their final incarnation in Garden Gaia, in which they would help Jesus convert other more recalcitrant spirit-souls."

"Yeah, that's right," Shel said. "Did I give an otherwise impression? I sure didn't mean to. Sometimes my thoughts do get crossed up. Maybe I should have said, 'Angels work with appCOG spirit-souls in minor heaven* until they are ready to work in Garden Gaia, after which they will ascend to, and remain in Heaven Proper as complete Humangel Cells Of God.'"

*{There is a minor heaven, also known as purgatory, as well as the even lower ghostly spirit shade, then below that a much darker shade known as the netherealm of hell; and then above all, there is the Major – or capitalized Proper Heaven known as the Child - God Jr.}

"Well, you know my thoughts sure can get crossed up too – anyway, sorry to slow you down – please continue, 'Me Shel, my belle'."

"You're cute.

"Anyway, to keep some of this generation from failing, Christ was willing to die on the cross, so our sins could be forgiven if we only believe that and become moral like him/her."

"Er, excuse me," Deepy interrupted, "Why do you say him/her and not simply "her?" Eno says "Her" includes him in the form of "he." I know I have said he/she and him/her, but people need to get used to the one pronoun that includes both polarities so they stop thinking in terms of gender."

"You're right. I guess I said it that way because I heard you say it like that. But, you're right; Jesus Christ is a Trangel, meaning an indivisibly-dual polar entity that can transition from Yin to Yang polarity,* or vice-versa, according to God's needs at any particular time."   *[Yin/negative; Yang/positive]

"I wonder if SHe could do that in the "gender" version of her polarities; I mean switch what would amount to genders?"

"It is my understanding that is the case and SHe did… but I don't mean actual body parts but rather polar essence. COG could only do that internally, while their physical bodies would remain the same. Although, yes, their spiritual Yin/Yang essence could reverse according to God's needs, which could make it seem a gender had become its opposite. These days when that happens, people don't understand the oft-times resulting physical confusion and wonder why a person in a male "physical suit," would act female, or vice-versa. Those with dark minds choose to see it as sexual perversion. It has nothing to do with such a desire, although it also can be confusing to those affected. God mainly has used it in hybrid times to teach empathy and override ego.

"Anyway, I wanted to make the point that people should understand they will be judged and rewarded or taught as God deems appropriate, in compliance with the exacting law of karma. True Christians (as judged by God) however, will be redeemed through the merciful Virtue of Grace.

"You need a break?" Shel wondered.

"Not at all - no, I'm okay – just a bit weary... unless you need one? We can continue tomorrow or whenever – up to you. Anyway, you said, "true" Christians, as if some might not be."

"They might not - not really, even though they think they are. People sometimes like to think they are doing the best they can morally, but ultimately that judgment is for God only."

"Makes sense," Deepy told her. "Do you need a break?"

"I don't need a break," Shel replied. "In fact, I want to bear down just a bit because some folks need to quit fooling themselves by thinking they already know everything. I mean, "Come on!" - People need to get real about the kind of God we have. We all want a loving God and we have one, but we need to give God more credit. For example, let's say if God really does live for eternity and SHE wants us as part of her life forever, then it does not stand to reason that SHE would only give us an infinitesimal part of a nanosecond, or what amounts to no time at all, to become "perfect." Would SHE do this based on life circumstances that appear to be vastly unequal in giving each of us a chance to achieve such perfection? - Hardly. It is karma that causes these seemingly disproportionate opportunities for success. People are not thinking logically if they cannot fathom that, but I expect some just do not want to understand. Some people are so thick-headed, I just feel sorry for them.

"Of course all spirit-souls started as virtual *'equals'* with their first life on Earth. It was their peculiar genetics that initially made them different, and then just the particular karma they developed that later put them morally ahead or behind others in each of their lives, until they reached their current state. Sometimes Egod finally just overwhelms hybrid humans. It always has been and will be up to them to call upon God for help, but especially now, if they are to receive any of God's Grace.

"Does the *Bible* not say, effectually''*... be ye perfect, even as your Father (or Parent) in heaven is...?* God wants our perfection to at least be within the margin of error of her Grace, which would allow us to finish our cleansing process within a more heavenly realm than this one. SHE will not have us contaminating her Home, not because SHE doesn't love us, but because SHE does. God knows we can only co-exist and thrive forever in a purely moral environment, in which we must make ourselves fit – with her help. It is there for the "asking," because of her mercy of grading on a curve and saving those with the most moral potential.

"God always knew SHE would not maintain a material world forever, in which to help us reach perfection, but SHE also would not give up on us after one or even a hundred negligible lifetimes. That would be illogical and SHE knows how attached most hybrid humans are to "their" Earthly home, and therefore SHE has had to do her best to turn it into a classroom before SHE must finally close this material realm forever. That is why we must learn to interact with each other in a moral, godly way.

"There are hybrid entities from other planets out there, and some are here with us now. Many of them look like us, while others do not. I'm talking about their forms, nor skin colors. If something as benign as skin coloration can divide us, think of physical differences as possibly more divisive because of Egod. They then surely could not come forward to help us advance morally and scientifically, so that we might save our planet. Racist hybrids on Earth would train their weapons on a different-looking species and those "otherwise" friends would have the right and certainly the capability to protect themselves while hybrids go back to their business of killing themselves and their planet.

"I happen to know from Eno that so-called space 'aliens' come in peace and do help in clandestine ways, just as the Heavenly COG are doing. In fact, most all "alien" hybrids have reached the appCOG stage of enlightenment, while Earthites still are in the process of destroying themselves, which they will do with the help of scientific hubris that already insists they must find another planet to colonize if they wish to survive as a species. The problem is not the planet. People are the problem. God is not going to just give people another planet if they don't preserve the one they have. They must save it from themselves.

"God absolutely will not turn her pure Heaven over to the more morally questionable of self-aware creatures among us. We can prove we are making a good faith effort by understanding the lessons of morality that Jesus taught and accept him as our gracious Leader. We cannot allow id/ego the ability to keep us from accepting the moral message of God, through the Essence of Christ. However, humans living now are some of the most stubbornly resistant hybrids ever to hear the moral messages of God through Christ, Muhammad, and others. Hybrids must try harder to change their intrinsic evil to godly essence. I'm told it is very close to "too late," although in terms of eternity, only God knows when?

"And yet, why risk not knowing? We must recognize God as perfect in the here-and-now and therefore as having the ability to save us all if we would but make the necessary effort. Otherwise, we will continue to adopt our usual pattern of ignorance and denial of God and God's laws. We elect to fool ourselves. We bury our heads in the sand or pull the wool over our eyes... if you'll forgive such trite expressions," Shel chuckled, excusing those examples that were 'trite' for good reason.

"Anyway, we hide behind ignorance in the idiotic belief that we can fool God into thinking we just don't know any better. And that is the greatest ignorance of all, to be that foolish, and it also is the greatest victory of Egod, to have fashioned us that way. It would be in the best interest of certain aspects of Egod to have us believe God is not omnipotent, or even great, so that we might question her very existence. It just makes me mad when I think about it. But, I doubt my passion will make a dent in the minds of ninety-six and three-tenths percent of the people who might read this, if you include it in your book, my friend. That's how effective the ego's system of ignorance is. It can render a person stupidly impotent."

A Deepy subthought registered (*96 and 3/10ths percent?*)

"I'm sorry, but I do get upset just thinking about it, and all I can say to people who want proof that what I'm saying is true, is just go right on denying God. Just go right on dancing with the one that "brung ya." {Shel resorted to her dialect whenever she was really ticked off or wanted to stress a point.} "And he'll be the one taking you from that party to his home in hell." Shel turned red, but then laughed. "I guess I just naturally come from a woman's point of view." she winked. "Besides," she added, "I like the activity of dancing. It's good exercise."

"I can tell you one thing for certain," Deepy told her, "you don't need to, and should not, apologize for your passion on behalf of God and her Son. The world needs many more such folks – a world-full, in fact," he emphasized.

"Thanks," Shel mumbled. She then told Deepy, "See what you get for being so nice – now I'm going to continue.

"We refer to Egod as a male, mainly because this has always been a man's world with 'his' male God, along with everything else that men think they own – no offense – but it's as if God were incapable of being a matched pair, and had to choose one gender (polar essence) over the other. You and I know by now that God is not a gender, but SHE does represent two so-called genders in her material world. But they are Twi-polar and those Aspects are equal in every way and perfect in their attraction of each other. The attraction should be of opposite spiritual essence and not to the outer physicality, which Egod propagates for profit. Craven sexuality is as addictive as a drug.

"We also know the societal negative essence we call Egod has the same powerful influence on women – as it does on men. Anyway, Eno says the *Bible* was written under the auspices of Father God, since a Yang 'Lord God,' primarily was viewed by a male-dominated society as responsible for co-creating this hybrid generation, which He partly was. They didn't know He was half of an indivisibly-dual twi-polar

Essence representing the much greater existential Essence of their Parents. And many still won't know it after reading what I just said, unfortunately."

Deepy really enjoyed it when Shel was relaxed enough to speak her charming "down home chat" with him. Maybe that's the kind of 'looseness' CHIP was wanting from him as well. Working in his profession though had caused him to lose his own southern accent, not because he wanted to, but because he had traveled a lot to different parts of the country and overseas, giving speeches and seminars. He had thus developed a neutral tone and cadence, or essentially no accent, although he enjoyed faking his own dialect at times. It could be colorful.

"But you would be wise to live your lives... okay, sorry – "We" – 'we' would be wise to live our lives, admitting that we really do know and accept that God is God. If you [Shel switched pronouns without realizing it] do that long enough, and try long and hard enough, eventually you're going to get better and better. Trouble is we may have run out of material lifetimes." Shel paused for a moment before saying, "Now, I will take you up on your offer to continue this conversation when we both are more alert, shall we say?" [She was actually feeling an adrenaline spike and wanted to calm down.]

Deepy didn't respond as she expected him to.

"Deepy?" "I say ... Deeeepy?" "DEEPY!"

"Whaaa? - Whaa? Oh, Shel... hi, what are you doing here?"

"Talking to the walls, apparently; Question is what are you doing here? Sleeping, by any chance?"

"Huh? What... Eno? Sorry, Eno, er... Shel?"

"Deepy, Deepy - sleepy Deepy. Come on now. Okay then, just tell me the last point I made... DEEPY!" Now Shel appeared amused that Deepy had managed to tune her out, even if they both were tired. She reached over and scuffed his ears together. "DEEE-PY," she said in a mock baritone.

"Knock it off, Shel. God, I'm so tired all of a sudden. Gotta get to my room. So tired ... so much walking today, not used to it, out of shape, too fat ... too tired, too ... too ... sorry Shel."

"... don't mind sleeping on the floor?" Shel was saying.

"Mind? ... Christ's sake, Shel, I'm a dog," his befuddled memory told him, and then echoed: "... sleepy Deepy, sleepy ... sleepy."

('Poor, dear sweetie,' Shel was now thinking.)

"Sleepy," Shel said one more time as she knelt down and kissed him on his forehead. "We were married in another life," she whispered.

"Sleepy Deepy," his tired mind wandered on – "married in another life... slee..." one eye tried, but couldn't quite open – "married - another life?"

"Good night dear," Shel was saying.

Deepy was committed to dreamland... "Married? - What the...? – I'm a dog... sleepy as a dog... married like a dog - dog tired... dog for heaven's sake... deep sleepy, deep dog, for Christ's sake... deep... dreaming... "Christ as Super Dog!" one newspaper headline proclaimed. "Wonder Dog really Jesus?" another read. "Miracle to End all Miracles!" still another stated. "Story of Stories: Dog claims to be Christ!" "Dog with southern drawl says he's Jesus!" "I never claimed that. I would never say that. I'm not crazy! Get away from me."

"Heretic! He's the antichrist!" someone in the crowd yelled. (Deepy rolled over in his sleep, whimpering) "Play dead!" he heard someone shout. (He rolled back the other way) "Kill him – he's playing dead!" "Sit up... roll over!" (Deepy rolled over) Someone kicked him. He yelped and barked. "He admitted it," a dog in the crowd shouted. It was 'Dandy,' who growled, and then yelled, "Traitor!"

"No, no, I'm confused." "He's confused," Shel yelled. "Run, Shel, run pell-mell Shel." "You could be," Eno said. "No, no, I'm not!" "You could be," Eno said. Deepy whimpered, and then yowled. "He admitted it!" "He's confused, leave him alone," Shel shouted. Help!" Deepy wailed, but it was too late. The crowd was all around him now. He could see a cross.

"Blasphemy! - he claims to be the god of dogs!" Dandy barked. "Dog – I'm just a dog!" Deepy cried, "You've got it backward... it's D-O-G, not G-O-D! For heaven's sake, people, I can't be God - I'm from Arkansas."

"We ain't buying it, boy. You don't sound like one-uh-us," "He could be," Eno said. "What? What?" Deepy yelled. "Eno, where are you, I can't see you." "I know Jesus," Eno was saying, "Jesus is a friend of mine, and believe me, Deepy, you ain't no Jesus!" "I ain't no Jesus!" Deepy shouted to the crowd. "You hear that... you tell 'em Eno!" Deepy shouted... shouted... "Deepy!" "Deepy! What's wrong?" It was Shel's voice. "Deepy, what's the matter with you? ...DEEPY?"

A woozy Deepy pawed one eye open and then tried to get up, but he slipped. Shel was standing at the bathroom door with a towel around her. She was dripping wet. "When I turned off the shower, I heard you squealing. Deepy, what happened? What have you done?" Shel was looking down at the floor where Deepy was now standing.

He appeared to be soaked through from sweat. That is sweat, isn't it? He wondered. He looked at his feet and sniffed. "Oh my God... Shel, I'm sorry, I had a terrible dream, worst nightmare of my life... any life. They were going to nail me to a cross. They thought I thought I was Jesus." Deepy moaned, "Can you imagine this poor pudgy dog body on a cross?" He sounded all choked up.

"Good Lord! That's a doozy of a dream," Shel said.

Still, Deepy thought, she might be upset. "Anyway," Deepy told her, "It wasn't a doozy," - he paused – "Doozy was my Mama... or was it Daisy? Let's see... Dipsy - that was my dad. Doozy, Daisy, Dipsy," he recited. "Dippy. That's it! Dippy! My Mama was Dippy for sure. Daddy was a dip... Mama was a dippy..." Deepy went on, in a singsong manner. By now, Shel had taken another towel and was mopping the floor with it. She was bent over laughing and mopping at the same time. Deepy hoped she was laughing with him and not at him. A thought flashed through her mind, which Deepy wasn't quite sure if he had read correctly: "Good grief - married to him!" is what it seemed like to Deepy. He closed his eyes and thought, "I heard that!"

Shel chuckled, but didn't say anything.

Deepy was now repeating the rhyme he had begun making up - softly at first and then louder "... Daddy was a dip... Mama was a dippy..." (Think, he told himself) "Mama let it slip, she's from Mississippi... (Um?) ... Daddy let her go ... back from where she came... he raised me Deep in Texas ... that's where I got my name. (And then from a sub-thought, he quickly added) And now I'm on my way... to fortune, love, and fame!"

He looked at Shel, hoping she was still laughing, but she only smiled at him, appearing to have something else on her mind. "All right, I guess I'm no writer of verse." He hung his head, trying for some sympathy.

"I know who you really are," she told him.

"Oh, good grief - what's that supposed to mean? Anyway who told you that we were once married - Eno?"

"It was CHIP who reminded me, the first day we were here together, since my thinking was a bit fuzzy."

"What do you mean... the first day 'we' were here? I thought you had been here a lot longer than me."

"Yeah, you do think that, don't you? And that's because you don't remember the first conversation we ever had, when we were getting acquainted. Tell you what, while you're doing all this thinking, why don't you run take a quick shower... get that doggie smell off you."

"Maybe I should just run along to my room, Shel."

"Not necessary ... I like having you here for now. Besides, you might have some more questions that can't wait 'til morning. Now here, let me help you out of those clothes and get that shower going again. No point in calling a quin this late. We'll get some fresh duds for you in the morning."

A little while later, Deepy called Shel back to turn off the shower. Instead she tossed his clothes under the water and set the timer for two minutes. I'll hang these up to dry later," she said, while drying him off. By now, Deepy was fairly awake and had thought of a question or two. Shel apparently had been lounging on her bed reading while he showered. She lay back down as they reentered the bedroom. She was still in her towel, he noticed.

"Whacha readin'?"

"Something Eno loaned me - a book about UFOs." She picked up the book and held her place while flipping the front around so he could read the title. He noticed the author was Jacques Vallee.

"Interesting?"

"Well, you know me; I like this kind of stuff."

"What do you mean?" Deepy inquired, "We've never talked about 'this kind of stuff' before, that I can recall."

"Listen, Buster," Shel replied, back in her 'down-home' mode, much to Deepy's chagrin. "Perhaps I should remind you yet again that there's so much you don't and can't recall, since you can't seem to recall that you have a very bad memory... that's all." Shel snapped the book shut. "Anything else on your mind?"

Deepy wasn't sure at this point if Shel was in a "mood" - or if he might just be imagining it. "Well... there was something else, but not if you're ready for sleep. It can wait," he added.

"DeePY!" - Mock exasperation. Shel smiled, "Let's not go through that again. With me," she said, "if you have something to say, just say it. I'll let you know if you're treading where you shouldn't."

"Just don't let me do any more dog-paddling for a while; I'm worn out. But, anyway..." he trailed off. Shel was smiling - but, still, Deepy wasn't sure. "Oh - okay then, on the subject of reincarnation - why don't you just tell me everything you know? It put me to sleep before - maybe it will work again."

Shel threw her pillow at him. "Smile when you say that, hombre!" She wasn't smiling. But then she did.

"Dang," he said, "I was hoping you'd throw in the towel."

"Funny dog. (A buzzer sounded) That reminds me, I'd better hang your clothes up to dry. Be right back."

"But anyway," Deepy pretended to pick up his thought as if Shel had not left the room a minute earlier "... tell me more about the law of karma. Skip the extreme example of murder - what about lesser moral crimes or sins?"

Shel pursed her lips. "Umm, let's see," she said, as she picked up her pillow and moved it next to Deepy, telling him he could sleep on it, that she had another. "Well, of course, all crime is breaking somebody's law, but sins are crimes against moral essence - a direct assault on the perfection and righteousness of God... that is to say, they are breaking the wise, intelligent, logical, and loving purity of God's Moral laws. And really I guess that means sins are virtually anything that can hurt or harm anyone, even ourselves for that matter. There's no doubt we certainly have sinned against and hurt God, because SHE does hurt for us - especially those who won't claim her - as we all are part of her.

"What about people who are just – say - ignorant, nasty, and mean; people who are too stupid or selfish to care about anybody but themselves and their own ilk?" Shel posed the question and then went about formulating an answer, while Deepy pondered the word "ilk" for a moment.

"People," she continued, "just get what they've got coming to them, usually under circumstances that are similar to those surrounding the positive or negative energy they have put into the world, if they're still in a physical life or when they return to such a life in the future. Let's say somebody was really racially prejudiced - just hated people of a certain race ... thought awful things about them, maybe even mistreated them - God could have that person undergo similar, hateful experiences, maybe even requiring the offender be born into that same race he or she persecuted in another lifetime. They would suffer the same sort of abuse they previously dished out, but, umm... surely at some point, mankind has to get over that kind of stupidity... one would think," she added.

"Those persons who have persecuted or harmed anyone because of prejudice or other injustice may find themselves the brunt of such suffering in a future life. That also is one reason some people "choose" to not believe in karma and reincarnation or even a God who would appear to "get even." But, any true God would mete out 'even' justice - for the sake of fairness and teaching, either before people die or when the time comes that they have a chance to reflect on their lives just lived - perhaps when they are waiting to find out what God has in store for them next, if they haven't already been told.

"Darn, I know I'm not Eno, and I always know what I want to say, but it just doesn't sound as smooth or authoritative as when he says this stuff."

"You're really doing just fine, Shel. You have a good way of explaining things, so we ordinary folk can understand. Sometimes Eno can kind of talk over your head, if you know what I mean; but I do like that 'ilk' word," Deepy chuckled. "Got ilk?"

Shel just beamed at Deepy. "Why, thank you. You're really a sweetheart, you know. And yes, I know just what you mean about Eno, although I probably would never have said so." She paused. "I wonder sometimes, and you may think I'm paranoid, but I wonder if they... er... CHIP or Eno or somebody might be listening when we don't know it."

"Nah!" he told her, playfully sarcastic, "Not to say you're paranoid, cause the thought has crossed my mind too, but I just have to go with my gut feeling on this. I trust them.

I mean, sure, CHIP has listened without my knowing it, but he always seems to find a way to tell me sooner or later. Maybe he listens just enough to know how he, or they, can best help us."

"Yeah - yeah, you're right, of course. Guess I'm just tired. So, if you're listening, Eno, I apologize."

Deepy and Shel laughed together. Deepy closed his eyes, reflecting on the conversation. He knew that CHIP or BB had to be tuned in to him practically all of the time... but why get into that with Shel, since he figured they would have no need to constantly monitor her.

After a few moments of silence, it occurred to him that this might be a good time to just say good night. He would just thank Shel, say he had a wonderful day, which he had, and end the evening on a happy note.

"Shel?" Deepy said, as he opened his eyes and then quickly closed them, "... for heaven's sake, get some clothes on!"

"Darn it, Deepy, you had your eyes closed - and that's what I'm doing - getting my P-J's on."

"You're right, Shel; I'm sorry, I didn't mean to embarrass you. I shouldn't have said anything. I'll just leave my eyes closed now since it's sleepy time anyway. Listen," he continued, "I had a great time today. You're really a lot of fun to be with. It was great, even though I'm worn out from that dog-paddling and the Frisbee chasing and what all. But, I do hope we can have fun like that again sometime."

"Oh, we will, Deepy dog, we will. Now, good night," Shel added sweetly.

End of conversation, he thought. "Good night, Ms. Shelena Dann," he announced.

After a few moments of quiet contemplation, Deepy then said his good night prayer. Deepy prayed a lot, so he couldn't always kneel, but when he could he would, as he now did. He knew kneeling wasn't needed nor was a designated time to have a word with God. It was just a specific heartfelt monologue in one's mind. All he needed was a moment of silence. He knew that much of prayer is personal and should be communicated in silence, by telepathy, unless your spirit-mind is bound to speak for others as well. But he also knew that the energy of prayer could be strengthened through communion with others, like holding hands with them if possible, while silently praying with a mutual goal.

Actually one should set aside time for silent contemplation and communion, in case God had some alpha wave thoughts to share through one's imagination. People don't know it, he thought, but their brain-soul-set (mind) is usually more active in those quiet times. There was one time in his Larray James life that he actually had his tiny soul sound off as a genuine, separate "voice" in his head, and he presumed that was the feminine voice of his O-Soul too. It was surreal, but somehow he wasn't shocked by it. It happened just that one time and right after he recommitted to a moral life, resolving to kick ego to the curb.

Of course now he was hearing God's Children all around him onboard this ship. In his Larray James past, God always had been there as a thoughtful feeling of Grace, through his own spirit-soul abilities and imagination. And he had felt what he thought might be God's touch many times. It induced a subtle shiver or vibratory sensation. Maybe God spoke to his subconscious mind that way, and the thoughts would come to him later in his imagination or dreams - maybe. He sure had no trouble imagining anything was possible with God. People still may not realize it, but they are tiny God consciousness cells or souls and could even become one of her permanent Mind Cells, which are the very essence of God Jr – her Brain Child.

These are the thoughts that were running through his mind now, in recognition to God for the wisdom SHE provided. Deepy always prayed for wisdom and guidance, whenever he prayed on a formal basis. Most of Deepy's praying, however, was carried on within himself, in the form of a continuing moral consciousness. He knew God was always with him, as his Over-Soul mate and his tiny soul, unless ego or Egod had crowded her out momentarily, as sometimes happened – but not as much now as when his Larray self was younger and all "sexed up." Whew, fuhgedaboudit! He was glad he could.

Deepy would address himself more informally to God, as a fairly constant routine throughout each day. He felt he had a personal relationship with his Heavenly Parent, and in Deepy's mind, it was always, "You and us, Lord". He always included his tiny soul mate and their O-Soul; and since the 'tiny' one was an adjunct to its God Cell 'above,' he had given them names: "Yarral," – his nickname backward for his 'tiny' soul and "Yar, his middle name backwards for his O'Soul. They sounded odd, but they were gender neutral; although that was not important.

Deepy also understood that if he ever intended a thought, or took action not worthy of God, then his soul would take a mental break during that time. She would immediately return when he dislodged his ego or Egod from around his thoughts again. Deepy knew this diversion still happened much too often, so he was continually on alert to improve.

//////////////\\\\\\\\\\\\\\

(CHAPTER 9)
Moon Beamed

"Deepy, I'll bet it's gorgeous outside again today, and I've got a feeling this is going to be one of the most wonderful days of our lives."

They were strolling down the corridor toward breakfast. Deepy had to think about Shel's comment for a second, and when he did, he felt perturbed. "I hardly think so, Shel. I'm a dog - remember? I can't imagine spending the most wonderful day of my life as a dog. I mean, really – could you?"

"Maybe you won't be spending it as a dog."

"What? Are you kidding me? I'm signed on here for a six-week commitment. If you know something I don't, I'd sure appreciate hearing about it. Come on Shel – what gives? Make my day."

"I think we're going to make each other's day, but for now, I ask your patience. Thank you."

"Easy for you to say, since you apparently know what you're talking about, and I have no earthly idea. Why do you women have to be so cryptic and secretive, anyway?"

"Why are you so surly, and please stop saying 'you women,' as if we're all alike. Don't you think that's just a bit patronizing? You're here as a dog, not a chauvinist pig."

"Sorry, Shel - Don't blame you for being upset. It's just an old, good-natured, teasing habit that's hard to break. I assure you, I would never intentionally patronize you. We're buddies, and I love you. Honest. I was hoping you knew that by now."

"Well... then," Shel laughed. "I love you more."

"Huh? ... Okay, if you say so. I didn't know it was a contest." Deepy winked and smiled to show Shel he was teasing.

He was a little distracted. He thought he smelled bacon as he and Shel passed through the doors of the Diner about that time, and took seats across from each other. Shel told Deepy she would remain with him, rather than venture into her "Shangri-La" virtual reality setting. Then "The Wayward Wind" by Gogi Grant, picked up from where it had stopped last time Deepy was listening to his jukebox.

Deepy tuned in for a few moments; then the song faded into the background when he spoke to Shel. "Not going fishing this morning, Shel?" He knew that her virtual reality was a favorite shady bank beside a gorgeous lake with snow-capped mountains for a backdrop. He had virtually visited her scenery with her several times, just as she often stayed in his diner setting.

Deepy had told Shel why he really didn't care to put himself in her setting. It was because she seemed so wistfully sentimental there. She said she just couldn't help it, but it hurt him to see her that way. He often found his mood turning to depression and he nearly always had a headache when he tuned out. He also experienced an almost overwhelming sense of déjà vu in that "idyllic" setting of hers. Such natural melancholy seemed like standard fare to her, but even she could not stay there very long, and usually returned to his diner setting with him or while he waited there, but not always.

Except for yesterday's excursion, neither actually left the seat they were in, so even when Deepy sat across from Shel in his diner, Shel's body spirit was there also, but her tiny soul was in an "Assembler" trance and her mind was in her 'Shangri-La.'

No one usually broke the spell of another's virtual reality with a loud disembodied voice, even though that person would be able to hear anyone who directly pronounced his or her name in a commanding way, as if needing their attention. CHIP could always relay messages, if need be, without breaking a person's trance reverie.

"Not right away," Shel said in response to Deepy's question about her plans to visit Shangri-La. "There's someplace else I want to go first, and I'd like you to go with me."

Deepy looked pensive to Shel and that prompted her to say, "In fact, I will be quite hurt if you don't start to show some interest, my Deep friend."

"Interest in what?" he wondered, but Shel just frowned.

'Hmm,' Deepy subthought, 'that's one of her no-nonsense looks.' Deepy was pleased that he had been keeping some thoughts to himself, this morning. It was a simple matter of closing his mental door. It was as if that same mental mechanism that kept most humans from saying everything out loud was now working with his telepathy skills. In either case, it was great not to have some capricious thoughts known by others. This still allowed him to read other people who were open, and he could start a conversation anytime, simply by directing a thought to someone.

Shel had been in conversation with a quin passing by, while Deepy was lost in thought, but now she was alone and staring at him, so he broke his reverie to say, "Shel, I'd love to accompany you anywhere, you know that, but right now I'm in the mood for bacon and eggs, and why not grits... and, oh boy... maybe some of Chef CHIP's creamed beef on toast, or maybe some homemade biscuits and gravy, or maybe all of that; I'm so famished." (His hunger and wandering thoughts allowed him to forget Shel's heartfelt appeal just moments before.)

"May I humbly suggest that our great adventure might call for a somewhat lighter meal? Perhaps you could restrain yourself for your sake and mine this morning. We can eat shortly after we get where we're going - what about just one sausage biscuit now to hold you over for a few minutes?" Shel said all that as tactfully as she knew how and yet still managed to offend her self-absorbed friend.

"Lordy, Shel, maybe we were married in another life, but... (Deepy left that thought hanging and took up another instead) uh... unless, of course, you're going to tell me that you have nothing but my best interests at heart ... Hmm? Deepy finished his thought more tactfully than he first intended. He now decided to smile at his friend for good measure, while a subthought dawned with a question mark, "...Get where we're going?"

"You sure do eat a lot... just like Larray... it's just that time is of the essence for one thing, and I do worry about your health... and his."

"Oh? You actually know Larray – er... me, as him? That's news to me, sweetheart."

"I just meant that you are him, so I would worry no matter which form you occupy, that's all." That having been said, Shel then shut down. After a few, long moments, Deepy realized he might have hurt her feelings. I guess dogs are not as sensitive as women, he thought. He would try again.

"But, Shel, I really am awfully hungry. That dream took a lot out of me, last night. And that Greek meal I had, while tasty, didn't stick to my ribs like bacon might. I could have eaten a whole chicken when we got back, but we were both pretty tired campers. You gotta know I'm tired when I settle for a moon pie and a milkshake.

Shel laughed; she knew in his own way, Deepy might be trying to smooth things over. "Maybe I could better understand if you were really thirsty this morning," Shel smiled and winked, trying to lighten matters a little herself.

Deepy groaned, playfully. "Ah, Shel, that's a low blow. Come on now '... *Don't be cruel... to a heart that's true,*'" he half-sang with his best Elvis voice. "And anyhow, I prefer having you address me as Deep. Coming from you, Shel - I don't know – 'Deepy' just sounds childish." He surprised himself with that request - not knowing where it came from and thinking it made him sound like a whining schoolboy.

"Oh, Deep, for heaven's sake, you had a nickname when you were growing up - A lot of kids do, and silly ones at that, oftentimes. You just happened to like yours."

"Yeah, you know I do like Larray, for Larry Ray, but... "Deepy?" - Oh, all right then. I'm sorry. I don't know what's wrong with me this morning."

"We sound like a couple of old married tit-for-tatters," Shel told him.

They both laughed, a little awkwardly, and neither was sure the tension was broken.

Deepy figured 'his' mostly came from hunger. "Aren't you just a bit hungry yourself, Shel? You hardly ever eat anything. And what did you mean about eating after we get where we are going? You didn't tell me we were leaving the ship again."

"Not so much hungry as in a hurry." She paused – "You're right, Deepy, er, 'Deep,' I have been secretive and I do have an advantage in knowing what awaits us as soon as I can tear you away from this table. Forgive me, I just wanted it to be a surprise, and guess I still do. You'll understand as soon as we get there, or at least as soon as we get back here."

"Huh? I mean I would love another outing, so come on and tell me."

"Yes, it is an outing – and that's all I will say."

Deepy studied her for a few moments, and then said, "Just give me five minutes, Shel. Hell, we've already wasted 'five' just talking about it. I promise I won't take more than five minutes - CHIP? ... Oh, CHIP?"

But Deepy was surprised to notice that Shel looked really hurt or maybe mad; he wasn't quite sure.

"MEN!" she thought, at more than full volume. She sounded distorted to Deepy. Painful to his canine hearing, she was, even though her voice was just in his head. The intent came along with it and it seemed piercing.

Deepy closed himself off. "MEN - Doggone it!" he growled. Last night she wanted me to remember I'm a dog. Well, I'm hungry as a dog, doggone it, and I'm gonna eat now, even if it makes her mad. Criticizes me for saying "Women!" and then turns around and says "MEN!" in a condescending way.

His stomach was raising hell about it too he couldn't help but notice.

"I'm going to Shangri-La for a while," Shel told him. "You can eat and then get lost as far as I'm concerned." She scooted her chair back a little, was enveloped by baffle headgear and her body immediately relaxed as she went into trance mode.

"Whoa, talk about mad," her stunned, but still cute dog friend was now thinking. The Greek excursion yesterday had been real, so Deepy now figured today's trip must be even more special. Shel was so secretive, but then why not? He wasn't really sure why he was in such a sour mood. Maybe he was just spoiled. He was now upset that he had made her mad.

"You keep catching me in your conversations. What is it with you two? Whoops, never mind, none of my business and I really don't want to know. I'm just the chief cook and Robo-gadget around here. May I take your order, "sir?" CHIP emphasized 'sir' in an unmistakably ceremoniously sarcastic way.

"Did anybody ever tell you, you're a pretentious prig, CHIP? Come out here and bend over, I feel like I need to kick something and you'll do nicely. Ha-ha, just kidding, CHIP old buddy. You do your job and I'll do my best to irritate everybody around me. Now, I'm in one hell of a hurry, so... ham, bacon, grits, biscuits and gravy and four eggs scrambled. Have I told you lately what a great cook you are? Now, could you hurry, please?"

"Oh, yes sir, boss!"

"Hi," Eno said.

Deepy's brain was so wrapped up in his stomach he hadn't even noticed Eno standing across from him... smiling brightly.

"I'm sorry, Eno, I didn't see you come in."

"Oh, I just slipped in quietly between the ham and eggs; but, why is Shel transduced? She had something really special planned for the two of you today."

"Maybe if I knew what it was, I'd be with her right now, but you know how women can exaggerate and how they like their little surprises. I thought I might as well hear about it on a full stomach. My stomach wouldn't hear otherwise, anyway. Can you hear it?" Deepy felt a little embarrassed.

Eno ignored his overture. "What did Shel say when the two of you came in here this morning?"

"Ah... I'm not sure, why? Is it important?"

Eno wouldn't let him off the hook. "Think about it."

"Umm, let's see, something about this maybe being the most wonderful day of our lives. So, you see what I mean about women exaggerating? I'm a dog now." He reminded them both, in case there was any doubt and perhaps to clear his conscience, which seemed to be prodding him more and more under Eno's penetrating gaze.

"And you're just sitting here on what could be a most wonderful day of your lives?"

"Crymeany, Eno, I'm a dog... damn it - Whoa, sorry!"

"And you seem to be more of one than usual today. So what? What if this was only a most wonderful day in Shel's life? Wouldn't that mean anything to you?"

Why are they ganging up on me? He wondered. And why did Eno always have to be so right, he asked himself, rather spitefully. Then he remembered he had the same thought about CHIP. He felt petulant.

"How can you eat at a time like this? You didn't go hungry yesterday even though you left the diner without eating."

Deepy groaned. His stomach moaned - "Et tu Eno?"

"Shel ... Shel!" Deepy seemed to shout and rasp at the same time, "Come back!"

Eno chuckled, and then added, "If you would, please, Shel?"

And then - there she was, un-baffled, in her conscious state.

Deepy was startled. Shel appeared to have been crying. "I don't understand all this, I'm only a..." Deepy thought better of it.

"Tsk-tsk," Eno muttered, "poor Deepy - only a dog, doggone it. When are you going to learn that things around here don't always have to be as they seem?"

Deepy heard, but he was looking at Shel. "I'm sorry, Shel. I'm ready to go now."

"Will this be all, sir?" the quin asked. She smiled at Eno, and began placing Deepy's meal on the table. She appeared to be a cute, but rather young, 1950's style waitress.

"Ooh," Deepy looked at his breakfast as though it hurt him. "Better take it back." Then, he added, "CHIP, I'm sorry, but I'm in a hurry now. I'll have to eat this stuff later... unless I could get it to go, maybe?" He cocked his head at Shel and wagged his tail, something he seldom consciously tried to do, but sometimes seemed to have no control over.

"We can eat as soon as we get where we're going," Shel told him.

"WAIT!" Deepy's stomach yowled.

Shel was smiling tentatively now. "Let's go my deep friend, before you make your stomach top priority again."

"Not a chance," Deepy told her bravely - thinking he meant it. "Thanks Eno," he said, as if grimacing in pain. It was meant to be a smile.

"Yes, thanks Eno, for everything," Shel agreed.

"Bye kids. Have fun," Eno told them, as he picked up a piece of wonderful-smelling, crispy bacon and seemed to study it.

Deepy managed to lip-lock it out of Eno's hand, as he went onto Shel's lap and a baffle closed completely around them to serve as a transporter, in whatever way CHIP or God worked their magic. "We're off to the see the wizard... the terrible wizard of Id. Umm, fried wizard didn't sound too bad," Deepy subthought, feeling giddy, as his stomach seemed to say in a grumbling way, "Gimme that bacon!" He bit it in two and gulped gratefully.

{'Scene Shift'}

<u>Heyday</u>

A young Larry Ray James was stretched out on his back, his knees bent to hang over the end of the bed, feet resting flat on the plush carpeting, eyes closed to the ceiling overhead. He opened one eye and squinted at something he had been sniffing. It was on his chest. "CeCe?" he called.

With both eyes open now, he saw his wife appear in the bathroom doorway. "Yes, my darling, you called? No," she said, looking at him, "We don't have time for that again right now. Hadn't you better get ready?"

Larray cocked an eye in her direction. CeCe eyed a _____ in his direction, causing her previous comment. [His was a lewd thought, he knew, but a future Larray wondered if he could turn it into a moral lesson somehow. It was a lesson for him – a reminder that his id/ego was still intact and would butt in when given the chance. Sure, the line was frivolous, but maybe too fortuitous to pass up. Okay, he would delete it, although it did seem to fit their lustful youth back then, during a time when he was irreverent about most everything and thought a little silliness might make a smile worthwhile. I will leave a blank space, so that the reader's imagination is as guilty as mine. We can all think again about the battle our tiny souls must wage against id/ego. Even so, this frivolity comes with an apology to anyone offended.]

"Beautiful, as always," he told her. "I have such good taste in wives."

"Methinks you might wish to restate your compliment just a tad if you want another taste of this wife later," CeCe told him.

"Uh oh – Oh, look at my chest."

"You mean that hair shirt you're wearing ... what's with your chest?"

"I don't think that's all I'm wearing, unless my mind is playing tricks on me, and it could be, after the best night of my life... but – and you might want to come closer my dear - closer... closer," he coaxed her. "Now, look closely… is that a piece of bacon on my chest, or not?"

"Not," CeCe told him. "Looks like half-a-piece to me." She picked it up, idly examined it and then tossed it toward the trash, just outside the bathroom door.

Larray grabbed her and pulled her down to face him, "And where might it have come from, Miss Smarty Pants? Some trick of yours? I'm starving, as you know, and yet you would torture me like this. It's not too late to have this marriage annulled, you know?"

"After what happened last night, I hardly think so. But, promises - promises, let me think about it, Mister No-pants."

"What?" Larray replied with feigned indignation, "I'm wearing shorts."

CeCe snorted, "Shorts? Ha, you mean that thong? I've never heard of a man wearing a jock strap instead of everyday underwear. Okay... I've thought about it," she quickly added, "and I predict we're going to have a long and wonderful marriage, my deep friend - er, husband-buddy."

Larray had been waiting for CeCe to finish up in the bathroom – just lounging on the bed in their honeymoon suite, remembering last night, as well as the weeks and days that preceded this most wonderful time of their lives. He and CeCe had just graduated from the University of Arkansas a month ago. They then flew from their wedding in Little Rock, to some of the most beautiful mountain country in Canada – hell, he told himself - it has got to be some of the greatest scenery anywhere. That was his humble opinion – shared by his new wife, who called it 'Shangri-La,' after one of the "top-forty" popular songs of the day. In fact, she had been singing snatches of that song, since their arrival, late yesterday evening.

"I've got to be the luckiest man in the world," he had told himself, while waiting his turn to shower and get ready for the day. "Yes sir, I'm a real lucky dog."

He had been laying there listening to an instrumental version of the Bobby Helms hit record, "My Special Angel." He didn't really know where the music was coming from, but it sure had fit, since he was thinking about the angel he had married.

This same angel was hovering above him right now; and that special perfume lingering up there and all around him seemed to say "...penny for your thoughts." He was in a world of his own. Heaven wafted down to envelope him, with a lyrical voice and sweet smell.

"I certainly hope they're worth more than that," he told her, "Otherwise I wasted my time in 'Hog Heaven,' - not to mention my – well, mostly my dad's hard-earned money."

CeCe now rose up to reposition herself above her new husband. She placed a knee between his legs and a hand on each side of his head, and sort of hung there, smiling down on him. But having closed his eyes just before she got up, he now said, "Now, who could that be? - My other wife, already? And I wasn't even through with the first one yet."

"I'll make you think 'first one,'" a stern voice told him.

"Ah-ha! - An angel from above. I'd know that voice anywhere." It didn't seem appropriate, necessarily, but with that salutation another part of him rose up in greeting too.

"Oh, and what have we here?" CeCe mockingly inquired. "Now I can better appreciate that restraint you're wearing."

"My little devil," Larray now introduced, "I'd like you to meet my special angel."

"Oh-ha! Not all that little," CeCe came back, "not when it wants to be big and bad, but I do think you picked the right name for it. Anyway, we met a couple of times last night, as I recall."

They laughed together. "Happiness personified," he thought, on hearing her laugh; "whatever that means?" he had to wonder at his thinking.

That happy person with the most gorgeous, big brown eyes, whispered to him now, "Would you rather stay here a while longer?" CeCe was grinning as she sprang back from the bed and stared down at him.

"You do look fantastic and inviting, as always, but I'd hate to mess up that hair of yours. Besides, look again... it was just a passing fancy. I think I'm still spent from last night," he said, and then added, "I think what I might need now, more than anything, is refueling. I'm famished."

"Yeah, I forgot," she replied, "You do have a deep hole to fill." He frowned at her, causing her to continue "... uh, I just mean, you're always hungry. Or so it seems."

"Maybe so - but with you a fellow's got to keep his energy up. I have a feeling I'm going to need it today especially - what with you talking about a hike for a picnic in the wilderness."

"It's gonna be a great day," she told him.

"But now, it's my turn in the bathroom." He stood up and kissed her, then looked around, "... where's that music coming from anyway?" He could hear it faintly again now.

She smiled at him. "You're so romantic. Would you care to dance, Big Boy?"

He laughed. "What? In this wardrobe, it could turn into a fertility dance."

By now, she realized 'what music' he was talking about.

"There's a radio in the bathroom, above the toilet. Turn it back up, when you go in there, please. No, on second thought, while you're getting ready, I think I'll check out the restaurant, and make arrangements for a picnic basket 'to go' ... for a later lunch. You like cold, fried chicken, don't you? And honestly, I don't know where that bacon came from." Talk of food suddenly reminded her of that.

Larray had forgotten about it too, but now could only shake his head and say... "Hmm - very strange, fell from the sky I guess, which I see as a good omen, since that is what I plan to be eating in about twenty minutes."

"Sky?"

"Ha-ha, only if it comes with bacon; tell you what, I'll meet you there. Go ahead and order in about fifteen minutes if I'm not there already: Three eggs over easy, with bacon, grits, biscuits, cream gravy, and a hunk of ham... ma'am."

"This is Canada, so likely no grits. If not, I'll get hash browns. Anyway, you expect me to remember all that?" She wrote it down, adding orange juice to the list, and milk. They already had coffee in the room. "Is that all, sir?"

"Just more coffee when I get there, thank you, ma'am." He kissed her on the forehead and spun around into the bathroom. A few minutes later, Larray James was singing in the shower, an odd little song that had popped into his head, *"I'm off to see the wizard - the wonderful wizard of Oz."*

It was after eleven by the time they finished breakfast on the restaurant patio, with its fantastic view of the lake and mountains off in the background. The waiter brought their picnic basket; they paid and got up to leave, taking another look out over the rustic railing, separating them from a pathway headed in the direction of the water. Larray nodded, "That the way to heaven on earth?" he asked her.

"I believe we're about to find out, but yes, I rather suspect it's the way to Shangri-La, which is the same thing. Let's go see."

"Down the path and into the woods, we're on our way to gram-Ma's house - and the big bad wolf is gonna get you again my dear." Larray sang the first part merrily without any tune in particular, and then growled the second line, as they skipped along through the trees, out of sight of the lodge and restaurant and they hoped any prying eyes. Suddenly, he jolted CeCe to a stop, and pulled her in his direction. They then partook of what he thought must be a textbook romantic kiss right out of the movies. "This is how it's done, boys and girls," he thought to an imaginary audience. "And I will have other lessons for you a little later."

Just then, though, he was swept away by the passions of returning pleasure. CeCe dropped the basket and they almost toppled over, and would have, had he not leaned one hand against the trunk of a tree, just in time, peeking through one eye, trying not to lose the magic of the moment. They were both breathing heavily when they finally untangled themselves. It took them a few wordless moments to recover enough for CeCe to whisper, "I think we need to get off this beaten path and find our own special place."

A little later, as they journeyed closer to the lake, Larray thought "Déjà vicw?" - "Does this place look familiar to you sweetheart?"

"Even "purtier" than the Ozarks; familiar, yes, but I don't think I've ever seen anything quite like this," CeCe replied, then added, "Well, maybe in my dreams... 'fer shore.'" she southern-drawled.

"We must have had the same dream. I could swear I've been here before," he told her.

"Well, if we're really good and lucky - maybe we'll get a chance to come back someday," she told him.

"A second honeymoon - while I've still got big plans for the first?"

And somewhere, music was playing he knew, and his terrific new bride was starting to sing her favorite song of late, "'... *your kisses take me to Shangri-La'... 'cause anywhere you are ... is Shangri...*" Larray planted a kiss where her "*La*" would have been. She gently pushed him away and sang it out as if the universe depended on it – giving it a vibrato, operatic flare. She then gave her husband a longer kiss, with a bit of added vibrato, ala French twist.

Finally, after much wandering, they ended up on a path that took them to an idyllic lake/mountain view setting. The first thing Larray did was stretch out to take a nap. He then had an odd dream of having lunch in his old diner, but with a really nice gentleman, and perhaps a dog? 'Weird,' he later thought, but then he always had strange dreams. 'Doesn't everybody?'

"What a day this has been ... what a rare mood I'm in ... why it's almost like being in love," Deepy sang softly across the table from Shel, who simply had been staring at him for a couple of minutes. "I'm really married to you ... the most gorgeous gal in the whole world ... and here I am in a dog suit - with just enough memory to be miserable and jubilant at the same time. Still, I do agree with what you said a moment ago. From this perspective, I'm not all that pleased either with the way we lusted after each other like animals but it was in the good cause of genuinely young and idiotic passion. Even so, it does feel a little lewd now, to say the least. In a perfect world, we now know there would be only a sense of purity and gracious respect in consummating our love," Deepy rambled on; then suddenly stopped, as though unsure of himself.

"You are married to CeCe," Shel corrected, "and have spent time with her, not me, these past two days and nights. No, don't ask; we'll have that conversation later. At least," she continued, ignoring Deepy's perplexed mug, "Eno tells us that in Heaven, every Soul will be in consummate love. Still, that was a nice sojourn for two "renewed" newly-weds, and you have Eno and CHIP to thank for that. CeCe, back home, was briefed on what was planned for you two and now recalls it as a luscious and very realistic dream – one which she will momentarily forget." [CHIP note: The Assembler didn't require much of her "time" to make it all happen - or much of Deepy's, as one can make time without requiring time... in God's eternal world.

[I caused Deepy to promptly forget Shel's remarks about her not being CeCe. Like she said, that would be for a later discussion – one he would forget he even had coming.]

"And," Shel continued, "you also are right to give thanks for the humble reminder that later in life, you did learn your way out of that lust conundrum into a more gracious, mature love."

Shel winked, "Either that or your hormones couldn't keep up. I'm teasing," she quickly added. "Anyway, it's healthier to allow nature to take its course in that regard, as hormone replacement is not natural, except in small amounts for health reasons in younger people. Sex for sex sake, meaning without genuine love, is not good for the soul." Shel then chuckled: "And, you are right," she continued "... to feel somewhat ashamed now, especially considering your pure surroundings in this Otherealm. Even so, I know it was great for you and CeCe to have a second honeymoon, and it was during a time she considers one of the best of your lives. That lasted until Sal was born, and then life just kept on getting better for the three of you."

"What? Huh? You mean 'us' don't you - the three of us? And we have a daughter?" Deepy looked perplexed again, amazed he had a daughter he couldn't remember. He somehow felt manipulated, but only for a moment, as his mind went blank.

[It was time for more memory surgery here courtesy of Dr. CHIP. When I returned CeCe and Deepy from Greece, they were together until Deepy awakened here in his diner only minutes ago. CeCe was "Assembler-entranced" as her younger self and played the part of Shel through the past two days. CeCe understood her role during the whole episode, continuing through the honeymoon celebration. She had been thoroughly briefed on all the facts regarding Larray. Later it all seemed like a dream to her after she awakened following a relaxing night of sleep by Larray's bedside. God is quite the Magician and I, CHIP or I, BB, or any CHIP for that matter can put a spell on anybody at anytime.]

"But imagine," Deepy now exulted, "all this time together here, and I was blocked from recognizing my own sweet wife - my Ce – uh – Shel... hey, my "CeShel"... I like that."

"My friend, I really hate to tell you this," Eno told Deepy from - wherever he was - "... but you have only a while to enjoy the full impact of your memories of being young again. Tomorrow morning, Deepy, you won't even remember that you and CeCe experienced your honeymoon again. I'm afraid, as your doctor, I don't think you need those kinds of thoughts in your head right now. We need you to focus your attention elsewhere, as you know."

Eno then suddenly arrived – actually popped up or in - at their table and sat down.

"Your adventure most importantly gave you a chance to refresh your knowledge that you, along with everyone else, need to subtract mental lust from gracious, tender love. Physical union of a sexual nature really always has been intended solely for those who want to have children. That was and is the purpose for it, as intended by God. Ordinary humanimals, as id entities, had no thoughts regarding physical mating. Instinct required no thinking. It's still a natural "no brainer" in animals, but in hybrid humans it is very much an id/ego "brainer" confused by conscious lust, which is the very essence of "Eve illness." Such evil also includes lust for all inappropriate or immoral behavior, although sex is most distracting from godly thoughts for most people. Hunger and violence still play big roles for instinctual id, but hybrid humans unconsciously always put an ego frame around everything they do that doesn't include moral thinking. All too many can still even rationalize some murders as "okay," – and the list grows longer for what some people would allow as long as they, their family and friends are not involved. Then again, they are not using their soul minds, if they have a soul still tending their thoughts, and not just an id-ego contrived from animated brain spirit.

"Humanimals, from which hybrids were derived, knew only the id survival instinct to mate cyclically, while having no mental sensation of being a separate entity from their mates. Their physical sensations never controlled their brains, but were controlled by their instinctive ids. Humanimals had no self-aware hubris telling them how impressive they were or making them desirous of satisfying an addictive mental craving. There was no mental connection then to the mating process. Thoughts, or lack of such, were not an on/off switch to sexual desires. Now though, the id/ego causes most hybrids to think "what turns them on."

[CHIP insert: *Romans, Chapter 1, (Verse 24) Wherefore God also gave them up to uncleanness through the lusts of their own hearts, to dishonor their own bodies between themselves. (V.26) For this cause God gave them up unto vile affections: for even their women did change the natural use into that which is against nature: (V.27) And likewise also the men, leaving the natural use of the woman, burned in their lust one toward another... (V.28) And even as they did not like to retain God in their knowledge, God gave them over to a reprobate* mind, to do those things which are not convenient; (V. 31) Without understanding, covenant-breakers, without natural affection, implacable, unmerciful: (V.32) Who knowing the judgment of God, that they which commit such things are worthy of death, not only do the same, but have pleasure in them that do them.]*
*(Evil; to foreordain to damnation)

"All immorality is ungodly, whereas, genuine, intimate loving could, and should, include morality as part of the equation. Again, just as with instinctual mating, there should be no thinking involved that would turn the love to lust. One should always love with the graciousness that comes with wanting to please the combined "entity as one;" and neither should take precedence or do what is unnatural. (more later, on the word 'unnatural;' but I can tell you now it means what God defines for her purposes, which always are Moral, of course.)

"With sex, married mates should feel spiritually bonded as if sharing the same spirit-soul, not simply having sex for physical pleasure. Each person has his or her own spirit-soul, but each needs to understand God's intention for them to become an eternal part of her, by co-creating their own spirit mate within themselves, specifically for her Moral use. SHE then can match them to the Over-Soul from which their tiny soul originated That essentially is the reason for the hybrid second generation, as each tiny soul must develop a spirit mate that is morally worthy of being its O'Soul's Mate for eternity within the Otherealm in between a Yin/Yang God. If you bond as such mates you become part of an 'indivisibly-dual' Entity as a Mental Cell of God Jr.

"Satisfying physical desires should not come between people and God. In other words, if you cannot have intercourse with gracious loving thoughts, then don't engage in sex, but especially not with perverse thinking. Instead, turn your vibratory energy into growing your angel self. Just concentrate on moral matters; but don't give up if you don't always succeed. Ask forgiveness. Yes, it will be difficult, but God can help you. In fact SHE is helping you stay the course on reading this seemingly eccentric book. If you are wondering how long you can continue reading, just know if the author really is eccentric… God is not. Trust <u>her</u>.

"Some people will think the loving procedure we have just described is unnecessary. It's needed. A so-called 'sex life' should be changed to a pure 'love life' filled with empathy and graciousness. This is crucial to any set of spirit-soul mates attaining heaven or Heaven, as it is a huge step in getting spirit-souls started along a moral path.

"Sexual lust should never be used as a mental stimulant. That's because in your world it seems to be an addiction almost impossible to overcome, because of that brain connection to the lib/<u>id</u>/o ego pleasure center. You may recall from an earlier lesson that the once "instinct-only" id became something of a thinker that reveled in sensual pleasures after it developed an ego (self-god brain) to bar what it saw as a transient intruder called a soul.

"That happened not long after God upgraded mankind, as Adam and Eve, with the ability to accept a peripheral, but adjunct, thinker in the form of a tiny mental cell or soul. It was meant to be a full-time "plug in" within the first hybrid couple. Unfortunately the self-god id forced its essence into the soul's chamber in the brain and virtually shoved much of the tiny "intruder" out the door.

"Now, the soul can be annexed only when a person seeks godly communion and ideals offered through one's imagination and conscience. If any of this seems revelatory to you, count your blessings. You have what many people are missing, but there's room for improvement in each of us – lots of room if you're staring into emptiness. You are not, since you have waded this far into such a seemingly odd tale.

"The id changed godly thinking from <u>id</u>eals into <u>id</u>eas that trained the brain to oppose the soul's influence on the brain, or in other words id subtracted <u>id</u>ealism from the equation. The id innocently was carrying out the duties for which God had programmed it for automatic protection against outside or inside forces acting on non self-aware humanimals. In most hybrids now, the tiny soul is seldom used, and id with its 'God-self' creation, aka ego, rules... unless WILL and Grace can be trained to act more authoritatively. They can learn that with God's help.

"God proceeded with the hybrid generation, knowing it would only work within a concept called "time" and with certain laws in place, such as karma and reincarnation, plus provision of various spiritual realms, such as purgatory or minor heaven, along with a ghostly dimension close to the heart of the problem of mitigating the moral differences achieved by individuals. They would vary widely over the course of time.

"This effort to save the tiny mental "homing" souls of former Humans by allowing them annexation of the human brain as linear beings did <u>not</u> allow the soul's input to be directly proportional to the id's response. Rather the id's electrolytic-chemical mode ran interference on behalf of the physical self, causing the fused-spirit body to become somewhat immune to the soul, until id finally became a proudly adversarial brain-set known as id/ego. That is when God sent us COG here to help until Jesus Christ arrives again for a Garden Gaia revival. In other words God's precognition had us here when the hybrid generation began.

"No thanks to the id, physical urges were brought to the forefront, especially the mating instinct that became hybrid lust through thinking. Id's power is the main reason Eve illness came about. Even though hybridism was God's only recourse to save tiny souls as potential Moral Mental entities, some unenlightened folks might wish to blame her, rather than thank her; but it would be wiser to call upon her to help you let go of your self-indulgence, whatever it may be. Your soul needs to help your spirit become morally worthy to mate with it as an indivisibly-dual angel form within God Mind's Heavenly Child. Most hybrids won't survive for eternity, but they also won't know they ever had the opportunity, since they would no longer exist.

"If sexual lust though was mankind's only illness, it would be cured by the absence of the id-ego sexual desire in Heaven where Spirit-Souls have no need of mating for procreation. Souls in Heaven remain in a state of Mental energy vibrational love with each other and thus with God. Angels formed from hybrids also would not recall material world sexual desires, as God's Memory contains none of that.

"For now though, sexual lust and other deadly sins or habits, that spring from self-indulgent desires, indwell the psyche of mankind to an extent that it effectually challenges God to a subconscious showdown of wills, if one can imagine an id/ego psyche rooted in enough ignorance and arrogance to contend with God that way. Yet, one need not imagine it, as it is the constant sickness among humans. Until now it has been indulged with ignorance. Now, each person simply has to look within to find at least one deadly trait of active influence in outright control of his or her psyche; although one might consider it a blessing to find only one such trait. Even so, it will be one that must be overcome. And, yes, it would be impossible without developing steadfast communion with God. Developing such communion might be difficult for folks not used to praying or taking time for insight into their purpose for living. What does God intend for your life?

"Meanwhile, humans have taken the acts (there should be only one) of sexual intercourse to a perverted art form of lustful fantasies, which they allow to take over their psyches, often to become spiritually debilitating. I repeat, mental lust is a result of libido artifacts in a self-conscious brain that allowed a self-captivating id/ego pleasure center, aka ego, to develop. Hybrid thought processes generally are held captive by this id entity. God knew that would be the case with Adam and Eve and hybrid humankind. And yet, SHE wanted you to have a 'tiny' chance since SHE saw it as better than none at all. Can you agree? And who are you anyway if you cannot agree?

"Evil is even more potent now than it was, and has grown exponentially, right along with mankind, as many children have been born as side effects of humans satisfying yet another sensual itch. That particular itch also is mental, and therefore in need of scratching – more often than not - to the extent of becoming *the* primary psychological trait and habit of most id/egos.

"Lust became the main attraction in the mating of Earth's hybrid humans, because it combined thoughts of sex with acts of sex and it became a tool for id/ego pleasure, rather than just simple instinct-driven procreation. Lustful thoughts are nearly always lewd and wanton, resulting from a mix of mentality and ego, which has evolved to make people even more ill than were the original first mates genetically disposed toward the illness. Hybrids consistently prove such to be the case when they put their "self" awareness ahead of the full God awareness they should strive for now. Adam and Eve were ignorant, but you can no longer use that as an excuse – not if you understand this work. And why would you want to excuse yourself into nonexistence anyway?"

"God could foresee all this since SHE is not inhibited by time or psychology, and so SHE knew some hybrids would compete with her for power. Nothing godly comes of competing with God. In fact it's impossible. It is only ego stupidity that would tell you otherwise. Ignore stupidity. Learn to praise and thank God for life you would not otherwise have. Try to make it last forever by earning God's Grace. Happenstance has no grace.

"The first mates, Adam and Eve, came to identify sex as the main comfort each could give the other, with its orgasmic buzz, which they called love. However, the original organic love attraction they experienced, and for which they were created, came from the conscious melding of their minds with the Mind of their Lord God, or COG Co-Creator. It was initiated by God and meant to be held as an ever-present Mental condition throughout the entire state of their Mental being, just as is so with COG. It was, and is, God's goal to teach hybrids how to initiate and sustain such mental attraction toward each other and her – in fact toward all conscious entities, whether self-aware or not and without any need of physical contact. COG still are working with hybrids toward that goal, but only God knows the results. Sharing both the goal and your results is what this work is all about. You can understand it through WILL and Grace. You can, if you will, but so many of you won't. Wisdom is just so inconvenient. [Hybrids tend to rationalize their way out of anything that calls for moral endurance and growth.]

"The hybrid-human love for conscious, self-awareness and God awareness should stem from each soul as the God-conscious Mind Cell that it has the potential to become. Each should relate in perfect harmonious communion with God Mind, through the power of WILL and Grace: Wisdom,

Intellect, Logic, Love, and God's Grace, along with the soul's own gracious love of God.

"The hybrid self-aware faculty initially happened as a result of COG cohabiting perfect Human Gardens. The "self" aspect of humanimals was primarily intended as a temporary addition to those fused spirit hosts as an ad hoc, subconscious adjunct, or simply a tiny piece of the initial cohabiting Over-Soul. That tiny fragment of soul was primarily intended to serve as a "homing" device for any COG arriving after departure of a previous Angel and O'Soul having completed their indivisibly-dual nexus and moving on to heaven. Essentially COG were changing shifts, so to speak, within a particular host. Their workspace was within those so-called "Perfect Garden" cocoons (or *'trees'*) of the Human fused spirit bodies, which ultimately would detach as Humangels from the interior and transcend to heaven with their Soul Mate Co-Creator.

"Those humanimals did not call themselves by any group or species name, so considering their use, COG simply called them 'trees of life.' The humanimals had rudimentary thinking abilities and didn't know what they were. They pretty much just tried to survive as all animals did, through their instinctual id in brains like that of the so-called serpent man; still the wisest (most experienced) of all animals at the time of Eden.

"The id-ego pairing is what separated Adam and Eve from COG and God, as epitomized by their artful disobedience through acquiescence to the instinctive power of their humanimal id serpent brain. It assured them a "tree of life," required sexual intercourse for pollination, which they thought was a power that equaled that of God's ability to create 'trees of life.' God knew the course of repeated natural human lives would be the result, but SHE created Adam and Eve as her only recourse to potentially save her tiny spirit-souls as Consciousness Cells for God Junior.

"Hybrid entities on Earth and elsewhere now represent these tiny 'homing' souls who, with God's help, are trying to create and save spirits within themselves to serve their eternal mates in the same manner as indivisibly-dual Angels or Trangels. They must co-create opposite polar forces within each moral human to live and function as God's twi-polar Mind requires.

"The 'ids' of these various physical entities were predisposed to incorporate some amount of tiny soul essence into a mental psyche mix, perhaps to extrapolate an antibody defensive measure to keep the tiny souls from taking over the whole physical organism, as COG had Mentally done with <u>H</u>umans. The id did not consciously choose such a procedure, but adapted and in the process created a 'self' god called ego. Once this ego brain-set took hold within the so-called "third eye*'" of the pineal gland it could intercept thoughts meant for the tiny soul and change them to suit the physical, rather than the spiritual self. That is what id/ego did, thus causing it to believe itself equal to God. *{Some ancient philosophers thought the 'third eye' to be the 'seat*' of the soul. The 'third eye' is said to allow hybrids to intuit possible futures and make sense of one's own potential. With id, it supposedly evolved to help humans <u>id</u>entify underlying patterns in their lives.} [CHIP Note: That is one hybrid definition of this gland, shaped like a pine cone or a serpent's eye. The id co-opted this "tiny" area, along with a molecule of tiny soul, which forced the remainder of soul into constant competition for attention by the brain. That miniscule spot in the brain is a "battle space" for a person's eternal salvation or eventual demise, as id/ego has a particle of tiny soul.]

Reading Deepy's thoughts now, "Don't give up," his Mentor told him. "God will help. Just ask.

"God did enjoy her perfect Human physical-world senses through her Children during the Humangel era, but SHE cannot do that within hybrid humans, many of whom constantly seem to be involved one way or another with sex and violence, often in quite bizarre and perverted ways. Yes, hybrids are ill, and yet God still has an opportunity, dwindling as it is, to cure many of you; and so SHE will fight – with her words and concepts – to do that – including through your book, my friend. All hybrids won't be called to eternity unfortunately because of id/ego mental illness, which would be like a cancer to God Mind. Their energy will <u>not</u> be lost to God, however, as SHE will use it in other ways, of which they will be unaware.

"One primary obstacle to solving the problems of hybrids is they deny God's authenticity, as if they created themselves, the world and everything in it – or that it just somehow happened willy-nilly without any forethought. It's true that God's birth was sort of preordained by circumstances, but SHE put a lot of life into her afterthought. So, yes, God Mind did fortuitously happen* over a period of non-time. SHE then brought about all other life forms as her Mental properties matured. *(To Be Explained) {TBE}

"Now, though, unmindful of God, the hybrid goal is to re-create themselves through upgrading their DNA; and/or building robotic machines to which they transfer their brain memory and activity, so they can live forever in a material realm. They should understand that God has the only eternal plan in place, virtually since her own inception as One Universal Consciousness. SHE has the ability to divide her Mental Prowess into living, indivisibly-dual Mental Cells or Souls, aka Angels. Understand, God's Mental Cells, aka 'Souls' only go where SHE puts them. SHE will only keep them in Moral containers for eternity in her Spiritual realm. Her material world is time limited and to be converted.

"Hybrids should be learning through this work that God's material world has a "going out of business" sign in the window right in front of their faces. The sign is growing bigger while the window's getting smaller, on its way to entering a black hole to return from whence it came, to God Mind. Where are you going?

"Hybrids obviously are not ordinary animals and so I make the point again that COG cannot directly cohabit them without being sullied by lustful thought processes. Instead we help from the Otherealm, through their tiny souls, to carry out the interior work of replicating their material forms and their mind schema into Othereal pure Spirit forms of angels, graduating to appCOG. Therefore, hybrids receive our assistance from a distance through their soul mates, as best any imperfect person will allow, since id/ego comes with their hybrid generation."

Three people sat quietly transfixed for a moment; one of them reflecting on the message just received and trying to sort it out. The other two had no such need.

"Eno, I know, and I do understand that my memory of CeCe must be suspended now for the good of the mission," Deepy responded. He felt blessed that he could understand the moral logic of what Eno was telling him. "I'll be thrilled every time I look at Shel, anyway... just as I've always been," he smiled. Shel smiled too - thanked him and told him how sweet he really was.

"Well," Shel said as she stood up, "if you gentlemen will excuse me, I'm going to turn in. I know Deepy, er - Deep, is a bit hungry again. If I'm not mistaken, he's had "Shrimp Creole" mixed up with thoughts of CeCe ever since he got back to this diner of ..."

"Yeah, but," he interrupted, "I mostly remember the greatest, most romantic, fireside evening of dinner and dancing of our lives – and twice now," he added, with what he hoped was a 'big-dog' grin.

[Shel just smiled, then thought to thank Eno and CHIP for making the second honeymoon possible – but now with a wiser perspective, granting some morally mature thinking afterward on the part of a deep dog who still thought he was speaking with a younger version of his wife. It would be explained to him in time for his future book.]

"Anyway," Deepy told them, with his thoughts still on food, "It has been hours since that meal. If you recall, Shel, most of the dancing came afterwards... and you know how all that activity can diminish a man's strength, even a young whelp like I once was," he chuckled. "And you, CeShel, you look as gorgeous as you did all those years ago. But, how come your eyes are blue here and brown there, and of course different hair colors, styles, and makeup also, but" he quickly added, "a beautiful twin otherwise."

"Thank you, sir… hair – makeup - wardrobe and eye color by CHIP's Wizardry Salon. Eno finally agreed," Shel told him, "that a second honeymoon couldn't hurt anything... as long as you aren't haunted by it, and he did say you could use it as a morality lesson for your book. He wanted to emphasize the real meaning of gracious love, which you and CeCe have had for many years now, old man."

"Which you and I have had," he corrected her; but there's something else that perplexes me," he told her. "How is it, CeShel, that you are here as a younger version of my wife, and I am an older man version of a young dog?"

"The older version of CeCe is by your bedside almost constantly, along with your daughter, Sal. CHIP allows you to recognize me now as a version of CeCe's earlier self and her memories of your life together as she now prayerfully awaits your recovery. I am acting as your comforter, under some pretty trying conditions that might otherwise be too stressful for an old man/young dog."

Eno chuckled as he scooted his chair back and got up, while saying, "I'll walk with you Shel. I'm ready to turn in too. It's really quite late. CHIP and BB are about the only ones around here who never sleep. I'm sure one or the other will be pleased to fix you some 'Shrimp Creole,' Deepy."

Deepy winked at Shel. "Good night, you two," he said, as he sat there perplexed and hungry.

"Pleasant dreams, Larray, my deep buddy," Shel smiled, while returning Deepy's wink. She then bent over and kissed him on top of his head and told him sweetly, "Nighty-night."

Smiling, she and Eno headed out the door, with Shel looking back to wave slightly, as the door slid shut.

"I agree," Shel now told Eno as they "popped into" the privacy of their room, "No reason Larray needs to remember that the younger CeCe played my and her own role during these last couple of days, courtesy of God's non-time machine. He won't recall any of it after he sleeps tonight." [It is amazing what can be generated by the Ship's memory 'Assembler,' with a CHIP at the helm.] {No flattery – just a fact}

"Deepy was entranced and CeCe was deep dreaming, but with full cognizance of her role, as CHIP had briefed her. Deepy didn't realize he never left the ship; and for CeCe, 'time' held no relationship to the events." [I will see to it this is all clarified to Larray later, for his book. He will be pleased to hear that he does have a CeShel wife, as they are virtual replicas, even if one is aged by time.]

"Sure, CHIP will tell him all the details at some point, but he has enough on his plate for now."

"Literally and figuratively," Shel laughed.

Eno laughed too, "That dog does have an appetite, but it's a nervous condition related to the stress he subconsciously experiences here with us. Well, Shel," Eno now inquired, "What about some communion, my dear?"

"I cannot imagine anything else, my dear," Shel answered, as the two of them melded to become their usual indivisibly-dual Trangel self, as a natural Mental Cell of God's Triune Entity. They then communed with God Mind for Mental updates.

[I, CHIP, made note of all the foregoing conversations and events for Larray's future book. With their melding, Eno's Yang entity again became the only one visible. Outward Appearance could go either way, but Dr. Mai's role of Commander took precedence aboard ship, during this mission. Oftentimes Shel and Eno separated to be with Deepy at the same time; but there was never a need to Soulfully separate from each other. Their mutual wave-length was immutable. Trangels seldom are apart in Heaven, but simply serve God's twi-polar needs, in communion.]

"... *Love is lovelier*," Deepy sang "... *the second time around ... so much lovelier, with both feet on the ground...*" then he was lost in memories of a human Larray James, awaiting his favorite meal as prepared by his loving wife. He sat there a few minutes before finally remembering to politely inquire of CHIP if he would mind making his special dish, 'Por favor.' CHIP said he would be only too happy to oblige, since he already had.

"Quite a lady," Deepy thought, sitting there in reverie for a moment. "I'm starved. CHIP? - sorry CHIP, but I wonder if I might also have a side order of fried catfish filets and some hush puppies, and a big glass of iced tea instead of the milk."

"Of course you may, oh valiant one. Your main dish is on the way and I'll have the other out shortly," CHIP responded. "Not very hungry tonight, are we?"

"No – er, thanks, CHIP." Deepy was lost in sweet, thoughtful feelings now. Gracious love is so much better than just sex for the lust of it, he thought. He sincerely felt that way, and thanked God for that. He was certain such thinking was easier for him now though, as an older, shall we say more mellow fellow. Still he felt good about it – cleaner and somehow purer. He also knew if he were in Heaven on a permanent basis, he would have no memory of 'sex' as a concept. It would be as if it never existed, he correctly remembered. That would be just fine by him. Who needs such crass, immoral nonsense as sexual fantasies? "Not me – not anymore," and he hoped Eno's illuminations could change many more tiny souls from brain thinking to mind thinking.

He enjoyed his meal immensely, while listening to his Jukebox, and then bloat-walked his way back to his room and to bed. He would need to remember to wash his red nose from the Creole sauce. His human self didn't like the thought of licking his nose. Yuck. Washing his nose after Creole was as habitual as brushing his teeth after every meal.

It took Deepy a long time to get to sleep. He was full of food and fond memories. He knew these memories of today would fade, just as they had in the fifty-five-year old mind of his true human self. [No fade needed. Gone after waking up.]

When he finally dozed off, he dreamt he had spent the day in a UFO with God, while trying to find the Angel he was betrothed to marry, as God waited patiently to perform the ceremony. He had a fitful, restless night that finally settled into exhaustion that stayed with him through most of the next morning.

IIIIIIIIIIIIIIIII
(CHAPTER 10)
Tiny Time

(Deepy's mind was in a fog. He thought maybe he had been getting too much sleep or not enough. He vaguely could recall reading about UFOs and napping on and off all day yesterday and then dozing off during his studies last night. Now he had read and slept some more and awakened just prior to his 11:30 quin "dress-up" call. Lying there, he remembered an idea he had last week when he first heard about today's special class presentation. When CHIP called to tell him a quin was on her way, Deepy asked if CHIP could meet him in the tinys' class room in about twenty minutes. He would need some help with his idea)

-Rehearsal-

"The story you are about to hear may boot you out of your mundane world. And I'm not just talking to you "tinys" here in the classroom either; I'm talking to humans all over the world, albeit in delayed written form, sometime after my return to Earth.

"Can you handle the truth!?" Deepy seemed to shout.

"YES!" the tinys teleped emphatically back to him.

But he was not to be outdone as he channeled a favorite actor* with great force: "You CAN'T handle the truth!" *(Film: 'A Few Good Men'; actor: Jack Nicholson)

"WE CAN ... WE WILL!" [The 'tiny's' played along.]

"Actually, I'm not sure that's your best approach, if I may say so," CHIP interrupted, in an offhand way.

Deepy swallowed hard because that momentarily hurt his feelings, until he quickly realized they were ego derived. He knew that CHIP always tried to be polite, but still it was a bit irritating to have him voice a seemingly negative opinion followed by the extraneous '... if I may say so' – which of course was polite.

"We've been practicing for ten minutes and now you tell me? But yeah, you're right," Deepy sighed. "I was close to thinking the same thing. Oh well, it was worth a shot."

They had been watching the third "take" of a simulated, synthesized scenario, generated by the ship's "Assembler." Deepy had thought the scene might be something of an attention grabber. Unfortunately he was out of time and his show-biz idea just didn't have that certain pizzazz he had hoped it might.

{When class time finally rolled around, Deepy was dog tired, even after three bowls of coffee, some hyper-activity, and a later than usual start time because this 'tiny' lesson was supposed to be telepvised throughout the whole fleet.}

"Class, we need your attention now," CHIP told the tinys, before turning to Deepy.

"Don't get me wrong; your idea was worth a try, but like I told you, nobody's expecting you to entertain them. You don't need that added pressure. They just want the basics.

"If I may, before you begin, Deepy, I would like a brief word with your future readers – those incarnate tinys in your audience."

"Of course," Deepy murmured, knowing it could not be otherwise.

CHIP then delivered a "disclaimer" which Deepy thought unnecessary, to wit: [The class you are about to witness in delayed form may seem a bit odd at times. Many of you will be shaking your heads in wonder or even disbelief and you may even be tempted to give up trying to understand or believe. Don't quit. God won't quit on you unless you force the issue. You have waded through some incredible concepts so far, so think of this as 'fantasy' if it suits you. I predict that someday you will be quite happy to have stayed the course. Thank you.]

"Thank you," Deepy replied; and then his mind went blank.

IIIIIIIIIIIIIIIIIIIIIIIIIIIIIIIIIIIIIIIIIII

"<u>Good</u> <u>morning</u>, <u>class</u>," Deepy finally managed. He was a bit agitated, which caused him to stutter momentarily as he continued. Then his myriad subthoughts caused him to lose his concentration. Must be nerves he thought, while trying to refocus on the mental teleprompter that CHIP provided. "Be steady," he told himself, before remembering that everyone tuned in could "read" him. 'How the hell do they do that?' he wondered. He really hated telepathy and sure didn't understand how it could work electronically. But not much was making sense to him these days. He might have to stop thinking altogether. 'Maybe he already had,' he now thought.

"Uh-Oh, more random, trouble-making thoughts," - Out of the corner of his eye, he could see CHIP wince. Could he help it if a human dog suffers a lot of internal dialog? – His whimsy causing his thoughts to stray even more now. [Note: Deepy had forgotten that only his audible thoughts would be teleped to the fleet, but some in the fleet were wondering why he seemed so hesitant and fidgety]

Dr. Larry Ray James, with his "Deepy dog" alter ego, was, to this point, one of a kind. There were adjustments to be made all around if this bizarre experiment was to succeed. It was, as one might imagine, difficult for a man to think like a man while "wearing" a dog body. "It has to be as crazy as it seems and yet here I am," Larray "Deepy" James now thought. He didn't like that thought either, or the fact that it came at a most inopportune moment. CHIP was now shaking his head, seemingly in awe. Deepy cleared his throat, from which the sound of Larray's voice would emanate. "Making sound" was not necessary, but it was done for the benefit of the tinys, who needed to adjust to human voice vibrations. Besides, Deepy still preferred to "voice" his thoughts, and so CHIP had made it possible. Everyone onboard the ship cooperated in that regard - thanks to Eno.

~~~~~~~~~~~~BASIC LESSON~~~~~~~~~~

"In the beginning there was no "time," and we do not know when time began, since there was no time," Deepy winked. He ad-libbed that last part, hoping to set a light-hearted tone. "Seriously though, 'time' as a measuring stick began when God needed that concept in her material world. But we don't know exactly when God began... meaning her Conscious existence; and of course, nothing exists outside her Consciousness. How could it? Nothing exists if there is no consciousness to perceive it. Without consciousness there would be no one and no way to perceive and describe anything.

"We think everything that "is," Deepy told his audience, "was"... and ... "will be." However, everything in the physical universe is always changing. Energy is in a constant state of flux. And so the energy forms of today are not the forms of yesterday or tomorrow, even though they may appear the same. And that includes the physical form of manifestation you currently perceive as your body." Deepy chuckled, and then commented: "Excluding the tinys on these Mother Ships, who as yet still are without integral incarnate forms.

"But, in fact," Deepy went on, "there are only three kinds of energy in creation. One is causal Mental energy. What do we call this Core energy?" he wondered to his class.

"God!" ... the tinys in the incubator classroom thought rather forcefully in one "voice," possibly still hyped from their teacher's previously intended introduction scenario.

"Yes indeed," Deepy acknowledged in a similar refrain of enthusiasm, "God is Causal Mental energy," he reiterated, warming up now to his main audience as he concentrated on his tiny subjects. All those eavesdroppers slipped momentarily from his awareness. He knew he had to convince himself that it was just another day in the classroom.

"God's Mentality or Spirit-Mind "virtuously" never changes. SHE is who SHE is, which means SHE is who SHE *"thinks"* SHE is and intends to be. This means that the Essence of God-Mind is synonymous with her Mental energy, which further means God is causative to every non-random creation and event. SHE can work her Intelligence into as many forms as her imagination can conceive. But, yes, there still are random events in God's material world, remaining from her "coming out" party, as SHE continues her coalescence of the universe. Eventually, all Moral Mental aspects of her material realm will coalesce within her middle Child, God Junior, who lives between her twi-polar Parental Minds. It's her Child that allows her to be an indivisibly-dual, singular Mind of three parts. Her middle Child is multi-cellular with myriad twi-polar, indivisibly-dual Mental Cells –

her Trangels and Angels working on a G'Host foundation similar perhaps to brain glia, neurons, gluons, and all else that makes a human brain, but providing perfect Mental and Spiritual stability now and forever in the Otherealm.

"Quite a few of her Humangel Cells have come from her temporary material realm, for which SHE chose only a few dynamical, physical and biological forms to receive "self" awareness; but there are some subtle variations of the forms. There are many erratic hybrid versions, but COG can help with such variants through spiritual guidance, when hybrids finally tune to God for communion.

Otherwise, the few varieties of forms essentially are the same across the universe. The Human form however was the only one meant for perfection when indwelled by a COG Soul, which was there to replicate an interior twin or clone of COG Mental Essence, or that is to say 'God's' Moral Essence.

Humans are the only forms capable of attaining Spiritual eternity. Other forms, such as whales or dolphins for example can compete with some hybrids on a practical brain basis, but not for Spiritual-Mental Soul replication. Essentially they are "anima *ids*," just as humanimal "stock" once was before it became superimposed with id's personality creation known as ego. Pure ids still can be indwelled by COG when God so chooses, as SHE sometimes does. In fact, COG have upgraded the brain abilities of some anima ids, such as the just mentioned ocean creatures.

"During Perfect Gardens, the COG energized the inner cloned-forms of Humans into Spiritual Humangels compatible with the Essence of God Jr. All such forms then became Mental Cells of "Junior," who God uses as her "Brain Child." We speak of that 'Perfect' process in the past tense, since it ended eons ago. It was replaced, however, through God's Grace, with a new generation designed to help save tiny remnant souls. Some hybrid humans still have such godly potential but most will not achieve success unless they understand these very words and change their ways to match God's essential Morality.

"The totality of God's Humangel generation was successful long ago, and that era closed, starting from where it began and extending to the farthest reaches of where God's Gardens lay. Earth's and Mars' were two of the farthest out from the 'big bang.' As Gardens were being closed, God activated her Grace to save the first hybrid 'tiny' souls from her "gardens" – now deemed *miniscule,* or not absolutely necessary for her needs. Notwithstanding its downgraded status, the hybrid mission has the same goal as that of the Humangel generation: to establish souls as Mental Cells within that aspect of God Mind known as her Child, in the Othereal realm known as Heaven.

"The first material world hybrid conversions began as near as possible to the inner edge of Junior's Spiritual Otherealm, then broadened outward to encompass all areas that previously held pure Humangel Gardens. That means layers of moral progress can be measured through that same extending hybrid ladder. Earth's hybrids, for example, are much later on the ladder than some alien hybrid visitors to Earth from planets closer to Junior's interior.

"The term 'Human' means the entity is both God aware and self-aware. Hybrid humans also are self-aware so long as God is gauging their ability to become moral beings through enlightenment regarding their Creator. They must become moral or pure enough to receive the mercy of God's Grace. To receive her Grace and eternal life, they must prove their worth by demonstrating godly traits of Wisdom; Intelligence; Logic; and Love, while displaying their own grace toward God and one another. Some Earthite hybrids already are God-aware, meaning they actually try to abide in God's Values. The vast majority is not so astute and some will stay oblivious, while many will be self-righteous.

"As you know, in the Heavenly Spirit world, or realm of God Junior, God's imaginative thought process works through COG, or Othereal Cells of God Mind, to include Trangels, Humangels and some hybrid Angels as well. Those Mental Cells, working within God's Otherealm, which phases through her temporary material realm, also are called Souls, a term more familiar to most hybrids as relates to God.

"COG - Children of God - are indivisibly-dual Mental Cells with co-creative license to perceive original thoughts from conceptual elements that God makes available, and to amend such thoughts, down to their elements, with her approval. This is called "Co-Creativity" as God's WILL and Grace would dictate.

"Naturally, when I say that God allows COG to Co-Create, as if they are separate from God, I simply mean that

God provides original thought elements and accepts re-created ones through her Cellular, Mental energy COG forms. In other words, SHE is thinking. This means that every missionary COG, or Cell of God Mind, is an extension of God herself and therefore all thoughts originate and evolve within God Mind. A single Cell (Soul) of God still represents, and functions with, the actual imago* of God. *(An idealized mental image of another person or the self, or 'Self,' in God's case)

"COG allow you tinys - as the indwelling holy spirit of hybrids - to act as mental templates for the material thought processor known as the brain of your hosts. Each of you has, or should have, the ability to combine your soul with that polar opposite fused-spirit brain, in order to co-create a personal twi-polar, indivisibly-dual Soul by cloning or replicating a moral spiritual version of the soul/brain combination, aka the mind. If you succeed in co-creating a spiritual replica within your fused-spirit (bodily) cocoon, you – the tiny soul – will transcend this world with that spirit into God Junior's heavenly realm. And if with God's Grace you are Moral enough your O'Soul will help you continue apprenticeship there.

"As you know, every Soul in Heaven is a twi-polar, indivisibly-dual entity, just as God is, although SHE is necessarily divided by her 'Middle Child,' so that SHE remains of stable Mind. Without her Heavenly Child, God's dual polarities would clash once again to disastrous results, as SHE did through unmeasured eons past.

Taking a momentary breath, Deepy added, "Of course, within all her universal realms, God is Producer, Director, set designer, all the actors and acted upon... everything Conscious or alive, to include the stage where life springs forth and grows. Such stages also are known as gardens, usually in planetary form.

"All God's Life is Conscious – meaning interactive with the energy of God Mind - but only COG – whether Trangel or Humangel - are Spiritually Self-aware at all times and in all God's realms, whereas human cocoon hosts now exist only as hybrids in the material world. It is with your tiny host-cocoon templates that COG can help you become a Humangel for eternal life with God in the Otherealm of Heaven. This mission gives you tinys here your chance to get there by the only method God now has at her disposal, meaning you must give your hybrid hosts the potential to internally replicate an Othereal form worthy of eternal salvation through Grace.

"If the replicated spiritual forms are morally vacuous, that pairing of spirit-souls will not be viable for an extended heavenly stay, and must return to the material realm in another fleshly cocoon to see if progress can be made. If the replicated forms lean too much toward evil, they may be viable only for potential reincarnation from within an earth-haunting phase known as ghostly. More egregiously evil spirits must wait in isolation within the confines of hell for either their final judgment or an upgrade to the ghostly realm or beyond. Some hellish spirits choose death. Be aware, however, that time is running out for all such events.

"When Christ said, *'Blessed are the weak in spirit for theirs is the Kingdom of Heaven,'* SHe* was referring to the body's replicated inner spirit form. In other words, the soul had overcome the sensual strength of the fused spirit body, so that the brain/soul could create an inner spirit replica of that form, even if weak. A "spectral" form would not qualify for heaven. Spectral forms are too weak to be anything but ghostly. Even weak spirits, however, can be moral and humble enough to be greatly strengthened in heaven for reincarnation and possibly to become appAngels for Heaven Proper. *(so-called 'gender' does not pertain to this personal pronoun used for COG and Humangels. It is a twi-polar Essence of Yin/Yang.)

"Tiny souls, such as those reading this lesson in the future, must fulfill their potential to act as liaison interpreters of God's Moral Essence for their hybrid brains – meaning they must be wise, intelligent, logical and loving enough to strive for God's Grace through overcoming their fused spirit's (id/ego) brain self, which can render their inner developing spirit weaker than the soul/O'Soul requires. Spirit and soul are required polar opposites of indivisibly-dual material entities, and the soul must replicate its fused spirit into an internal form that can survive physical death.

"God, being everything, also becomes Humangels in her perfect forms; but Earthite hybrid humans are not perfectly majuscule and thus are not God in a present perfect sense, even though their consciousness also derives from God's. Therefore SHE is them, even though they are not yet morally of her Essence. They are deficient in that regard, but do have the potential to be 'future perfect,' which they must become in order to abide within a perfect God Jr. One could say that God is undergoing a "hybrid experiment" at this point when it comes to Earthite and other humanity within the universe. It's working for her in most other planetary gardens, but not so much yet among Earthites. The "experiment," however will soon be completed to the good fortune of many, but not all. As the *Bible* states in *Romans 8:28: "... all things work together for good to them that love God and who are called according to [God's] purpose."* [That purpose is moral perfection of her Mental Cells. Those *'called,'* ultimately will be allowed perfection through her Grace to become eternal Spirit-Souls.]

"So, each of us, with God's help, must create a "savior self" within, by saving our hybrid moral essence as a spirit aspect (even if weak) through our Over-Soul. That only includes all us hybrid humans who would care to live with God forever.

"In the pure Spirit dimension of God Mind, the twi-polar Child of God Spirit-Soul or Mental Cell who became Jesus as a Yang material Spirit also was known by her Soul's Yin name of Christ. To be Human, each fused spirit body needs a Soul; and the 'Christ' Soul also incarnated through the perfect Human Spirit Body of Jesus, to co-creatively share the "Word" of God – as an indivisibly-dual Yang/Yin entity. Jesus provided the Yang Spirit... Christ the Yin Soul. Together they were the only such moral 'imago' of God perfectly present on Earth, since the time of the Perfect Human generations, and the only one ever to be born through the natural birth canal of a hybrid woman whose Heavenly Child was beamed to her, in a flash, with perfect godly Essence – both Spiritually and materially. Jesus Christ was a Mental energy DNA pattern provided to the mother, Mary, directly from God, through the breath (liquid crystal insertion beam) of the Christ Soul herself.

"Jesus Christ was the only Cell of God Mind ever to be born – Body and Soul – into, but not OF, the material dimension through a hybrid mother. Jesus essentially followed a similar course as the COG who occupied perfect Humans in God's universal planet Gardens, prior to the hybrid generation; only He did not step forth as a mature adult Humangel. His physical body went through his surrogate mother's womb, but only as a passageway and not developmentally in the way human babies are born. He (Jesus) was never physically connected as a fetus to the mother. He came forth as an infant Spiritual Child that materialized inside the mother's womb just moments before birth into the material world. After He was in the world physically, his Soul Mate, Christ, rejoined him as the Trangel they were. SHe then was fully *COG*nizant of herself from the moment of that inception as a "Be-In." He was his total "SHe" Self of Jesus Christ, or essentially a full him/her or Yin/Yang Trangel in baby form.

"In a somewhat similar, but opposite, manner, Humangels were Co-Created by COG as adult spirit "gels," inside Perfect Human matrixes and then were transposed into Heaven as Mental Cells. This restored more of God's 'Big Bang' loss of Mental Energy Essence to her Spiritual Self in her God Junior Child. COG formed fully mature adult "Spiritual Replicas" of their own Essence, Co-Created with God Mind to serve God as Mental Cells. Those "twins" stepped forth from the Human bodies as fully grown Vessels of pure Spirit-Soul Essence, newly reclaimed from fused (material) Spirit as indivisibly-dual Soul-Mates to serve God in her Otherealm.

"You tinys in the reading audience who already are incarnate as soul adjuncts to your spirit entities must understand all this, in order to help your fused spirit brain-mate *'believe'* it and *'live'* it, in order for your spirit-soul to be saved as a new appAngel. If your spirit-soul unit comes to truly believe in moral virtues and the practice of mental activity that goes into bringing them to life, you will grow to your fullest potential. You must believe and practice the teachings of Jesus Christ, whether you learned morality through Muhammad, Buddha, or whomever. Even though you may still have some karma to pay, God can sort that out to your mutual benefit and save you through her Grace.

"Mental Energy, or Will Power, is based in Morality, and upheld by the five Virtues of God and her Children. God is God. Her Children are virtuous images of her, to include Humangels, but Earthite humans are not. However, it should be the goal of each person who can fathom these revelations, to become* God. *(meaning to complement and enhance her – to be as SHE is)

"Becoming God means you must practice living in the light, or Wisdom, of God and her Son, until you realize a change of mental persuasion, or conversion. Your converted essence then will become the main representation of your life in your world and the next. But, practicing godly principles and making them your own, are only the first steps toward becoming One with God, or essentially Humangel-COG.

"As you now know, Humangels are Angels who were created as Othereal entities from within perfect Human matrixes in previous "Gardens" on Earth and other planets. They are the type of Mental Energy Cell that makes up the God Jr aspect of the Triune Entity of God. Human forms served as protective cocoons for developing Humangel COG, much as the caterpillar of a butterfly serves as progenitor of an entity meant to serve a greater purpose than just itself. Hybrid tiny souls likewise are protected in their human body enclosure, but they are transient and oftentimes must step aside if id/ego thinking takes hold. With all too many fused spirits, their tiny souls never make meaningful changes that benefit God and themselves, most unfortunately.

"You tinys here are special, in that you already have served God as heavenly appAngels, transposed from moral hybrid beings, and therefore you should quickly adjust to what awaits you in the flesh. For love of your fellow humans, you have agreed to risk the worldly temptations you once overcame, although re-infection is unlikely since before long you will be serving side by side with Jesus Christ in Earth's new majuscule "Gaia" Garden. Temptations will not flourish then as they do now; but you also will have some immunity through knowledge.

"Obviously God does not wish to lose any portion of her Self to immorality or Eve illness and that is why SHE has given spirits with tiny soul-mates multiple lifetimes to adapt to and overcome the material world's character pollution. Your mission will be to help the spirit-souls who reincarnate but who have yet to achieve angel status. You will help form a more perfect breed of potential appAngels than other missionaries who have preceded you. Some of you, in fact, were those very missionaries. Now you are apprenticed Angels, ready for your new mission prior to, and with, Jesus Christ."

Deepy paused for a sip of water, and then surveyed the tinys in their machines. Most of the Holy Spirit Essence of which their spirit-souls consisted was swirling around as suffused light, which occasionally coalesced as individual points, like fireflies. CHIP had said that such coalescence indicated thoughts were being shared among them, or they likely were full of questions for their teacher. It was their polite custom though to wait until it was time for conversation. Deepy had told them to speak up whenever they had a question, but usually they waited for a signal from CHIP.

Deepy continued...

"Tinys always retain their inherent ability to commune with God, even while their moral mental essence is at risk of influence by the brain's id/ego. For those of you who reincarnate prior to the coming Gaia Garden with Christ Jesus... Over-Souls will maintain you tiny Angel souls as mostly pure Spirit transponders, attuned to God 'sense.' However you also will be constantly challenged and even possibly thwarted at times by the id/ego of your fused fleshly spirit as you try to keep it in alignment with God's Moral laws.

(Romans, Chapter 8:Verses 1, 3, 4, 5 and 6:

There is... no condemnation to them which are in Christ Jesus, who walk not after the flesh, but after the Spirit.* *[or spirit-soul]

3. For what the [Moral] law could not do, in that it was weak through the flesh, God sending her own Son in the likeness of sinful flesh ... condemned sin in the flesh; 4. ...That the righteousness of the law might be fulfilled in us, who walk not after the flesh, but after the Spirit. 5. For they that are after the flesh do mind the things of the flesh; but they that are after the Spirit the things of the Spirit. 6. ...For to be carnally minded is death; but to be spiritually minded is life and peace.)

"Your mission once again is to overcome the evil aspects of the world and then to assist the more recalcitrant tiny souls to vastly improve their own spirit-soul mates toward receiving God's Grace, so as to attain eternal life in Heaven. You and they can only do this by following the teachings of the one who is sent to be your Savior. When that time comes, you will recognize her as Jesus Christ – even when SHe appears as Christ Jesus; and while SHe will know you as the angels you are, you will not recognize yourselves as such; just as the disciples of Jesus did not know they had formerly served as tinys of Angel status, but of course Jesus knew it.

"During the halcyon time of Humangel development, the pure Mental energy of COG cohabitants, within Humans, enveloped the whole organism and strengthened it for healthy development of its interior Angel Spirit. During that prime era of Gardens used for growing God's Heavenly Child, those COG Cells were not "Over" Souls, but resided directly within their perfected humanimal 'Human' hosts. Those Children of God Cells along with you tiny 'nesting' or 'homing' soul partners gave Human spirit brains – to include the 'id' instinct - a subconscious awareness of self. It was the subconscious selves that later during hybrid time affected the instinctive 'ids' to unduly influence you tiny souls into becoming a combination of id/ego, also known as a personal god self. Every one of you essentially is Adam or Eve.

"Previous COG cohabiters now serve as your 'Over-Souls.' God Mind communicates with them, and they with you; but now from a distance. God shares thoughts with all her pure Children, whether they were materially embodied as Humans or serving as Over-Souls; and obviously within the pure Spirit-Souls or Cells of God Mind Proper.

"Yes, I do speak in past tense when referring to COG Cells that cohabited perfect Humans of planet Gardens. As I have mentioned: that project was completed during a non-time prior to the concepts of time and reincarnation. The only perfect Humans now operating in the material realm work and reside within this support fleet and others like it across the universe. We are missionaries dedicated to the hybrid generation. These garden fleets are specifically designated to assist tiny hybrid souls, some of whom we "borrow" at times to provide them more direct and immediate assistance. [Deepy was unmindful that he was speaking as one of "us." He was flattered when re-reading the transcript.]

"Last week, you'll recall, I told you 'Othereal Spirit' is a Mental medium that permeates annihilated non-polarized Spirit (AKA the Holy G'host, God Jr "foundation") for its transmissible support throughout God Jr. That dark energy area, as seen from the material realm, consists of twi-polar "hot spots" of indivisibly-dual COG Spirit-Souls (AKA the "dark matter" of Conscious Mental Spirit). It is within this Otherealm "Host," which cannot be perceived as light by humans, that your Over-Soul mates reside. COG TranShips operate in and out of the farthest fringe of that aspect of the Othereal dimension that sparsely envelops the material one.

"I know I have given you a lot of information, class, and told you some things you already know, but that is for the benefit of our wider audience. Before you arrived here, you already knew all this as part of your total Angel selves and you will remember it again through individual epiphanies as you fight to overcome id/ego after incarnation. These classes will help trigger your memories when that time comes. For now, that concludes this lesson plan and I will take your questions."

"Where do hybrid thoughts originate?" Ceepa had that first question.

"Most moral thinking originates with God and endures for material world use as long as God sustains those thoughts within her Othereal Spirit energy. If hybrids change them or no longer use them, then God stores them in her Assembler's "Library," removing them from her immediate Consciousness. SHE has them for recall if needed for karmic reasons, or otherwise.

"When pure thoughts become perverted, many hybrids sadly continue to pass them along according to the wishes of their egodly essence and they are retained in human memory or recorded works. That is why sex and violence continue as desired concepts in the hybrid thought library; and that's quite sad and such a deterrent to moral thinking.

"What are those concepts? What do they mean," Angst wanted to know.

"Angst, I'm sorry to tell you that is something you will relearn after you reincarnate. Be pleased for now that you don't remember. God doesn't hold those definitions in her memory, although COG must, as they continue their missionary work.

"However, Earth's hybrids do have God's Othereal memory energy available to them, even if outdated. They are within her Assembler's so-called Akashic Library.* It can be referenced by brain/soul minds connecting with their O-Souls, but perhaps not quite so prolifically as psychic/prophet Edgar Cayce managed in the twentieth century. He accessed a "timeless" record of viable thought energy available to tiny souls with pertinent, moral needs. This timeless record bank includes moral thought history and future events made available to some hybrid humans who engage their souls toward moral goals. Also, an amoral section of the *'record'* is available to anyone for retrieval. Immoral thoughts and deeds are not recorded but they remain in constant use by hybrids who usually take them to new levels of supposed cleverness. You likely can get some from a neighbor or through a variety of technology. Egod will continue to perpetuate evil on all hybrid viewing screens, in your books, and other media, as long as he can enrich himself materially. Egod has no working soul. If hybrids were to cease their demand for atrocities, eventually society would become a safe haven. Sex and violence are not sports and not to be celebrated as *"that's life"* normal.

  [In theosophy and anthroposophy, the Akashic Library is a compendium of all moral and amoral human events, thoughts, words, emotions, and intentions ever to occur or that will occur. They are believed by theosophists to be encoded in a non-physical plane of existence known as an etheric (or Othereal) dimension.] {That definition is COG given.}

  "All fused spirit-souls retain and sustain some polluted or warped memories through brain cells influenced by psychoses and body chemistry, to include the id/ego, mainly as the libido, as well as thought processes colored by narcosis. Polluted thoughts and memories make up the bulk of those contained within the societal entity of "group thought" that we call Egod. You can guess which resource – the mind/brain or the id/ego brain – that hybrids access most often. Yes, the polluted thoughts are in great demand and accessed on a regular basis, especially by lazy or under-educated or undisciplined thinkers and/or those of weaker moral fiber. Unoriginal, regurgitated thought is contained in *Egod's* library, of which most humans are card-carrying members, and at the same time – shelf stocking assistants.

  "All good conceptual thinking originally comes from God. More often than not, Egod manages to change that to suit his world. That being the case, God will not sustain her original thoughts to build upon if Egod has corrupted them into criminal or immoral activities. Her "Assembler" will retain the originals.

  "Most egodly genres of individual memories are accessible through hybrid media forms, whether verbal, printed, electronic or other means generated by humans using their free will to suit their id/egos and Egod. Such human thought energy dissipates relatively quickly, but it is constantly being accessed and thus renewed before it can be completely forgotten. Most human thinking is innocuous at best, but is outright evil in its most harmful varieties. There are plenty of those around."

At this point, Deepy's mind started to wander until it locked onto something he and CHIP had been discussing the previous night, and before he could stop himself he shared something vaguely related.

"Thought energy will remain in the material universe until God coalesces into a single state of Mind to include some universal hybrid humangels. This period of time constitutes the diverse life of thoughts born to God in the universal realm, which includes our current state of existence."

"Huh?" Ceepa said.

"Huh?" was Deepy's response to her.

"I thought you said there was no such thing as 'time,'" Ceepa wondered.

"Did I say that? 'In the beginning'... in the beginning, there was no time as a Mental construct, until God gave birth to the concept in order for Earthite humans, not God or COG, to measure their existence within each of their incarnate states. Pure Humans also did not need time, as their animal bodies lived as long as God's physical laws allowed under virtually ideal conditions. Time became a material concept after God decided her immature hybrid humans, with their individual egos, would need to be given terminal, physical lives, and a multitude of them in many cases, in order for them to conceivably process enough inner-angel spirit to reach a high quality of "moral intelligence," within the operating purview of God's Grace.

"Whew!" Deepy sighed, somewhat flustered.

CHIP allowed another of the tinys to weigh in with a "Sir, could you please elaborate a bit more?"

"Time, or the idea of it, does not affect an eternal God in any way, but it does exist in the physical-mental world - that is to say: effects of such a concept can be perceived by the physical senses, even as spatial coordinates can be perceived. Sometimes those coordinates and temporal moments are even calculated as one or the other - affecting the other." Deepy paused to reflect on that for a moment, as a subthought of another "Huh?" flew by. But that didn't stop him.

"Also, time's temperance upon objects and events can be perceived mentally by an observer of those objects and events that have been acted upon by physical laws. Time is said to be a temporal coordinate, a fourth dimension, and that is fine. It serves a purpose. But as a strictly mental construct, or concept, it exists only to serve the physical world, and we have a way of measuring what we refer to as time. We break our perceived reality into increments based on analogical thinking, coordinated with perceived events taking place in the material world, and proceeding sequentially out of the so-called past into the so-called future.

"And so if time does exist in the physical world in that manner, where does that leave the present? We could say simply that effectually it does not exist, because its mental framework is memory and anticipation. The present is only a point from which to measure or remember what we perceive as our past, or to extrapolate a potential future. The ever-present "now," is neither here nor there.

"However and paradoxically we could live in an eternal "now" that incorporates both a past and a future if we allowed our mental energy to strictly come from God. SHE is a constant of Virtues, based in Morality and driven by her own Conscious State of Essence; but even though most of us are out of alignment with God's Virtues, our conscious state remains steady for the most part as God's Grace and mercy allow us to remain as upright as possible, depending on how much we use our tiny souls and O'Souls. Most unfortunately, Egod usually conducts our trains of thought through our brains and minus our godly mind cells or souls, causing most of us to live with varying degrees of Eve illness. That makes Egod (society at large) better able to communicate with us, due to our willful ignorance or denial of God; and yet God will not give up on us unless we quit on her.

"I would also note, there is nothing but the past or future, as far as our physical energy patterns are concerned, because they are constantly changing. Therefore, God created time as a Concept to help us keep our mental equilibrium, while often imperceptibly watching ourselves and the world change all around us on a continual basis. We break this equilibrium concept into increments in order to form it into patterns that keep us grounded or please us mentally. We all want something from each precious moment to carry with us from our past into our future, because what we call 'now' essentially is neither one nor the other. It is so fleeting as to be immeasurable. There literally is no time like the present. It's passed. Time does not stand still, although its physical effects do slow down with less gravitational pull, as in 'space' for example."

Deepy now knew he was ready for a "time out." He wasn't especially pleased by his immediate past or looking forward to his immediate future. His moments felt neither fleeting nor precious. He was both exhausted and dizzy. But no breaks were allowed during a class, except in emergency. He felt himself sinking into a hole he continued to dig, seemingly without effort. He continued.

"Ironically, we, as mental entities, do not immediately live in the past or in the future... only within the moment of a single breath, hopefully followed by another. Each breath constitutes an indefinably tiny increment of recessions into memory or intended future consciousness. It is only memory of physical relics of sensory perception that allow us to construct a reality passing from what was, into an extrapolation or anticipation allowing for a future what is, as represented by what is now the "past present," meaning an increment that virtually passed at the very moment of its existence, so far as our consciousness is concerned.

[CHIP note: Deepy was offering a valuable lesson to the tinys, one that would be clarified to them later as an example of human ego, because whether the information was right or wrong, Deepy had vested himself in making it turn out right, without thought of longer-term consequences if he failed. Ultimately I made sure he stayed true to the concept we devised, and for which he was giving himself credit, but to his own dismay.]

"Essentially what I'm saying is that while we live in the eternal now of our physical perceptions, our thoughts live in either the past or the future, as either God's or Egod's. That does not mean that material world life is outside God's purview. SHE keeps it in Mind, as an anomaly that SHE must resolve to her ultimate satisfaction, because it is a piece of her that slipped away during her birth. It also means we are blessed if some of our original thinking comes from God. Whether we are wise enough to think godly thoughts or not, it is God's Mental "thought energy" that enlivens our spirits. In other words, God's thoughts are our breath. We are God's thought forms. God thinks, we breathe, which means SHE can take our breath away, which SHE must do with the most evil among us who have outlived their ability to ever become Moral Cells of her Consciousness.

"In the meantime, if we don't care to commune with God for creativity, Egod is only too happy to mix old perverted thoughts into new ones to make recipes that our id/egos love to feed on. In fact we usually just pick from those thoughts we have on standby with our chosen mentor. For most of us, that seems easier than abiding in God to co-create new thoughts worthy of her. You tinys will come to see that most humans usually opt for the easy way out, and for instant material gratification.

"Now... I took so much time talking about time, I can only take one more question, and hope it's an easy one," Deepy told his class.

"Doctor Deepy, excuse me, but there is something I'm not quite sure about. Could you please tell us again, who is this Egod?" Macie asked.

"Thank you, Macie.

"Egod* is both the personal and collective subconscious of ego evil, which is a form of insanity. Two id entities in Eden were the first to pervert original, godly thought, thereby creating this social entity. This 'Egod' is now the size of all humanity, past and present, because he contains virtually all evil deed-and-thought confluences of hybrid humans. Basically, Egod is a societal "thought-cancer" inflicted on those spirits who allow a materialistic society to have more influence than godly morals in their lives. We definitely will be talking about this Egod a lot."

*[Egod is "id^" coupled with ego, and taken to the level of societal attitudes and lifestyles. Egod affects both genders, and has the audacity to try to pass off "ego props," as idols for worship. These can include societal groups, man-made "stuff" or even types of people – for example, politicians or celebrities – some of whom revel in ego). Other examples are "personality" ego props, whether individuals or groups; "peer-power" ego props; "brute power" ego props, whether the power-person's intimidation is literal or symbolic; and, of course, there is general, societal hubris, sometimes in the forms

of personal elitism, reverse snobbery, and nationalism, to give a few examples. Hybrid has become a synonym for hubris.

[^Id is dictionary defined by humans as: 'the one of the three divisions of the psyche in psychoanalytic theory that is completely unconscious and is the source of psychic energy derived from instinctual needs and drives — compare ego, superego.']

This group of soul "tinys" composed a class that Deepy and a few others in the crew were teaching a variety of subjects. The tinys were only forty days old at this point, as time is measured in the material realm. As part of their current training as tiny angels, they were getting no input from their primary Mental Essence – in other words no help from the 'Over-Soul' aspect from which they originated. That would come later, along with a fused-spirit body. The difference between them now and the humans they were to become could be summed up in one dual "slashed" word – id/ego, packaged in hybrid bodies. The tinys were learning about id/ego now from an objective point of view, as the burden it could become for their spirit's emotional reactions or as a tool for their own thoughtful proficiency in surfing a fused-spirit brain.

Deepy understood that each ship in the fleet carried a representative number of one-hundred-thousand project tinys and he had been told there were millions more "in the neighborhood" who would be receiving these lessons as well, via telepcoms. At the moment, Deepy stood at a podium in the center of a small room in TranShip III looking at small glass compartments all around him, flashing with the pulsating, co-creative thoughts of effusive, tiny souls. When they focused and directed their vibrations, CHIP transmitted them as sound, while teleping Deepy's voice as vibrations to them.

Deepy had no idea how the exact mission of the tinys would unfold, but he had to settle for this incomplete knowledge, while curiously awaiting more information to come, which Eno had promised. For now, he simply marveled at the tinys' natural ability at telepathy and the rate of their advancement. He was pleased to be teaching them about things that related to the human realm, as well as the broader information that he also was learning from Eno's and CHIP's lesson plans.

It was true that they all could simply be "programmed" with knowledge directly from CHIP, or any COG for that matter, but this human touch of interactive teaching was deemed more appropriate at this time to the life awaiting them on Earth. So whether Deepy realized it or not his faults as a teacher and his failings as a human offered invaluable insight to the tinys, as they were told of his real status, and how it fit with his good character.

"I'm honored," was his first impression when this part of his mission was explained to him. After all, he was the first human spiritual entity chosen by the COG to fill this unique role of teacher and friend to these now delicate, tiny entities. Larray really appreciated being a pioneer in this experimental program, known as the "dog project," or "D-P," which also included another important aspect to his work on board the ship. Still, he knew his teaching was just an honorary position, and that he was a student also, with most of his own knowledge being supplied from CHIP's or BB's data bank. He also very much appreciated the COG interaction with him, especially from Eno. In essence, they were doing the teaching... so long as Deepy managed to stick to the script, that is, and didn't call his befuddled memory into play as he was wont to do, but knew not why. [He failed to realize his own ego wanted some attention.]

{After he had swelled with pride on hearing of his teaching position, his new friend CHIP told him that feeling "pride" was an ego problem and insulting to God who is the font of all conscious perfection. 'Personal pride is arrogance and does not honor God who is composed of pure Energies and Essences of which honor is inherent. Considering God's traits, there is no honor in doing "good" since nothing else would be acceptable. Those who do 'good' simply are sharing God's Essence, and therefore pride would be superfluous.' "Okay, CHIP, thanks. Uh, does that apply to everything a person does?" "As long as it's not immoral," CHIP told him.

Deepy had found himself saying, "Okay, CHIP," a lot as the only way he could logically accept CHIP's pronouncements, which he didn't always understand. He did understand the 'pride thing' though. It was okay to feel pride as satisfaction, for God's sake, for her accomplishments through morally intelligent beings.

CHIP also had told him that only hybrids have the need to distinguish between good and evil, such as honor and dishonor, love and hate, and other less than perfect characteristics, since hybrids are the only "self-aware consciousness" to experience such opposites, or any moral impurity. 'Earth's hybrids and all those elsewhere,' he had said, 'carry within their spirit-souls the potential to convert all their imperfect flux of characteristics to godly essence, but can only do so with the steady assistance of their tiny souls and O-Souls; but Earthites rarely call upon their souls for help.'}

"What about bad thoughts?" Addi now wanted to know.

"Excuse me, Addi; who was thinking bad thoughts?" Deepy wondered, as he snapped out of his brief reverie.

"How can God think bad thoughts when God is pure good?"

"Good question, Addi," Deepy told her; while a subthought told him he had already explained this.

"And the answer is that all original thoughts come from God in pure form, and that is how they are received by God's Children or COG, who then pass some of them to those Earthite humans who have made the effort to call upon God for answers. But since most humans generally are still hiding from God, through arrogance and ignorance, they cannot break through the barrier of the ego to commune with her. Ego's nature is to recognize itself as separate and independent from God, whom it goes so far as to either disavow or ignore.

"This means that most hybrid thoughts are recycled versions of once original and pure thoughts. These thoughts are tainted with changes found acceptable by individual egos as they relate to one another through the psyche of a societal Egod.

"COG and Humangels still pass God's pure, original thoughts to deserving humans who are diligent and who faithfully and fervently seek answers for *'good'* reasons. Occasionally though, God may grant ideas to inquiring minds not so deservedly insistent or persistent because there are problems SHE wants to have understood on a timely basis; problems her more ardent seekers may not be contemplating. Her intermediaries usually succeed in getting her pure thoughts accepted without perversion by these more naturally inquisitive people. However, those thoughts often make their way to ego-influenced brains that are not quite so well intentioned or moral. They then can become quite distorted, even dangerous. On the other hand, sometimes a broader percentage of people can learn from misdeeds by others.

"So, humans must still contend with ego directly, as well as the gross entity of Egod,* which does offer a surrogate psychological life for interested subscribers - or most hybrids.

*[Again - Egod is the collective thought library or lexicon of words, concepts and ideas used by human egos, as summed up in societal attitudes by people whose brain-sets usually are at work without their tiny souls, much less their O-Souls. Individual egos constantly pervert pure thinking or re-create 'evil' from rehashed thoughts. About the only time that Egod uses an original, morally pure thought is in the process of corrupting it. Unless seekers set aside their egos, it is extremely hard for God's COG and Humangel Assistants to filter godly thoughts through the human psyche.]

"Egod-evil (egodevil) is aided and abetted by the human id/ego in tempting spirit-souls away from the moral purity of God. Egod, as a whole, essentially is the brain experience of everyone's combined "id entity," which wants the mental power of God, without the intrusion of obligatory moral thinking. Individual egos and thus Egod want no moral inhibitions placed on them, and rarely call upon their guardian Angels unless circumstances are dire. Then that call often comes forth grudgingly, in which case God usually just allows karma to continue its work without recourse to insincere prayers.

"This "id/ego-as-god" entity influences the spirit-mind essence that otherwise would develop within humans in a pure pattern, allowing each one to become an Earth angel and subsequently an appCOG and Heavenly Humangel."

"Dr. Deepy Dog, sir?"

"Yes, Bain?"

"I'm sorry, sir. Does time exist or not?"

"Yes, Bain, it does, but only because mankind needs it. God would have no use for it on her own, as SHE is eternal. So, right now it only exists through God as it works for mankind. Nonetheless, folks should realize that they only exist as part of God's eternal "now." In the material world, the 'present' is a relic of the past... a memory since it flies by. The future is a potentiality, but may cease to exist at any fraction of a moment for mortal beings. Life was and will be your last breath, heartbeat, and brainwave. And I'm sorry if this is confusing to any of you. If you're still having trouble understanding it, please take it up with CHIP. He's the real master of time here, of which we are just about out for this session. Deepy was just about to say a final word when Edam spoke up with another question: "When will you tell us more about God the dynamic Father/Mother duo, Dr. Deepy - er... sir?"

"Sometime next week, Edam, but I can't say for sure which day, as I don't have my lessons plans yet."

"Who invented God?" Caye was curious.

"That's right – "Who," is the answer to the question, because it is a question without answer, as there would be no questions without God. So, I can tell you who invented, or created, me and you and everything else in "our" conscious world. Sorry Caye, but what I'm saying is - it would appear that the energy of "what would become God" influenced the elements of God, which were already in place. When that happened, Conscious Essence was brought into existence within an entity that first defined itself by a single word – that Word being the one we Christians know as "God." This same entity of God is the cause of both the Othereal and material, or fused-spirit, realms of our aspects of God's Consciousness. Since the elements were there and were causal, one could safely say that God always existed, and that SHE 'invented' everything else as well.

"In fact, I would like to address future readers of a certain book to be cautious in trying to assess God on a scale measurable or definable in human terms. It might be tempting to look out at the vastness of the universe and believe there is no way it could contain a God that controls it and somehow relates to life as tiny as the smallest living form. That of course is partly true, because the universe doesn't contain God. It is God, and God is life. Every living aspect of the universe is an aspect of God, and God Mentally senses and serves her Spirit energy throughout."

Deepy paused, and then unintentionally took another question, right after he got a private telep from CHIP telling him "nice adlib." "Oops, sorry," he subthought, hoping no one noticed his almost pride.

"Why is God both male and female?" Marny wondered.

"Marny, it is because God is divided into two polar opposite regions that live in mutual attraction on either side of a chasm between those two halves of God Mind. This chasm is called Heaven, or God Jr, and it has taken shape according to God's plan. One half of God's Mind {refined Mental Spirit Energy Essence} is termed Yang, which is said to be male, or a positive polar force. The other half of God is Yin, or what is called the feminine or negative force. The Heavenly chasm between them consists of an annihilated polar-neutral fundament for a twi-polar stream of life of Mental Cells living there. One might think of it as an ocean of "Liquid Crystal" containing God's Other life forms known as Cells and used by God Mind in her Mental processes – so that effectively it is her 'Brain Child.'

"Jesus referred to this ocean as 'living water,' although it is liquid crystal. God has filled this heavenly "life stream" with twi-polar Mental entities that alternate their polarity according to God's needs - meaning they can be either Yin or Yang, or polar neutral as called upon, because they are indivisibly-dual, perfectly balanced, and always Mentally ready to serve.

"You will be hearing more about this, but I will tell you that even though God's polarities are equated to the sexual gender opposites of male and female in the physical world, it is wrong to equate her innate powers to sensuality. They are Mental – even the so-called "touchy-feely' Concepts of Love and Grace.

"In God's world of matter, gender serves only as a sensual twi-polar, attraction between opposite mind and body energies. On Earth, the physical or fused spirit, hybrid body attraction is brain-enhanced by the id/ego to the extent that gender becomes a psycho-illogical sexual attraction based on what would be benign "procreative" body urges if the id did not interfere with the tiny soul to create id/ego brain thought. The way to at least try to overcome that is to constantly strive to think with one's mind concentrated on morality.

"Now," Deepy paused... "I appreciate your interest and curiosity, class, and we will eventually tell you everything you want to know. Meantime, it's almost lunchtime, [He was thinking of himself, since tinys don't eat] then naptime, [again, himself] then study time, then time for your physics class. No time to waste. What would we do if we didn't have time? Have a fun time studying with CHIP later, and as usual he will explain "me" to you. Bye for now."

~~~~~~~~~~~~~~~~~~~~~~~~~~~~

"God – ergo ergodic COGnitive conditions -
Or more simply put...

"Yin Yang - Big Bang"
(CHAPTER 11)

[The Commander gave Deepy the following information not long after he came on board with us. At the moment, the 'deep' one has opted for a long nap, so he asked me to share this with you. This was 'then,' and we will get back to 'now,' later.]

[The Commander spoke:]

"In the beginning, there was no beginning. God awoke and there SHE was. And SHE hasn't slept since." Eno winked at Deepy, and then continued, "Prior to her awakening, God Mind existed as "potential" within an unconscious bilateral condition, in which two parallel universes of opposite polarities had come together to form a singularity, the pressures and interactions of which were to create what we know as Mental Energy, which later would recognize itself as "Consciousness" named God.

"All the fundamental activity unfolded over a course of non-time – a lot of non-time, but of course no one was aware of that, because no one existed. At some point though, this Consciousness eventually discovered itself through perception of vibrations, through perhaps many such noiseless episodes of coming together, imploding and then exploding away as mixed polarity in different directions. Eventually, a Conscious Mind was randomly created while contained at the core of the mixed, but mostly polar opposite universes, which still were being drawn together, only to just as necessarily implode and explode again and again, until... the word 'God' and Consciousness met at the axis of "Intellect" – a vibratory sensation that understood and pronounced its Self. It vibrated as the word "God," without knowing any meaning, other than to recognize its Self as "God Aware." It could only happen because there was no *time* to constrain the possibility; probability; "inevitability?"

"Eventually, prior to the "hatching moment" of our particular singularity, the entirety of the combined two-part God Entity had become imprinted with Mental echoes of more "word" vibrations within its infinitesimal space. And thus the "God Egg" hatched, followed at some non-time point by re-*cognition* of each polar aspect that it would need the other as its mate, in order to live in Conscious Awareness, while likewise also intuiting that peace and harmony would be required. In the beginning all thinking was mutual and intuitive, and it still is, with a variable allowance granted alternately to the Child this married Couple would Co-Create during the process of sustaining their creation.

"They came to know that as a permanent, Singular, indivisibly-dual Entity, they would not allow any more "head-butting" or clashing of minds. They would be One 'God,' with some lingering chaos as they preternaturally formulated "plans" for remaining forever married. Of course they knew they needed 'plans,' which would take continued, evolving intuitive ability.

"God devised her main plan while in one last "at<u>one</u>ment" stage, before being split by the distance of her final Yin/Yang explosion - or present state of Consciousness, which was to include all indivisibly-dual Mental Cells. We were formed by our Parents to serve as a middle <u>CHILD</u>,* keeping God's equally adept and wise Minds operating as one Mental Entity through her Children Cells. Perhaps one might think of those Cells as providing thought processes similar to that of the human brain, since humans are made in God's image. *(Acronym for: <u>C</u>rystal <u>H</u>ologram <u>I</u>n <u>L</u>iquid <u>D</u>isplay)

"God's so-called Brain Cells are self and God-aware Conscious, twi-polar Spirit Cells living inside a foundation of God-aware - but non self-aware - "living" liquid crystal.* The Angel Self and God-aware Cells primarily are self-contained, but still interdependent as a triune Entity. One might say the Cells Of God within the Child function similarly to glia, neurons, synapses, etc., or in some cases more akin to something of a different nature, such as gluons. Her indivisibly-dual Cells are "Latin" to God Mind, to be called upon as: "et aliae" or feminine; "et alii" or masculine, and "et alia," or neutral (non-polar). They are electro-magnetic, dual or neutrally polar Mental Energy.

*(liquid crystals (LCs) are matter in a state which has properties between those of conventional liquids and those of solid crystals. For instance, a liquid crystal may flow like a liquid, but its molecules may be oriented in a crystal-like way. There are many different types of liquid-crystal phases, which can be distinguished by their different optical properties.)

"Yes, we can agree it is complicated to grasp God's birth and life as a serendipitous series of events leading to her Conscious Awareness, but it happened, and I must say there is little point now in trying to explain it further. I know human scientists express doubt about anything they cannot prove, since doubt seems to bring their best thinking to the fore. Opinions are not acceptable. Everything must be proven. Scientists likely will never be able to prove God, even if they approve of "a" God concept as a societal or even scientific tool for psychology.

"About sixty-percent of God's middle Child Otherealm became the annihilated Spirit life foundation for God's Trangels, Angels, and Humangels, as well as animals and plants. That 'sea of tranquility' is what humans call dark energy; but mind you this word 'dark,' is a misnomer, simply because humans don't have *'eyes to see'* the light that exists there. It's of a different spectrum. Its Othereal continuum flows through the prism of liquid crystal* and God can "aim it" where SHE pleases. When you die, if you see a "light," go to it and pray it's not one you left on in the bathroom."

[Bemusement and a little laughter from Deepy, with a hint of a smile from his Mentor who told him the silliness was meant to refocus his attention. It worked; but did he need some caffeine he wondered? - 'No,' because he had some right before he could think 'yes.']

Eno was quick to add, "If you have enough moral spirit to deserve God, SHE will aim her light at you and draw you to her.

"The Children Cells and other Spiritual life forms make up about forty percent of what this world sees as dark matter within that Energy foundation, which when taken as a whole, we call God Junior. The Yin God Mind on one side of the Child and the Yang Mind on the other side are split about fifty-fifty between their separate Mental Energies. The material realm accounts for about five to eight percent of the universe as fused energy – give or take a little from each aspect of God Mind, with some of it formerly Mental, and some not.

"Jesus Christ called the dark energy foundation of the Child, "Living Water." It lives without intellect, but subconsciously aware of God's existence as its own. It's Life Essence supports that Mental Kingdom of Heaven, just as material oceans support life. It, however, is unaware of itself as a living crystal Entity.

"Since her last rude awakening, God has expanded her horizons and re-membered her original Selves by revitalizing her separate polarities, cognizing and re-cognizing her new-found Mental Essence. We are happy to report; SHE has, for a long non-time now been a thriving family of three. God's Yin (polar negative) Mind aspect and the Yang (positive) aspect now cling to one another through each side of their middle Child - God Jr – some of which God Mind partially raised from the mostly "dead sea" of the fused dimension, which is held by the gravity of her Love at the edge of her Othereal Yang Self.

"Prior to cognizing her condition of dual existence, God first woke to Consciousness, and then Self awareness, which one might say constitutes a birth from within the potentiality of Spirit, which pervades and is the basis for everything."

"Huh? I mean, okay, if you say so, but it sounded as if you were beginning the story again," Deepy thought before realizing he was summoning up a nagging, bewildered feeling out loud. "It just confused me momentarily. Sorry."

"No problem," Eno smiled his reply. "By the way, I will be repeating some information you already have... because hearing it again could help you understand it. And yes, I know some of your future readers won't be as patient as you are, but then again you are a captive audience. Wisdom, however, should at least allow some of your audience to be captivated too."

"At some point in non-time, there were separate, but virtually equal amounts of polar opposite Spirit Energies. They collided. They merged and then melded ever more compactly into a tiny single Body of unfathomable, pent-up energy. Each polar aspect within this singularity finally, at some point, infused the very essence of the other, igniting an eternal Mental Energy known as Mental Consciousness or Mind.

"They had come together this way countless times, and each time* imploded and then blasted apart, setting off huge vibrations, one after another - diffusing, fusing, and confusing untold amounts of Spirit Body and Mind energy. When at some point they became consciously aware of themselves and each other, they began to get an idea that they had experienced all the mindless melding already. *{after Consciousness and Memory dawned, it was during the quiescence before another such event, that God developed a plan for eternal survival of her dual Self. It helped that many of God's opposing Mental Cells had "married" during much of their melding and un-melding chaos and they had begun getting acquainted on a Mental Consciousness basis as indivisibly-dual aspects of one another.}

"After a final "AtOnement" round, with her plan in place, God aimed some of her energy at a specific spot that seemed to vibrate the most after her previous eruptions. A relatively small amount of that energy was sent flying through a "hole" that her violence created in her own Spirit body. The hole became a portal into an arena that then filled with "fused spirit," or a density called "matter." That material dimension seemed to spread apart to accommodate the energy ripping through it; but it was just a fraction of the total disruption.

"That fused dimension was a very small part of the entire breach known as the Othereal Spirit realm. That "other realm" came to exist, as God planned, between her twi-polar opposite Aspects or Minds, which stabilized themselves as the perimeters of her Heavenly Othereal Body chasm or Child. Her dual Minds were set on each side of those perimeters. Both her annihilated 'Othereal' Spirit in-between, plus the still living opposite-polarity Cells within that Spirit held her divided Mind together, but apart. It was tenuous though, and SHE had much more work ahead.

"It turned out that the majority of her Mental Cells between her dual polar Minds remained focused and intuitive enough to be guided by her plan to stabilize their movements. SHE sent them where SHE needed them. SHE then set about matching and marrying opposite-polarity, free-radical Cells to create indivisibly-dual units that SHE could switch from one polarity to the other, as needed to stabilize her Middle Child between her Selves.

"The initial and ensuing forces propelled the two original polar halves of God Mind apart from the conjoined hybrid Entity they had become. That final breach birth to include their middle Child continually increased the distance between the Parents until their inertial energy dissipated enough to be overcome and stopped by the attraction of their opposing Mental polarities, which they then began to orchestrate through their Child. The Parents had control of God Junior's conglomerate body of mixed polarity; and they choreographed the Cells between them to suit their polar needs to remain 'married.'

"Initially, however, the Othereal Child was a mix of bipolar disorder; and much of the large, newly transformed middle portion of Cells was shattered into liquid crystal. Those Mental Cells contained varying amount of liquid crystal but otherwise were largely unscathed. God termed them "Trangels," as they had remained indivisibly-dual polarities that had participated as whole Cells within God's pre-bang Mind. There were many, to include Jesus and Christ as one such.

"As bipolar entities of various sizes, the Trangel Cells offered more flexibility and were capable of many phase changes, but always on display to the Parents equally and alterably as they became ever more Mentally acute. Essentially, they were enhanced by the kinetic process of the Mind altering experience, plus their new challenges. Eventually they overcame their initial bipolarity and phased into a more Mentally stable twi-polarity.

"Their Parents quickly helped former or non-Trangels to phase from bipolar to twi-polar, meaning uninhibited by confusion and amenable to intuitive guidance for their sake and that of their Parent's. They in turn helped the Spirit Cells adapt quicker to God's plan, by guiding them to polar opposite mates.

"It was the Othereal God Jr. arena that played host to free-wheeling, annihilated Mental Cells that were blown to bits from an interpolated God Mind, to take up subconscious life as the new Holy God Host (G'Host) foundation of the Child. Throughout that maelstrom, loose and polar opposite Mental Cells were flying about and mating without any preliminary romancing. Their mating instantly created twi-polar Cells attractive to both Parents, depending on their whirling-dervish waltz within God's Heavenly Body. God learned to control their thoughts (polar vibrations) to direct which polarity SHE needed them to be. When formed or reformed Trangels learned this, they began teaching newer Cells updated practices presented by their Parents - to whom all will remain students for eternity.

"The two halves of God Mind used the free-flying Cells to commune between her main Polar Selves. All this made up the integral third aspect of God Mind – her Child, which was necessary to hold her polar opposite powers - both together and apart - as dual Minds of a growing "Triune Entity" – in effect, two Parents, plus a Brain Child within a Holy G'Host operating as One Supreme Entity.

"This divisive, but unifying, genesis fashioned God into two interdependent Minds, one Yin and one Yang, separated by an interspersed brain-body of multi-Cellular twi-polar entities. Many of these Children Cells were Trangels, while many more were pure Spirit Mental Energy as Humangels added later from the material realm.

"The LC* Trangels gave structural Spiritual substance to the much improved potency change in the somewhat mixed, but mostly pure Mental Cellular structure of God's dual Mind Cores - split across from each other at either side of their Child's Otherealm. That newly formed realm was a vast Ocean of Othereal Spirit in the great divide between the dual Minds of God. That divide is called Heaven. It is the Body/Brain of the entity or Child known as God Junior. *(Liquid Crystal)

"Jesus referred to the whole expanse as "living water," which was the best Earthite term he had then for liquid crystal. It was the living Spirit "G'Host" or fundament for Junior. It was Conscious of God, but not self conscious. It was animated by God Mind and sections could be moved about by the activity of the Child's Mental Cells, according to God's instructions. God used it as building blocks to suit her imagination. For example, SHE has a new Earth filled with those Angels who were Co-Created on Earth. That new Earth subconsciously remains alive.

"Each Parental Consciousness enfolded its own Mental Spirit energy that was created by the pressure of their singularity, prior to the so-called "Big Bang" event. God then used her Mental Powers to help guide stray, 'free radical' Cells to connect with an opposite polar Cell, rather than being swallowed up by an opposing Parent. Trangels protected many of them until God could create polar opposite mates from her material realm. Trangels knew "why, when, and how" to switch their outward polarities in order to remain independent within Heaven and thus made certain they blocked single cells from attraction by an opposing Parent. Many Trangels became multi-cellular until mates were provided for Cells needing to become indivisibly dual.

"In a later phase, Trangels would lead material world Humangels to the polar opposite Cell that God had chosen for them to "marry." They also taught them polarity switching, in order that they then could remain free of absorption by God's twi-polar Mind.

"God's "Triune" Spirit energy was the Conscious Essence of a living Mental Force known as Mind, but now "God" existed as a permanent indivisibly-dual Self with an added Child composed of Cells existing as a permanent adjunct of conjunctive alternative polarities.

"I know, my deep friend, we are perhaps offering too much detail for your future average reader, so I will ease up soon to give everyone a break, including you," Eno assured Deepy.

"I have virtually no memory, so I'm happy CHIP helps me with my weekly log, and will be there when it is time for "us" to write that book I keep hearing about," Deepy told him.

"Together you will get the job done," Eno replied, before resuming his presentation. "The fused-spirit material world is the one aspect, or dimension, of God's triune polar division, that represents a rift within the Othereal Spirit Realm. It lies at the boundary of Father God, just outside the Otherealm. Its mass is gravitationally wedged at the edge of the Yang Father Mind. It's a sore spot for Junior as it causes fluctuations in his/her intuition.

"God and her COG long ago transformed most of the material dimension's fused mental properties into Othereal Spirit beings or new Mental Cells called Humangels. God now is regaining some of the remaining tiny amounts of the former 'Holy Spirit' within hybrid humans for transmutation into Angel Cells. This process has been ongoing for eons and soon will be coming to a close. The material dimension then will subside into a period of transformation that eventually returns all its otherwise usable properties to the Othereal dimension through "black holes*" or just the opposite of the white or light hole that blew fused Spirit into the material realm in the first place. *(According to the general theory of relativity, a black hole is a region of space from which nothing, not even light, can escape its gravity. Black holes now serve as one-way portals from the material realm into God's Otherealm, and are placed where they can do her the most good.)

"How many hybrid humans end up in Heaven for eternity depends on the will and grace they develop quite soon. God will not take any chances on anyone's purity, and of course SHE does not expect any of you to become perfect without the help of your O-Souls and their leader, Christ Jesus. We pray this message registers with the many human egos on Earth who still have time to change. All of them should want Heaven, but too many will allow apathy to continue ruling them through ignorance. They will never be amazed by what they are giving up.

"Now, if you'll excuse me," the Teacher abruptly told his student, "I'm needed elsewhere at the moment. But since I am repeating myself, I'm asking BB to take over. He's a very agile repeater too, if he thinks it necessary. In fact, he can put you to sleep."

With that, Eno popped out of sight.

"Good, I could use a nap anyway. Wonder what's going on? What's going on CHIP?" Deepy knew CHIP or BB was tuned in. They both were CHIPs, so he settled on that one name.

"Sorry, buddy boy, but that's highly classified information, available only on a 'need to know' basis."

"I don't need to know, CHIP... just curious. Could I get another strawberry milkshake, please?"

"That one I can answer - No way."

Deepy smiled to himself, but didn't respond. He thought he knew CHIP pretty well by now. Sure enough, a smiling quin placed his order down half-a-minute later, saying, "CHIP decided you needed this."

"Thanks," Deepy smiled back.

"Hear that CHIPster - You scalawag? Thanks."

"Please, no name calling. Anyway, you're the "wag" around here. Get it?"

"No, I don't get it, you old scump."

"Scump?"

"Yeah, it's a cross between a scamp and my rump."

"Very nice," CHIP told him.

Deepy had to laugh. He needed some humor, even if he made it up.

"I did pre-read you," CHIP then told him, "but you did need that laugh."

"You're my buddy," Deepy replied, as he continued to chuckle. "I'll take this milkshake and be in my room awhile. BB can get in touch with me there, if he has a hankering to."

"A hankering? Wow, you really are from Texas."

"Shucks, Ah reckon... but mostly Arkansas..."

{DEEP ASLEEP}

[BB Interlude: So-called Humans were humanimals cohabited by Mental Cells of God, aka COG. The animals remained conscious vessels that tangentially became aware of themselves as separate individual entities. They believed themselves to be what their COG Minds were thinking. They were naturally instinctive but after the Perfect Garden generation ended; their brains remained somewhat smart as a result of some osmotic seepage from their COG benefactors. The once-again humanimals were superficially endowed with some COG qualities when their forms were inhabited (cohabited) and mentally guided by COG. They became able to think in rudimentary ways; apart from their naturally reactive instincts to physical events. When cohabited with COG, they were "Perfect Humans," but much less than perfect with only a tiny "homing soul" onboard, which was the case during the animals' mating cycles, as COG vacated them.

[Those with Yang fused-spirit bodies were referred to as "Sons." Due to polar attraction, they naturally were cohabited by polar opposite Yin Souls. Conversely - Yin "Daughters" attracted polar opposite Yang COG Souls.*

*[Therefore, each Polar opposite Human Garden usually was on a nearby planet, with a Yin or Yang, so-called Guide or Lord. Their necessary mates for physical procreation were untended by COG and were available in both gardens. When mating time came around, Souls would leave their cohabited Humans so that the animals could rejoin their herd for that season. Afterward, the Souls would find their 'homing tiny cells' and return to their co-Creative Humangel Spirit processing. And by the way, Yang Souls never allowed Human

hosts to become impregnated. There were plenty of humanimals already providing new bodies and often more than needed.

[If they shared the same Garden, one can imagine a scenario in which cohabited Yin and Yang Minds might get too close to one another with their host material bodies and just how attractive those fused opposite polar bodies and strong Polar Minds would be to one another. Then - what if they physically mated as animals do? That essentially turned out to be the case with Adam and Eve. They did not understand the so-called "tree of life" was in the center of their personal "gardens" - their physical bodies; and it was that procreation asset of Eve's material form that tempted her to try the instinctive act with the serpent man. Adam was psychologically persuaded by Eve that the experience was 'good fruit' and would not cause death."]

(BB pondered for a moment if he might be repeating something Eno already had covered with Deepy.)

{Slow down, you move too fast
... got to make the moment last
Ain't you got no rhymes for me?
Life, I love you, all is groovy
We're feeling groovy}
Simon & Garfunkel <u>1966</u>

Deepy yowled and tossed back and forth and his eyes popped wide opened. "Damn," he thought, "that was a weird, but funny little dream. Actually, CHIP's chirpy singing is more of a nightmare." He chuckled to himself, rolled over and was plying the ZZZzzzzs again moments later.

"Why did you do that, CHIP? I had our friend in a deep sleep and he was fully locked-in to the story."

"Yep, and that's why I did it, since you wondered if you might be repeating some subject matter. You were. We already covered that with our friend. And too, we both know Deepy's sense of humor, and so he can include this short break in his book if he wishes."

"That's fine. He can decide on that, but I must say you sure made a mess of what Paul Simon wrote and your singing was atrocious, as I'm sure you know by now."

"Sorry, brother buddy, but he's REM snoozing again if you want to sing him a different tune."

"Nah, not really, I was just teasing to see if you would "save the day" for some weary readers who don't see the need for repetition. Okay, I fess up, the devil made me do it."

"Just because you think you're funny, I'm going to advise Deepy to skip all this in his book."

"He won't though because he knows some repetition is relevant and this was, except for the interruption. Now, let's go get a beer."

"Now that's funny," CHIP chuckled, "and good timing since Eno wanted me to get Deepy back at the table pretty soon – but not for that reason, obviously."

"Slow down, you move too fast; got to make the moment last." "Whoa, Simon says" – "Sorry, Paul - about my weird brother here."

"Or it could be my weird sister," one of them said.

Pray for Wisdom, Intelligence, Logic, and Love; so that God's Grace may be added.
IIIIIIIIIIIIIIIII
CHAPTER 12
"The Grace Era"

Eno and Deepy sat back down at the table they had left an hour earlier. Deepy requested a strawberry milkshake. Eno told CHIP he could make that two. That surprised Deepy, as he had never known Eno to drink anything sweet. If he ever had anything, it looked like water or tea with ice cubes. He never ordered food during their lessons. Eno was aware of Deepy's musings, but got down to business.

"The dimension known as the material world is almost drained of all its attainable godly mental resources, except for the relatively few hybrid humans willing to trust God and become one with her, and God already knows who they will be.

"The final time on Earth with Jesus Christ as the principal Co-Creator is right around the corner as far as God is concerned. No matter what transpires - moral progress will be required for those spirit-souls that have survived and reincarnated from previous advanced hybrid civilizations. God judges advancement, based on moral quotients, and this lifetime could very well represent the final opportunity for some to become worthy of one more incarnation with Jesus

Christ in Garden Gaia. That will be the time of judgment for all hybrid souls with outcomes still pending.

"Before this world changes completely to that Othereal, Heavenly One… God must collect the remaining hybrid spirit-soul mates to be co-created as angels. There will be spirit-souls to reincarnate from Earth and purgatory, and possibly a few from the ghostly, spectral realm in order to learn directly from Jesus Christ. This will take place within a one-thousand year "Grace Era" of reincarnations into Garden Gaia. The Era will constitute a time known as "appointed death" to the material world. It will require every hybrid spirit-soul's participation, except for those already adjudged unworthy of a final incarnation.

"All recovered spirit-souls must gradually adapt to the Othereal Body of God Jr by processing through the intermediary purgatory, aka minor heaven that lies within one of the shaded areas between the fused material and Othereal Spirit dimensions. This will be a time to make Soul Mates indivisibly-dual and for learning how to switch polarities. After this internship, eternal Heaven will be the final destination for new Angels."

On that note, Deepy slurped his last bit of milkshake, wishing he had more. Eno then pushed the other shake over to him, saying "I got this for you. CHIP is meeting with the quin now and I knew you would want more."

"Bless you." Deepy unwittingly said, being distracted by his taste buds. "CHIP makes the best milkshakes. Quin Ami's are pretty darn good too."

"Your future writing will consist of much unusual information, some of which may go against the grain of what many people think they already know. However, they don't need to accept it right away, or ever, but God knows who will. We have the privilege of knowing that most of what results from your work here will be recognized to have the best possible intrinsic value to one's potentially eternal life. Even so, some of your readers may never be able to swallow, much less digest, the thoughts we provide, simply because their systems for accepting and ingesting God's Morality are hopelessly jammed by id-ego's mundane material brain processes and constantly interfered with by their sensate tastes."

"Hmmm…slurp…" Deepy was only half-listening, absorbing more sweetness than light. [The Commander knew I would help Deepy later.]

"Just know that thoughts provided by God serve as the only Essence for growing a spirit-mind worthy of Heaven. If any information seems confusing to you, just do your best with it and expect it to become clear later as you pray for guidance, and CHIP comes to your rescue."

Eno paused briefly to see if his friend had questions.

He had a statement, "I know what you just said applies to me as much as anyone, so I will be praying a lot."

"I know you will."

"I just know all this is God's WILL."

Eno smiled at his friendly, furry God creation.

"I know much of this information seems familiar to you but we do repeat some of it, while mixing in a bit of new material.

"In the beginning, the Word "God" as a vibratory sensation was both a thought and a feeling as God awoke from her prior state of what SHE now calls deep sleep. That one "God" Word gave God her Conscious presence and prescience… allowing her to reCOGnize her Self through all her many past singularity states. SHE would then use the Word 'God' as a code vibration to regain her composure following each Big Bang event. SHE sent the Word forth at the exact moment necessary to cause its reverberation throughout her reawakening and expanding universe. Natural elements constituting her Consciousness were reborn each episode, along with memories of her internal life in her singularity states, even if SHE had no need to place a chronological order on each of those states.

"It was in her singular states that SHE formed a language using the many variations of vibratory sensations that sprang from the initial Word Of 'God' that SHE perceived, along with the distinctive vibrations that came along afterward within her Single Mind of dual polarities.

"For eons, God has been able to envision images of her Self in her Imagination and then display them in phases of the Liquid Crystal canvas that is Host to her Child. SHE sees her Self as every self-aware form SHE has ever created throughout the universe, but her favorite Self image is her original Human form, which SHE created for her Children's use.

"You might be surprised to know that with God's Polar help any indivisibly-dual Mind Cell can use his/her own twi-polar powers to attach to virtually any life form. God has little need for this ability, but uses it on occasion. SHE can have a COG peripherally attach to the brain of any animal. Really, you might ask, 'Who is this dog that loves me so much... or cat?' Of course they do love to eat and be loved too, so most of "what you see is what you get" and your pet is not otherworldly; but sometimes attachments are used to help hybrids overcome temporary or even permanent needs. [All that insight gave one human-dog pause to reconsider his paws.]

"God chose the Human shape SHE shares with all her self-imaged, self-aware "be-ins" as the most versatile tool for her polar molded creations. Her Children use the multi-functional human forms in the material realm to help God physically create many structural forms for their use. Many of those forms were first styled in Heaven. All God's favorite Spirit forms are on constant display throughout her Holy G'Host fundament for use by the Children Cells that compose her Child. Those of you who make it to Heaven will be amazed at how areas of it appear to be your, or some other hybrid species,' own material home world.

"Even with all the life SHE co-creates with her Children, God only thinks of her Self as a "prescient presence." SHE senses or feels the Spirit energy that incorporates her. SHE refers to that part of her Spirit energy that comprises her Consciousness, as "Mental." SHE calls her Mental Self, "Mind," and refers to her sensory Spirit Self as "Body." Her Body's dual polar interplay between her Selves and across her Child's Essence is the inter-dimensional attraction that hybrid humans call gravity. SHE calls it "Love." Those polar forces penetrate the Othereal veil between her Child's Heavenly dimensions to also pervade her material realm, which has served as something of a nest egg for God Jr; but is very close to being free now of those who would fly.

"Love is the glue, or polar essence, that holds the two polar halves of God together, through the alternating polarities emitted through her Othereal Child, which has grown between her Selves. God Junior's alternating current energy will hold the Parents both together-and-apart, as necessary to maintain their existence. Effectively, God Jr. serves as a buffer between the Yin/Yang dynamics of the dual Parent Mind. The changing currents within the Cells of Junior's Body keep a predetermined and required distance between the two Minds that operate as a trinity.

"I would ask your future readers to be patient with us, due to this brief repetition, which we don't care to risk as unnecessary for some of them. We will keep it short.

"As entities that are separated from the core of God Mind, Earth's humans must mentally heal or convert themselves to a state of equilibrium with God, in order to create a mutual love attraction. Humangels learn to do this in their transcendental or Angel forms, which allow them to literally switch to either of God's two polarities as called upon by her Mental energy. Earth angels in minor heaven or purgatory get to practice this to perfection.

Eno paused, as if reflecting.

"All humanimal bodies, and of course perfect Humans, originally were created to function perfectly, with proper nutrition and conditioning, and without artificial intervention - whether from genuine science or cockamamie hubris. Every one of the perfect Humans raised in God's Gardens had those natural options for maintaining perfect bodies, and their COG cohabitants made sure they used those assets. Hybrid humans also should become wise enough to choose natural options of diet and exercise for proper maintenance of body and soul, allowing for more precise communion with the Over-Soul. Of course, you would need to return your food, air, water, and general surroundings to more pristine conditions. One way or another, that is going to happen, but many hybrids sadly may never witness it. If that doesn't make you want to cry, you lack wisdom; either that or you're working and praying to see it again as Garden Gaia. That would be wise.

"Much spiritual work, in the form of godly thought, is required of virtually every human being, and is long overdue. Husbands and wives must become gracious, thoughtful partners to the extent that sex is not necessary except for procreation, or other joyful, loving union, free of perverted acts and thoughts. Keep in mind, there never has been a need for sexual activity in Heaven, or even in Perfect Gardens, and no new Angel misses it because it cannot exist as part of God's memories, as it was never held within her Memory in the first place; nor was any type evil, except what is recalled by God's Assembler for karmic purposes.

"There will be no memory or knowledge of any evil among hybrid Cells that attain eternal life within God Jr. That id/ego slate will be wiped clean. You would be extraordinarily wise to begin erasing any immorality now, to the extent that you can. No, it won't be easy, but it must happen for your continued existence as an eternal entity. You must show a willingness to adjust your attitude. It is one measuring device for God's judgment.

"Essentially now, God is whole, as in healed, from her "breach birth" experience and the raising of fused spirit from her material realm. Just as soon as her Spirit-Soul Mind of God Jr officially is completed, following the thousand-year reign of the Lords in all her various Gardens, God will be her Trinity Self forever. Some of you will be there to understand what you have accomplished as a final generation from the material world."

Eno paused... then caught Deepy off guard.

"Where do thoughts come from, my friend?"

Deepy was still sub-thinking about sex and wasn't quite ready for another subject and a test as well, which Eno was using to get him back on track.

"Uh - God?"

"One definitely would hope so. That is the ideal, and is how God intends her Mental Cells to live, keeping her in Mind always. With hybrid humans though, hardly anything ever is ideal. You choose to consider idealism a fanciful dream, with the same old excuse of – 'We're only human after all,' as if God didn't create you for eventual perfection – with her assistance, which some of your egos just cannot abide or appreciate.

"Hybrids help each other think the way they do. While God didn't create any human junk, as some folks like to say, some have turned themselves into trash with the help of many others of you. You tend to think for one another – as you reprocess original, godly thoughts over and over, until they are about as far from godly as they can get. This is known as egodly thinking - wherein one relies on what other people think, rather than what God thinks. That just seems easier and that's how most folks want it of course. They don't need to worship anyone but themselves, or praise or thank anyone but themselves if they so choose. Why bother with prayer and communion, or to trust one's tiny soul to relay godly thoughts?

So much moral thinking would seem strange now to most people, which is quite tragic, but another sign that God's _shades_ (crystal phasing) are shifting into place to close out this realm. For some hybrids, 'Hades' is in sharp focus.

"See you back here in thirty minutes," Eno now told his deep friend.

After a few moments, a chirpy voice wondered if Deepy would like a burger and a shake.

The chirpy one was standing there with a burger and a shake.

"Thank you. I wish I could get this kind of service back home."

"Someday, maybe," CHIP told him.

{Thirty minutes? – no time for a nap - Maybe? - Naah! – He would tough it out, while thinking maybe he should have a cot in his diner, since he didn't want to sleep on the floor like some sort of animal. Slurp - Chomp}

(It wasn't long before he heard the pot calling.
He hurried to his room to answer it.
Being physical was just so gross he thought.)

(CHAPTER 13)
THINK AGAIN!

"In the material world of God's perfect gardens past, when some 'thing' became necessary that was not already a thing, an object to be detected by the senses, it was defined by God's Mental Sense, as a concept to fit God's image of what SHE wanted it to be or represent. After God conceived it, her perfect Human Children created it, whether organic or inorganic. How it looked depended on its function. Now, in God's hybrid world, everything depends on how well her Over-Soul Children can communicate with their cooperative tiny mind mates to get an idea across and some 'thing' created or accomplished, even if it can be converted from good to evil, which of course never happened in Perfect Human times.

"In any case, God began doing what SHE does, through the use of letters and numerals, to make words and numbers, in order to make thoughts, from which concepts can be built, so that hybrids can have a meaningful life, if they follow a moral path.

"Communications depend upon the strength or weakness of each of us when it comes to patience and understanding, in the use of our building blocks of numbers and words for ideas and concepts. Attitude can, and often does, affect communications. Some people who don't understand certain words or thoughts want to blame other people for having that knowledge. They won't take responsibility for not knowing what they are unwilling to appreciate; whereas God says 'I AM the WORD' – meaning SHE is all and ultimate knowledge. That should cause sensible people to understand the importance of the communication concept with thoughts artfully received and graciously perceived, as a primary means of communion.

"Options include math, art, sign language, and of course music, as well as concepts of which hybrids have yet to hear or see, but will - if they ever adjust their attitude regarding moral, hybrid visitors more advanced than Earthites, but who perhaps are not as "pretty" as hybrids think themselves to be. Many, perhaps even a majority of hybrids simply judge other people by the way they look. They cannot seem to conceive of moral "insides." So, you must get over any cynicism you may have pertaining to the words in this book and learn to perceive the goodness in others; regardless of their exterior makeup.

"People with the wrong attitude about education might be willing to let their meager vocabulary get in the way of communicating. Who knows what profound thoughts they might have if they just had the building blocks of myriad words? God... God knows. SHE also knows many such folk do blame others for their own failings. Of course, sometimes Egod has tried, and continues to try, to withhold equal education from certain people or groups. Along with that, apathy has a very strong grip on people's attitudes about so many godly concepts these days; and people do rationalize all sorts of excuses for simply not caring. That is why COG sometimes refer to "Apathy" as the eighth deadly sin. It is on its way to becoming first on that list of eight.

"If you think you do not understand the concepts offered in Deepy's book, you might care enough to swallow some pride and ask someone "wiser than you – God forbid" to help you. There is never time for pride, 'false' or otherwise, so don't risk your eternal life because "man's best friend" failed to commune with you." Eno winked at Deepy while saying, "The two of you may simply be at different word processing levels, through no fault of your own or his. Pointing fingers of blame has become too much a way of life for some. Give it up, as it can be a distraction to the point of being deadly, as politicians have proven time and again. On the other hand, own up to any responsibility you think is yours and correct any situation caused by your words, actions, or inactions. Sometimes you can do it discreetly, unless others need to know. Be totally honest with yourself and others as you know they would expect, and without equivocation.

"And too, it is *not* always a good idea to communicate at the lowest common level IF certain ideas need to be advanced – such as some of those in Deepy's book-to-be. It underscores the overarching importance of a good vocabulary to attain a higher intellectual level of communion. Strive to raise your levels, so that no one else needs lower his or hers. It's a worthwhile, gracious goal."

"May I ask you a question?"

"You know you can and should anytime you wish."

"Please don't take this the wrong way; but do you ever get tired of preaching?"

"Have you learned anything since you've been with us?"

"Of course I have. I've learned more than I could have imagined – a lot of incredibly amazing things."

"Then I guess that makes us "teachers" who seem like preachers because of repetition. A preacher is someone who tells you what you already know or should know. A teacher teaches you new material, so that you become prepared to learn even more new material and can advance from one grade to the next, so to speak. Preachers are mostly well-intended folk who think you should be hearing the same message over and over, just because it doesn't seem to be sinking in and you need to be reminded. Sometimes though, when you are learning new material there is good reason to repeat some of its more difficult aspects. We COG know it is necessary for some folks, but not for others. My brother and sister, Jesus Christ, had amazing new lessons to teach during her earthly sojourn and SHe repeated much of it to her disciples, some of whom never quite seemed to "get it." It can seem as strange as

Cross Wise

learning new pronouns (SHe) that include both polar (aka gender) aspects of a person.

"I know many people can become quite weary of listening – or reading - if that is the case. If you are experiencing that now, we can take a break, just as your readers can and should, anytime they grow weary. Please know repetition of new knowledge is needed for some, while not so much for others. Need a break?"

"Sure, sometimes I do, but I'm okay for now."

"Fair enough, but I will put you in charge of "breaks," so just say "break time," whenever you need to, with no apology necessary - Deal?"

"Thanks, Eno."

"Of course, but no thanks needed, as COG know intentions. Now," Eno smiled at his friend, "I just want to make another point or two.

"Any idea of "talking down" to people is part of a rationale by some folks that slower thinkers might be left behind in their understanding. Those "thinkers," though could be insulted that the person speaking to them might think they should understand what they don't; meaning they think the other person is talking to them differently because they are "stupid." It is a delicate situation because sometimes people can have learning parameters different from what is considered "normal." There are "other," but still valid ways to think. When someone who seems slower - "gets it," he or she might get it at a deeper level than your average learner. They might have more imagination interfering with assumed knowledge. Ingenuity could be at work.

"Then there's the opposite idea that some words or thoughts would be offensive to people who might term so-called intellectuals "*elitists*" and interpret their communication method as a personal "put-down." That also is not a logical way for others to help themselves develop their higher potential. Just don't assume anything if you think you have knowledge or wisdom to impart; but do be patient and insightful in the role of teacher or advisor and even as a student. Hopefully if someone is slow to understand, the problem can be discerned and mitigated. It also could be the teacher is not as "ept" as he or she should be.

"'Ept?' Is that really a word?"

- 211 -

"No, I just wanted to make the point that students should ask questions when in doubt. You might not be the only one not understanding something in particular, so apply the reasoning some folks use: "there are no stupid questions."

"If we were talking childhood learning, there are special-education classes for those who develop slowly. That is a reasonable compromise, but some adult attitudes need to change, so that no one is blamed for being more intelligent than someone else whether receiving the same instructions or not. Raise your Wisdom Quotient (WQ) unless you would be satisfied with a mediocre God. God would not return such sentiment. SHE wants all of you to be much more than mediocre; and Wisdom is one of her Virtues, which means it should be one of yours as well. Just don't ever embarrass yourself or someone else by seeming to flaunt your intelligence (IQ) over theirs or by somehow judging them, since you may not know their precise circumstances. I use the term 'seeming to flaunt,' because you might be surprised to know someone is taking you that way. But, if humility is not part of your character, perhaps you need to practice it more. Humility is vital to being a well-rounded morally intelligent and wise person. Humility ultimately always wins over arrogant intelligence, whether intentional or just seeming to be. Be wise enough to cater to various "quotients."

"Know this: you don't just awaken to understanding the absolute need that society has for moral essence unless you have some fundamental attributes in place, just as God did, so that eventually, through serendipitous orchestration by Mother Nature, God became God over a period of non-time. Then, with the right attitude, SHE taught herself how to learn. Inherently, SHE understands morality as "essential." That's coherence.

"The more complex and well honed your attributes, the more awake you potentially could become, especially if one of your attributes includes the wisdom of prayer. Don't forget to pray for understanding and all aspects of WILL and Grace, and then don't forget to thank God for supplying those needs. SHE will, in accord with your sincerity, appreciation, and efforts.

"Prayer itself is a most fundamental way of proving you at least have an understanding that God does exist, and SHE takes care of her own. But, until you claim her through the

Moral guidance of her Son, or your own O'Soul, SHE will not be able to claim you as a Child. SHE will toss you back into life's "briar patch," where you might survive among a bunch of thorns that stick, scratch and bruise you, even if some of that hurt could equate to growing pains. Too much of it though could kill you.

"There are persons who would proclaim that God and her Children are unworthy of them because their egos tell them they are just too intelligent to believe in something they can't see, in some form that they can't seem to imagine or recognize. They might be intelligent enough to understand the words of this book, but not the essence of its concepts, especially if their character is apathetic. Of course apathy will not have allowed them this far into the book. Therefore, wanting to understand is vital, but it doesn't come easy to arrogant people. If you do not care to understand; then you won't know God as morally essential and you won't be wise, intelligent, logical, and loving in spite of any great secular education. On the other hand, if you are politically ambitious, there may be enough similarly morally uneducated or opinionated voters to elect you; although God won't select you.

"Is that really where some of you wish to leave this matter – as in resolved to "your way of thinking" because you have a deep notion of faith in your ability to think apart from God and to exist forever without her? Your choice is to accept the teachings of God's Children as your own, and as coming from her. SHE then can return that bit of moral wisdom multifold. God helps those who know enough to pray in the name of her Son and Daughter's dual Essence of Jesus and Christ - to confide through them; then ask forgiveness, while striving to live healthier, more moral lives. That's not possible if one is not acquiescent. Your tiny soul must strive to defeat your id/ego – with humility. It can - since you really are this far into such a moral work.

"Jesus Christ and Christ Jesus were both a Son and Daughter of God – in an indivisibly-dual, Yin/Yang material form. What made him a 'Son,' in the material world, rather than a Daughter was simply his outer fused Spirit Yang form. He had to appear in male form then because many men thought women were unworthy of life. That attitude came about because Earth's Humans of the perfect generation were of Yang or male outer essence, with many humanimal females serving merely as procreative mates. That means only male hybrid humans had tiny souls left behind by Humangels. That changed when God transferred many wiser species to Earth from other Gardens.

"On Mars, the opposite was true. "Tares" female or Yin polarities made up most of that human/humanimal population. The humans there had Yang polarity souls. As always, humanimals were soulless. Most humans on either planet had been moved to Earth from the Antares region. A mixture of hybrid human genders was later moved from Mars to Earth, where God was to upgrade all remaining humanimals to accommodate souls. SHE did this through the family of Adam and Eve. Eve was given the first female tiny soul on Earth and she had children who married other humans already there or brought from Mars.

"To repeat an earlier point regarding narrow or stubborn thinking: with mankind's "what you see is what you get" mentality, most humans still judge people by their looks, rather than seeing and considering inner, deeper Spiritual levels. However, such a single aspect as outward appearance applies only to the material world. In his/her primary Heavenly home, both Yin and Yang Essence is intertwined in the form of a Trangel or Angel. That means outer appearance is switchable at God's discretion, so that Jesus just as often appears there as Christ. Either way, SHe* looks virtually identical as male or female. *(reminder: personal pronoun spelling for God's COG or Children Cells)

"It is that outward polarity that makes a Trangel negotiable to a particular Parent's use in drawing it closer or sending it away, as part of the dance that keeps God's dual Minds both together and apart. Never forget, all God's Cells must be alternately dual. It is a Heavenly requirement, so get used to the concept and know it's easy enough to pray in the name of the Child's dual Essence, just by mentioning both names, e.g. Christ Jesus or Jesus Christ. It is time to recognize God as SHE is. Cognize the information in this book and then re-COGnize it, because you once were an integral part of God Mind and could be again.

"Break time," Eno said, "I can sense you are sleepy."

"Do I have time for a nap?"

"We may not meet again today, so plan whatever you wish. If my plans change, I will ruin your plans," Eno winked. I will let you know later when we can meet again."

~~~~~~~~~~~~~~~~~~~~~~~~~~~~~

"CHIP?"

"You rang, Master?"

"CHIP, have you been feeding me "Othereal" food instead of real food?"

"Yea, verily, want to make something of it?"

Deepy had to laugh at CHIP's tough guy posturing. "No," he told him, "I want you to make something of it – a burger, again – and thanks, by the way. I do appreciate you."

"That's good to know. I'll put this box of arsenic back on the shelf."

"You know, CHIP, ol' Buddy Bot," Deepy told him; "You're getting to be fairly funny, for a multi-faceted hunk of crystal or diamond or whatever causes you to gleam and sparkle.

"Ah, you're just saying that because you think I'm precious."

"That's it – end of conversation," Deepy told him, but a moment later was saying, "Er, but I really do love your cooking, so I would request... er, uh... let's see... maybe I will try something different."

He decided to have two burgers, fries, onion rings and a milkshake, while telling himself he would cease and desist allowing his taste buds to control his better judgment, just as soon as he returned to "civilian" life. That came to mind because he had once pictured himself as a "soldier dog" on a heroic mission among alien life forms. He knew for now though that if there really was an alien form around, it was his, until such time he could return to just being Larray, the man – "Thank God." That thought caused him to think more deeply about ultimately returning to his Heavenly Parents, as a Child or Mental Cell of God. He was too humble to allow many such thoughts along those lines though. Besides he wasn't sure he understood everything he was being told. "It's all so deep," he surmised, feeling a tad bit sorry for himself. But that only lasted a couple of moments before he was lost in his taste buds again; slurping - chomping...

IIIIIIIIIIIIIIIIIIII

AND Just Thinking

[Larray "Deepy" James – author-to-be of the material version of this book – ruminated over his meal. CHIP - his Buddy Bot - put these thoughts of his in parentheses, for possible use later by the author.]

(The truth is I've been blessed in so many ways, I wonder if people will understand that I have no ulterior or profit motives for telling anything but the truth as best I can understand it, so help me, God – and quite literally, I think.

(Besides, 'You can't take it with you,' and why would anybody want to make up a story of this magnitude except to help others? No, I just want to tell a godly tale as best I can, with whatever gifts of imagination God has given me. Eno says most of this stuff he's telling me will recur in due time, through the imagination of my real Larray James self. Imagination I know is just one of God's means of communion, if and when used for her purposes. It also can be more important as a godly conduit than most people realize, because such imaginings can equate to reality if they are godly and it's God's will. That is 'co-creativity' that could become reality, but also might not. Everything is God's "call." Even so, I think we should all believe the very best we can imagine about God and ourselves. That is more likely to be the truth than anything else. The truth is what we make it, together with God – again if it's her WILL. With faith, God eventually will show us as much total truth as we can understand at any given time.

(Anyway, I pray the book that CHIP and I will write can enlighten people in ways that could save their lives - their spirit-soul lives for eternity, to serve as new Mental Cells of God Jr. in Heaven. Of course that was always the purpose of the *Bible* too, and the founding of God's churches; so I hope folks will understand this is meant to be a continuation of that type of moral work – even if they allow themselves to refuse believing much of it. I admit some things are hard to believe, especially if you don't believe in the One who could make anything happen.

(I really do think we will be telling God's truth as it needs to be told now, and that SHE will help us in the endeavor. How can I not believe it, since I'm having this crazy, wonderful experience? But I know I would believe it if I was just sitting home reading about all this as someone else's experience. That's just me. Call me gullible if you will – I don't care. I'm just grateful for my imagination and for the fact it is

God focused. Isn't this what all of us should be doing - imagining 'life' in godly ways, since we are said to be created in her image, which also would mean for her purposes? Of course I guess you have to believe that, as I do, to make it work. We just need to get beyond our id/egos which prevent godly thinking, and that's 'much easier said than done' for too many of us, and of course me too at times.

(I truly thank God for letting me know that if I did not believe the Word of God, through Christ... the book we are meant to write would still exist because God would find another person to work with the COG to tell this truth. I mean come on, if you're God and you need to tell a truth that might seem far-fetched, how would you go about it? People have a tendency to shy away from the truth anyway if they don't like it. I expect there will be quite a few who won't like God's truth as we're going to tell it. A lot of people didn't like it when Jesus told the truth either, and they still don't like 'his' truth – not that I'm comparing myself to him – just my belief in his Moral principles, which don't sit well with egodly types.

(I may not know full well who I am, but I do know whom I am not; I'm a long way from being Jesus Christ, which just makes me love him/her all the more. Who knows anyway, besides God - why or how SHE finds whom SHE finds to serve her in a particular project? And while only one hybrid human appears to be writing this book, this human co-author is learning what that truly means – thank God – just as I believe a coterie of Souls is taking part in the Co-Creation of God Jr – meaning I believe what I'm being told here. I hope readers will get the same impression of truth.

(Yes, of course I believe Christian tenets wherever and however expressed. I know some Christians may take exception to the karma and reincarnation aspects of our religion cited here. That's quite all right, so long as they truly know and follow the teachings of Jesus and know He paid their karmic sin debts for them, if they would accept that huge amount of Grace. That's really all a person should need to know to cause them to want to lead a moral life. But then again, too many people are not morally intelligent. They refuse to think deeply, which is not wise at all. They find thinking beyond sensual needs to be unwelcome.

(To me - sitting here in a dog body, the book is <u>not</u> going to seem like a work of fiction, despite the characters and settings. It is only fictional if one cares to view it that way. I believe that God may have declared the truth of the *Bible* and all such moral works '... *in the beginning.*' SHE has no limitations except those we place on her, and that means SHE has no limitations, but we do. We should thank God if we at least know that much. It would be a good starting point for some folks, I imagine. I certainly know that God has shown more faith in me at times than I have in her.)

[Deepy chewed on his thoughts and food a while longer and then got up and left the diner, but not before he took a prayer pause.]

"Dear God: Help the writers write, so that readers will be patient enough to come to understand you better. I pray they also will ask for your guidance as need be, in trying to fathom some of our more abstruse renderings on your behalf. We ask this in the name of Jesus Christ and for his and her sake. Amen."

~~~~~~~~~~~~~~~~~~~~~

Back together now, Eno's pooch pal told him. "I did need that respite, even with the fitful nap I got. Also, I've been thinking," Deepy laughed, and then confided, "There's something I'd like to say to family and friends of mine who might be paying attention to what you've told us, if that's okay?"

"Of course."

"Some of you back home may be shaking your heads in disbelief at the information Eno has put before us. You may be wondering, yet again perhaps, how you ever managed to read this far. Look at it this way; you are blessed with potential. Even so, everything Eno says and will say is true, no matter how many of you consciously experience God's truth as the self you now are. Unfortunately you have an "eject" button labeled 'id/ego' which many of you have come close to pushing or soon may rationalize your way into doing. Try desperately to <u>not</u> do that. I know some of our "group" thinking together back home was not really what I wanted to express and didn't, only because I wanted to fit in with all of you. But now, my "beliefs" are so well-founded that I want you to fit in with me and God, and so from now on I will express myself accordingly. Hopefully you will respect me for it, even if you disagree." Deepy concluded his comments with a sigh and a bowed, shaking head, before wistfully looking up at Eno.

"Well, that was some 'Deep thinking,' my friend, and on God's behalf," Eno said, and then added, "Anyone who wants immortality must understand God's plan and his or her part in it. Adam and Eve institutionalized "Egod" through the serpent id brain of Eve, who then was able to tempt Adam. Since then, mankind's part, or cause, has changed to that of fighting for survival of one's spirit-soul. God knew this was the only plan SHE could activate at the time. It has evolved alongside hybrid evolution. There's hope, but it needs to be in the form of prayer."

IIIIIIIIIIIIIIIIIIIIIIIIIIIII

{CHAPTER 14}
"May I Help?"

"Even though God helps her own, that doesn't always seem to be what SHE is doing. While SHE could temporarily cure you of all the illnesses of your lives, it also would cure you of being you, once you prove to yourself who you are. SHE and you must know the "moral you" capable of becoming her. Not proving yourself is not something SHE can allow. God needs you to voluntarily be you and to remain you by proving yourself to you. SHE already knows whether you will resolve yourself for her. Do you know? If you have read this far, you may be finding out.

"No, you don't want to be an automaton, and so in fact you can only be you by actually living your life as you choose. That is what makes you 'you,' even if you don't become acceptable to God. If you don't choose to live as God lives, then you cannot become* her; and since God will not force you to change, you are the one who must change yourself to be compatible with God. If you are to live with her for eternity, you must change yourself to enhance her. There is no other you than one you help co-create, either with God or Egod. *{complement and enhance God as a Moral Mental Cell}

"God, however, cannot help cure you of any evil aspects of yourself if you won't admit they exist. Without your acknowledgment of her, and your dedication to her, in the fight of your life for your life, SHE cannot help you cure yourself of your id-entity problems for eternity. You can't be her Child unless you enhance her through a self that is co-created by you and her.

"Not only must you recognize needed changes to your character, you must do your part in helping bring them about. Even though you don't currently remember your previous incarnations, the essence you created in each carries over to the next. IF you do manage to help God save you for eternity, then someday SHE will re-member all of your moral, godly essence from each life and you will be made whole. This will make the total and final 'you,' as you will be reunited with family members from prior incarnations who also were 'made whole' within themselves from their previous families. Because you all had different family members from previous lives, essentially God Jr. will be made whole as one godly Brain Child with moral properties from each Cellular life.

"God also wants you to remain you - albeit a voluntarily changed you - so that you will fully appreciate what it took to become the new you. Ultimately you **must** co-create yourselves with God instead of Egod. Your mind **must** become synchronous with God's through your tiny soul and Over-Soul so as to override immoral influences by the superficial world of "appearances." Allow the word "*must*" to inspire, not deter you.

"God will influence you by helping you change your very essence, so that you can define yourself for both you and her. Prove how intelligent you really are – how wise, logical, loving, and how gracious. Overcome this world as Christ did. SHe, of course, never catered to Egod at any time. SHe knew better, so become as SHe was – in this world – but not of it. Become a Child of God.

"God appreciates diversity, but you must be certain you are co-creating yourselves in the moral image of God. God will not force a mind-set on people by overriding the id/ego entity they allow themselves to be. However, immoral character is not acceptable to God. You must learn to stop making yourselves sick. Of course you could be paying off some karmic debt that might require your suffering in specific ways, but with an alternative course of working through it with God. Paying your karmic debt (i.e. living your life) with humility would make it easier and ultimately would garner you some Grace."

Eno chuckled, "I realize all this might seem like a commercial trying to "sell" God to people, but they can "own" her by living up to her, since they are a part of her that will die as her cancer if they don't help her cure them. I guess we could call that a "pushy" sales pitch, except that it is truth, which you must accept or deny. Are you happy to have a choice? We simply want people to understand they have the option of being an eternal part of God by being what SHE can help them become: purely moral.

"God should be promoted, and that is what your book will do, so we don't cast aspersions on anyone who does so honorably. But who are they? Can you ascertain if their messages ring true, as they did with the late, Reverend Billy Graham, or if they might ring much less true with *"the son of a preacher man?"* Can you tell if they ring true, as they do with Dr. Charles Stanley or less true with your personal choice of a Pastor?

"If you don't like *religion*, just forget that word, but don't negate God in the process or her need of your genuine moral essence, so please do show up in a church you like, as often as you can. Most Pastors have godly intentions and some have talent in the way they interpret God's Word. For some others though it's just a business, or perhaps they are training for a political career, which would be okay if they truly promote morality at their core.

"Dear readers," Eno said, "Deepy's book definitely will be somewhat repetitious at times because of new concepts. We know it could make you weary, but no COG is about to apologize for loving you. Even so, if ever you feel harangued, don't give up - just take a break. And, for God's sake, don't let any of this depress you. If you do, it simply means you are not yet enlightened that all this really is not just good, but "Great News."

"It boils down to this: Because God cares so much about saving every potential Mind Cell confused by the chaotic transformation of their separation from her at birth, SHE will allow you to re-create and co-create yourself to mental purity by using _her_ WILL power (Wisdom; Intellect; Logic; Love - plus her Grace) if you would just allow yourself such a blessing through Jesus Christ. That would help fulfill his mission to save you.

"Let's take for example, my Deep friend, the book you will write about God and Egod, and your experiences here with us. There will be persons who dispute that God underwrote your work, and there will be discordant murmurings in one form or another from Egod. There will always be those who condemn godly works. Some can do so quite respectfully and with good, if misguided intentions. God understands and will continue to bless them for their sincerity, just as SHE continued to bless Job of the Old Testament for his loyal sincerity - troubled as he was at times.

"Readers, please understand that the *repetition* in Deepy's book will only be aimed at those of you who don't recognize it as *"love."* You will know it is necessary for those who need it, whether you number among them or not; so don't be insulted on your or their behalf. One who is wise can appreciate the guidance being given. We congratulate those of you who have come this far with us. Maybe your own morality can influence those whom you care most to influence as a role model. If so, you will improve your own chances for God's Grace.

"What would you learn if God did not try to teach you anything, but simply left you to the societal god of man and the vagaries of material life? If religion had never existed to teach morality, you might learn that you would do what many others now are doing to compete for the *'stuff'* of your world, in the here and now of it; and that would be whatever it takes – to include the death-dealing in which many id/egos participate, while, with each passing day, many more consider that to be an option. In fact, if God had never existed, it is likely mankind's evil would have eliminated the species by now, although it still indulges in a slower process of doing exactly that. WHY? It isn't God's choice for mankind, and it doesn't have to be your choice as *politicians – preachers – teachers - psychologists – psychiatrists – moms/dads – or whatever?*

"You can only overcome your ego selves with God's help and in the process you must learn to be humble, if not meek before God, and gracious with your human brothers and sisters. Cooperation and a Moral Essence are fundamental components in the Character Essence of God's Children. These are the same characteristics most parents once appreciated and expected from their children, and so it would be wise, as a potential child of Heavenly Parents if you recognized those traits are good for you. It seems some of you prefer to learn the hard way through suffering caused by ignorance. That makes God's Love tougher and at times unbearable. Can you even bear hearing about it?

"It is tough, but it's also 'Just,' as that too is a godly characteristic. I would say to parents, when it comes to your own children - or anyone's child - physical abuse is psychologically harmful; but so is spoiling a child by not teaching proper behavior. As to the maxim, 'spare the rod - spoil the child,' think of the so-called "rod" as divine and not physical. Verbal lessons based on morality can be used. Be morally prepared to discipline children with practical knowledge as well as ideal wisdom. Take some time to teach them love with morality; and know too that 'shame' can be a teaching tool, so long as you don't scare a child with threats or emotion. In other words, you need to be a role model, so they know what they did is not something a good person would do. Children need to be guided toward morality by following you because you are following God.

"A child's psyche is fragile and can suffer long-term harm imposed by an angry adult from whom he or she expects love. Loving guidance is the answer, so inform and teach the misguided. If God allowed her Self to become angry with humans, there likely would be no hybrid humans. Instead SHE tries to guide them. People really still need to learn the lesson that *'shame before God'* should logically teach WILL and grace. But they have to first believe there is a Perfect God who would teach them. As for God's Justice, SHE has her law of Karma, but it is not for innocent, immature children. It's a teaching tool that God uses with more mature humans who are ignorant and not innocent.

"Unfortunately though, it appears that too many children are becoming more demanding of some material means to happiness, whether such means are conducive to high moral standards or not. All too many parents simply give in to their children, sometimes through a sense of guilt for not spending enough loving time with them. Effectively, buying their love with more stuff, means spoiling them in a way that can ruin their adult lives through fostering a view of this being a strictly material world. Teach them about a better world with God. That's the goal we COG have with many hybrid *adult* children.

"Too many kids are in competition with their peers regarding who has 'what' and how much of it. Who teaches them to think that way? Simply growing up in mankind's society has become the same rat race for some children as for their parents. More stuff with the most preferred brand names seems to be the answer for the competitive, oftentimes, greedy nature of people. And advertisers know this and foster it. They have become quite savvy taking aim at whichever audience they target for ready and willing id/egos."

Looking squarely at Deepy, Eno said, "God has an end in store for Egod's greed. Your book, my friend, will be a forewarning of what is coming for your vain society." Eno made that stern avowal without emotion. In fact, Deepy knew COG never were possessed by emotion. Even empathy was not a "pity party,' but rather part of God's 'WILL and Grace' conceptual thought process.

"I sure don't want to be counted as part of Egod," Deepy mumbled... before speaking loud and clear: "People who do moral good, usually have been trained from childhood to rely on their inherent goodness and to recognize its intrinsic value for making a better world. Even so, personal egos and society's Egod are making it more difficult for loving parents to raise their children in moral ways when there are so many, ever-growing immoral distractions."

"Well said, and I couldn't agree more," Eno told him. "Please continue."

Encouraged by his Mentor, Deepy went on, "It is best to teach by example, but it is quite all right for children to occasionally be in awe of one or both parents who can be sternly moral enough to teach them disappointment for not meeting the high expectations of people who love and respect them for their goodness and who are there to protect them. They must know that correcting them is part of love and protection, and know it also is your duty as a parent to chastise them when necessary. You must tell them each time why it is necessary. Reaching out to them with moral lessons could be most beneficial, if kids come to view shame as a form of teaching personal responsibility for their thoughts and actions. Just be sure you're setting good examples and are not hypocritical."

Deepy looked at Eno, who again encouraged him.

"Kids should not fear admonishment but should expect to be cautioned by simple, firm disapproval, when that is called for by especially loving parents who are good role models. If children feel loved, their occasional burden of shame is not debilitating, but rather enables them to be guided by someone they don't want to disappoint. As they grow older they will realize their parents cared enough to practice some tough love, while guiding them down a Moral path rather than Egod's immoral one."

Deepy's 'shame sermon' got the better of him and caused him to sigh heavily at this point, so Eno took up the refrain from his student.

"Child-rearing has changed considerably, along with core moral values in today's selfish society. Some parents now even rationalize their child's stubborn ego individuality as an expression of their child's uniqueness of personality, while blinded to the fact their child simply might be just another misguided or unguided spirit, some of whom are bullies. Bullying can be caused by not enough love and moral mentoring from parents and teachers. In fact some parents think their bully kids are just being tough, and so they often accept the child's unverified story about what actually might have happened. If lies are unknown but accepted, more lies will be forthcoming in other circumstances.

"Nowadays, many parents don't want their children corrected by other adults – not even teachers – perhaps because of the guilt they feel in not doing it themselves, or because of the id/ego self-righteous protective mechanism of knowing what is best for "their" child. They don't want their personal power of raising a child their way taken from them, even if the child could otherwise have been helped. In other words, they effectually are saying, 'mind your own business, while we - "my" kid, along with Egod and I do things my way.' In effect: 'I own this child – so butt out,' because I know he or she is living in a bad "village," and I know what to do about it. Oftentimes those parents can be right about that 'village' aspect, which hopefully means they are trying to teach morality, and simply are being misunderstood, or they need guidance regarding a better way. Moral adults should always work together on behalf of all children.

"Parents who truly love their children, will find the time and patience to raise them using God's Wisdom, Intelligence, Logic, Love, and as much grace as they can muster toward everyone around them. Hopefully they ask for God's help through prayer, as well as for human help through compassion. They should begin early to teach their child respect for adults, while they engender in them their own moral traits, which should include those godly ones just mentioned, as well as sub-traits such as… honesty, humility, patience, kindness, gentleness, and just plain common decency toward everyone. At this stage of mankind's history, after all you have been through, there simply is no excuse for remaining ignorant or apathetic about the need of morality as a means to ultimate survival for each soul out there.

"Unfortunately, some time ago, many parents had to renege somewhat on their responsibility to their children because just "making a living" was forced on them by the greed of Egod, who wanted more work in exchange for longer hours and less pay. Outsourcing jobs to cheap foreign labor also became one way of achieving that. In Japan, for example, people literally have worked themselves to suicide for their capitalistic bosses.

"Greed has no shame in causing people to take their lives, or allowing a virus pandemic to do so, while Egod, as personalities are worshipped.

"It also might have been much better for children, had women not been so dependent on men for their self-esteem. Too many of them found little self-worth in parenting, cooking, and house-keeping, but it wasn't because they did not value those needs. It was for a variety of reasons that women became more anxious to share what was deemed a man's world. In some cases they simply had no choice as sole provider for their children. Others no longer wanted to entirely depend on men for all things monetary. That was especially true because men in general often reminded them they would have nothing if it were not for their devoted working man, even those who stooped to domestic abuse.

"How could such dependency and disrespect sit well with anyone? It couldn't. It didn't. Things changed, but kids also paid a price, and yet women's roles were bound to evolve in the modern world. Even so, most women still sacrifice as much as they can for their children. This rhetoric is not meant to disparage women, but rather those men who still feel superior and who always would cause women to sacrifice if they had their way. Most women are psychologically stronger than most men, and so they manage under diverse, even adverse, circumstances.

"Women often were given little or no credit for their heavy responsibilities centered on child-rearing and house-keeping. That provided extra impetus for women to get out of the house for what they viewed as a more independent life. Some also wanted to show they had, or could learn talents and skills to prove themselves *'equal to'* or *'better than'* some patronizing men. They had something to prove, and even now that remains a challenge in any number of areas.

"Many women hated the dependency required by not having their own source and amount of earned income, and of course some women had children but no help mate, and so had no choice but to work. It's doubtful any such working women ever intended to somehow reprioritize their children's well-being due to short-sighted envy of men, or pride. There could have been a few, but it also is true that no person really wants to feel dependent on anyone else, especially an unhelpful, critical, or even abusive partner. On the other hand, children cannot help but be dependent. Very few mothers will let them go unloved. Dads also love their children; but one, if not both parents, still have to fight a greedy Egod, which means less time with the kids.

"Still and all, envy, pride and other egoistic feelings can be killer sins, as shown by the number of abortions taken by working women or single women not wanting to change life styles so important to them. Pregnancy often is rationalized by some women as unfair because they want to stay creative outside the home. It's as if they would take no responsibility for becoming pregnant. Times have changed and so have people, but often in ways harmful to them or others, especially to children, which eventually means to all society. It would appear Egod is winning; God losing and that is true for some people.

"Even so, we are mindful of the vital parable regarding judgment: 'Discern character; shun evil; but judge not; that's God's job.' God will judge you for judging others. SHE, not you, knows all the circumstances for people's decisions and they vary.

"I also would say what you and many like-minded people believe and that is: "Thou shalt not kill;" Also, 'judge not, lest ye be judged,' meaning women should retain the 'right to choose' to have an abortion, because it is obvious that God ultimately will judge them and those who assist them, just as SHE judges all humans – on a personal "one on one" basis, because circumstances are individualized and one's whole life must be weighed in God's judgment. People don't need a "hunt them down" mentality that punishes women according to their own opposing wills or opinions. But that seems to be what the situation with abortion has come to. This is an issue that is ensconced in politics and nearly always has been. Those same persons who bring up this subject around election time do not bother to pass stricter gun laws when little children or teenagers, or people sitting in church praying, or attending concerts or whatever are torn apart by very powerful military weapons.

"Many politicians take so much money from gun-rights activists that they cannot allow too much weeping and mourning over those who lose their supposedly precious lives in such hideous ways – more hideous than abortions and more acutely traumatizing to the family and friend survivors. It is good to have the 'hunt them down' mentality in those cases and new stricter gun laws should be passed every time criminal killers take more than one life with a gun.

Eno continued, "That is worth keeping in mind when you might wish to judge women who elect to deal with their bodies and even their mental health by having an abortion. Allow them their choice and allow God to do her job of judging them and their helpers in that regard. God knows all circumstances regarding a woman's decision to have an abortion – even some that the women themselves may not know. God might know and help them rationalize what turns out to be the right decision for them for whatever reason. A soul is not lost to God even if a human fetus is caused to die. God retains that soul for use elsewhere as SHE chooses. No, that fact is not a rationale for abortions. Simply trust God to do her job of judging people.

"A woman's so-called "right to choose" what to do with her body is just one other human decision that must be weighed as morally right or wrong by God and not by another human. Abortion doesn't necessarily come under the commandment, *'Thou shalt not kill.'* That caveat though is not a license permitting abortion, but every woman will know extenuating circumstances for which she is willing to put her own soul on the line for God's judgment. Each case can be its own manifestation of morality or immorality. Allow God to take on the awesome responsibility of 'judgment.'

"Mankind has made other laws based on moral beliefs and rightly so. Therefore, if an otherwise safe, legal abortion can be humanly rationalized as patently more unfair to a mother than to a normally developed fetus beyond – for example - a trimester, then a law specific to that circumstance could be passed, to include a trial and, at most, a nine-month sentence of working in an orphanage or another exclusive "human rights" facility. Who wants to take on God's judgment of such situations, or put women's and fetuses' lives in danger by way of illegal, unsafe abortions? Everyone is up for God's judgment at some point. YOU are not God.

"That being said, however, mankind should not punish a woman too harshly, if at all, for how she uses her God-given body. God will take all her circumstances into consideration and judge her; but a human court ruling might be part of that judgment. Study the issue; debate it; and pray about it, but stop using the issue for political purposes. It is a moral issue. Just know that God can remove a soul from anyone at any time and so, as I said, that soul is not lost to God, even as a 'body' dies. Any of you who really know God, know that what I'm telling you is true.

"As to having an unwanted child, adoption arrangements can be made for the baby, as some women cannot have their own. Perhaps some churches can morally justify orphanages with nurseries and moral, loving caretakers. Perhaps the ever-growing hate cults could return their attention to a loving God while caring for children in orphanages. Such a turn would require some so-called 'Evangelicals' to recognize that God is not political.

"Is life fair? That can depend on one's mind-set regarding the ability to think morally and rationally. Life obviously can be tough, but that's not God's fault. SHE will never be off-the-mark with her Essence. Remember this: God gets credit for all good; mankind gets blame for all evil – simply because God creates no evil. That essentially is the lesson to be taken from the garden of Eden. If you don't understand, it's because you don't care to. Morality can help one rationalize and adjust to life in a godly manner; especially if one understands God's law of karma, her remedial reincarnation, and her empathetic Grace."

When Eno paused, Deepy rendered a long sigh and let him know, "I'm glad I didn't need to say any of that, but I'm happy you spoke up for the rights of the unborn – and women too, for that matter. That said, I expect some women are not happy with you - even though from the outset of my time here I learned that there is no so-called "glass ceiling" for women when it comes to God. Women in the material world refer to breaking the "glass ceiling" as their objective, when it comes to having equal rights with men. I wonder how many women have noticed or even care that a Yin, Mother God is equal to a Yang, Father God. I wonder more though how many men have taken notice. All hybrids, men and women, are equal in God's sight and one might expect that to include fetuses of a certain age. On the other hand, I know God's truth ultimately wins out, even when disputed. But, if people dispute it belligerently enough, karma takes over in the case of faulty judgment. That is why God ultimately is the One to Judge."

"You're right," Eno agreed. "'Life trumps death' and humans don't give life; God does, just as SHE gave each set of parents their own lives. The fact remains that women and men should take precautions, including abstention, to prevent unwanted pregnancies. They both otherwise will answer to God for wrong decisions regarding abortions, as will those who assist them. Men often are negligent in birth control. Wise planning and abstention should rule romance. Heat from lust should not.

"Parenting also is a matter for two and therefore the responsibility of mom and dad. Many though, rationalize their way into allowing "society at large" to raise their kids, because generally speaking, many employers haven't been benevolent as regards parental priorities. Society fortunately is coming to understand this and many employers are changing. Many more now are trying to accommodate women during and after pregnancy. In the past, a lot of businesses didn't want pregnant women working for myriad reasons – some valid, some not.

"Making a *'living'* has demanded more parental time be taken from kids who are then raised through whatever forces might intervene, such as parental immaturity; surrogate irresponsibility; peer pressure; electronic or other media nonsense; and a host of other unwelcome influences. Some tired parents have the attitude of "kids, I'm just too tired to do anything but watch TV right now. But you know I love you."

Deepy interjected, "That may qualify as misguided love, but it also meets the test of ignorance and denial of morality by those who don't provide jobs at livable wages, but instead hire more part-time workers with few to no benefits, while those same working parents must find second or third jobs to make ends meet, and with little or no time left for family. Shame extends to capitalistic as well as egoistical greed. A fair minimum wage must keep up with the economic times."

"It doesn't help," "if some people hold the world view that there's only one life and every smarter, more competitive person is going to win out, while everybody else will be okay if they just say they love Jesus. The latter of course is true if those *'Jesus-loving'* folk are totally sincere; in which case they ultimately will be the ones who win eternity through morality.

"What it comes down to is this: everyone – employers and workers alike must show they care about all children – born or unborn - because those kids are society not that many years down the road. However, with societal mores and attitudes being what they now are – no one needs wonder why kids are taking drugs, having sex, and becoming killers – even of themselves. The reasons why are as obvious as those heads buried in the apathy of vanity and selfish living – to include greed and power. Don't sacrifice kids. Love them like there's no tomorrow, because some day, and relatively soon - there won't be – unless you and those you love survive this ever-growing more hateful, immoral world."

IS THIS A GOOD TIME TO PRAY? ANYTIME IS GOOD!
[CHIP Note: That was <u>then</u>, and this would be '<u>now</u>'.]

(CHAPTER 15)
The End is Always Near
Eternity is now and always!

This day seemed rather like an illusion to Deepy. It had somewhat of a surreal quality to it. First off, he had awakened from his nap with the strangest fragments of a dream – that he had been married to Shel in a previous lifetime. And, he was somewhat confused about what he had done with yesterday. He remembered Saturday just fine, but yesterday, was a blur. He thought he had spent most of the day in his room reading and napping. It was an Eno assignment. CHIP had programmed some books and other material about UFOs into his compod... very fascinating stuff and Deepy could recall a lot of it vividly.

"Oh, well," he now mused, "I don't even know who I am half the time, much less what I'm doing."

What he also could not recall at the moment was where he had gotten much of the information he had passed along to the tinys today – but even more worrisome was the fact the entire fleet had been tuned in via what he called TelepVision. He wondered why he couldn't seem to stick to his prepared text. He couldn't resist the urge to stray, and he knew that what he said always seemed right *'at the time.'* In fact, at times, he had felt as though he might be Eno standing up there, reaching out to the world. Still, for the life of him, he just couldn't remember anyone ever telling him some of those things he talked about. All he knew was that CHIP told him afterward that he had made certain alterations – nothing serious - so as not to confuse the tinys. CHIP said he would provide Dr. Dog with a transcript for his edification.

"Edification...? Ha!" Deepy thought. But then he thought, "Why not?" God intends for all her words to be used by people who care to be intelligent enough to know their meaning. "God's certainly not stupid and we are made in her image, so..." his thought trailed off. He shrugged. He knew what he meant. He usually stated the obvious to himself, but he was trying to overcome that useless habit.

Before class, he had asked CHIP to let Shel know he would be having a late lunch, in case she wanted to join him. According to CHIP, She had returned to the ship the previous night from wherever she had been.

Five hours and twenty minutes later, he was on his way to the diner to have dinner with her. He had canceled lunch right after class, opting for a long nap instead. She had called him right after class to tell him 'nice job'. Now he was lost in thought again. He began to worry about everything that was taking place. A sense of foreboding swept over him. Anyway, it's something to talk about over dinner, and it beats fantasies of being married to a shipmate you shouldn't be dreaming about. I am a married dog... just because I don't remember CeCe doesn't mean she's not waiting for her old pooch to return. So, I sure don't need to be playing mind games with... a younger woman? Wish I could remember what CeCe looks like. All I have are pictures of Shel in my head – shame, shame.

But, it's not my fault," he reasoned, "that my memory's all screwed up. And it wouldn't even be fair to blame CHIP, I don't suppose." He halfway expected CHIP to butt in at that point, but he didn't.

Deepy was surprised to see Shel waiting for him for a change. "First time for everything," he thought, quite tritely.

"Hope you don't mind," she said. "CHIP assured me he could start the song from the top for you, if you wished."

"Huh? Oh. It is one of my favorites, but then, they all are." Shel had been listening to Paul Anka. "No need to start it over. I'm glad you're entertained. Have you ordered yet?"

"I'm not hungry - just having some tea."

"Didn't anybody ever tell you, you can eat strictly for your taste buds here? All CHIP's recipes come from the same low-fat stock of seaweed, I do believe."

"I'll just have my usual a little later. Hard to imagine, isn't it, that I actually like the taste of salad?"

"What? Speaking of seaweed?"

Shel ignored that. She just sat there with a big grin on her pretty face.

"My, but aren't we beaming today? Your secret outing yesterday must have been quite relaxing. You look even happier than you normally do, if that's possible, for a perennial sunbeam." Deepy said this, realizing how silly it must sound. He blamed it on the "groggies."

Shel ignored the 'secret outing' remark, "Just sitting here reliving my weekend - Did you enjoy our picnics as much as I did?" Shel smiled and arched an eyebrow.

"Nics," did you say - as in more than one? I enjoyed our Greece episode immensely, except for perhaps you know who. But, if we had another 'nic,' I don't recall, Ce – er, Shel... sorry, seems I've had CeCe on my mind... straining for memories, I guess, 'cause she seems mixed in with you and all the UFO material I've been reading, all day yesterday, in fact. It's so weird though that I can't recall what she looks like, unless she looks exactly like you; but I can't imagine anyone so pretty marrying a dog like me. And really I don't recall what I look like as a man."

"Thanks, but you just want me to say you're beautiful inside. No doubt she loves you for who you are as a person."

"And what about your Sunday?" he asked, trying to prod some tidbit of information from her. "Take a day off, did you? – go out and get drunk or something?" Deepy realized he was making some fairly inane conversation.

Shel's face, Deepy noticed, had gone from quizzical to a smile, while he was speaking, and now she was laughing out loud, causing him to say, "Hey, I've been a bit worried about you."

"Now, you know that project I'm working on with Eno is something we can't talk about just yet, but you will hear about it in time to include it in your future book if you wish. And this evening I'm helping Eno prepare for the next phase of our "little secret," or did I tell you that already?"

But Deepy was just half listening. He was too self-absorbed. "I'm not sure. Man, I was so tired when I woke up this morning, like I had been on a binge myself and it has been years since this old pooch had more than a couple of beers. Come to think of it... I'm still not energized. I think I'll have a burger and go back to my room for another nap. I sure can't think straight. I do know that. Please forgive me; I'm not very good company right now."

"I always enjoy you, and not to worry; you'll be fine. Maybe you just had too much Shrimp Creole last night."

"Honestly, I don't even remember eating yesterday, if you can feature that, although I should be able to remember if I had my favorite meal last night. On the other hand, the way my memory's been acting up lately – apparently not. I'm going to have to talk to CHIP about this 'memory' thing."

"Forgive me for interrupting," CHIP broke in, "but Dr. Mai wants me to inform you, Deepy, that something has come up and he needs to change the schedule. He wants to have a session with you in half an hour."

"I had something I wanted to ask you, CHIP, but now I can't remember what it was," Deepy winked at Shel. "Thanks for the message, CHIPster. Half an hour," he repeated, "Okay then."

"Are you ready to order now?" CHIP was all business.

"Just a burger with fries, please," Deepy responded. "Better give me some onion rings with that too, I guess. Well, there goes my nap," Deepy muttered. "Oh, CHIP – send me a big bowl of caffeine too. Thanks."

Shel poured herself a little more tea from her pot.

"Having memory problems, eh? I mean worse than usual."

"Oh God, yes," Deepy groaned, "and I'm really worried about what I might have said to the tinys and the entire fleet of ships this morning." He went on to explain to Shel his day thus far, wondering if maybe that's why Eno wanted to see him sooner, even though Shel said she watched his class and he did just fine.

~~~~~~~~~~~~~~~~~~~~~~~~~~~~~~~

Deepy was sitting at a corner table in the diner, across from Eno, who had already reassured him that CHIP had smoothed over the morning lesson with the tinys, so not to worry. They had just sat down to enjoy a more relaxed setting for Deepy's informal discussion with Eno on lesson plans to come.

"Eno," Deepy finally said, since his Mentor seemed to be preoccupied with a nearby wall, "What about cats?"

"Cats?" Eno swiveled his chair slightly to face his friend, "Oh, I pre-read you - no need to explain."

"How do you do that, Eno?"

Eno had already said, "No, we..." but now paused for a moment, "It's because I am so close to you, Deep; close enough to pick up thoughts coming to you or from you."

"Thoughts coming to me... wow, you mean from God? How close do we have to be?"

"Ah, I see what you're thinking, Deep. No, not like that, not physically close, but spiritually close," Eno answered. "You know the expression of being on the same wave link – it's something like that, but I suppose you know not all your thoughts come from God... not yet anyway."

"Oh yeah, right... yeah I do know I'm not perfect by any means and some of my thoughts are rehashed through society; even sometimes perverted by that bogyman, Egod," Deepy mulled in acknowledgment, not really wanting to change the subject from cats.

Eno laughed. "That's true," he said, "Oftentimes your temporary CHIP O-Soul allows you to recall some of Larray's memories. Mostly though, for your time with us here, you are granted thoughts to help you construct a dialog that will be especially meaningful to your future readers."

"That explains why I'm not nearly as smart as my ego would sometimes have me believe."

Eno ignored that. "No... Deep, to answer your question, we don't have any cat projects, at least not yet.

Funny you should ask though, as we are researching the matter at the moment. Being a cat lover, you have probably noticed that cats are very skittish, easily startled creatures. That, of course, is instinct, based on mistrust or fear. You know how sensitive your own human spirit is to what we do here. We don't know that you could take the pressure of being connected to a cat's instinctual sensitivity, rather than that of the more trusting dog. Still," Eno concluded, "we're looking into it, and perhaps we will try a cat, if we feel the need is great enough to override or amend some of the cat's nature.

"Now," Eno continued, "your other question reminds me of a system God has for pre-reading her Children's intentions. Intuition, or direct perception of truth, is something that God has relied on a great deal since her chaotic troubles caused by all her 'Big Bang' events. SHE has needed to establish systems to commune with her Children in both the material and Othereal realms of her universal fields. SHE uses her systems to commune more precisely, while they also serve as something of an early warning device. God can telep thought signals to COG after reading, or even intuiting, the intentions of each, through a process we call correlative collaboration, or C-C for short." Eno paused and chuckled as Deepy expressed in a hushed tone, "Huh?" as his own 'CeCe' had come to mind.

"First let me clarify that God warps the fabric of space-time through the use of Othereal crystal prisms with shades or phases that fluctuate into microwaves, according to God's need in sending specific thoughts or thought patterns to individuals or groups close to or directly in the material realm... whether to COG operating in Human forms or even Over-Souls in touch with tiny spirit-souls. Essentially it is telepathy."

"Whoa, I'm afraid I didn't quite absorb all of that."

"It was a mouthful. Let's try it again." Eno then repeated it verbatim.

Deepy was still trying to make it make sense, when Eno said, "Moving right along, God's Othereal Body *'Host'* always acts as her medium for moving thoughts around within areas of her Otherealm that coordinate directly with material realm outposts. Some of her thoughts are meant for material world operations, with her irradiative prisms serving as transmitters for communion."

Deepy put his head on the table as if to say "... This is all too much."

Eno didn't let up, so Deepy perked up. He had to stay tuned, figuring that CHIP might help him out later.

"God usually just provides Othereal Humangels and COG Souls specific thoughts that are to be shared among themselves. Every Soul will have a whole library of such thoughts in reserve at any given time, for recalculation and use as needed.

"God also always knows ahead of time just which thoughts a hybrid human will "check out" of either his or her Over-Soul's library or Egod's library, and any use that will be made of those thoughts. But, of course, because of the Earthite human's artful dodger willfulness - aka 'freedom of choice' - much of hybrid thinking is flat-out immoral and therefore censored by the tiny soul or O'Soul, so that God is not subjected to it directly. All too often, a hybrid's mind is consumed with the regurgitated thoughts of society... usually enough to make them sick... literally, both physically and psychologically. On the other hand, godly thoughts are always healthy and life sustaining, but one must specifically seek them through right living and practiced communion with one's O'Soul.

"As to the "C-C" or correlative collaboration process... God keeps in Mind a memory base of each individual COG life, since each COG is in fact a Cell of God Mind. We are Mental Cells, and our entire record of service to God-Mind is contained within God's memory. God remembers the work SHE has done through each of us, and her memory is perfect, so SHE can pre-read us quite well and nearly always knows which of her thoughts we will select. SHE offers us choices in order to give us guidance prior to major decisions and we don't take it personally, of course, since it is God reading God. SHE also does this with the Over-Soul Children and Humangels who make up a network of so-called guardian Angels giving guidance to all hybrid human spirit-soul mind mates who seek it. There are many throughout the universal fields.

"God always tends to mitigate imperfection, especially of the magnitude that has caused so much suffering for mankind. God does this even though most of Earth's humans never seem to understand when Grace and mercy are bestowed upon them. So many are arrogant and consider themselves to be self-made in terms of their perceived material success and thinking ability. So, rather than giving a moral "hand-up" to those they judge as less worthy, they often just ignore them or blame them. That also is a way of implicitly judging God, and then blaming and/or ignoring her. Ignorance and judgment are serious violations of grace.

"God expects and needs her potential children among human beings to finally awaken to their true purpose and to use their co-creative abilities toward those ideals that will benefit God in both the Othereal and material dimensions. Of course, that would mean doing only good works, just as all Cells of God do. Obviously, SHE wants all of you to have all her attributes and develop them to perfection. You will only receive the Grace of God's remaining "matter of time" to accomplish that, so you must accept the moral way as your path through life, without excuses.

"God's attributes are essential in order for any Cell to function as an eternal element of God. For hybrid humans who become angels, those attributes will turn into virtuous, moral essence, as they proceed through the angel hierarchy, homeward bound to their Parents, as part of God Jr.

"God for a little while longer will continue to expand the Consciousness of her main Mental lobes at each side of Junior. We are talking quantity, not quality. Perfect is perfect. Her Essence is always perfect, but her Mental energy continues to expand at the outer limits of her twi-polarized Minds. That also means dark energy and matter will, at some point, envelop and transform the material world into G'Host Spirit, discounting tiny spirit-souls that attain Consciousness as part of God Mind."

"I would ask you to repeat some of that, along with just about everything else I've heard since coming here," Deepy now told Eno, "but I'm afraid I still might not understand it all; so I will just spend more time later with CHIP - my facilitator mentor. I'm sorry, Eno, but I just cannot seem to think straight today."

Eno acknowledged Deepy with a quick nod and smile. He knew that most Earthite humans would need to spend more time with their 'tiny' soul facilitators and their Holy Spirit Over-Soul Mentors - if they were to understand much of this same information. Then again, so many unfortunately might not have the wisdom and patience to understand and appreciate the concepts explained in Deepy's book to be.

"God can do anything and SHE does know everything there is to know, because SHE is the Sum of all power and knowledge. While her Omniscient, Mental energy forms are eternal, they do not represent a static God, as the 'be-all, end-all' of her Self. SHE long ago conceived of a much faster way to separate annihilated Mental Spirit from former non-Mental Spirit. That, as well as her ability to absorb and transmute more energy from the Cosmos outside her Self also means an expanding God. God will continue to grow in her perfection, not in Essence, but through converting materials into Spirit from outside her Main Minds. SHE can refine new Spirit into Mental energy and Moral Essence. A "more perfect" God just means more of her. Otherwise the term is a misnomer. If anyone or anything is perfect, it can never be 'more perfect.' Perfect is perfect."

Eno paused and Deepy told him, "All that is more than amazing. In fact it's mind-boggling," Deepy reflected for a moment, and then said, "I was wondering - are all COG alike?"

"Essentially... but there is a notable mixture difference between Trangels [mostly liquid crystal within] and even more so within Pure Spirit Mental Cells that spin within God's dual Parental Minds. There is a moderate amount of liquid crystal in Othereal Angels of Human origin, but only a 'tiny' amount in the relatively few hybrids who become angels.

"God, in all her forms, works on all manner of ideals or concepts virtually all at once and all of her time. SHE can do this because 'time' is of no consequence to her processes, except momentarily in her material realm. Also, God really is a triune Entity, when one considers her Brain CHILD* or Mental Cells of *'Crystal Held In Liquid Display' in God Jr.

"Some COG, such as Over-Souls, or those onboard our fleet of ships, are missionary Cells in this material realm of God's existence. That means we get precognitive input of activities from everywhere. When we relay information of impending hybrid processes or proceedings, we also include any of our own co-creative thoughts we think might be helpful. But here is what you might call a paradox; since the COG essentially are 'ONE' with God and instantly share all thoughts as a conglomeration, it can be said simply that God really is doing all the thinking. That being the case, I guess we only think we are thinking. That's a joke," Eno stated, while chuckling slightly.

Deepy couldn't help but laugh too, partly since it was rare for Eno to tell a 'joke,' as he called it, even though Deepy thought that particular joke also might apply to hybrids who subscribed only to Egod's rote and unoriginal thinking. They also only think they are thinking since so many of them provide no godly co-creativity whatsoever. Anyone with moral sense would not care to think evil thoughts, knowing such thinking could cost their eternal life? It did tickle Deepy to think of God somehow laughing through Eno, or any of her Children, for that matter.

Having read Deepy's thoughts, Eno said, "Very astute of you to make that correlation, and I'm glad you were tickled.

"There often is much irony in the way God's Mind functions, as it would seem that COG are interdependent Cells of God Mind that act independently, while instantly being absorbed by the whole. It would be as though you knew every thought that every human is thinking at the instant realized. Of course that makes the totality of God Consciousness precognitive, because of Correlative Collaboration, and that makes for some awesome Parents, Brothers, and Sisters.

"Now then, I would like to point out we all think for, and through, ourselves, including humans. God depends on us to do that, in case we and SHE wish to be Co-Creative.

"Sadly," Eno continued in a more somber vein, "carried to the dense mental level of Earthite humans, other things come into the thinking equation - one being id, as in the case of 'libido' being influenced by ego; and ego itself, as greatly influenced by id's numerous alterations through the societal 'Egod.' For most humans, these influences of a phony god, whom they seem to worship, far outweigh those of God. But God is able to keep such evil or confused thoughts in context, thanks to our collaboration. Of course there are some human thoughts SHE will not accept in any context. When we COG are back with her permanently, we no longer will remember anything that SHE doesn't want to know – anything immoral.

"Even with everything that's going on, COG actually do much more casual thinking than what our so-called 'work' requires of us. Yes, we do get time off for our own personal lives and thinking. Most of our work and thinking is based in creativity, and so for us it's all pleasure, except for the mental anguish we experience through humans. And we constantly share any moral Co-creativity. God has never been left "out of the loop" because God is the 'loop;' meaning so are we, since it takes all of us to make God's connections. Yes, you could say God has lots of riders on a "merry-go-round" that never stops. But, we all constitute One God... sharing all the same Virtues of her perfect Morality of WILL and Grace, and it is a very merry ride."

"How do COG and God think while at the same time receiving the thoughts of every other Cell? That would seem impossible."

"You said the key word – "time," as there is none for us, except as it applies to the material world. But, perhaps I should clarify that not all God's Cells are on the same 'merry-go-round.' SHE has multiple 'merry-go-rounds,' because SHE has innumerable separate projects going on, with specific Cells assigned to the tasks involved. SHE can absorb every bit of information that comes her way, since SHE compartmentalizes it and has perfect memory.

"God always has the right answers and only hybrid humans would risk their eternal lives to prove they can do without her input of shared moral thinking. Of course, most hybrid humans don't cognize or recognize requirements from God. It is because of id, ego, and Egod, that most humans are not even close to quin angel status, let alone that of Humangels and COG. They simply do not know God – at least not as we now are praying to introduce her to them through your book – at least those with minds willing to understand. The right attitude equals a mind-set of brain/soul and not brain/id/ego or what amounts to one's self god.

"I would also mention that God has long since known those persons who have a fundamental problem with "wanting" to understand her. Even so, SHE would help them know themselves and what they have to gain or lose, because SHE cares enough to be repetitious in the process. SHE offers reincarnation with repeated opportunities. However, to repeat our warning: the time allowed for such godly Grace will be ending relatively soon; even though SHE hasn't told us what SHE considers relative as compared to eternity? Time becomes irrelevant on that scale. Even so, at some point you will have either whole life or no self-aware life.

"God has your lesson plan, but most humans won't even abide by ten simple rules for their specific spirit-soul needs as individuals. We have often tried to give you the co-created "seven deadly sins" as another moral guide, but you can't, or won't, hear over the roar of Egod. Could it be you are apathetic?"

Eno paused for Deepy's quizzical look to turn into a question.

It finally did, and it was "Huh?" followed by, "Uh, sorry, I guess I was lost in thought."

"Many people are," Eno told him. It was a fact that flew right past Deepy, who had a couple of questions in mind.

"Did you say "seven" deadly sins?" he now inquired. "I thought you said 'eight' at one time."

"No, there are the seven you already know, but there's another one that enhances the seven. It is Apathy. We call them eight "Mind Killers." (Eno put a list in front of Deepy, who took time to look it over once or twice)

Apathy: This sin enhancer allows you to ignore the seven deadly sins; to deny God, or deny the concept of moral perfection as possible and necessary. Apathy lets you retain and maintain your perceived pleasures, no matter the cost to others or to your own wisdom, intellect, logic, love, and grace, as well as to your potentially eternal life.

Anger: Manifests as ugliness, from disturbed passion.

Envy: A brooding for the material pleasures of other people.

Gluttony: An overwhelming appetite to selfishly consume more of anything actually required by someone else, bringing harm to oneself and to others as well.

Greed: Excessive desire for material wealth or ego power, which causes thoughts and actions detrimental to one's potentially immortal spirit-soul.

Laziness: The deliberate avoidance of giving extra effort in one's endeavors, to include the pursuit of "deep thinking," as it pertains to mind (spirit-soul) enhancement and advancement.

Lust: An inordinate, often perverse, craving for sensuous pleasures of the physical world.

Pride: Allows the ego to take full credit for one's abilities, rather than acknowledging one's essential traits could and should be moral essence from God, for God's purposes in one's life. {Her purposes are not based entirely on anyone repaying karmic debt. A person's good attributes, just as often are gifts to help them overcome certain aspects of their debt, so be grateful for that.}

Deepy thought about those deadly traits for a few moments, before struggling to remember a question he had wanted to ask prior to the diversion. It didn't seem all that important now, but he thought he had better ask before he forgot.

"Since God provides your thoughts, why would SHE need to read your intentions? Wouldn't SHE already know what SHE is going to do through you – especially with her precognition?"

Eno essentially had already addressed this, but did so again: "God does not always provide specific thoughts to an individual COG, but rather thought patterns in specialized categories from which COG can Co-Create their own thoughts. In other words, God allows us to follow her ruminations when SHE wants to lead us in a particular direction in whichever endeavor matches a specialty. We are vital Cells in God's thought process, relating especially now to her material world. SHE is pre-cognitive about her own intentions, but we can change her Mind with the appropriate input. That's Co-Creativity.

"COG and Humangels offer Co-Creativity with God through interactions and intentions. Earth's small hybrid angel corps also does this, to some degree with COG. Earth's incarnate humans were meant to provide God the same offerings, but 'id' skewed that likelihood. God has made her Children Co-Creative beings, Deepy, my perceptive friend, but Earth's humans are seldom ready to become God's children. Most simply have not reached a state of *"WILL and grace"* that would allow that.

"And so, we have 'a say' in what God does through us, by providing her with suggestions and information along the lines of her generalized thought patterns on various matters, and on more specific issues when consulted. God helps inform our thinking according to how we interact with her energy and what intentions we have for continued interaction. The process would seem to be psychic on God's part and intuitive for COG and Humangels.

"This Co-Creative process means we can reform or restructure any thought patterns God has given us and thus become somewhat independent thinkers and actors. That being the case, God does not automatically accept all our input, but usually SHE does. There is never any question as to its Moral value, as there would be if we were less than SHE is. This 'C-C' process affords God the chance to get much more return, shall we say, out of any single thought, which is very wise of her. We are here to give her cogent feedback regarding, for example, the societal life of Earthite humans, as well as information about certain specific persons at various times, such as tyrants, dictators, or other idiotic megalomaniacs and of course outstanding moral leaders as well, and everyone in between. There is a catalogue of the in-between ibidem types, but they still have recourse to the same 'One' God as everyone else.

"Since mankind's beginning in the garden* of Eden, human beings have suffered Eve illness, and that is reflected in the way you live your lives. God has been dealing with your illness from before "day one," and has received our helpful insight and input since before your physical inception, but Grace was confirmed from the time that Jesus came and laid down his life for all who would "live" it. *(miniscule from imperfection)

"God is perfect, but, for reasons of her own, SHE does not share all her thoughts with us, or her reasons for thinking as SHE does, but SHE makes thoughts available to us to serve her purposes. Besides, we could not contain 'all' the thoughts SHE is capable of generating. Even so, sometimes SHE lets us have a say in determining her purposes. We never question her motives, as there is no doubt SHE is inherently Moral to include every part of her Consciousness, except hybrids; although COG and 'Other' Angels are working hard to correct that situation. We guard God against immoral human thinking, so the inconsistency of hybrids does not change God's Perfectly Moral Essence. Nothing can. As I said, it's 'inherent.'

"No - we could not contain all God's thoughts or reasoning... just as your temporary dog brain cannot contain all your human memories; nor could the brains of humanimals who served as perfect Human vessels contain all the cognitive ability of any cohabitating COG Soul," Eno told his student friend.

"Yet, God will share the thoughts of your book with Earthite humans and its explanation for your chaotic world; illogical and irrational as it is - born of fusion and confusion. Even considering the imperfection of humans, God is willing to gather information from any source because ultimately it can be put to godly use, since God is all there is; but we do filter hybrids who take God in vain, in whatever manner they do so.

"Since their beginning, hybrids have allowed themselves to continue lowering God's morality bar, based on what their fellow humans do. Many are affected primarily by "bought-thought." That means they are brainwashed and/or otherwise manipulated by "big money" propaganda or personality cohesion, espoused by the greediest aspects of Egod, to include most everyone who worships Money over God – business types, politicians, lobbyists, spokespeople, and Egod's entire imprinted-brain consortium. Many are lemmings and copycats who cater to their physical senses rather than any "God sense" that still may lay dormant within. At some point in all their ugly lives, they may give in to every deadly sin, and with apathy, just as Egod would have them do. You might be surprised at how many of these people believe themselves to be extremely intelligent, just because of so-called material success.

"All human faults result in karmic incidents that come about as a result of Eden's paradigm. God saw everything that would be coming as consequences. The bad would outweigh the good, but God's Essence could not allow her to abandon that good. Wisdom and Grace allowed her to institute her program of reincarnation and karma immediately and to allow the first hybrids to know about it.

"The *Bible* tells us that Adam and Eve's son, Cain, who killed his brother, Abel, knew of God's law. When the Lord purportedly told Cain what his punishment would be for killing Abel; Cain said: '*My punishment is greater than I can bear... I shall be a fugitive and a vagabond in the earth; and it shall come to pass, that everyone that finds me will kill me.*' *Genesis 4, verses 13 and 14.* Now, how many times can someone be killed? That depends on how many times they reincarnate and what their Karmic lessons require. Abel, by the way, was reincarnated to Adam and Eve as their son Seth.

"Adam who purportedly was 'Lord' of his garden actually thought he had some powers of God, and so he ruled that anyone killing Cain would pay seven deaths for killing him. He marked Cain to show that anyone killing him would know his penalty to be seven deaths. *(*Biblical* scripture can be confusing at times; e.g. there are too many 'Lords' in the *Bible*. There was only one 'Lord God,' however.)

"When the actual *Lord God* of the time gave men authority over women; many men began calling themselves 'Lord,' meaning "Master" of their families. Adam's children called him *Lord*. As father of his first sons, he was unwise enough to praise one over the other, thereby leading to jealousy, spite, and the eventual killing of Abel by Cain.

"There is much rhetorical confusion in the *Bible*. I would make the point again that the actual *Lord God* was a COG. He, like all COG, did not eat material food. COG imbibe pure Spirit as provided by God. The Lord God also did not stitch clothing for Adam and Eve. A CHIP provided it at the *Lord's* request.

"As the tiny cells you are, you simply cannot know everything, nor can we mature Children retain everything that God accumulatively knows; but we can and do know her Moral Essence as ours also. We are her in that regard and we know the amount of knowledge we can contain is perfect.

"Most of your readers have the courage of their convictions! Congratulations to them for succeeding once again in being who they are – wiser than so many others who gave up on God and your book long ago.

"You want to take a break?"

"That would be nice."

IIIIIIIIIIIIIIIIIIIII
(CHAPTER 16)
Karma & Hitler

"Some Christians would say that Christ negated the law of Karma, but that is only true if Grace* comes into play, as it does when God recognizes a person as sincerely moral, which SHE did with most disciples of Jesus. Such Christians always come under God's Grace, and therefore have no need of reincarnation, unless returning to the world in missionary status. Some have volunteered for such service, even if they can't recall doing so.

*(Normally, "graced" Christians and other moral religious persons remain in the Otherealm to be tutored by their Over-Soul COG.)

"Non-graced, insufficiently moral persons reincarnate or they are consigned some other fate. Many self-declared "faithful" to God types simply are fooling themselves. They cannot measure up to God's moral standards enough to qualify for her saving Grace. Some church-goers are immoral and conscientiously unaffected by their bad behavior. They can be quite adept at rationalizing any evil that suits them, along with a God who will forgive them such evil.

"While it is true that even the most ardent God believers are not perfect, and can only be saved by Grace – God knows sincere from insincere, as well as one's deepest intentions. One's attitude, as well as one's spirit-soul, must be sufficiently God oriented, which is to say *'grounded'* in faith and good conscience. If God deems you are sincere at the very moment you give your life to the principles of morality, then you are graced* – which means that even though you remain vulnerable to sins, you also remain as protected as your conscience allows. If you sincerely regret your sins, God will save you into purgatory through her mercy and that of her Son, especially if you are trying to emulate his moral Essence. You may have karmic debt in need of purging, but at least you will know where you stand with God.

"*(Do not judge anyone, as that awesome responsibility belongs only to God. We all must discern good from evil, but judgment of persons is a matter only for God's perfect insight. That doesn't mean you are required to like all people. You may know of some in particular that you find disgusting. If that's a non self-righteous opinion, pray for them.)

"Non-Christians and Christians in name only, may reincarnate many times, but eventually will either attain Grace or prove their own undoing. A person with too much evil momentum likely will continue that way, lifetime after lifetime, until finally God must segregate him or her. It's quite difficult when you're on a slippery slope to change direction; but God can help you if you are willing to ask, and then strive for redemption. Even so, it won't be easy. Most folks will not be able to do it.

"Most spectral-spirits that remain in the earthly realm as so-called ghosts after leaving their bodies generally will end up in purgatory, learning lessons for reincarnation. Meantime, as temporary ghosts, they sometimes try to serve as "guardians" of loved ones left behind. They are not quite ready to "see the light" of Heaven or to proceed there, as they choose to believe they are in a good place to be helpful to still-living family members or other loved ones. Some even try to make themselves known through "psychic mediums," and a few succeed if their efforts are well-meant and judged by God to be helpful.

"Sometimes those who grow impatient in the ghostly state will try to force themselves into incarnation through whatever means they can make work. It's fairly rare now that a spectral-spirit can enter a fetus for which God specifically has made ready for another spirit-soul, but ever so often a spectral-spirit will force itself into a body in that most unwelcome way. God deals with such spirits as required. Those uninvited incursions were quite prevalent in biblical times, often involving multiple spirits - [*Examples*: *Book of Luke; Chapter 8, verses 28-33; Chapter 9, verses 38-42; Luke; 11-24*]. Such spectral-spirits encountered by Jesus often were referred to as 'devils.' Devils are of Egod (meaning hybrid spirits) and are not of God's Child, Satan.

"Reincarnation is only a good thing insofar as it is necessary. Essentially it means you have failed God and yourself; but still it is better than forcing God to judge you as being so evil that SHE cannot allow you to continue living as a self-aware being. Every person has an eventual appointment with a final death in this temporary material world, followed by a judgment and permanent dispensation of his or her spirit-soul. In the meantime, there are multiple material deaths followed by judgment of that particular life episode, followed by guidance into another incarnation with new opportunities, which usually incur other karmic debt. Wanton immorality generates the worst debt and incurs the strictest karma.

"Where might you end up after this life? There are interim and permanent possibilities: You could be adjudged worthy by 'Grace' of becoming an angel apprentice or – you could be pronounced effectively dead, so far as conscious self-awareness is concerned. In that case, your energy would be transposed into a form of God's choosing, perhaps into a material world animal, or an inanimate object living as a tree, or bush, possibly to later become an Otherealm version of one of those entities serving in the Spirit fundament of the Holy G'host. God has countless options. You have five: accentuate God in order to enhance her forever; go to hell; to minor heaven; to reincarnation; or God will choose your non self-aware fate.

"If the judgment is not a final one, you could be in heaven* or a shade of the material realm prior to reincarnation into karmic debt or you could transpose into the netherealm of hell.

*(This interim heaven [small 'h'] also can be referred to as purgatory, depending on why a spirit-soul is consigned there)

(The need for hell will no longer exist when God finally closes the door on her hybrid generation of spirit-souls from the material dimension. If you are in hell at that time, you will be transposed into the non self-aware Spirit-Body G'Host of God Jr. You will be able to "sense" God, as plants or animals do, but you will no longer have self-awareness and the capability to become a 'co-creative' Cell of God, as you now have. That's a lot to give up.)

"Heaven (capital 'H'), on the other hand, is eternal, Mental, self-aware life, as an integral part of God Mind. You will be well aware that you are a perfect Mental Cell or Child of God, abiding within the Holy God Host Essence of God Jr – the third and final summation of a whole God. You would enjoy the full complementary traits of godliness, along with endless godly experiences. How could any godly-wise Soul be more blessed?

"Some people create such vast amounts of karma that they can only fit so much into one lifetime. How many times can you be murdered in one life, in order to be punished for multiple murders you may have committed in a past life? You obviously can only die one physical time per life but you could experience multiple psychic deaths that would seem just as real to you. If God judges your spirit irredeemable, any material death could become the appointed death of that spirit, with loss of its soul.

"Otherwise, you (as spirit-soul) either receive a renewal of the essence of your spirit for reincarnation, or it is held in an interim state in purgatory. You can allow your tiny soul and O'Soul to commune with you in that interim state and tutor you, but that's your choice, just as it now is. God eventually will render a judgment of those in heaven (purgatory) as to which direction they go – whether to hell; into another physical life, or angel apprenticeship. Those spirits consigned to hell are transferred there after a brief counseling in purgatory. If they become bitter rather than humble, they will suffer more.

"Sometimes a portion, or all, of karmic justice is carried out during the interim of purgatory/heaven if the sins were relatively minor and God chooses to forgive a spirit through Grace. On the other hand, if your sins were heinous and caused great suffering, God could recall those sins precisely and substitute your spirit for that of the victim(s), causing you to "live through" every one of your evil deeds, exactly as your victim(s) did. In effect, you "become" them – as they were – with all their thoughts and emotions prior to, and during, their suffering and death. You will feel their pain, both mentally and physically, but will know it is you punishing you, even though your victim's suffering also was karmic, which is true of all evil.

"This is one way God can exact justice that would otherwise take too many physical lifetimes; although God's Assembler memory is just as real to you as the actual experience was to your victim(s) since it consists of the original energy patterns – revitalized through the Assembler. But, even though it is the original scenario, the victims of the original do not re-experience those events. You live them instead. You are both perpetrator and victim. Will you ever understand God is God?

"God's law of karma has been in effect ever since Eve and Adam corrupted themselves and since Cain murdered Abel, as related in the *Bible*. The tree of knowledge of good and evil is all about karma – or good rewards good, while bad punishes bad, as in 'like begets like.'

"Isn't it comforting to know that such a logical law is in place? It's good to know for example that if you murder someone, you also will be killed, either in that lifetime, or another, or through God's "Assembler" memory system in purgatory or the netherealm. If repayment is made in the material world, it's often under similar circumstances of age, lifestyle, and environment as those of the law-avenged victim. If it happens in hell, then God's Memory Assembler provides every nuance of a time-machine episode of the actual event, only this time with your consciousness identifying you as the victim of your own crime. Would you agree ONE could hardly be any more fair, just, or logical than that?

"Would you doubt the power of God's practical ability to mete out justice as her karmic law dictates? Would you deny your own existence – even as some of you deny God's? Would you deny that mankind is venturing to make cognizance-computing machines in his/her own likeness, while denying an Omnipotent God the power to replicate perfect Mental Cells in her/his image through spirit-soul "be-ins" of biological entities. Your non-logical id/ego would have you deny God any power you don't wish her to have. Mankind is failing the WILL and Grace Test through the audacity and ignorance of trying to usurp God as God.

How good is your imagination? We only ask, because we are going to tell you a story now, which is part of the bigger story; NEXT PLEASE:

ADOLF HITLER?

Picture, if you can, Hitler standing before God's judgment throne. Better yet, imagine him lying face down, twitching, as his Othereal body is too nervous to support him. He is shielding his eyes, as the power of God is way too effusive for him in his shame. Yes, he is ashamed and he knows he is guilty of all the charges brought against him. Then too, he remembers this place. He has been here before, and he recalls a Justice system that was perfectly fair, and he wonders: "How could I have forgotten? Dear God, have mercy!"

"I shall, but strictly on my terms, which obviously exclude my grace now, but not my mercy. However, when it comes to my mercy, you have a choice to make.

"To answer your question: No spirit is able to have memories during a material life that don't coincide with that life... so you wouldn't remember this place. But your Soul never forgets and so you do remember now, along with every detail of all your previous lives, your brief visits here in between, and what transpired as a result. You could remember all of that now if you were not so stressed about the life you just completed and the coming judgment you dread. So, for now, I will spare you those other memories because you have a decision to make.

"As you know, it is because of you that millions of human deaths are emblazoned in my Energy Assembler. You are directly, or indirectly, responsible for these people dying, by genocide and in war and its aftermath. This of course does not take into account the entire suffering you caused.

"I was with all those people who suffered and died, as well as those who suffered and lived. They all had debts to pay, but I was there too, even if they never cried out to me. I am always there for as much comfort as allowable in a karmic situation, whenever someone calls upon me or not, throughout his or her life. You remember that now, don't you? I know each person because their lives are etched in my recall Assembler, and I guide anyone who asks... as best they will allow, and in keeping with the circumstances of their karma.

"Now I am going to give you the opportunity to know all of those people you killed, directly or indirectly... all those who called upon me, and those who did not. I always have more than enough stored energy to recall any part of my entire life, which includes all of your lives, as you are part of me. Unfortunately, many people elect to not have me as part of them.

"When my memory is used in purgatory or hell for karmic debt payments, I do not suffer through such tragedies repeatedly, as I have a memory system that re-assembles the events exactly, to include whatever part I may have been called upon to play. If there are multiple debts, I replicate all memories as needed for debts to be paid here rather than in other lifetimes. Upon full payment of every debt, I let all evil memories wane. As of now, not enough time remains in the material world for you to live enough lives to die enough deaths to pay for all the suffering you caused.

"You cannot plead insanity here because you were responsible for the very mental aberrations of which you now are about to be purged. Your mind will be cleansed. My CHIP memory Assembler is perfect and so I can allow you to relive the final thirty days of each of your victim's lives, even though they suffered much longer. Since you are responsible for millions of deaths and assorted suffering, I hope you can appreciate my leniency. Needless to say, you will know every thought, have every memory, every feeling throughout your victims' final thirty days, including how each one felt about me. People do tend to think of me in their dying, suffering times, often with great bitterness, or with extreme graciousness.

"I will provide you with intermittent memories that you are Hitler, and responsible for torturing and killing your "self" in the bodies and thoughts of all your victims. You will know that I suffered with the original victims too, but only because I want all humans – yes, even you – to be part of my eternity. If I willingly suffer with victims who call upon me, millions of times over, are you not willing to pay your debts so that you can live in Grace forever? Your answer to that question is your sanity test, but the question remains – can you endure so much of the suffering you caused?

"If you do not like your fate as payment of your karmic debt, your choice is... you may kill yourself, by asking me to end your conscious existence. I can do that by simply forgetting you, since essentially you are a "thought form" that decided to play god, rather than 'complement' me in exchange for eternal life. I will forget your spirit, which is the ego personality with which you identify; and I will cleanse your tiny soul of the evil residue of your God-defying, soul-denying spirit. It will no longer recognize you. It will be safe. I also will put that purged soul to good use.

"In order for life to exist in heaven as it does, within my active mind and memory... I must re-member and re-cognize every Cell of my Self on a continual basis in order to keep it living. That's not a problem though. Neither is forgetting you. I have forgotten many before you, as they chose eternal death rather than payment for their sins. Considering the egregious life you just completed, I expect you also will choose death. But, keep in mind – while you can – that this would be a final death for eternity. You would be without a "mind" to change later ... as you won't get to re-think this decision or think anything at all."

"Your Honor, please, I beg you, have mercy on me. I cannot survive all that suffering and all those deaths, but I don't want to consciously die forever. What can I do?"

"The suffering will be as horrible for you as it was for your victims, but you will survive, just as they did. They did not truly die. Physical death occurs when the spirit-soul leaves the body to pass over here for judgment, but it is still you who passes over. You are only dead to the material world. Eventually everyone must come here to be judged and to pay the debts they have incurred, or to make arrangements to pay in another earthly sojourn. Yet, even then many of them get the choice I am now giving you. Choose to pay, or die for eternity.

"Everyone comes here with full memory and knowledge of their one continual life... that one life the tiny soul and Over-Soul mate have both endured and enjoyed at times. If spirit-souls are salvageable through Grace, they get reincarnation or appAngel training. They of course remember their latest material sojourn and why it ended the way it did. They must come here to find out what will happen next. If they become too evil for rational salvation, I allow them a temporary suit of Othereal Spirit, until a decision is made regarding their future. Once again, for what may be the final time, they make a choice. And some do choose eternal death rather than endure any suffering they caused other "living" entities. It is only thorough mercy that none must also suffer the anguish and heartache caused to relatives and friends of their victim(s).

"The second choice I give you is also merciful, since you would not remember anything at all. You would become a non self-conscious Othereal Spirit Cell, rather than remaining one of mental, self-conscious energy. Your self-aware eternity would cease to consciously exist along with your hybrid spirit or what could have been your angel form, had you lived your life attuned to my life. If you choose the first option, at least you will survive. That period of debt repayment will pass and then you will have the same eternal life as others. Eternity is eternity, after all. So, if you pay your debt as described, you will be allowed a peaceful life, with an Angel tutor who will assist you to maturity as an Angel in your own right. You no longer will be Hitler; you will be christened anew.

"I will return in a while for your decision. If you can't decide, I will decide for you."

[Eventually, all of you will need God's Grace and mercy, so maybe you should not bemoan the fate of anyone else who receives that. In fact your prayers for them could help strengthen your own grace, even though it's really difficult to pray for a soul as despicable as Hitler's, or of any dictator or "would-be" dictator/strongman. You can do it, but that's one more reason God is Judge. Of course, God doesn't answer all prayers as one might wish.

[Why would a loving, forgiving God want retribution for evil? 'Retribution' really is the wrong word. Purification is the right word, preceded by enlightenment. As you read Deepy's book, hopefully you will come to see God's purpose is to purify any imperfect aspect of consciousness that would become part of her Self; and you temporarily are just such a potential aspect.]

//////////\\\\\\\\\\\\

(CHAPTER 17)
Dia-Logos

Walking – talking - Man – dog - Beautiful day - beautiful woods - a black forest measured against the light, with wispy white streaks and fluffy cotton-ball puffs, high overhead and off in the distance - some floating like halos around mountain peaks, or lounging high above vertical stalks of looming green giants. Those shadowy hulks crowd together and take wind-moaned umbrage at the intrusion of sun shafts bouncing and falling and playing among them, in spite of the almost mystical presence of those spires. Deepy told himself he could even hear a babbling brook. No, it's really there. Of course, it would have to be. This was heaven - "Eno's universal version." But much to Deepy's surprise - shock really - an hour before, while the ship was hovering and they were surveying the scenery, Eno had told him that they were inside Mars. "Yeah, right," Deepy had said, thinking his friend was joking. "Not kidding," Eno had emphasized. "There are artificial seals covering pockets, rifts, and valleys of underground space and we are in a valley. This is a staging area here... with a variety of flight missions coming and going. We will traverse one of our connecting tramways to a living area in just a few seconds."

"Yeah, right," Deepy had said again, "People are not going to believe that; it's too trite. I know you are incapable of lying, so I do believe it." Deepy said, and then the ship monitor showed what looked to be hills with cave entrances, as he finished his thought, "Our scientists know there's no intelligent life on Mars now. They are looking for specimen of past life."

Eno had to laugh then. "There you go again," he had told Deepy, "concerning yourself with what people will believe or not. You know, God doesn't force anyone to believe anything. As far as that goes, most people always are able to rationalize their way out of accountability to God, and most will do so, even after reading your book, if they manage that journey; but that only works for them psychologically and not for God at all. So their effort instead should be to recognize their real accountability, because the time to start making amends is always now. At some point there will be an end to 'now,' and it will be too late, but everyone of course still will be accountable.

"Ah, but there I go again. Besides, we're not on Mars; we're in it, or better to say underneath the general surface area. Anyway, you might be surprised at what your scientists don't know. They know a lot, but most would tell you they sure don't know as much as they would like. We will see if they are willing to learn anything from what folks call religion, because we are not quite ready just yet to provide material evidence."

"I hope you're not counting on the book to teach any scientists anything," was Deepy's cheerful response.

"God will handle that and all hybrid matters, as SHE sees fit," Eno replied.

"We know most of your scientists are dedicated and hard working, but often give God little or no credit for the information they receive. Christ said… *'Ask and you shall receive,'* and that is true, if the 'asking' comes from the soul of a person, which would include the O-Soul-to-God nexus, or just a heart-felt desire to serve fellow humans. Ego gratification won't get the job done.

"Then too," Eno continued, "there have been times we purposely did not assist human thinking, in order to protect you from information for which you are not yet psychologically prepared, which sometimes seems like just about everything. Most people are not prepared for what they will read in your "co-created-with-CHIP" book, but we must present it now, as an initial step in a process of people learning what is imperative.

"The situation on Earth has become desperate," Eno had continued as their craft approached docking, "People are more and more blinded by Egod's power of materiality and that situation must improve in order for your society to survive, even for as long as it must, which, relatively speaking, won't be much longer. Your world is undergoing disorder that may prove apocalyptic, if not worse.

"All mankind's pains began with ignorance and then denial of God and long before any political elections or disease pandemics. Always as before, it will be - or was - brought about <u>not</u> by God, but by the power of man to ignore God, to include incompetence that Egod may justify to protect his recalcitrant hubris, such as misinformation; harmful inaction; possibly even harmful action."

Reflecting on it now, Deepy remembered asking, "Eno, couldn't our scientists bounce some sort of laser beam or something off Mars to find these hollowed out spots of yours?"

"All matter is hollow to Othereal forms. Your scientists will only see what their material eyes allow, and we do have some crystal shields for adaptive irradiative cloaking." Eno had responded. "You won't find us until we know you are morally ready and we allow it. Fairly soon after the return of Christ Jesus to your planet, we will begin to allow Othereal visitations here, my friend. That, however, will not be anywhere near as awe-inspiring as the return of our Lord God, who will be Lord of the Gaia Garden for another thousand years. 'Time' will end when Gaia does and it will become 'on Earth as it is in heaven.' After the Garden Gaia era, Earth will be known as "Hearth," a combination of Heaven and earth and it will be a vital, creative center on behalf of the Otherealm, with a Heart of Holy empathetic Love. It will be a part of the Otherealm, as the material realm will no longer exist for those who survive the hybrid world.

"By the way," Eno had said after some reflection, "those 'connecting tramways' I mentioned were once visible from Earth. They are still there, but in altered form. A few of your early scientists referred to them as "canals," until we allowed some cloaking camouflage. They decided their eyes and equipment had been insufficient, which it was, along with their imaginations."

Deepy's mind had wandered then, as it now did, thinking back on their arrival "inside" Mars. He had been overwhelmed by everything, not to mention a bit incredulous, so after a slight pause, he had mumbled, "I see," as he looked out the porthole or glanced at their shared topography screen. There was a fascinating display of ships swooping, hovering, lifting and dropping vertically into well-choreographed patterns above towers into which they extricated or inserted themselves via stacked slots that fit at least two shapes Deepy noticed. There were huge, elongated oval craft, like the one he was in, as well as the saucer shapes, better known to most humans. There were a variety of sizes, but Deepy did not see any triangles. Everything seemed automated, as Deepy saw no sign of life. No, wait... he did see several figures.

"Where is everybody?" he had asked. "All I see are a few Marsians."

"You have been mistaking our biological humanoids for Marsians. Those 'little grays,' as your Earthite UFO fans call them are the Marsian version of our CHIPS. You may remember 'Hoster.' The basic difference in them is that the humanoid CHIPS we use were developed to function primarily in the Otherealm and therefore are of crystal, diamond structure, with liquid crystal coursing through their circuitry. Marsian humanoids are biological, primarily for use in the material world. They have veins with a blood-like serum, which carries their nutrition and breathe of life, but like plants they take in carbon dioxide and exhale oxygen. We need that here for Earthite visitors and for other reasons.

"Actual Marsians look exactly like Humans. You can't see any difference. There are many Marsians among your hybrids."

"Are they spies?"

Eno laughed, "Of course," he said, "if surveillance is considered spying."

It had been some time ago, upon arrival, that Deepy had first asked his "Where is everybody?" question, while thinking that what he usually perceived as reality wasn't going to seem all that important today. Now, walking through what Eno had earlier referred to as one of the "living areas," and not seeing anyone or anything but Nature, Deepy was thinking of the noncommittal answer he had gotten the first time he asked. "Just wait," Eno had told him then. But now, since this was supposedly a 'living area,' he posed the question again.

"There are many COG here. When they are within Marsian or Human forms, they are attached to and in control of those Othereal or physical bodies. Human forms of course also include Marsians bodies, lest one forget, and as I said, there's no telling them apart from Earthite humans. In this underground realm, COG nearly always cohabit a Human form to suit themselves, although there is a small coterie of Earth-bred Humangels here, of which my immediate staff consists for now.

"Marsians were a species of humanimal that was located both here and on Earth when God created her perfect Gardens. We transferred one Earth species here for awhile for their safety; then back again after the dinosaur's reign ended.

They were an endangered species among the other animals of Earth. When COG finally cohabited them, we made them farmers, not predators and their sensibility became moral humility. Now, we have many in the Otherealm as Humangels and some who have returned for our mission here; again to function as perfect Humans.

"Now when you see Marsians, you are looking at the perfect Human aspect of their Humangels. As with any Humangel – one sees a perfect Human form. I would also point out; there never were Mars apprentice angels since the Marsian species was not included in the hybrid generation, as it wasn't necessary. That means _none_ of their Humangels would go through an apprenticeship program such as Earth's tiny Angels do.

"Marsians were the default type of God's standard program during the generations of perfect Humans Co-Creating Humangels. They were given shorter material lives and so their tiny homing souls were cleansed to return to the Otherealm as part of the original Soul. There were many Mars (Ares) type Gardens. They all used the same formula. A new 'tiny' homing soul followed by a COG entered a humanimal, making it Human, and upon completing a Humangel, the 'tiny' was released to purgatory for a cleansing, in order to be inducted into its Parent Soul. The tinys were cleansed as a precaution even though they did not have time or circumstances to become seriously tainted by animal id instincts."

Eno paused, "The humanimal forebears of Angels here were polarized for mating purposes, but we long ago had to relocate their remaining Yin and Yang fused spirit forms to Earth. That was before we built this underground world and were returned here as a support fleet for hybrids. To digress just a little more, I will tell you that some former Marsian animals still survive on Earth to this day. They mated with humanimal remnants from other gardens, also sent to mix with the hybrid generation. God does not kill her species. The laws of physics do.

"The large, hairy Marsian animals, of which we speak, are known to humans by various names. They never had tiny souls and are as wild as any other animal living a wilderness life. They never evolved beyond the animal stage. The only humanimals that did evolve were those with tiny souls on planets such as Earth where Human lives lasted longer, providing a greater number of Humangels. Unfortunately some of the hybrid follow-on generations have used their souls sparingly through multiple lifetimes. Many are bound for hell because they find no fault with their lives, no matter how they act or think.

"We therefore now are trying to save the tiny universal souls who need to be healed of Eve illness through essentially no fault of their own. Now they have faults of even greater magnitude for which they must be held accountable. Their only chance for eternity is to escape id/ego's influence and conform to morality. Fortunately a majority of them will come to want that. Succeeding is another matter.

"Like all Gardens prior to the hybrid generation, 'Ares' aka Mars was strictly a planet for Co-Creating Humangels. As I was saying earlier, it was different from Earth, because each COG cohabitant here took its own tiny soul to Heaven with its Humangel after only a 50-year physical lifespan. In fact, this curtailed physical life procedure was used almost everywhere in the universe. Earth was one of the exceptions, as God Mind wanted to explore more of her material realm and thus SHE required longer physical lives in some Gardens. Limited life cycles were normal most everywhere else, to include Mars. The Marsian Humangels you see there (Eno pointed) are some who have returned for this hybrid mission on behalf of Earth.

"By the way, the Ant/Ares, 'Serpent' species that mankind now refers to as Neanderthals was originally from Antares, as you may recall. That is where they acquired their tiny souls. They lived underground there and were both above and below ground on Earth, before God directed them all below the surface where they have thrived. Technologically and spiritually, they have evolved even more rapidly than mankind on the surface. Some of them have been helping surface humans for a long time. Even so, there is a small group that remains bitter and they often have damaged surface conditions for the sake of their leader who has reincarnated many times since he was admonished by the Lord in Eden.

"The friendly Ants have advanced quicker morally because they remained in communion with God Mind. They were never followers of the adamant "Mant*" as their vengeful chosen leader now calls himself in his present-day incarnate state. Fortunately the 'good' outnumber the 'bad' on the surface and underneath it; but all you hybrids struggle between those two characteristics. *(Mant called himself Adam Ant in his garden of Eden life. Oddly (innocently or suspiciously) a hybrid human of this era adopted that name for his musical and acting careers. 'Mant' though is spiteful, hateful, and dangerous, just as he was in past lives that, like most all hybrids, he can't remember.)

"Other human forms that God sent to Earth from other planets became a variety of multi-ethnic species after Adam and Eve's arrival. Those other ethnicities derived from several races brought in from different planetary Gardens. Except for the Ants, they were all 'surface' related.

"A relatively small number of Humangels here came from the final Earth Garden and they help us with our Earth-related hybrid missions. Some of us COG cohabit them if they invite us to be guests in their bodies. Many of them hibernate here while serving with us. If we use their bodies they often just mediate their Souls into synchronization with our activities while sharing our thoughts. They do so in a trance state, which also provides rest, similar to sleep.

"All Humangels are as morally pure as Trangels. Unlike Earth's hybrids, Marsian animals never dealt with id/ego illness. Even so, our testing stations still are in place for all Angels returning from this realm and mission, which puts us into such close contact with hybrids. As I have mentioned, even Jesus Christ was analyzed through varying shades or phases of God to include the Netherealm after leaving this realm, and his/her COG brother/sister – Satan Nasat, also was often tested for possible contamination."

"Satan? I don't understand."

"I will tell you more about him later – and her.

"There are multitudes of Marsian Angels here, awaiting future use in the physical world. Most are the very 'homing' souls and COG who went to Heaven from here eons ago. They eventually will serve as Angel adjunct, perfect Human Disciples to Jesus Christ. That means they also will be administering to the tiny souls of reincarnated hybrids in Garden Gaia. There also are incarnate Marsians sleeping here now, as each awaits its COG partner's return from the Otherealm. In fact, my Marsian partner, 'Hodo,' is asleep now, since I am cohabiting within a Humangel of Earth origin for this project for now.

"But more specifically to answer your question - as you know, COG are strictly Othereal Spirit-Soul entities, and if we were not "suited up" as a Marsian or other style Human, you would see no indication of our presence, unless you had the Othereal form we have provided you for your mission with us. Right now though, most of our mission's Othereal forms are operating in both a material and Othereal world, under the Mars' surface. We can appear or disappear as we please in these confines to those eyes that have no need or authority to see us."

"Ah!" Deepy acknowledged, adding, "I don't see many suited-up versions. Is it always this slow around here?"

"It's really not as you see it. Many here are not allowing you to see them. They value their privacy. Usually we either are coming or going. What you see here is primarily a physical staging area for COG and Humangels on duty, but this is the actual home of a fairly big Marsian population, along with some Ant/Ares Humans and a few Earthite hybrid humans temporarily assigned here."

"Really, you have hybrids assigned here? Who are they?"

"Yes, we do work with some incarnate spirit-souls from Earth, some of whom have been with us for decades and some for centuries. These are people who voluntarily "disappeared" from Earth to come to work for God. They were quite dismayed with moral circumstances on Earth and needed an escape. We provided one, for which they have been grateful, as they can eventually transition into angel apprenticeship from here. We also have disincarnate spirit-souls from Earth, who stop here on their way to minor heaven – some even as recent as (Eno paused ever so slightly) about six seconds ago – a party of three spirit-souls transcending your realm.

"One Muslim and two Christians are stopping through, on their way to angel lessons in heaven. Those who tarry here also lend us a hand as we go about the business of preparing for the return of Christ. Most of these visits are brief layovers, but sometimes we call on a few of these spirit-souls to return here when they have become more mature Earth angels pure enough to function as Humans with COG cohabitants. In fact, some of our ship personnel are Humans, while others, such as the quin, are apprentice Angels. At times we have required some of our incarnate Marsians for brief missions while on temporary duty within your realm. In the meantime they live and work here, quite happily."

"Excuse me for interrupting, but why are apprentice Angels called quintessential? Isn't that a term more appropriate to Trangels?"

"We use it as a term of endearment and encouragement. None of us has ego to be flattered, so it's to remind them of that.

"We also have newly-minted Earth and Mars Angels who gather here for relaxation. This is a rest and recreation spot for them. We have several really nice golf courses, fishing lakes, hiking trails, and gorgeous scenery..."

"Really?" Deepy had to chuckle; "So, this is a country club for Angels?"

Eno laughed. "It's a site where appAngels can materialize for awhile, for some good clean fun. Apprentices are not yet qualified to enter God Junior's room, where they could partake of most sporting activities in their Othereal bodies.

"No kidding?" Deepy had to think about that for a moment. "I had no idea there would be such similarities between Heaven and Earth. Is that why Earth will one day be known as H*earth*?"

"Yes, that is a good name that one of our appAngels came up with. Of course, Moral experiences do include good, clean fun of an earthly origin, as well as a variety of activities from other garden planets around the Universe. Hybrids who do make it this far in their moral evolution are in for many wonderful surprises, such as no injuries or harm in sports or other activities that could produce those results in the same material activity. But that's just one small example."

"And what supports this dome? I see no structure." Following his thoughts, Deepy switched subjects, as he had been studying his surroundings, somewhat lost in thought.

"It is self-supporting. The dense raw spirit, of which the seal is made, supports it, along with the volume of atmosphere within. Even so, many of the "apparent" mountain peaks are also structured into the seal. The mountains are hollow pyramids, serving as power sources, as well as housing and recreation areas. This shell structure is virtually indestructible. It would take an almost unimaginable amount of chaotic energy to make a dent in this place; but God could whisk it away with a thought."

"Eno, this is truly breathtaking scenery, but, if you'll pardon my saying so, it sure looks a lot like my own home sweet planet to me. Not that a dog could find fault with a tree, but I can't help saying I'm more than a little shocked by all this. No offense, but are we not actually in the Alps, Himalayas, or Rocky Mountains somewhere? I'm teasing; but if we are underground, how do you get that sunlight down here and is that real snow up on the mountains, and what about those clouds?"

"The Spirit Dome is a natural refractor, and we have crystal reflectors in strategic places. Also, the sunlight is supplemented by artificial light, which can be switched between material and Othereal - either equal in every way to the solar or Spectral models. So the ceiling is like one huge light emitting diode, I guess you could say. By the way, some of this scenery is holographic, that is ... created through the use of crystal lasers. But, these scenes are not from Earth. This is how Mars once looked, but you are correct... very Earth-like. We want our special guests to feel at home, as well as relatively new angels who join us here at times. And yes, the snow is real, but it is showered in place from those artificial clouds that are programmed to move about.

"Now, let's just continue our walk for a while," Eno said, "Any more questions?"

Deepy figured he could think of plenty, but he also was anxious to dive into the subject of UFOs and humans, since that had been on his mind so much lately. "Right now," he said, "Just a comment – God truly is amazing and magnificent, even knowing that no 'word,' other than the Word 'God' can do her justice."

"Amen, brother Larray."

As Deepy, Larray laughed, "Your brother – the dog," he said, and then added...

"People have reported all sorts of creatures arriving on the Earth in space vehicles in the distant and not so distant past. What gives?"

Eno guided them down a trail that Deepy hadn't noticed. It seemed to parallel the water, which Deepy could glimpse between what he took for red cedar trees. Being from pine tree and oak country though, he wasn't sure.

"Deepy, my friend, your underground neighbors are more advanced than surface humans. Not only that, this also is our world too. We COG lived here as Humans sharing physical bodies eons before the hybrid couple you know as Adam and Eve. Both Mars and Earth have again been our material homes since then, when we are on hybrid duty. Even now, we have a large contingent of Humangels, Trangels, and humanoids in areas of Earth. We also visit your neighbors underground, and in the waters there. As I said before, they are scientifically and morally advanced and they also have some anti-gravity, underwater "Ships" in your skies at times.

"Sometimes our craft are spotted by hybrids and sometimes they belong to your neighbors. Our ships are Transitional in service to the community of Othereal COG who act as Over-Soul guardian Angels, or godly tutors, supporting hybrid human souls as id/egos allow. Unfortunately, we have had limited success, since hybrid mental, moral illness has become so psychologically ingrained.

"It almost sounds too simple, or too complex, to be true, depending on how one views it? That's because it's so familiar. Religion has always mentioned souls and spirits, heaven and hell, without really having a grasp of all the many facets of reality those words portend. Religion correctly has pointed the way to Angels and/or COG, the Children of God, all along. Don't you think now, there was good reason for that?"

"It would sure seem so," Deepy cautiously replied. "But, I have to tell you something, just to clear my conscience, if nothing else."

"I already know what it is, but tell me, so you remember to include it in your book."

"Many of us hybrid humans essentially are "nutty," and by that I mean schizoid. If we don't understand something, or if it seems too strange, then we invent theories or even conspiracies to explain it. You know we have 'alien conspiracy' theories that you guys want to take over our bodies and minds for whatever reason, and it seems you essentially have been making the case to support just such a theory."

"I somewhat agree, although we are not material world entities and therefore not 'aliens' or hybrids from other planets, even though Earth sometimes does have such visitors. In fact, some visit here to support our mission, just as your neighbors support us.

"As purely Otherealm beings we COG only "invest" in your limited-life material bodies what we can take out of them. It is through them that we co-create Othereal bodies for humans who will qualify for Heaven. Your minds are only attached to, and not immersed in, your physical bodies, but both are needed to help you ultimately create an inner-angel, spirit self. However, most of you only manage to create a spectral apparition described as a ghost. However, the difference between ghosts and angels can be quite stark, depending on their moral fiber. All too many ghosts are ego-derived and eventually prone to dissolve into the netherealm. Some however resolve into purgatory/heaven.

"If your spectral inner form does become a ghost, it means it is evil to the degree that heaven is at least temporarily off-limits. It must abide alone in a surreal state within a nethereal shade* - meaning a dimension between Othereal purgatory and the material realm. As it starts down this path, it deserves neither hell nor reincarnation. If closer to reincarnation, the spirit is said to be in a "switch" mode. If closer to hell, its 'shade' is referred to as being in a more serious 'Hades' state. *{Shades are veils that hide one irradiated realm from another.}

"Ghosts briefly sometimes can be seen or felt by hybrid humans who are on a character path coinciding with, or closest to, a particular 'shade' of ghost. God regulates her shades for a variety of hybrid conditions, but the switch and Hades states are both very common. The degree of separation between the dreamlike switch shade and the Hades shade can vary through a multitude of moral or immoral character stages. 'Switch' has one range so close to the material one that oftentimes such spirits don't immediately realize they are dead to the material world. On occasion, such ghosts – to include poltergeists – can even affect objects of matter; and/or they briefly can appear as apparitions – some even seeming solid. They usually also are quite confused and disoriented. Oftentimes when they realize they are 'beyond the pale,' many begin to pray for God's Light to transfer them to purgatory, which usually happens eventually, depending on their sincere resolution, understanding and communion.

"Depending on a spirit's determination, its ultimate fate will vary according to how much time it fosters with its tiny former soul to revive and enliven its moral memory essence into a learning mode open to wanting more knowledge of God. Over time, a spirit's growing willingness can take it to purgatory to learn even more moral lessons for reincarnation with its tiny soul.

"If your spirit-mind does manage to develop an angel spirit rather than a ghostly specter; even if its spirit is weak, its soul works with it in heaven toward completion of a character Self good enough either to qualify for God's Grace, or at least reincarnation on a loftier scale that will give it a better future.

"A tiny soul is Othereal and essentially eternal because of its Over-Soul Mentor. Then again, everything belongs to God and what God would give you hybrid 'aliens' in return for her investment in making you compatible with her, is simply eternal life. Seems like a pretty fair deal to me, if only you could be convinced of it. Hybrids, though, are too cynical about one another and carry that cynicism over to God. Way too many are beginning to see God as alien to the types of lives that Egod would have them live, and because many humans have virtually no contact with God – for them, there is no God. They could get to know God through faith and communion, but most hybrids still seem to favor imperfect lives through personal hubris. They replaced God with themselves in the garden of Eden. Hello Egod.

"As I have said before, hybrid humans have the evil aspect of the knowledge of good and evil down to a science. But God always has had the good aspect down to her Essence, which equates to pure Morality. If hybrid humans are going to survive, they must determine now to do it in the only way possible – by the moral means offered to them through God and all her 'Other' Children and Angels, including Jesus Christ, the one we call 'Lord God and Master,' of your particular solar garden.

"All of this means hybrids must gain enough of God's Wisdom, Intelligence, Logic, Love and Grace to overcome their schizophrenia. We know that most of you will not be able to do that. Even so, it never has been and never will be something that God can force on you. The hybrid id/ego "free will," will be the death of those who cannot both understand and welcome the moral religion and eternal life that goes with what we have been trying to teach since Adam and Eve. Those who allow the instinctive id of their old serpent brain-stems to continue ruling their heavenly, executive cerebral hemispheres will have one final Adam and Eve experience and it will be deadly.

"What time do you have?" Eno suddenly asked – causing Deepy to wonder, "You mean now? I don't know the time. I tried wearing a watch but it kept falling off."

"You're a funny guy, Larray" Eno told him. "I was just recalling your explanation of the temporal dimension to the tinys. It was quite good actually, considering the direction you took. Of course, CHIP helped you go that way, but one can go in other directions also. For example, COG live in the present, future, and past of time as Earthites record it. God sees the future because SHE knows her plans without regard to time, but they are subject to change. The future is what SHE plans to happen now, meaning it also exists in the present, along with the past, which SHE can selectively remember or forget. In accordance with her thinking, everything is simultaneous."

"I'm afraid I don't quite understand that. I wish I understood how precognition or clairvoyance works."

"You do, if you stop to think about it. God's activities don't happen within a time frame or period. SHE always knows immediately what SHE is going to do and thus can project her WILL and imagination into what you call the future. Sometimes SHE will allow COG to access that place in her Mind where a certain energy pattern will come to exist. Occasionally we are meant to share that information through a human being. On the other hand, SHE does sometimes change her Mind and negate what SHE might term a fleeting notion. "Mind-changing" has nothing to do with imperfection. It's a critical aspect of thinking."

"That makes sense somehow, but it's amazing how little I understand; so please, do tell me what God has planned for the foreseeable future." Deepy, was intrigued by the concept of precognition.

"I have been telling you that since the moment you began your visit with us and I have said repeatedly, material world time is expiring. God set a limit for time, as humans understand it. That limit was based on her need for reincorporating fused spirit, meaning 'matter,' into more Holy Spirit Mental Essence for her Child. That 'need' was met and her need now is to gather all her material world energy into the Otherealm, from whence it came. SHE must negotiate that soon, but SHE won't allow us to give a specific date. In fact,

SHE has not shared that specific time. Of course we know the end of time means some hybrids will cease to be self-aware. Such entities will change to Othereal Spirit and be added into the Holy God Host foundation, aware only of God.

"Remember, practically speaking, there is no past and no future for you, other than what God intends. Time is only assumed by humans as a modus operandi frame of reference. The past exists only in memory and the future only in expectancy. So I am telling you what you can expect in the ever-present 'now' to come, but God doesn't want panicked minds that can't think clearly and so we can't offer you a specific time. We do know there's none to waste though and never really has been.

"God and COG live with eternity, meaning without past or future, but with immediacy. Before anyone can even contemplate the 'present,' it is 'past,' and before one can anticipate an instantaneous 'future,' it is 'now.' So, God has a big advantage in not needing to depend on 'time' as a coordinate. Among other things, that means God requires memories only of previously established thought patterns used to make objective energy models that SHE wishes to retain, maintain, and sustain for recall. God does create original energy patterns, shaped into models as desired, and/or SHE recreates energy patterns from her perfect Memory or Assembler. That's why 'Déjà Vu' is sometimes relevant. Many things happen over and over and some human minds can vaguely recall such patterns or events too.

"As for material world creatures, your next breath does not exist until you breathe it. So, breathe your next breath for the purpose of purifying your spirit-soul for a "change for God's sake." And the one after that and as many as it takes for you to realize that you cannot breathe without God. God breathed life into you and will take it away if you do not eventually come to be perfect, as SHE is, as COG are. You must know that every moment you perceive life should be "dedicated" to God. When that finally becomes a reality for you, you will be in Heaven, perceiving each godly moment as often as you will, just by accessing its energy location through sharing God's Memory. You should know by now that God holds only Moral Memory, which also will be the case for any of her Cells.

"In the meantime, 'time' is a powerful, conceptual tool for humans within their material realm, as they need a way to measure and categorize changes. So, we will continue to refer to "now," as a familiar part of that concept. So, now – addressing you readers – how many of you have the wisdom to use the concept of time to measure the most important change of all – your change from a material brain-set of id/ego indulgences to a spirit-soul mindset of moral life for eternity?

"You may continue into your mundane future by staying your past course, or you may change that future by deciding on a more godly way. Don't fail to use this God-given power of your ability to co-create with God, by exercising it for your salvation. Every time you get ready to speak or act, you might allow mindful thoughts to be your essence: "I had the power 'then' to change my future to one of perfect morality. I am using that power now." You should know it is what you will, and it will become who you are – a self-aware entity compatible with God in order to Savior Self.

"So much mystery surrounds religion on your planet, but some people actually like it that way. That though does make it more difficult to uncover the universal truths that Christ said would be revealed, and to have them accepted – so much so that many of the things I'm telling you must seem like fantasy. What would you expect God's truth to be, otherwise? It is tragic that so many minds are closed to the wonder of God, or that so many would limit her to misinformed thinking – such as God being a single Parent and only of male gender. To this point, one might have accepted that, but beyond this point one must know better.

"Does that really mean that people should turn their imaginations loose and that every moral thing one can imagine is going to be true? Whether anything becomes truth to material senses is up to God, but realize SHE also gave you some "God sense" through your tiny soul, especially when it operates through its O-Soul or Cell of God Mind. Does this mean all good things are possible? Yes, it does. What about all bad things? – Only to the point of one's destruction at one's own behest. That means all bad things soon will be coming to an end, but that doesn't need to simultaneously portend your ending, unless you would have it so. Would you? That might be the most important question of your life, because you will need to prove the answer, one way or the other. A wrong response equals ignorance and death.

"Now, did that information leave more of you "Deep" readers shaking your heads in bewilderment? I know it did for some of you who have yet to learn how to tone down that self within you that seems superior to such "imaginings?" By 'superior,' I mean your own id/ego assessment of the 'you' that you think yourself to be – contrary to God's knowledge of what (not who) you really are. You are 'essence'- either good or evil.

"We pure Spirit and Othereal 'Be-ins' are still here serving the material world, ages after our Parents instructed us to give birth to a final crop of humankind within former perfect Human Gardens all around her multi-dimensional universe. Now it's about time for these hybrid human gardens to bear some final fruit.

"Yes, we are here to test your incredulity, as part of your id/ego testing, but our tests are based on credulous truth that many of you will simply refuse to believe. Still, we won't spare you incredulous truth just to keep you in your comfort zone with a God who "suits you." Go ahead and close Deepy's book if you feel absolutely safe in doing so. If you really seek safety, then don't be afraid to continue with us until we have our say – on behalf of God. Have you had the good sense to fear yourself, your fellow man, Egod, or God at any point during your reading? If so, that is a sign of sanity. Give thanks; even though it's unfortunate that 'fear' is even a concept. It won't be for much longer, but the worst is yet to come for some of you; sadly – quite sadly.

"All too many of you have had your say on behalf of the devil (Egodevil) for much too long – tens of thousands of years, in fact. So, hear us out, even if you don't care to trust us because you are not hearing what you want to hear, or you're hearing what you don't care to hear. Yes, you are being challenged. If you are just now feeling that challenge, then perhaps CHIP and I are not doing our jobs. If so, I accept responsibility for the inability to communicate, unless you are not open to understanding this truth – in which case you are killing both time and yourself. However, I can safely say you haven't come this far without good reason. Perhaps you are inherently wiser than you know.

"When it comes to understanding, I would say to some "feel-good" preachers out there that you are allowing people to drift comfortably into hell, even if one or the other of you does not mind, so long as some coinage of the realm is deposited into "God's" account. Some hypocrites pay rather than pray, but that should not be okay with you teachers and preachers of morality.

"There never has been time for complacency – but especially not now. So, revive some fearsome, erstwhile "fire and brimstone" lessons that hit people in their moral solar plexus. Those dire warnings of tough love really are the most loving biblical messages of God. Some people should not leave their churches feeling comfortable with how they are living their lives, because most still do have the ability to recognize the truth when they hear it, even if it makes them nauseously uncomfortable. If you fear they won't come back, you simply then are "just another politician."

"Tell it like it is, even if you lose some lukewarm donations. Many of those who truly know they are living with godly morals will appreciate the fact you are trying to reach those who are not. The number of self-righteous, pseudo Christians is dwindling anyway, as they become part of the growing secular community; some are even being teased into radical violence against democracy in the name of democracy or sadly in the name of Christianity. That's how smart they perceive themselves to be; too smart for a God they can't see or touch and don't care to consider. Perhaps they believe they somehow are scientists, even if many of them don't believe in some things they can see and touch, such as climate change, social and economic injustice or virus pandemics for example. Maybe they just haven't been touched enough or seen enough yet by what they have caused or will cause others to suffer.

"If you presenters of 'God' truly are holy, SHE ultimately will reward your work in accord with the truth that you cause others to perceive as reality. Help your audience understand the gospel truth, not for your own earthly rewards, but for your, their, and God's sake. Yes, of course we know you are putting much of your coffered money to godly use – but are you saving spirit-souls in the fast, furious way called for by the "end of time" scenario that already has begun to play out in this world? Are you? God knows. You should too. Some of you might want to consider revamping your programs somewhat. Make yourself more of a teacher than a blissful preacher. This is a horrible world. You would be wise to hate it and try to do something about it. You may recall that Jesus hated this world. It truly is hell for so many people, as well as disappointing to God. God and Jesus love the suffering people who cause themselves and others to suffer, but they cannot love such a world society. How can you?

"These are "end times," if for no other reason than they are materialistic, idol and ego worshipping, immoral times. But that has always been the case with this species. Lives are ending every day. Where do you think the once living essence of those entities go after meeting their personal 'end' time? So, what makes this time different? It is because God's time limit for this generation is about to expire. Jesus Christ soon will be returning. How soon? Are you ready to find out it's tomorrow or day after tomorrow? What if I told you, day after tomorrow, ten years from now? Do you really want to know when – now that you know why? Either He's coming or you're going, but either way there will be a reckoning. I'm asking you this much right now: "Are you ready to be judged?" Know for sure God knows your true status."

"Here's a question for persons who witness for God professionally: "Do you really know what to do to meet your own, as well as God's, time constraint challenge? Would you say it will take more money in your coffers or more wisdom in your soul, or both? For your part and God's, it could take some hard reminders to your audience, even some scolding that makes people squirm in their seats because they know they have reason to squirm. It means the 'still, small' voices of their tiny souls still are alive and they should be grateful for that and to you for helping them realize it with whatever godly lesson you can teach them in the process.

"As pastors or other clergy, you already know your audience should not see you as judgmental or self-righteous. Even if you don't have a booming, melodious voice, just stand up there and preach-teach the biblical verses and stories that you can put into moral context in a meaningful way. That is what Doctors Billy Graham and Charles Stanley did and will continue doing through video recordings, writings and sermons. They are blessed that way because they deeply love the God who created them, all of us, and all Consciousness. That's why they are so beloved.

"Deepy's book should separate out those lukewarm, hard-core egos looking for an excuse to stamp 'nonsense' on this work and excuse themselves from further thought of responsibilities they knew they would not or could not meet anyway. We pray they eventually will no longer second-guess God's powers or limit her to "nuanced" misunderstandings that seem to work for them - for now.

"This work may seem like poppycock to some of you who make the choice to see it that way, but it makes God-sense on behalf of God, who Co-Created her forms through COG on an "as needed" basis. Therefore, if you don't meet God's standards in a timely manner, you won't be needed and will never have existed. Then again, God has always moved on without certain of her immoral and useless thought forms. God regrets all lost spirits, but so many of them would not or could not recognize they needed to change in order to be saved. Do you fit that mold?

"You might allow a cancer to spread within you if you won't take a doctor's word that it is cancer. Your ignorance might let it continue to feed on every part of you? God is anything but ignorant and if you are immoral, you are her cancer. SHE would rather cure you with your help than let you kill yourself, but SHE will not allow you to spread through her, killing her Cells with your poisonous influence. For now though you still are a tiny creation in her final generation. It's your move. Bend at the knees: Pray.

"I wish we could save you all; but you won't let us.

"Okay, enough "preach-teaching" again for the moment. Some of you are getting weary. "Am I right, my Deep friend?"

"Huh? - Of course. Okay, I think I may need a bit of a break. In fact, I wonder if the CHIP chopper could find us here. I'm having energy withdrawal. I could sure use a bowl of caffeine."

The two trekkers both sat down on a flat rock to enjoy some silence.

A few minutes later a quin stepped out of a small, round, one-seat CHIP ship and put a bowl in front of Deepy's face. It did not look or smell familiar. "What's this?" he asked to her back, as she walked away. "Guava juice, sir," she said, glancing back. "It's feijoa – pineapple guava and really quite good."

Deepy tried it. It was 'yum,' and shortly after he had lapped the bowl clear, he felt much more alert, thinking he might need to ask for feijoa guava java juice more often. He liked the taste better than regular guava – sneaky CHIP.

"What else is of interest to you at this time, my friend?" Eno asked, as he waved goodbye to the quin about to fly away. Deepy teleped a big 'thank you' in her direction and heard back, "You're welcome, sir."

"I know the tinys eventually will take human form. Mind if I ask when?"

Deepy figured Eno must have forgotten the question, as he did not reply for what seemed like a long time. "Or maybe I have," Deepy then thought. "What was the question?" he chuckled to himself, but went on to inquire, "Wrong question – Wrong time?"

"It is exactly the right question, my friend, but the timing is a little off for now."

'Dom-da-dom-dom!' Deepy simulated a sound he thought denoted intrigue. He then expressed some gratitude...

"I will thank you in advance for sharing that. In fact, thank you for sharing all of this."

"You're very welcome. Pity those who would read your book and "choose" to not understand, simply because you, my friend, have your own limitations. They will gladly notice your faults, but not their own, which is to be expected; and yes, Jesus said something to that effect about how to treat a brother.

Deepy knew that Eno had no id or ego, of course, so he did not give a hoot about human criticism unless it harmed the critic or the critic's audience. He had the 'Self' confidence of God, who simply cared about human beings, who loved them in spite of themselves, and wanted to save them for eternity. Deepy was not as optimistic regarding humans as Eno, but he had no doubt that Eno effectually was God – "is" God, he corrected himself – and all that he said ultimately is truth, or could be, for those hybrid humans who could imagine God imagining it. Deepy, however, did not want to tangle with Earthite scientists regarding physics, but he trusted Eno enough to try to translate his manner of speaking into what he hoped was within range of Eno's expressions. CHIP helped in that regard. Deepy had great confidence he was bound to fashion some errors anyway because CHIP had so much going on that Deepy had to trust himself too. He then rumbled a thought out loud at the end of his surmising.

"I guess I'm pretty simple – somewhat eccentric too, but not innocent. I usually think I know what I'm doing, even while knowing I am a sinner who is about as Christian as I know how to be, while making excuses for not being better. I try hard to not do things for which I have regrets, but I also know I live in sin every day of my life and often fail miserably in my thinking. I know too that I will never cease asking God to forgive me and I will never stop trying to do better."

He paused, and then added, "I'm sorry," apologizing simply because he thought what he just said might somehow have been an ego-contrived sentiment. His thinking often stopped him in its tracks, while he tried to clarify to God what he thought he had meant. Once again, and at the moment, he made no sense to himself, but hoped God could interpret his motivations.

"Your wisdom and honesty are becoming," Eno now told him, "and as good a note as any to end this session; so, back to your room with you and I will let you know later when we shall meet again. However, to partly answer your earlier question, your classroom of tiny angel cells will be among the first to reincarnate to serve as assistants to Jesus Christ. We don't know exactly when that will happen. We simply are speaking in relative terms when we say 'soon,' but prior to the time some of your readers address the new reality we offer and for that matter even before your book goes to print."

~~~~~~~~~~~~~~~~~~~~~~~~~~~~~~~~~~~~

Right on cue, a voice chirped inside Deepy's head: "Robo Chef, here – Are you hungry, Sir?"

"You had better believe it, CHIPster."

~~~~~~~~~~~~~~~~~~~~~~~~~~~~~~~~~~~~

Deepy felt someone's hand shaking him. One eye opened to see a quin standing over him. "Here's your breakfast, sir. Sorry to wake you, but CHIP said you would want this." He pawed both eyes wide open. His nose was telling him he was awake enough to know he really was quite hungry, and in his own bed and the time literally "on the wall" showed a digital seven. "Thanks, CHIP," – "and you," he quickly added to the departing cheery quin, who smiled brightly with a "You're welcome, sweetie".

Must be a down-home, southern quin, he thought – to call him 'sweetie,' as it seemed almost a southern custom.

He then recalled parts of a dream and put a little of it together before his hunger took over. He decided either he or the Lord God was from an alternate universe.

"Forgive me, Lord," Deepy mumbled, thinking once more as he often had in his Larray past that even crazy dreams may have some necessary message to them, if one could just figure out what it might be. "Dear, God!" he muttered. Then, looking at the food on the tray table, he remembered to say, "Thank you for this food and all your blessings...especially the spiritual feasting.

Amen!"

\\\\\\\\\\\\\\\V/////////////

(CHAPTER 18)
Foxes & Wolves

"That's just the way it is, folks," Deepy thought to himself, as if to emphasize just how "matter of fact" this whole experience should seem; as he had long ago determined to take Eno at core moral value and try to sort intellectual matters later as necessary. He at least now knew that wisdom somehow superseded intellect, but you needed intelligence to achieve wisdom, and then logic to separate the two. Love was a natural attractor between opposite polar forces, but it then was enhanced by God's empathetic *Grace*, which Deepy knew had saved him, if he was saved, through her Spiritual Son, Jesus and his polar opposite Christ Soul Mate, even as he prayed he was not being presumptuous. He knew he at least was becoming a better man wise enough to pray for Grace and mercy through humility.

After eating, Deepy studied some UFO experiences had by humans; he later took a brief nap and then made his way to the diner, knowing he was to meet Eno there, even though he could not remember how he took leave of him from the leaves of the forest floor to awaken in his own bed about twelve hours later.

~~~~~~~~~~~~~~~~~~~~

"In the woods again; here I am, in the woods again musing with my Mentor friend; it's such a happy life... walking here – in the woods again." Deepy was thinking somewhat tunefully of Willie Nelson's* *"On the Road Again,"* even as his Mentor friend seemed full of questions and answers. *(singer/songwriter)

"Some politicians really do know right from wrong – good from evil. Some others base their priorities mainly on money for their reelections and their continuing prestigious material life. Would too much real social goodness cost those politicians and their self-serving greedy supporters too much money? Many politicians and their investors have priorities that fall well below moral intelligence and so the answer is "yes, too much moral goodness is not good for the bottom line of selfish egos in any profession. By all means, don't shortchange Egod (yourself) on behalf of God."

"That is so depressing," Deepy responded, as Eno paused to clamber over a rock. "Nobody wants to hear that."

Eno acknowledged Deepy's poll results by saying, "You're right on the first count, but wrong on the second. It is depressing, but most people do want to hear the truth, except of course for politicians who oftentimes are wolves in sheep's clothing to quote a brother of mine. Some sheep types really *'need'* to hear truth and let it sink in. Some folks can never have enough money or power to cover the investments they make in their own id/egos. Society should define that type of thinking as naïve, if not stupid – because ultimately it harms everyone, to include perpetrators with vaunted social status – down to the core of their ignorant essence, <u>IF</u> – or quite likely <u>when</u> - they die for eternity.

"As it is, it would seem that moral intelligence is that 'Othereal' intelligence that just cannot be applied to all people. Obviously, id/ego's opposite brain-set runs rampant through the lives and deaths of others, because some 'elite' individuals are not morally smart enough, or just too greedy, to condemn all immorality. Yes, of course tiny souls know evil from good, because 'good' inherently amounts to God within the souls of hybrid humankind. Even so, many 'humanimals,' aka former humans, no longer have the tiny soul they once had to know 'good from evil.' Multiple id/ego reincarnations caused the loss of those souls, leaving only a spirit-brain humanimal who gives no thought to life beyond this one. But, God gives them a final chance to recover their souls. A relative few have done so.

"Do you suppose babies don't inherently know what a smile means and how to return it? Be a child in that regard, and always verify a child's trust. Be a child in your innocence.

You, my friend, have <u>not</u> lost many of your childish, loving attributes and you won't. You were raised in the ways of a loving Lord."

"And I thank God every day for that," Deepy told him.

"If moral goodness, as defined by godly thought, interpreted by WILL and Grace - cannot be legislated into mankind's laws (as politicians say) what does that leave within the realm of legislation – "immoral actions and deeds?" Of course – such as murder! Therefore, immorality, as interpreted by God's 'WILL and Grace,' must be legislated out of existence with appropriate shame and penalties. Politicians will claim that they are not sure what's immoral and what's not. They are politicians and like "publicans" during the time of Christ, most are "re" publicans just pretending to be saved by religion and pretending in a way that will get them reelected by their likewise pretentious followers.

"Too many politicians don't know God and don't care to because it portends too much responsibility in always doing the right thing. Instead, they must pretend to believe what most of their constituents pretend to believe, because votes equal money. Unfortunately too many voters now are more concerned with watching sports live or on TV, than going to church and paying attention. They seem to have lost the inherent moral caring their tiny souls could provide if they used them. Unfortunately for them life is more than ever "materiality." It is their "reality," and religion is "unreal," in a way that suits them.

"What I'm saying does not, in any way, mean a theocracy* of officials is the answer to governmental problems. It is not. *{Dictionary-defined as Government by immediate divine guidance or by officials who are regarded as divinely guided}

"As institutions, Church and State should be separated. But that hardly means that morality should be separated from your elected officials or from the laws of your government. Of course when Jesus Christ returns, SHe will offer immediate divine guidance^ with angelic helpers to teach personal governance by one's own morality. Divine guidance^ would equate to always being guided by moral intelligence. Humans should strive for that, as they await the return of Jesus or their own earlier end-of-life judgment by God. ^ [God would be the only One to say if an entity is a divine Trangel such as her son and daughter – and not born of humankind.]

"The United States of America is a Republic that embodies capitalism as its working financial concept with democracy (rule of, by, and for the people) as its core foundation – 'said' democracy having been undergirded by a comprehensive understanding envisioned by a majority of highly-principled founders and written into a governing "Constitution," that sadly can be, and has been, disputed by evil politicians named "Egod.' They can make it seem that some people are above the law and thus in their case nothing is unconstitutional. Democracy must be preserved where it takes root; otherwise lives have been sacrificed for a grandiose, temporary state, simply awaiting Egod's ultimately evil take-over.

"Generally, most of the United States' founders were morally smarter than the average citizen, unless they were slave owners, in which case they were self-righteous, even if they otherwise meant well. On the other hand most of them accepted laws that freed slaves, even if slave descendents to this day still are fighting for civil rights and equal justice. That fight must end now with a final, fair solution, to include stiffer penalties against known racists. That should include anyone who uses their free speech to denigrate any race and condone or incite racial hatred or unequal treatment based on race, religion, creed, nationality, or any self-declared 'polar' gender – or so-called 'sexual' gender they know themselves to be, regardless of outward appearance. People usually know themselves for who they are "inside," and you are not their judge. God is Judge. Do you still not comprehend that final point? People who love each other know it, regardless of how they appear to "outsiders" who are not one with God.

"Many politicians are sly like foxes, meaning too phony for God's greater good. Nowadays more and more 'publican type' politicians come from the most morally ignorant among you, because some of their constituents also believe they are wily, even without moral intelligence. One big-time political donor owns a cage full of fake-news "sly like foxes" commentators, at which viewers keep tossing fresh money, because they are hooked on the hatred and lies that sell advertizing. That faux fox team definitely wants a big "helping" from the cream at the top of material wealth;

therefore most of the world's politicians are for sale to the highest bidder – Rupert Murdoch being one such "shrewd" buyer. He will learn the hard way he's not the god he thinks he is. He has not created a spirit-soul to last forever. Evil bought Mister Murdoch with a bad bye-buy forever sign $. But, it has bought so many others as well with that power sign.

"Capitalism is a good system when it promotes fair, honest competition. It also easily invites corruption among those who see money as their god – thereby stopping morality in its tracks. Right now, the United States seems bent toward corruption among the foxes and wolves. What will cause its final destruction from within? – Greed by too many misguided humanimals will. Or can the USA finally energize the core moral intent of its "One Nation under God; 'Indivisible,' with freedom and justice for all" pledge? It can. God surely would welcome that vote of confidence and obviously live up to her side of that once-proposed, but never resolved "covenant." That blessed nation has not been absolved of its godly duties.

"Of course at the outset, American democracy was divided against itself and fought a civil war to uphold or overthrow its own fledgling government. The issue was divine guidance versus the self-righteous '*right*' to "own" other people also created by God.

"Much of the populace remained unguided by a federal government that would make slave-owners answer to a central authority. They could disagree with God and apparently get away with it (or so they thought then – and maybe now again) but government laws based on divine guidance were a different matter. The most egregious slave owners were ignorant of the Christian religion most of them claimed. They were immoral. Many of those same or kindred spirits now are around in reincarnated, slow developing minds. Some have paid their karmic debts, but many still are shameless and downright evil with more serious lessons to learn. Just know that God has an end in sight for all hate mongers. Those with debt still to pay may end up hating each other with a vengeance; but whatever happens, they will suffer as God deems necessary. If they fail this life as a final chance to 'believe,' in God, they simply will go "poof" afterward as God waves them away. They will give up eternal life for – stup<u>id</u>ity, <u>id</u>iocy, ignorance or denial – all of which ultimately mean lack of wisdom and grace.

"Citizens of every country remain divided against themselves on a host of civil issues – to include laws that would try to lead them down a moral and more divine path as nations. As a COG, I am here to tell you that divine guidance is a model of wise, intelligent, logical, loving, and gracious moral leadership worthy of serving the only types of governments that have any chance of survival on your planet, whether deemed socialist or democratic or a combination thereof, such as sociocratic.

"We COG know better than to expect perfection from 'mere mortals' (as you so excuse your sins); however, sometime within the predicted one thousand year guidance and tutelage of Jesus Christ, it shall become '... on Earth, as it is in heaven.' Therefore we suggest any presiding politician or candidate for office, come with a large dose of moral grace toward all citizens and other countries. That means raising the moral bar for democratically elected leaders. Meanwhile, some of you really do look forward to the return engagement of Jesus Christ. Congratulations. Make your plans now and carry them out if you want to be here during his/her time in Garden Gaia. By now you should know what's expected of you."

~~~~~~~~~~~~~~~~~~~~~~

"Need some refreshments, Deepy? CHIP's catering service is just a thought away," a chirpy voice said.

"I especially cater to furry critters with half-a-mind," CHIP continued with his interjection, having taken his Commander's silent cue.

"Really? I always suspected you did everything with half-a-mind." Deepy retorted, with a smile and a wink at Eno.

"Oh my! Touché. You got me. I'm at your service for life, or a couple of minutes, whichever comes first."

"You know my standard fare, CHIP. A couple of burgers with a milkshake... no wait, make that iced tea, please, and I do thank you, Sir."

Eno asked for some space juice, [as he called pure Spirit]. He had a canister of water with him, some of which he had shared with Deepy a couple of times. About a minute later, none other than CHIP himself showed up to serve them, as Eno was telling Deepy that 'space juice' was a coded message private joke, while not saying how he could imbibe Spirit from a 'space' cup. CHIP was friendly, but all business and didn't stick around to chat. He waved and smiled at Deepy, gave a thumbs-up sign to his Commander and then disappeared.

The two friends refreshed themselves in silence for the next several minutes... Deepy concentrating on his burgers, Eno apparently lost in reverie. They then continued on the trail after a brief respite in which Deepy fended off another nap. Eno caught his friend's attention, with a very pronounced word that seemed to sizzle.

"DEATH!

Let's talk about it, as humans often seem to perceive it."

(Oh God, I'd rather not, Deepy subthought, suddenly recalling the first funeral he had ever attended – that of Howie's mom, Mrs. Sanders. Howie had thanked him later, as Larray had been the only one of his classmates to attend. Between then and now though, it had seemed people were dropping dead all around him. His grandparents – both sets – had "ascended," as he now liked to think of it. His parents and wife's parents seemed to still be going strong and he and CeCe were grateful to have them for so long, but there's no escaping death, as he had lost a lot of friends, relatives, and acquaintances to it. But he did know what Jesus said on the subject. He said, '... *let the dead bury the dead.')*

"And that's the point I want to stress here," Eno now confided – having been tuned to Deepy's reflections. Eno had paused to allow that introspection, as he knew most humans have strong emotions regarding the 'death' topic. "That may have sounded callous, but of course," he now continued, "By 'dead,' Jesus meant those people not living with the knowledge of a godly afterlife – or in fact one's only real life – the Othereal Soul life in Heaven. People see it as their loss, if a loved one dies to this world, and that's logical, but we would rather they know it is God's gain to have a potential new angel apprentice in many cases. Although those who mourn the most should be those who are not sure such is the case with their loved ones. God, however, is merciful and prayers can help, especially if one is within the purview of her Grace.

"Certainly you will miss those who precede you in this passing over, but you must realize that the vast majority of departed entities are more alive than ever if they reach heaven, even those who may face some serious consequences in purgatory for the life just departed. Of course each of you will mourn in your own way. Even so, mourning can be seen as something of a misunderstanding of Christ's own teaching. As his/her final lesson, SHe taught that SHe had overcome death and that anyone could; and they would be foolish to not know that. SHe (the COG pronoun) led the way in such teachings.

"Obviously people will be sad to lose those they love, but if their loved one is a Christian, or likewise moral, they should try to be happy at the same time, implausible as that may seem. That takes a deeper understanding, which is appropriate with respect to God's judgment. Naturally it is better to live a life that leaves little doubt as to your next and perhaps final destination.

"Of course, people will miss those they love, but there is no point in feeling sorry for oneself, whether dying, or having lost a loved one. God loves each entity, and even though some spirit-souls may represent her badly during their physical incarnations, usually SHE will give them another chance. Sometimes, however, they are so far gone in character value that God's energy is put to better use than offering such a failed spirit another lifetime.

"Reincarnation can never be a realistic goal for anyone, however. Its value is in keeping you alive until your spirit-soul together can fight a more successful moral battle in order to attain eternity if possible. It's only possible if you work with God.

"If you were not the flawed form of beings you are, as Earthite humans, you always would see "life" from God's perspective... through God's own eyes, or Mind, with which your mind should be able to commune, even if indirectly. You would see that God's "Life" does not include death, and so it would serve each person to live "God's life," as offered through her Yang Son Jesus with his Yin Christ Soul Mate. However, as imperfect beings, God can be situated within your thoughts only to the extent you allow. That is why you should and must reach out to her by way of your tiny mind through your Over-Soul, which abides within her Heavenly Child.

"Death," even though imperfect humans may not wish to celebrate it, should be looked upon as an opportunity to pass from one plane of existence into another higher plane – or from life to an alternate more godly life, even if it is only a brief respite from starting anew in another body, if reincarnation is needed."

Eno took a moment to tell his friend to watch his footing as he clambered over another rather large boulder.

"I would remind you yet again, that unless you are truly moral enough you can't expect to live just this one life in order to reach God. Nor can you expect those loved ones who preceded you to heaven to necessarily be there or stay there, if they did not go as committed, Christ-like* moral beings. [Even if not still there, God can allow brief family reunions through her Memory Assembler.] All of those who are incarnate now have lived before and this is a final opportunity for many. Those scheduled to reincarnate for a potential *'biblical'* end-time scenario will do so, and those intended to return for the new Garden Gaia will do so when that time comes after Armageddon or the Apocalypse."

*(You don't need to be called Christian, in order to have godly moral values, but you must love and appreciate Jesus Christ as a Child Of God, and understand his teachings. Other moral leaders sent by God also should be loved that way too.)

"Eno," Deepy interrupted, "Pardon me, but I thought that anyone committed to Christ as one's Savior meant an automatic ticket into heaven, if you will pardon my vernacular. I mean there's no reincarnation in that case is there? I'm a little bit confused. It almost sounds as if everyone has needed to reincarnate, even Christians."

"'Committed' is the key word. There are so many who are now, and have been, Christian in name only," Eno replied. "They judge themselves to be okay, in spite of knowing they are sinning without much if any remorse. Morally faithful Christians do not need to reincarnate except for a future passage through Garden Gaia, to assist Jesus Christ and other moral leaders and Souls."

"Excuse me again, but can people be saved in purgatory? Can they make a firm and believable commitment to God through Jesus Christ then, and not need to reincarnate?"

"That is where God's Grace can come into play if a person's sins are not egregious. Grace allows for committed Christians and moral 'others' to occasionally backslide, so long as they continue to pray and get back on course. So, yes, some of the least harmful sinners can be guided to salvation while in purgatory. Even so, there will be a final, if brief, reincarnation of virtually all border-line spirit-souls during that thousand-year period in which Christ will reign. Some recalcitrant spirit-souls will be in desperate need of salvation during that time and will benefit from having family members there from all previous lives, all of whom will likewise benefit."

"Woe is me," Deepy sighed. "Sometimes it all just seems so complex; I have a hard time absorbing it all. All those families won't be there at the same time, will they?"

Eno just smiled and said, "No, they won't. Wait here."

"Hey, where are you going?"

"Just relax, I won't be long," Eno said, as he strolled off in the direction of the woods, but seemed to evaporate before getting there. He had, however, left his friend in a beautiful, sunny spot.

ZZZZZZZZZZZZZZZZZZZZZZZ

CHAPTER 19
"I'm Woke!"

"Deepy! Wake up! ... Wake up, my friend – Time to get moving."

A drowsy, droopy dog tried pawing his eyes apart, even as the Voice of God rang out.

"So," Deepy said, as he struggled awake, "I don't know if it's my horrific dreaming or my weakness for CHIP's cheesecake, but I'm afraid we are about to be inconvenienced by a gross physiological need on my part."

"No problem. That's a friendly looking tree, or we are only a "CHIP-shot" away from the ship."

"CHIP? – Hurry!" Deepy regretted wearing clothing at the moment and he didn't want to inconvenience Eno with any nursemaid duties.

Eno was sitting beside the lake when Deepy returned a short time later and perched beside him. "Whew," Deepy told him, "thank goodness for the speed of thought. CHIP knew I really didn't want to mess up the pristine beauty of these woods. I'm not a bear, after all," Deepy winked. Eno smiled and said, "You're not a dog either. You're more of a comedic angel."

Eno immediately got up and began walking at the edge of the water. The non-dog, 'comedic angel?' dutifully followed, asking Eno if he liked country music.

"I like most kinds of music," Eno told him.

"Good, here's a little ditty I wrote. It's a miserable tale."

CHIP's Hillbilly Headband played along, as Deepy sang

"The Downhill Bar…"
When she finally left me
I wasn't standing tall
She knocked me over
But I knew enough to crawl

I'm on my way to crazy
It ain't very far
Just around the corner
From the Downhill Bar

She said she took me back
One too many times,
Said I couldn't change
No matter how I tried.
I giggled and I laughed,
I broke down and cried,
That's when I knew
I was losing my mind

I'm on my way to crazy
It ain't very far
Just around the corner
From the Downhill Bar

There's a blue moon above
Dark angry skies
Pouring salty rain drops,
Stinging my eyes,
But I can still see the flash
Of that big neon sign -
Welcome in loser
To the Downhill Bar,
If you're going crazy
It ain't very far,
Move on, move on, move on
{HEADBAND BREAK}

She hung me out to dry
Three sheets to the wind
She wouldn't let it slide,

Said she was smelling whisky
For the very last time
Now ain't that ironic
I was drinking vodka tonic
With just a twist of lime

She said she took me back
One too many times
Said I couldn't change
No matter how I tried
I giggled and I laughed
I broke down and cried
That's when I knew
I was losing my mind

I'm on my way to crazy
It ain't very far
Just around the corner
From the Downhill Bar

There's a blue moon above
Dark angry skies
Pouring salty rain drops
Stinging my eyes
But I can still see the flash
Of that big neon sign
Welcome in, loser,
To the Downhill Bar
If you're going crazy
It ain't very far

Move on, move on, move on...
Move on, move on, move on

So they did and Deepy realized his singing had taken some of his wind and that hill just up ahead looked like a mountain.

"Well, I'm no talent judge, ol' chum, but I found it entertaining in a hybrid human sort of way," Eno told his now-panting partner.

"People should be praised for a job well done, so long as they know their talent, skill, and other laudable abilities, in fact come from God, but must be practiced," Eno said, then added, "They may not be so blessed in a future lifetime, *if* they don't understand, appreciate, and use their abilities in this life, in a moral way. That's just part and parcel of God's law of karma."

It was time for a break, Eno then said. They took a short one – Deepy to his place in the sun; but this time, Eno needed to take care of some official business back at the ship. "See you back here in about twenty minutes."

A dog laying in warm sunlight... what could go right? – And so it did. *ZZZZZzzzzzzz*

~~~~~~

When Eno returned, he decided to talk in Deepy's sleep, knowing he could do so without disturbing his friend.

"Do not despair. Evil is a curable cancer – IF you take your moral medicine as prescribed by God. Ask God to help you "stomach it," until it reaches your mind and stays there. God wants you cured. If you are willing to kill Egod with the wisdom of morality, God will assist you. Those unwilling to kill Egod should get in touch with their Over-Soul - their guardian Angel - to get First Aid. Their essence remains evil, and if they do not change it, God will act upon it to render it benign, inert, or otherwise of no consequence. If that happens to you it means you no longer will exist as you. If that is okay with you, then don't worry about it. Otherwise, also don't worry about it – just do what you know will make a difference. If you have learned nothing to this point, then blame whomever you will and worry as much as you like.

"Yes, I know some of your readers, my deep friend, may be high-strung and quite emotional. Some might think they are ready and willing to just give up. Why? I would ask them: Is the alternative to what you now are doing really so impossible to your current state of mind? If so then, while 'giving up' might be understandable, it could not and would not satisfy you. That solution could change your fate to zero existence forever. If life is so inexplicable or unfathomable to you, then understand if you cannot knowingly reason death, God will help you reason life. Try asking her help for as long as it takes you to become humble. SHE already knows how repressive many of you are when it comes to believing in her.

"I am addressing all of you nail-biting fretters directly. Considering your condition, quitting life might even seem logical, but it isn't and God can help you overcome yourself. SHE can change you if you work with her. SHE really can and you may trust her, but you also must trust yourself. At least consider asking her to help you. You're important – too important to be impatient with yourself or especially with God. Therefore, be prudent and approach God for the long haul. Instead of giving up on yourself – give up what is killing you, namely id/ego and Egod, through some form of distress. Pray and then continue to pray. Once done, suicide can't be undone.

"Any faithful Christian will tell you they understand something crucial: they know you can be saved for eternity by simply accepting and practicing the moral lessons that Jesus taught. He died in order to prove how much that creed of morality means to God... but part of God's lesson was to show that Jesus Christ did not die at all. He suffered – yes, but his true life continued in his home realm of Heaven. He escaped this life for eternal life with his Parents. You don't need to escape life for eternal death. Humans must live morally in this life before they can attain Heaven. You can do that. You can, and you should know that God is a loving Parent now pleading for you to live in your physical realm until you have paid your karmic debt. Trust your life to her, so that SHE can help you change it before allowing you to live her eternal Life.

"When God changes, everything changes. All that remains of "what was," is God's memory of it. If God chooses to not re-member it and re-cognize it, then it may as well never have existed. Who's to say it did, if God doesn't? When imperfection is deleted once and for all, it never will be recalled. What would be the point? Look again at the statement that imperfection is deleted "for all." It must be; otherwise, like cancer or an incurable pandemic, it would spread. The point now is that you have only a little time left to insure your life is cured and secured for eternity.

"And while God knows none of you can attain perfection within a single lifetime, SHE expects you to recognize the need for making a sincere, moral effort at the very least. If you do not make that moral effort, you may never get another chance. If you can add to that effort through believing that God gave her only begotten* son, Jesus Christ, to suffer physical death and then be revitalized in forgiveness of your sins, you will accomplish about as much as you can In any one life. *{passing through a physical birth canal} You should understand that even though life in physical bodies is hardly ever free of suffering, you could, through Christ, be reborn into an eternal, heavenly form. In the meantime, God's sustaining Grace will carry you through the karma of this lifetime. Christ said in Matthew 7:7-8:

'Ask, and it shall be given you; Seek, and ye shall find; knock, and it shall be opened unto you. For everyone that asketh receiveth; and he that seeketh findeth; and to him that knocketh it shall be opened.'

"In other words – TRY! Make the effort. It is up to you to have the wisdom to understand that some things are worth believing in, seeking, finding, knowing and experiencing. For it is only through finding and understanding the truth of what God and her only begotten Child did for you, that you can understand what you must do for yourselves and each other. Seek, find, and understand, if you really want eternal life with God, and if, in the meantime, you really want your lives on Earth to more closely approach her heavenly ideal.

"Ask God to give you that chance you may not think you deserve. SHE won't give up on you unless you give up on her and force the issue. Please remember that. Allow it to galvanize your will with hers, so you gain Morality- "the Heart and Soul of God."

Deepy lay there, wondering if he had been asleep. For some reason he wasn't sure. He knew he had been listening to Eno, but it must have been part of a dream.

"Alright, let's change the subject somewhat, before you go back to sleep."

"Huh?" I must be dreaming in the voice of Eno.

"It is a shame that more people, especially those who consider themselves religious, have not paid closer and particular attention to the early twentieth-century psychic, Edgar Cayce. (1877-1945). However - many have done so, and even now there is much to be learned from his family's and foundation's* compilations of Cayce's work." *(A.R.E. – Association for Research and Enlightenment – in Virginia Beach, Virginia)

"What in the name of heaven?" Deepy tried to shake awake.

"A young minister, with a doctorate degree from Harvard, learned a great deal, both from Cayce himself and his archives; and Dr. Harmon Bro wrote about much of it in his book, *"Edgar Cayce – On Religion and Psychic Experiences."** It was in that book, edited by one of Cayce's sons, Hugh Lynn Cayce, and copyrighted in 1970 by A.R.E. that the author made the following observations about Cayce's reincarnation views, which Dr. Bro referred to as "retro cognition," as opposed to precognition. *(first published by Random House, then later by the Cayce Foundation)

"To quote Bro:

'In dealing so naturally with reincarnation, Edgar Cayce was handling the one phenomenon of his work, which more than any other alienated him from responsible people in his times. Doctors were often keenly interested in his medical diagnoses and detailed prescriptions, as well as the theories of physiology which streamed through Cayce in thousands of readings^ - until they learned of the reincarnation material. ^(personal insights into subjects, offered from an entranced Cayce) Ministers and priests were fascinated by his detailed descriptions of Biblical times, which included accurate accounts of clothing, coins, food, languages, customs, and even the correct distribution of names of the time in various languages familiar to scholars and archeologists - until they learned of the reincarnation material from the same source. Scientists responded to the chemical analyses, psychologists to sophisticated descriptions of hypnosis, government officials to theories of social change in various nations – until they came across the reincarnation material.

'It did not help that details had been so often verified, by old court records, or archeological finds or history books – for this might only demonstrate that some part of Cayce's mind had access to factual sources about the past.

'... The writer was fairly convinced at one point that he had located a massive error in the Cayce materials, when he came across frequent references to the Essene group of Jews at the time of Jesus, or to similar groups of Covenanters, described in the Cayce life readings as significant precursors of Christianity.' '... Yet not long after his death the Dead Sea Scrolls were found, and confirmation poured in of many of Cayce's reports on sites, practices, and even the presence of women in the retreat centers – so long denied by scholars.'

"Normally, my friend," Eno now stated, "I would allow you all quotations of pertinent material from your material world, but I found this a convenient time to mention the foregoing. We do want Mr. Cayce's work to receive its due recognition."

Eno seemed to stare into space for a moment, causing Deepy to say something from 'the back of his mind...'

"I hope you know I am way serious about all this, Eno... even when I sometimes act silly. I guess it just helps me relax."

"That does works for you, and that's fine. You're under more stress than you care to admit and frankly you handle it quite well, Larray. That makes it easier for all of us. So, don't worry... your silliness has been helpful and a good thing. I think maybe even CHIP enjoys it as much as he seems to. I know he's getting pretty good at it. He says it's an art form. Anyway, some people might think it's silly that we had you play the role of a dog in this endeavor. That could mean they don't understand some of the essentials of this work.

"No, my friend you don't need to apologize. Relaxation techniques are important, so long as they are not inappropriate to a situation. You have done well in that regard. Those who judge you will be exposed to being judged, as always." Eno paused as Deepy mumbled "thank you," not quite feeling up to the praise.

"Now then, I suppose we need to continue being serious for the moment," his smiling Mentor told him.

"When societies and families become more morally enlightened... people will realize they need to be their 'brother's and sister's keeper,' when possible. That way, each spirit-soul combination will have a much better chance for survival, because the societal Egod also is diminished in the process of everyone looking out for one another. Your book, my friend, will bring much enlightenment to those who care to know and know to care. That, by the way, is a greatly diminishing number at this time and it will only grow larger.

"All human spirits, unfortunately, begin life as id and ego-centric, rather than God-centered; and each well-intentioned soul must work to overcome its personal would-be god. Parental help in this regard can go a long way toward making a child's life happier. That is why it's immensely important to have everyone helping everyone else as brothers and sisters. That means someone, or more than one, will be helping you too. It is critical to begin godly influences at birth. Too many humans still are being raised with evil in their families... in the form of intolerance for others who are somehow different from them. Essentially these families pick someone to pick on or bully throughout their lives, teaching their children and grandchildren the same traits of bigotry and bias. It is one epitome of <u>idiocy</u>, and a moral disaster.

"Parents, teachers, ministers, and all right-thinking people must serve as moral role models; otherwise they serve only themselves and Egod, in a temporary role. And by all means, people should continue to commune with their local church ministers. Most of them know the only permanent way to Heaven is through moral living, even if some Christians choose to disagree with the concepts of karma and reincarnation. It's quite okay to simply trust God to be God.

"Men and women who have been serving God zealously and lovingly will continue to do so, but they too should always be open to God's "living Word" no matter the source, and be practiced in how to recognize it. Yes, that will require their own will and grace, but usually it only takes a modicum of intelligence to recognize morality; although admitting and adhering to it takes 'moral intelligence,' which takes wisdom. I will tell readers again that karma is playing a huge role in guiding them through the life plan that God designed for them, based on lessons they must learn according to how they lived their previous lives, as well as this one. Everyone has troubles along the way. Everyone should ask for help and be willing to assist each other.

"Karma, as you know, is attributable to cause, and is a hard-core teaching method of true justice. For every thought or action, there is a reactive thought or reaction, and many occur immediately, rather quickly, or relatively soon – and usually are reflective of how deeply the lessons must be felt in a person's life. Hitting your finger with a hammer is no accident. It should teach you to pay closer attention and be more careful in what you are doing. Most people usually just get angry at their 'bad luck,' and curse it or a scapegoat.

"More consequential karma however can draw God's reaction to grossly immoral lives, which might result in untimely physical death to a particular spirit, followed by strong counseling and further moral education and then reincarnation, although some sessions do take place in hell. If a spirit ultimately can't be saved, its tiny soul works with a new spirit. It moves on, as directed by God and its old spirit is dissolved, meaning forgotten as never having existed. That old spirit could be you if you fit the "Hell-bent" category.

"Regarding karma in general, one might logically ask: how can a person learn if he or she is not corrected in a manner similar to the way that person may have harmed someone else? What is fairer than receiving as you give? Of course some reaping has come, and still may come, in reincarnation, even though the seeds are sown in one's current life. Eventually all karma catches up to the perpetrator of deeds and thoughts, good or bad. God picks the time and setting that will have the most impact on one's growth potential. People can gain wisdom by trying to see such matters from God's perspective. All hybrids inherently know right from wrong. It is coded into your tiny soul, but ego can teach a false version known as self-righteousness. Do not go there.

"If you sin against God, SHE can forgive you without karma being involved if SHE thinks you truly are regretful and can be taught without her natural teaching tool. This forgiveness can only come through her Grace and ultimate understanding of your duality (either spirit/brain or spirit/soul) and where you stand morally in relation to her.

"If you commit a crime against another person, that person can forgive you, without karma becoming a factor, unless God deems there are more, or even harder, lessons you need to learn. Generally if a person forgives another person, God likely will forgive the perpetrator of the misdeed, if it is relatively minor and rare. SHE also will be more forgiving of the person who forgave, when his or her own judgment is due.

"Such acts of forgiveness come under the virtues of mercy and Grace. God will not use corporeal or direct punishment lessons if enlightenment (simple understanding and acceptance of ultimate truth) can be brought about in a spiritual way.

"God allows one to process through life, pretty much as one sees fit, while SHE gives guidance and protection when and where SHE can. SHE can though, only if one allows one's Over-Soul to interact with the tiny mind of spirit/soul. SHE can then give each of you the words and thoughts you will accept in order to continue building the individual combination of spirit-soul experience that you call your life, in accord with your own developed abilities, intentions, and karmic debt. Essentially you are in control of your destiny, except for karmic debt you already have incurred. Work with God and gain some Grace.

"Yours only becomes a life worthy of God when your spirit-mind reaches out to God Mind for guidance in the form of godly thoughts. Pray for such thoughts on a regular basis, rather than being content with corrupted thoughts from Egod. Do this and eventually you may grow a spiritual mind, which can supersede and/or transcend much of the evil you may have nourished in the past. There are stages to this attainment of a godly life, as you must know by now. Ask God to help you along the way, so that you may possibly attain the next and final stage as an Angel of God. SHE knows that your spirit mentality is morally cluttered because of id/ego, and SHE will grant some mercy through Grace when it will suffice and not hinder growth.

"Choose the reprocessed and oftentimes perverse thoughts presented to you by ego and Egod... and your next incarnation, if you have one, will be that much more difficult. It likely will lead to further corruption, as spirits nearly always attract people with similar spirits during each earthly sojourn, until finally the spirit may be lost to evil through default. If you are a social being, gather with persons of moral intelligence, as you can best discern.

"Remember, as humans, you are trying to develop the type of spirit-soul that eventually can become one with God. God is the Mental energy foundation for thought. SHE is the Mind Center or Core, which we call the Father (Yang) and the Mother (Yin). SHE and SHE are One. When the name "God," is used, it is understood to include both aspects, with all indivisibly-dual Cells (COG) scattered throughout the universal fields of Consciousness. In other words, God's Triune Essence is One Supreme Entity, to include her CHILD.

"All in all, God predisposes circumstances to allow for lessons that one needs, or seeks, to learn in each life. SHE then leaves it up to individuals to select used or new thoughts and actions, according to the study, work, and prayer they are willing to put into their own abilities. So, essentially then, you build a life of your own choosing, in accord with your character – good or bad. That character usually influences you to add more of the same type essence to your spirit/mind, aka soul or spirit/brain, aka id/ego – depending on your thinking and your karma.

"Warning: Beware of the gross established pool of recycled thoughts or excrement of the collective evil subconsciousness of Egod. People with evil or less than godly intentions automatically draw thoughts from this polluted pool. Egod's evil societal brain-set corrupts God's pure thoughts and returns them to any incarnate or disincarnate spirit willing to accept them. Egod has a vast library of such memory energy, much of which no longer has any resemblance whatsoever to the original, godly thought that may have spawned it.

"I hope to have made it clear that people have freedom to think as best they can, and the lesson here is that you choose from either good or evil thinking. God will share original thoughts with you, but 'yes,' they did originate with her. Humans can degrade any 'good' thought into evil, no matter how creative it might have been. More often than not, too many of you take the easy path of allowing Egod to provide you the most dreadful, dire, dangerous, or otherwise negative and harmful thoughts that he selects from among those that his minions have co-created, often choosing to spread such thinking through various media forms. Instead of thinking for yourselves by co-creating thoughts with God in logical, loving, intelligent, wise, and gracious ways, many of you resort to the borrowed or even 'bought-thought' that is perpetrated by the least morally thoughtful among you. One of mankind's most dangerous propensities is always to seek the easy or lazy way out. That can become a journey to hell.

"You, as Larray, recognized the changes over your own lifetime, from your youth of the 1940's and 50's into your present time and beyond. [*We allow our friend some precognition of a future he will experience*] You saw how immorality took over television, movies, and other art forms, and how it has gotten much worse and become accepted as normal. People have been led for so long to believe it is what everyone wants and therefore they also accept it without much, if any, thought as to why it should not be that way and what it has done and is doing to society. Laziness and apathy are growth factors for Egod.

"One can easily offer the excuse that people are just so overcome by the pressures and stress of working for a living that all they really want to do is relax, without having to think – and so they accept thinking from others in line with their character essence. Many even take drugs to help them *'not'* think, or they engage in reactive non-thinking or shallow pursuits. That is exactly what the political Egod expects. You seldom fail to disappoint him anymore, even as many of you continue paying hypocritical lip service to God.

"I know that some of your readers, my friend, are a bit weary of hearing about humanity's failings when it comes to God and morality, but I would ask them if they really think life is not supposed to have some higher purpose, such as an opportunity to grow into eternal life? Very few people consider the purpose for life, as if there really is none. It amazes us COG that most people do not even question their existence. They exist to become Co-Creative Mental Cells of God, namely COG. Hopefully by now we have made that one point at least.

"Okay then, enough thinking so deeply for awhile. This looks like another beautiful spot for a break and some refreshments. I can read your stomach too."

IIIIIIIIIIIIIIIIIIIII

Homo Sapient
(CHAPTER 20)

"Homo huh, what - I mean, 'pardon me?' I must have missed something."

"God does not want anyone to be unhappy." Eno stated and then said, "Homo Sapient" again.

"I would like to digress here for a few minutes to say really all I care to say regarding a subject you had earlier wondered about, Deepy... that of 'homosexuality.' However, the subject is a bit complex, so I'm going to stick with the fundamentals and try to keep it short for those who just find it and any LGBTQ* activity surreal, or even immoral as the *Bible* "did teach" at one time. I express it that way because the *Bible* intended to denounce same-gender-sex as perverse, but only IF it was for strictly sensuous lust gratification, having nothing to do with genetics. *(Lesbian, Gay, Bisexual, Transgender, and Questionable)

"Genetics, however, have since come into play, as God, through COG, is working to make it easier for people to evolve into the Heavenly, "indivisibly-dual" entities SHE needs them to be. And since time is growing short in the material realm, SHE wants as many hybrids as possible to be modified for a much faster conversion to what Othereal, Spiritual life demands. So, I do ask your readers' indulgence because the subject is of utmost importance to some folks who want to be treated as equally moral to other moral humans.

"I bring up the subject now because I wish to make a point regarding some spirit-souls who have reincarnated. It might seem that some of them have been impervious to God's Spiritual Law *"that every vital entity, whether physical or heavenly, has no choice but to consist of opposite polarities."* For example, in the case of a Yang or polar-positive, fused spirit body, the unfused tiny spirit soul must be Yin, as a tiny soul increment of its polar negative Over-Soul Self. Conversely, a fused Yin body must have both a Yang tiny soul and Over-Soul. Each 'tiny' and O'Soul must co-create a replica inner-spirit of its fused body host; hopefully with appAngel potential that can progress to survive forever with God.

"Because time is growing short, God has a plan in place that benefits her in getting eventual Humangels from the hybrid world to heaven for more rapid development. SHE pairs two Over-Souls and their tiny spirit-souls in one hybrid body, thus allowing the 'tiny' aspects to form a common bond consisting of dual polarities. Essentially they become friends who learn togetherness in making their minds transitional when it comes to working with each other and their O'Souls to co-create a twi-polar spirit. With the body's eventual demise, that moral spirit-soul would go to heaven with enhanced ability to learn polarity switching there. Before that happens, such spiritual "twins" naturally will be attracted to the opposite (gender) polarity within themselves in the material realm, resulting in someone who can be transgender, meaning twi-polar. It may look like "gender" confusion to what heretofore was considered 'normal,' but this new arrangement is set to God's teaching standards and really is all about polarity. Any such twi-polar entity who is confused or distraught over how society reacts to them often can become bipolar confused at times. That makes life all the more difficult.

"Normally two tiny souls work well together in one body because their Over Souls also are working to make it happen. They could work together in any 'LGBTQ' arrangement* such as bisexual or homosexual, but the ability to be indivisibly-dual and polar switchable in heaven makes up for most material world problems caused by ignorance, which usually is based on faulty judgments by self-righteous humans.
*[fluctuational rather than steady transitional]

"All that being said, hybrids need to understand there will be many more "homosapients" incarnating now and into the future, as material world time dwindles. That should be viewed as a necessary 'polarity' arrangement rather than one of gender.

"Opposites attract, as you know. Therefore, what might cause people of the same exterior polar "gender" to attract each other? With two tinys and their O'Souls combined to assist each mate or partner, they sense their soul/Soul's spiritual essence more than any fused-spirit attraction. They are drawn together for the right mental reasons. Of course, those "right" reasons essentially should be the same for opposite genders or polarities, but since ordinary hybrids have only one soul each, the id/ego desires of the flesh can remain stronger than any higher Spirit-Soul attraction. Let's recall the following:

(Romans 8:1, 3, 4, 5 and 6:

There is… no condemnation to them which are in Christ Jesus, who walk not after the flesh, but after the Spirit.*

3. For what the [Moral] law could not do, in that it was weak through the flesh, God sending her own Son in the likeness of sinful flesh … condemned sin in the flesh; 4. …That the righteousness of the law might be fulfilled in us, who walk not after the flesh, but after the Spirit. 5. For they that are after the flesh do mind the things of the flesh; but they that are after the Spirit the things of the Spirit. 6. …For to be carnally minded is death; but to be spiritually minded is life and peace.)

*{Homosapients *'walk not after the flesh'* (in lust of), but after the Spirit; (with moral communion) and the *Bible* says, *'There is no condemnation to them.'* They practice gracious and wise love, not homosexuality for the lust of fleshly desires.}

"Homosapients each have two indivisibly-dual polar opposite souls in one body, but with an inherent ability to learn from their Over-Souls which polar aspect is needed from what is being put forward by their mate at any given time. That coordination is arranged by their O'Souls so that dual "twi-polar" spirit-souls work as one, within the physical body of each partner. It is a sacrifice for those partners living in a judgmental world, but with moral intelligence they are allowed much grace by God to endure. You also must let it be according to God's will, or suffer karmic results for wrong and possibly hurtful judgment.

"Two Over-Souls agree to allow their tiny souls to share the same physical body because they know time is growing short in the material world. This is a very unselfish, loving act by them, and God agrees to this Co-Creative duality to suit her Souls as SHE, and they, will never be aware of any sexual activity* after these hybrid Angels-to-be reach Heaven as their forever home.

*The relationship between biology and sexual orientation is being researched. While scientists do not know what determines an individual's sexual orientation, they theorize it is caused by a complex interplay of genetic, hormonal, and environmental influences. That's true, but what God needs is the key factor. When scientists theorize, you can usually expect to see the word 'complex;' but it really is quite simple for God, even if not simple to explain, or for many others to understand.

"That brings us to a few points we would make regarding anyone's sexual orientation.

"One should keep in mind that one's sexual deviations never infringe on God Mind, as they are not explicitly shared with her by COG or other Souls. That means there will be no memory by anyone in Heaven of any kind of sexual activity. God knows there's too much perversion in the hybrid id/ego brain set. SHE doesn't need to know details about any of that. Her MIND stays clear and perfect, so that all her Mental Cells eventually can become as SHE is. COG working in the material realm always are spiritually cleansed of hybrid evil prior to reentering Heaven.

"Yes, I know my deep friend that you find some of this information fantastic, but I also know you believe it; even as you may wonder otherwise on behalf of some friends who could think this is all just a bit too 'otherworldly,' shall we say? They might surprise you, especially if they feel underestimated."

Eno was right about Deepy's concern.

"So I am grateful for your faith," Eno continued. "Many of your readers will tune out at various times, I'm sorry to say, but I know you are thinking of them when you seem stunned by what you're hearing. I do read sub-thoughts on a constant basis and yours are pretty altruistic for the most part.

[The Commander knows how complex this sounds to many of you. Just realize it is a quite workable model for God.

If your brain is tired, engage the imagination of your tiny soul. And do take a break anytime you feel a need to un-boggle your mind.]

"Having explained homosexuality, possibly to no one's satisfaction, let's be generous and say spirit-souls are placed by God where they are, for her needs and their salvation. Even so, they have, in the past, created a bit of a problem for the person they came-to-be in their lifetime. That is changing though as people become more tolerantly enlightened. Judgments regarding sexuality are more of a "grace test" now for those who would judge such entities harshly because they are unusual, even while harming no one with their love. Yes, empathy is a part of your test... as is wisdom: You should trust God to be God, since SHE has enough empathy to allow your own existence... at least temporarily.

"God will judge your graciousness in accepting her variety of spirit-souls who simply try to live peaceful, loving lives in a way that God ultimately will judge as either worthy of her or not – just as SHE will judge your judgment regarding her needs. And, just so you know – the reality of material "indivisibly-dual angels" can assert itself in various ways when it comes to love and/or sexual preference, whether you agree with God or don't. Virtuously, <u>NO</u> physical-world potential appAngel should lie down for the purpose of sexual gratification having nothing to do with genuine, spiritual love. Abide in God and your trust in her will be automatic whenever SHE judges you as SHE will.

"There are so many sexual depravities in the world between opposite genders that make it difficult for anyone (other than God) to say that a "loving variation" between same genders is a depravity when compared to opposite-gender thoughts and actions that often involve depraved thinking while <u>absent</u> anything remotely resembling gracious love whatsoever.

"We will leave the subject there, as I cannot explain it any more succinctly or easily than I just did, and so I would ask readers to re-read the foregoing until they can understand it, or at least praise God for eventually rendering them gracious judgment for their faith. It is God's job to judge people, as we say time and again. What right does one sinful person have to judge another? Jesus was the perfect discerner of evil and He prayed that his Parents have mercy on all sinners. You are in a group for whom He gave his life.

"Many, if not most, material-world appAngels are bright and gracious people who likely already have qualified for God's Grace in her judgment of them. That does not excuse perverted activity by anyone regarding any moral requirement. There remains only the need to be cured of the same character ailments and deficiencies that most all hybrids suffer. Every hybrid human is a sinner and most all are sexual sinners (having variations of sex without genuine love) in addition to all their other sins. Would you care to see a list of your sins – to be shocked by the not so obvious ones? Are you ready for God's judgment or would you first care to make amends by perhaps asking forgiveness for being and acting judgmental? Those are not rhetorical questions. Answer to God."

A Rude Awakening

Deepy found himself awake enough to wonder if he was awake. He seemed to be in the woods with Eno again.

"Sorry to wake you up so early, but we need to be on the move. We're running out of time... your time," Eno told him.

"My time? – It just seems to get away from me." Deepy tried to snap out of his lingering slumber. He remembered going to bed in his room last night, but this was his first hint of trying to wake up. Thinking he must be dreaming, he shook himself vigorously. That didn't help; he was still seeing Eno.

"Did you bring any coffee," he now queried his blurry hiking partner? Then eyeing the stream beside them, he went down and stuck a paw in the icy mountain water. "Ain't about to go in there." The chilled paw did help shiver him a bit more awake – enough to lap guava from the bowl Eno sat before him. Dawn was now dawning on him. He was pretty sure he would still rather be in bed. This dream was too real, too soon.

"Your helpful quin noticed you twitching quite a bit in your sleep. Bad dream, or just sore muscles?" Eno inquired as he picked up the empty bowl and returned it to his backpack.

"Umm," Deepy mused; "Probably a bit of both. I was reminded by my dream of the seemingly peculiar actions toward mankind, of the COG Commander, the Lord God, during some of those biblical times. I'm not saying that punishment and retribution may not have been called for then, but some actions just seemed a bit bizarre during that time."

"I'm quite glad you brought this up, Deepy, because it is a worrisome subject for many modern-day Christians who try to discover and get to know God through the *Bible*. They want to know a compassionate, loving God, as reflected in the Son and Daughter, Jesus Christ. But, in reading the *"Old Testament,"* many become disillusioned to the point they become judgmental of God and give up the truth without ever fully knowing it.

"The *Bible* is truth, but is incomplete and often lacking proper context. It was passed through the brains of hybrid humans, just as your book is – even to include a hybrid dog. Mankind's biblical interpretation could not tell the full story and Jesus said there would be more to come. In fact, He said everything hidden would be revealed; and so your book will explain a good bit more.

"COG actually never liked the idea of manipulation, but we did try some psychology at times in order to make a dent in Earth's Egod of earlier eras. Psychology can be naturally manipulative, but it should not be regarded as necessarily inappropriate. It simply can serve as a tool, and it has worked effectively in other hybrid gardens much older than yours, but it has its limitations.

"The Lord God of the Earthly realm was at various times waging a battle with the 'collective ego,' aka Egod, of mankind. As an example, He tried to set the Jewish people straight, by turning their thoughts back to God and away from so many evils of the material world. They had become some of the worst offenders of "society-as-god," – even if much less offensive than the Egod of this age – simply because society was smaller then.

"But the Othereal Lord never made any empty promises. He did with, and to, the Jewish people exactly what He said He would, while using their own karma against them. He took no reprisals for spite or revenge, even though He made it sound as if He would, because they understood that kind of tough talk because of their own id/ego brain-sets. Many still are paying the price, as a result of not heeding his warnings. Some of them have suffered through lifetimes, still as stubborn as they ever were, while adopting some of the same selfish, greedy materialistic principles as their forebears, who also suffered in the same arrogant way, as do all hybrids essentially. *'Vanity of vanities; all is vanity,'* said the *"Preacher"* in the biblical *Book of Ecclesiastes*.

"Even so, many Christians now stand before God as more worthy to be "chosen" for eternal life than the original 'chosen' tribe whom God claimed as her people, while most of them later refused to claim her Son as their Savior. Some do. For others at the time, doing so would have wreaked havoc on their ill-advised lives, just as it now would with most hybrids of any ethnicity. Will the warring factions of persecuted tribes, including the Jews, of ancient southwestern Asia never learn? A few have; but many more will, as usual, read these words as anti-the-superior ethnicity they perceive themselves to be.

"By the way, God was not playing favorites when SHE chose the Israelites as "her people." It was a "WILL and Grace" decision at the time. At their outset, they were the most moral as a social entity. Their bloodlines were truer to the original hybrid couple, with less intermarriage among some of the wilder humanimals that still remained on Earth then.

"God chose the Israelites as a moral multitude, but they rebelled against her – in wanting to do things *'their'* way... to suit their egos, which meant complying with the societal system of a materialistic Egod. The Lord God became disgusted with them after Egod deceived more and more of society into "idolizing" and coveting material wealth and power. Their lack of grace, or even love, bereaves the Lord to this day, and God is still calling many karmic debts due from that ill-mannered, unrepentant bunch; with ethnicity being of no favored consequence in today's society.

"We are here to help set the record straight. We leave it to our Parents as to which of their devotees will accept this work of God, of which all hybrid humans are a part. Everyone is a part of this work, whether in acceptance or denial. Anyone who reads it will render one verdict or another for themselves and God. Those who don't read or understand it will be at a disadvantage.

"God is Master of the Word. And there are many hidden messages within the *Bible*, but some are right on the surface too, waiting to be uncovered by those with a mind to perceive. Through God's word play, the *Bible* was written for two different eras at the same time – the beginning of the hybrid generation and the end of it – the Alpha and the

Omega. The question is 'can humankind decipher the correct version for the time?' People are working on it. One alleged cipher has the Korean peninsula being destroyed by nuclear war. We will not confirm or deny that, as Egod will decide which course to take. Pray for mercy.

"During today's times, you must discover other morally correct, logical, wise and loving ways to interpret the *Bible*, or even decode it in some cases. This process must take place with lots of prayer for guidance. You have to believe that your Heavenly Parents, who love you, will not lead you astray, even as God wants you to increase your wisdom through Deepy's own moral work. SHE can speak to you in today's language, or even through an old vessel, an old covenant called the "*Holy Scriptures*," or *Bible*. All you need remember is to walk a moral path, even though it may be circuitous at times and laden with Egod's mine* fields. *(ego or vanity: as in I, me, and mine)

"Different times call for different measures. In those olden days, as the number of human descendents of Adam and Eve and their extended human family increased greatly, the only guidance available to those people was offered by the COG commander, or Lord God, as well as his competitor, and would-be claimant to a world title of his own, namely society's Egod.

"Whenever there are biblical passages that appear to show hubris or other human traits within God, be aware that either some egos who called themselves "Lords," were full of themselves, or the actual Lord God was trying to relate to humans psychologically in the egodly ways they were adopting. In many cases, the "scribe" in charge of the storytelling also is interpreting God from the human id/ego perspective, and perhaps without discerning a deeper knowledge.

"One might be able to unmask even more of Egod now, within the *Bible*, with the knowledge offered in this book, if one wishes to use it, but keep in mind that God dealt with humans from the most logical perspective they could understand at the time. They could understand threats of power and vengeance, for example, so long as the threats were carried out. God keeps her Word and the modern "warnings" we offer through Deepy's book will not be idle speculation. So, do pray for Korea, the world and all mankind while praying you can overcome the treachery of some politicians, and others, who may be as ignorant as humanly possible about God.

"Able to see ahead of events, God's so-called vengeance usually was a foretelling of what was going to happen anyway, for karmic or natural reasons, including events brought about by mankind. Even now, in these times and in this book, God is offering a perspective some humans can understand, even though there would be more to tell, if people were capable of knowing the full truth. There is more to come in heaven and during the tutorship of Jesus Christ in the new Garden Gaia. For now though we are telling more truth than some folks can fathom, tolerate or appreciate.

"Even so, we COG are here to level with hybrid humans for their sake as well as God's. The Lords of hybrid planetary gardens have always used the best methodology for dealing with recalcitrant spirit-souls, and our end results mostly have been positive. We had no experience when it came to moral imperfection, so we did have a learning curve to overcome. Sometimes our psychology worked better than other times, especially since logic has not always been a strong suit of humans.

"For example, one can look at the *Bible* now and see as much vanity in those days as some of the id-ego on display within hybrid humankind today. Even so, the "I AM" of the Lord overwhelmed id-ego then with the moral messages we also now want to impart on behalf of our Parents.

"Later, of course, God was to send her Son/Daughter, Jesus Christ to teach about a moral God in a more direct way and without all the psychology some of us COG used during that 'learning curve' period I mentioned. Jesus though was fairly disdainful at times regarding the potential of Earthite people. Still, He loved them then and now.

"Yes, we are perfectly Moral as Children of God, but we have not always known best how to teach that Morality, as we had no experience with imperfect or immoral spirit-souls prior to the creation of hybrid humankind. Fortunately for us though, vanity could never be part of our Essence and it was only one of the many reverse psychological ploys we used in trying to teach morality to Earth's hybrid humans.

"Vanity always has been a part of the psychological essence of hybrid humankind and we COG used it as a means for trying to communicate our messages that mankind would have to change "or else I – even I - the Lord God" - could use my power to force or coerce such change as necessary. It was a scare tactic, but it was no bluff. We tried using that 'vengeance is mine' line to portray a tough, no-nonsense God, scarier than a mere human being could be. It did help at the time and society began trekking more moral paths – although some were quite superficial at best.

"Nonetheless, we came to realize that any change brought about using those methods was only temporary, and the heart of hybrid illness lay much deeper than simple blind obedience. "Honest-to-God" change would require intellectual knowledge.

"Jesus Christ was a real hero for doing what he did and He will return soon. Meanwhile, through Deepy's book, we have been explaining the core of hybrid illness and its roots, and how we finally came to recognize it through our own deeper understanding of vanity, although now we have to step it up a notch because humankind's religious essence is growing weaker at the very time it needs to be stronger than ever.

"Human language in biblical times was uncomplicated, and did not necessarily need the benefit of more intricacy in explaining God's powers, which were shown in abundance. But the ability for more subtle communication grew along with the human race, because so many new experiences of a divergent population required it. God usually wants to communicate with the most morally understanding of her children first, especially those who will spread the word SHE wants known. Language must evolve along with the people who use it – in order to share the thoughts of God. Egod often does not require much in the way of language skills, but at the same time he also wields power through some personalities who can vividly express themselves, especially if they have consuming character flaws that resonate with persons handicapped by the same temperaments.

"Now, let's talk about something else that will evolve when moral understanding does. It can be called the language of the spirit-soul. It is the trait of 'character' expressed in an often-silent communication skill that speaks volumes. It can be either good or bad. Let's focus on the good.

"Why don't you take it from here, for a while, my friend?"

"What? Are you sure?" Deepy was glad he had been paying close attention, but still he was caught off-guard, if not stunned.

"Yes, if you would, please."

After some hesitation and with some doubt as to where to begin talking about good or bad character, Deepy weighed in with something he had been contemplating during some of his meditative, quiet times. But he also had to wonder what he was going to learn by being put on the spot this way.

"You want me to talk about good character? Okay, first I would say God does not recognize personalities, as such. SHE recognizes character, meaning the moral essence of human beings, of which personality should only be a small part as a natural side effect. Often when we say that someone has a good personality, the word 'good' is not being used in its literal moral sense, but rather as it relates to entertainment. All entertainment ideally should be morally good, but isn't, obviously. Personality also can relate to congeniality, but it's only of value if sincere and not for show. Good character makes people more honestly congenial.

"An entertaining personality often is not a 'good' one, since we know that many people expect entertainment these days to involve a lot of sensuality in one form or another. So, a good personality often does not mean 'good,' in the same literal, moral sense as when applied to character. I think we all know what 'good character' means. And that same good character can build a good, as in godly, or at least virtuous, personality that reflects character over and above a personality that is contrived for show business, politics or other vain impressions."

"Am I making sense, Eno?"

"Indeed you are, my friend."

Deepy hoped he wasn't talking in circles. He also knew he didn't care to be 'preachy,' and so hoped Eno would feel his uneasiness [which he did].

"Just being different, sometimes to the point of being bizarre, is a sign that Egod is shaping a personality in order to gain the attention of others, meaning to put 'ego' on display to be idolized as such. Otherwise, caution must be taken by people who recognize vanity within themselves. It is a brain or id/ego trait that lies at the heart of all hybrid humans in varying degrees.

"Too many people now put too much emphasis on adoring the personalities, or showmanship, of others, rather than respecting a person's character, which is accountable to

God. This does not mean we should judge anyone. It simply means we should discern a person's character in spite of his or her personality. Moral goodness is essential to God; personality is not. One can generally tell whether people are moral or immoral from their actions, inactions, words or silence. This discernment is how we must choose with whom we wish to associate – God or Egod. We should perceive how a person performs, as defined by God's laws or commandments, and the "WILL and Grace" extensions of those laws.

"Something odd is going on here, Eno. I sometimes sense that you are speaking through me. It's freaking me out a bit."

"Well, in that case, my friend, I'm insulted," Eno laughed and quickly said he was joking. "No, what you're sensing is normal and goes to the very point you are making. We often are influenced by the "company we keep," by the character or personality traits of those with whom we have the closest associations. That is what makes moral kinship so imperative. Please do continue for a few more minutes, if you would."

"Sure, thanks. That's encouraging. And I liked your joking personality," Deepy chuckled. "Really," he added.

"Using one's own moral intelligence, in a manner befitting God's WILL and Grace, gives us the right and obligation to decide whether we like and/or respect someone, or feel just the opposite. This is discernment, and not judgment, because we cannot, and should not try to pass a karmic sentence on someone we deem is breaking God's laws. God will handle that, and oftentimes through the scope of mankind's similar laws derived from her Essence.

"We should only associate with people we dislike or don't respect 'IF' we are fairly certain we might be of benefit to them in godly ways, while not being corrupted in the process. We might determine that 'fine line' is not worth walking with some people. Help them if they are willing and they do not try to sully or take advantage of your graciousness. Otherwise, try to be certain your differences are irreconcilable before you break a prolonged relationship in the most diplomatic way possible. You could just be abandoning a lost soul, so at least pray that God has something else in Mind for him or her. Suggest other avenues of help for them if at all possible, but do not feel guilty if you did your best.

"Eno, this moralizing is quite disconcerting to me, knowing as I do just how imperfect I am."

"Discard that term 'moralizing,' as it is ego-invented to be derogatory. God truly understands just how far down the path to perfection you are, so let her be your judge and go easy on yourself when you know you are doing the right thing. As you well know, it comes easily to me, which it does for any Child of God. You could become such an entity. By now you know that."

After a few moments reflection about how difficult his future book might be for people unaccustomed to thinking morally on a constant basis, Deepy continued:

"If breaking a commandment is also breaking one of man's laws – such as murder – we have a legal justice system to handle that. Unfortunately though, it is not always "just." More specifically, many personalities serving in the justice system are themselves morally inept, if not corrupt. The system itself is not necessarily broken, but some of its people are, when they try to work that system to their, or another's, benefit whether moral justice is served or not. Oftentimes they just serve their own prejudices, which can be anathema to God.

"While it is true that all lives matter, if police departments in my country consisted mostly of black officers and they, along with a few white cops were involved in what appeared to be a multitude of "seemingly" senseless killings of unarmed, unresisting white people... then it is reasonable to presume some demonstrations might take place on behalf of those unarmed folks, with people displaying signs that "white lives matter." It's only logical. It's also logical that it does not mean that some lives do not matter. It also is logical to know that the protests adopted by some people to kneel at events when their national anthem is played is a sign they could be kneeling to pray to a higher power for true moral justice, and why wouldn't they? That is showing proper respect to God and not to vain, unfair political or nationalistic, prideful thinking.

"Here is the larger point I wish to make: Like politicians, most police officers (men or women) are citizens who come from among our ordinary mix of cultures, mostly from the neighborhoods and households of middle-class to highly educated job seekers. Such public officials bring all their diverse societal backgrounds with them into their law enforcement training, but their character flaws may not be tempered enough. They don't automatically become saints when they put on their blue uniforms with badges. In fact some of them may have become cops in order to shield their bad character and possible future criminal behavior from the type scrutiny other citizens might get, if caught in violation of the laws of man and God. That is something we would rather not believe, but it definitely happens; and that is not meant to denigrate police departments as entire groups.

"Many police officers receive ethics and civility training; but all of them should consider the simple concept of common decency to fellow humans, regardless of ethnicity, race, religion, and gender, and display such concern while honorably carrying out their duties. Some of them simply pay lip service to such a code, while patting themselves on the back for getting away with "murder," in some cases or whatever they think is clever. Badges may keep killers out of jail, but not out of hell.

"None of the foregoing assessment intends to overlook how stressful law enforcement can get at times or how "afraid" some officers may be of losing their own lives in certain situations. But we should not overlook the fact that some cops do bring life-long prejudices - to include hatred, and other bad character traits to work with them. Some of them even decide in advance what they will do if confronted with a situation that remotely resembles their wildest nightmares or even 'hopes,' sadly enough. Some simply are ignorant haters at their core and seek opportunities to do harm or take unfair, if not illegal, advantage of situations.

"Cops, like politicians, unfortunately <u>are</u> <u>us</u> – meaning imperfect humans who should align ourselves foremost with a Moral God and serve the public only from that perspective.

"Lord Eno," Deepy seemed to sigh, "I can't say I enjoy this "morality teaching" business. I think I may be preaching more than teaching and it's not in my nature I guess. It depresses me even though I know how really necessary it is for some folks to hear "morality" spoken, if mankind is to have any hope for survival on this planet. Would you mind if I give this teaching of morality back to you before I have a nervous meltdown?"

"I will just say you did an admirable job under some rather trying conditions and so I thank you for that, my friend and agree that assessing humankind should be psychologically hard for any imperfect hybrid being. So, yes, I will briefly pick up where you left off, with just a few more thoughts to underscore your point about the dangers inherent in attitudes, because essentially that is what you were talking about.

"Specifically some of the harm that bad attitudes can bring about can be found in how they affect much of the next generation. Attitudes – much like DNA - can affect character traits in those who need role models.

"Kids and even adults die every day from their own stupidity, often taught to them by bad role models, whether parent or teacher or some media personality; or a morally corrupt person running for public office, or someone celebrated as being a "star" in whatever they do. There can be many repercussions when a person's life is cut short due to negligence, ignorance or stupidity because many enterprising people usually are invested in one another to keep their livelihoods going for the sake of financial independence.

"People who allow themselves to be distracted while driving are acting selfishly, even if their IQ might say they are above average thinkers. Should eating a sandwich while driving be outlawed? - Only by one's own conscience, knowing one is not immune to accidents and could be endangering others. It's an odd human characteristic that most people think accidents are something that happen only to other people.

"Not every law or regulation is going to suit everyone, but a majority of rational thinking officials sometimes make rules before other people suffer the consequences of what would unquestionably be life-threatening carelessness – such as doing illogical, distracting things while driving. It is an all-too-common practice and that's why wearing seatbelts became mandatory, or why helmets are required for motorcycle riders; or special car seats for little children or facial coverings and vaccines during a virus pandemic. There are many among you who need to be protected from yourselves, and others who need protection from you. Attitude is important and should be taught as a moral imperative.

"Look closer at one of the worst examples of horrible attitude set by a narcissistic moron in what once was described as the most powerful political position in your world, as well as one leading in human rights. He had followers willing to do as he said, even giving up their lives and taking other people's lives by not protecting themselves during a virus pandemic. They would protect their "brain-set," of freedom at any cost to anyone who got in their way; meaning they suffered the same illness as their 'role model' in an office for which neither he nor they are qualified. There are so many hard lessons to learn in your world and so many folks are just not up to the moral challenge. Their thoughts don't go much beyond the common sense of id/ego, which is becoming more and more dangerous, as one of your nation's political parties has crested in that regard. It is insane, due to money and power.

//////////////////////////\\\\\\\\\\\\\\\\\\\\\\\\\\

NEED A BREAK? GOD CAN RELATE.

(Chapter 21)
Egod's Other Nemesis

"Anything in particular you would like to hear about now, my friend?"

"I'm not exactly sure, Eno – "Satan - Maybe?" Deepy replied with an apologetic look, followed by a hapless chuckle.

"All right, let's start then with this bit of information," Eno told him: "It says in the *Bible* that Satan deceived the world. He admits to being complicit in that because he did nothing to prevent or dissuade people from thinking it, but he meant it in an entirely different way. Effectually, and with his Parents' tacit agreement, he deceived the world into thinking he was evil. Why?

"It actually benefited God to have a nemesis that people might believe worthy of going against an Omnipotent Power. A mere mortal would never do. Something or someone with the power to take on God would need to be some sort of scary supernal entity. Satan nearly would need to be a God in his own right. Since there's just one God, Satan at least had to be a Trangel and of course a he if he was to be taken seriously. Can you even imagine any Angel being powerful enough to go to war with God? Satan is neither that powerful or stupid. A hybrid society would never be that powerful, but it would be that stupid for eons to come, pretending it knew of an entity it could scapegoat for its own uses, possibly even too stupid to believe it was taking on God with such idiocy.

"Meanwhile, Satan agreed to play a role to benefit his brother/sister, Jesus Christ, in order to expose a distinct difference between the concepts of good and evil. God obviously represented 'good,' but SHE needed a nemesis entity until an eventual time came, in which mankind would recognize itself as the true face of evil. And thus, Satan was written into history through the *Bible* as an entity of evil. He grew in that role by the word of mouth story-telling of society, until finally Satan was clearly viewed as the primary enemy of God and, of course to a society that would cozy up to God in word, but not in deed. Satan was to be the fall guy.

"The true devil though was the entity unknown at the time as a societal 'Egod,' and his goal became to convince people there is no God or at least no invincible one, and so Egod was quite pleased to have a "Satan" in his corner. Considering the immoral state of today's society, it does seem Egod is having great success, just as he had with other egoistic civilizations.

"The real devil is within the sick psyches of humankind. A Child of God named Satan is not to blame. One of your comedic entertainers – Flip Wilson - used to say, 'The devil made me do it,' whenever he needed a scapegoat. He did not know the 'devil' is within each human hybrid entity as id/ego. Egod's (d)evil (not Satan) is mankind's societal moral failure.

"Yes, there was a time when God actually needed people to be afraid of God – as a stern "Father-figure." (Obviously men did not fear women and certainly would not equate the female gender to God. SHE is God, although the Essence is polarity, which equates to gender in the material world.) People were so dense with ignorance in biblical times, why not try to scare some sense into them by whichever means might work whether good and righteous or in the case of God's Son, Satan, giving the perception of a powerful force of evil mighty enough to contend with the almighty power of God? Absurd perhaps, since mankind's faults logically should implicate mankind, which they do as far as God is concerned.

"Egod, being vain as he is, wanted people in "his world" to believe in an evil Satan, because Egod always wants to detract others from himself as mankind's evil-doer. Every hybrid human has some id/ego illness to offer Egod, and most want someone else to blame – even for being so much as tempted by evil - assuming they likely will give in.

"People blame Satan for mankind's moral weakness – because if mankind is at fault, then each person is susceptible and responsible for his or her own sins. Why not blame some bogus evil entity that even God her Self must fight and somehow defeat? In that light, mankind doesn't look quite so frail or guilty. Even now, some of you might say, 'Satan's doing it again – trying to fool us with his lies. Next thing you know he'll claim he's God.'

"No," Eno laughed at his own analogy, "Satan has no need to claim anything, but the truth is that both he and I, and our mates, are Children of God, just as our brother and sister, Jesus Christ is. God is us and we are her. Essentially all COG share God's moral purity. Mankind also has the potential to become (enhance) God, through being morally obedient as Children, meaning you become the same moral Essence as God. Egod, however, rails at the word 'obey' and therefore only a relative few persons will acquire enough godly Essence to join the COG.

"So, yes, Satan deceived the world in the sense that he was so successful in his godly job of testing people that Egod had to put the onus on him for the evil that Satan found within those people He tempted on God's behalf. That's because many of those who failed Satan's tests ended up in hell. Satan is a Trangel and a faithful servant who was doing the job that God and the Lord God assigned him as an assistant Angel to the Lord during mankind's early years and later as well, working with Jesus.

"Many of your older readers might decry this new profile of Satan as blasphemy, as if it were against God her Self. They subconsciously know it is blasphemous to their own egos and to a society that fooled them to the extent they could mischaracterize one of God's Children. Do you really believe God incapable of ridding her Self of Satan if He truly were her nemesis? If true, what would that say about an Omnipotent God? Think about it. Of course some you would believe that neither God nor Satan exists. Perhaps there are no Angels; no Heaven, and no Otherworld. That could be true for you, if you believe that.

"Satan (and his mate, Nasat) is a pure Son and Daughter of God – a Trangel - as is our brother-sister, Jesus Christ. For awhile, Satan-Nasat was required by God to tempt people into evil - and to the extent God deemed necessary, depending on varying circumstances, most of which had to do with karma. Of course, Egod embellishes the idea of Satan being of evil character in order to detract from his own evil. Egod – aka most of human society - is anti-Christ in trying to portray both mankind and God, as pitiable, wretched fools being taken advantage of by a wicked fallen angel who would blame humans for their own evils.

"The devil often is mentioned in the same context as Satan, but the devil lies to some extent within the very eyes now focused on these words – but way more so on those who closed this book too soon for their own good, or those who will shun it for its moral reasoning. God knows the devil as Ego\d/evil - mankind's vain societal entity. Egod comes from the brain-sets of hybrid humans who want Satan as a scapegoat for their evils. It's that vanity or pride of Egod, which God has required her Son, Satan, to test; although such testing now has become fairly moot for the vast majority of persons who seldom think of God or Satan at all. They don't really care if some major single entity is to blame for evil as long as they seemingly are getting by with their own versions of it. Greedy politicians are especially egregious.

"Someday soon, Jesus Christ will set everyone straight about our brother/sister, in enough detail to satisfy even the most skeptical among those of you who do manage to overcome this world, as Jesus did. However, I will tell you a few things.

"First of all I will tell you that particular Son of God that mankind has made the "fall guy" for its evils, deserves an apology from Egod - not for the Son's sake, but for God's. Of course, Satan won't get one; is not expecting it, and doesn't need it.

"I also am telling you that Satan could write this very book you are reading, and that would cause some of you to condemn him – just as Jesus Christ was condemned by many people for doing God's work. Even though one's own godly attributes naturally should persuade anyone this work is godly; the fear and distrust of Satan will cause some of you to ignore the Moral Essence herein on behalf of Egod's fear of seeming foolish in the eyes of his peers and followers. May God have mercy on so many who would fool themselves that way – but deny doing so.

"Satan is helping arrange the id/ego tests associated with this book, and for some of you there are many such tests to be found herein. Allow me to 'id' test you a bit more now with this information, which basically is a summation of prior rhetoric:

"The Garden of Eden was not a garden as mankind thinks of it. Humans don't think of themselves as 'Trees of Life;' but that is how they were characterized in the hybrid beginning when words were still being "invented" for those very basic entities. They were trees which would bear "Angel fruit" known as Humangels. God reaped as much as SHE needed to fill her Child with thinking, Mental Cells in Spirit forms. Eventually when SHE had all SHE needed, the perfect Gardens were closed. Somewhat later SHE opened a new generation of imperfect gardens, in order to give 'tiny souls' and their Over-Souls a chance to become perfect gardeners of what could be termed tiny apprentice angels, formed in like manner to Humangels.

"God began her imperfect hybrid 'trees of life' with two humanimal forms of opposite polarities, named Adam and Eve. You now are being told 'the rest of the story' in novel form. So, your id test is: Do you believe it? You have known all along that would be the bottom line. But since we are not quite done with the story, you can withhold your answer until you are ready. There, of course, is only one answer that will work for you and God. It won't take luck to get it right. It will take WILL and Grace.

"Now, I want to refresh some thinking.

"This garden generation of ancillary tiny souls became jeopardized from within their physical world bodies by the brain's id/ego. The 'id' had served as a protective device for their animal's body and brain, while the body served as an incubator cocoon for Human/Angel development during the perfect generations. However, in hybrids, the brain became so ingrained with the id that the pair became a nemesis entity fighting the tiny soul. We have termed this pairing 'id/ego.' You are one such entity and all of you as one hybrid society are known as Egod.

"God's original spirit program of id still works wonders through its protective instincts, but it also is protecting your whole organism from what it instinctively sees as interference by the transient tiny soul. Your tiny soul and its Over-Soul are trying to incorporate moral thinking into the brain for the purpose of formulating a sturdy, morally-minded angel spirit inside you. It was this initial effort by Adam and Eve that caused the id/ego to 'feel' its material form was being superseded and diminished as an entity in its own right. It is hindering the brain's ability to accept the soul's input. The brain still has the option to override the id and allow a 'mind' with soul. That option can only be started voluntarily and sustained through communion with the tiny soul, its Over-Soul and God Mind.

"Therefore, God has developed a coded pathway of moral thought. It is enveloped within radiative and irradiative waves of whichever type is best at any given time, whether just plain old sunlight, microwaves, music or just a form of noise, such as "white or pink" noise. It sometimes can be random noise from virtually any source. It is translated through the soul-O'Soul nexus. Souls understand all Spiritual code and translate it into languages and quite often do so through one's imagination. Of course Egod is usually right there to undo any moral good on the spot if one's mentality leans to moral corruption regardless.

"With suggestions and other input from her Children, God decided to turn our efforts in the material realm to a mission of un-melding the id/ego from the hybrid brain, so that fully-functioning spirit-angel aspects can be returned to God as Moral Entities worthy of becoming appAngels within minor heaven. God's latest concept for achieving this came about through Co-Creativity with COG working in support roles in the material world. The concept resulted from close study of mankind's psychological aspects, as well as physical DNA. It is in progress now and results are meeting expectations. Initially, the program will be accentuated within some of the more repressed spirit-souls in Garden Gaia.

"I now have summed up the basis of what we have been explaining throughout Deepy's work as regards this id/ego/Egod concept. Let's diverge some more before we get back to Satan.

"The id was programmed as a protective "recoil and reaction" device. 'Id' was left unchanged in the new Adam and Eve hybrid generation, as it always had worked perfectly. God knew it would remain perfect, but the Lord God (COG Commander) hoped the id would continue to protect the humanimal's fused spirit body from everything as usual, while not interfering with the difficult to detect tiny soul and _id_entify it as a foreign invader.

"However, when the brain/soul tandem began to override some of id's natural instincts, as in knowing, for example, when a danger really was posed by another animal or not, and stopping id's reaction, if there was no threat, the id finally was able to hone in on the tiny soul and contend with it, and has done so ever since. The id alone cannot think, but it can make adjustments to *id*self within the brain. Id finally rendered an electro-chemical process that essentially could detect and interfere with the soul. That new element of the brain became known as id/ego and that re-thinking alignment by id was equal to the task of constant battle with the soul over what id naturally deemed its "territory." It was, and still is, doing the job God designed it to do. Id/ego, however, has ended up costing more lives than it ever has saved, and that includes would-otherwise-be eternal lives - yours, perhaps?

"The Lord of this realm at that time had hoped to guide the genetically upgraded hybrid couple into godly thinking by appealing to the power of their new cerebral hemispheres. God allowed the Lord to try. He was determined, and SHE respected that. He, by the way, is still trying. It would take 'time' – God's allotted time, which almost has run its course.

"Every Perfect Human had the original 'id' in place, without any problems, while their Humangels were co-Created. The id was perfect in its functioning, but it could not overcome the power of indwelling COG. However, in hybrids, the 'id' did detect the 'tinys' as invaders and without an interior COG protector, the id got a stranglehold inside the "Third Eye," pineal gland in the center of the brain which was reserved for the tiny soul. With the brain's cooperation, this "Spiritual center" allowed id to become the self-fulfilled thinker known as ego. This id/ego Eve illness became a formidable foe and the tiny soul became transient, as it could not abide living with evil on a full-time basis. It now only touches base there when called upon by a higher brain hemisphere aspect known as "conscience," which works through WILL and Grace. There is no shame without conscience.

"The first id/ego test of hybrid humankind was directed at Eve, and she failed it. Without enough trust through wisdom, God knew Adam and Eve – even with cerebral brain capacity - would succumb to the old instinctual id serpent brain stem which was well-rooted in kinship within the humanimal 'trees of life" and their instinctual knowledge of the physical world."

"Humanimals who never served as a host for an Over Soul did not have the intellectual capacity to understand they were instinctively attracted to mate with an opposite gender (polarity). There was no evil involved as all "wild" animals mate without giving the matter any thought. They never make a choice to mate because they liked how it felt sensually. This is where Adam and Eve, as "advanced" hybrids, failed God. Sex felt good and they wanted more of it.

"The COG Lord God at the time had taken a "wait and see" attitude as to which frame of reference, either brain/id or new brain/cerebrum would dictate the fate of the tinys. The Lord God obviously was disappointed that the old id brain tempted Eve to succumb to its sensual, material nature. God knew what the outcome would be, but SHE never removes hopeful thinking from her Children, to include the Lord Commander at that time. So-called precognition can only come from God as communion.

[So now, dear readers, Larray and I will need to make our writing as simple or complex as necessary to help your understanding, as we work together to tell the tale as straight-forward as we can. Can you even imagine putting such a story into words? Perhaps you can; but you don't need to, as we have done so for you.]

"When Eve failed, God also knew Adam would defer to his own id and "RNA*" essence *(ribonucleic acid) and be persuaded by Eve to ignore the Lord God's instruction to not obtain the knowledge of good and evil offered by certain 'trees.'

"There also was a Spiritual so-called 'tree of life' in that part of the garden. Could Adam have eaten from that 'tree' and gained eternal life? Yes or the Lord God would not have been concerned enough to move Adam and Eve away to their original grounds. That particular 'tree' next to the TranShip lab was a "Spirit-well" resource that provided the food of life-sustaining pure Spirit Essence to the Othereal Entities known as COG or Children of God. Having received a Soul directly from his COG Co-Creator, Adam would have benefited in the same way as the Lord God and other Children did. He could have lived forever as one of them, but by then he had been compromised by evil, through material world id. Then again, he was needed for that particular mission assigned to him by God, and so it was meant to be.

"Since God intended Adam for her hybrid garden the Lord God took necessary precautions; for if eternal life ever is granted by God, it truly is forever. After his initial failure with the other (simple temptation) forbidden tree, Adam was no longer trustworthy. Eve's id and his own had overruled God.

"Adam and Eve unintentionally downgraded the psyches of the hybrid species to a lower level of intelligence through physical sensuality. Essentially, Adam, at least, had been of a purer spiritual nature, but they both became "naked" in their awareness of the knowledge of just how effective evil could be in pleasing their sensual selves. Hybrids have been addicted to their material senses ever since; seldom living up to their moral potential.

"God's reasoning in creating and testing the first hybrid couple was meant to upgrade the humanimal species to humans with potential to Co-Create themselves with God to an extent that would garner eternity. Our friend Deepy has pretty much covered that aspect of the story in his writing. It was to reach this point now of understanding, as you should, the Eden garden creation and its ultimate mission. Now, all hybrid humankind essentially is Adam and Eve in what they must overcome to reunite with God for eternal life in Heaven. The responsibility and burden grows with each passing day, as time is running out. Even so, God is Gracious and there's prayer.

"In fact, God made the hybrid human commitment as a gift to the tiny souls who had served her COG-Humangel Co-Creations. SHE, however, had a lot invested in the old instinctive id brain of humanimals and id's perfection in its role kept her from simply discarding it. It is needed by all physical creatures.

"So now back to my brother Satan, who knew all along what his mission was in carrying out God's plan. He has been doing his job since the hybrid inception in the garden of Eden. He has been as loyal to God as any Son, even the "begotten one." Satan always has been God's official 'tester' of hybrid humans to be sure their tiny spirit-souls are becoming worthy of God's Grace. Some are on the right path, but most are far behind where they need to be. Some of that fault goes into teaching children what they learned from their parents, in spite of calling themselves Christians, or whatever other religion they claimed.

"By the way, Satan's official name is He II (He2), and hell is named for him, as rightly it should be, since a bad spirit-soul appraisal from him can put people through it or in it.

"Even so, many men and women officially standing up for God have a lot invested in Satan as God's nemesis. If they truly believe mankind – evil as it is – really needs a scapegoat, they can go right on condemning Satan if they choose and he will go right on forgiving them, because he loves them. But - woe unto Egod – that beast wedged into your id/ego brains, to the detriment of your souls. Humankind has an Apocalypse or possibly even an Armageddon coming to Egod.

"Satan has been testing Earth's hybrids ever since he translated the serpent's invitation to Eve in Eden. One of his biggest tests has turned into a celebratory season surrounding a fat man in a red and white suit and sporting a flowing white beard. Now, jolly old Santa Claus has become the reason that so many people often overlook the birthday of Jesus Christ. Satan invented Santa simply by moving the last letter of his 'Satan' name into the third position. That concept has proven to be one of his best id/ego tests, showing that most hybrids in Egod's world fail the "commercialized Christmas" test every year – as the biblical story of Christ slips off to the side, if recalled at all.

"Greedy Egod especially loves Santa or anything that puts religious thoughts in the background of the best sales season of the year, and in the process rewards Egod's bottom line. Giving to people you love is worthwhile, but you should also give them a greater understanding and appreciation of what Jesus Christ wanted them to have: eternal life. Of course, feeling cheerful and optimistic during a celebrated season, such as the time from Thanksgiving Day to New Year's Day is a wonderful thing, as are other holiday occasions, but wouldn't it be great to always feel that way through God's WILL and Grace?

"Forgetting or just vaguely remembering the recognized birth of the Son of God is wrong, and happened when the substitute of material profits became glorified as the reason for the season, not necessarily in words at the outset, but in deeds.

"Satan's 'naughty' list is growing each year as people pay more and more attention to that big jolly "cash cow" than they do to Jesus Christ and his role in their potential eternal salvation."

Eno paused for a moment to allow Deepy's comment.

"But even Christ made Satan out to be God's nemesis. I don't quite understand that yet."

"Christ knew that God needed a 'bogeyman,' and so SHe* did not interfere with mankind's thinking of Satan that way. It was not the mission of Christ to defend Satan. Satan's ill-repute suited God for her purposes, and so Jesus even enhanced Satan's role at times. However, Egod, not God, perpetrated Satan's reputation of 'deceit' as part of Egod's self defense strategy for his own evil for which he, as mankind, needed an invisible devil. Ultimately, of course, all things work together for God's good – or in God's favor, but Satan always did anyway, in spite of his maligned and false reputation.
*(personal pronoun for COG)

"Jesus agreed before his human birth that - even as a pure Son of God - He actually should be tested to make sure that id/ego and Egod had not unduly influenced him during his earthly sojourn. God and all her Children know the power of matter (fused spirit) because it once was pure Spirit. As fused or "compacted" spirit, it can be quite potent under some conditions and circumstances. Jesus asked that Satan test him for evil as each was steadfast in his position of protecting God Jr. Yes, Satan gets tested also before reentering the Otherealm, and He does come and go with us at times.

"Since the Holy Spirit Body of God Junior's Otherealm consists of 'annihilated' once-pure Spirit, Satan always has tested the spirit purity of COG Co-Created fruit (Humangels) of God's perfect Human Gardens. All COG and their Co-Created Humangels were tested for viruses, prior to their release into the Otherealm, because the material world essentially is under quarantine. The only begotten Son of God, humble servant that He is, also requested his brother test him, during and following his earthly sojourn.

"Jesus even said early on in his ministry that the "prince of darkness" was on his way, without mentioning He was coming to test him, as part of his mission to test mankind. Satan's reputation with mankind preceded him and that was just fine with God. Satan was coming from the Otherealm, which now is perceived by your scientists as 'dark' energy and 'dark' matter.

"People who don't already understand should finally realize that "time" is God's concept for mankind and has nothing to do with her otherwise. Her Prescience of Mind and Omnipotence are unaffected by her 'time' concept. It can waft from past to future or vice-versa, as God intends. For example, my friend, God always has known the very words of your book would be written in a certain locale and when and how the book would be made available. SHE also knew it would be as close to perfect as your ability would allow; which is to say "imperfect." SHE even knew the words you would first choose, and then change for other ones, because you are guided in your writing and rewriting. You pray for it often enough. [Larray was praying as he wrote these words. He was praying the words would somehow be made good enough for now, with more to come from Jesus, and soon he hoped. He also prayed his work would not 'fall by the wayside.' God knew who would receive it and who would not and who would equivocate and lose a golden opportunity.]

"Yes, Jesus Christ wanted his princely brother to test him. He would never want to put at risk any Othereal Soul by making an "unclean" entry into the Heavenly Body of God Jr. He was, after all, preparing for a return trip home to that so-called "dark" realm – which is suffused with a light invisible to material eyes. All COG who deal with matter must be tested, even God's first-born, plus Satan and all us COG. Jesus even agreed to pass through hell in order to be purged (ethereally washed clean) of any potential detritus of a world He took upon himself, in order that those who lived the moral lessons He taught would not need to suffer in that netherealm. He reached out to spirits already there, in order to summon up some vestige of the need for morality and their need to pray consistently and with conviction.

"To sum up this Satan revelation, God is all there is, but SHE comes in different forms, as SHE chooses. One of her pure Cellular forms is named Satan. He puts humans to the test to see if they share enough of God's Moral Code and Virtues to qualify for Grace – meaning God's empathetic forgiveness of lesser egregious sins. However, Egod has pretty much taken over that testing role; because human greed and other immoralities have grown so much, that testing by Satan is superfluous in most cases.

"When it comes to both perfect Humans and hybrids, it always has been Satan's job to make sure that "two halves make a whole." This is especially true in the case of Over-Souls producing angels from hybrids as they must now do by assisting tiny souls from the distance of the Otherealm. The dual polar entity of graced persons has to measure up to God's morality tests, thus insuring the eventual perfection of the Soul Co-Created entity, still referred to as an appAngel or COG.

"Hybrids are graded on the karmic curve, as you know by now, and a varied number of life times can be needed for spirit-souls to adhere to moral Christ-like values to attain Grace.

"Satan's job has been to make sure God's perfect standards were carried over to the COG production of both Humangels and hybrid, potential angels. Perfection can only be attained when polar opposites essentially become one. In the case of hybrids, fused spirit essence must be infused with Othereal Mental essence by way of the Holy Spirit nexus known as a tiny mental soul along with its Othereal Over-Soul when called upon.

"That 'tiny to O'Soul' nexus represents interaction between the fused spirit brain and the tiny soul to the exclusion of the id/ego. The brain rises to a higher more godly level when O'Soul thinking is in the mix, usually through prayer, meditation and sometimes even dreams. It then can reach a Spiritual strength wherein it can be received through God's Grace. Apprentice angels also remain in that O'Soul state of 'Holy Spirit' until they someday graduate to their Original Holy Spirit of Heaven as indivisibly-dual COG Angels, or pure Cells of God Consciousness.

"Those tiny holy spirit 'souls' and their co-created good spirit essence are what God wants to rescue through the hybrid human species. Because tiny souls such as you the reader, and all your brothers and sisters became so "God aware" through eons of cohabitating perfect Humans with COG, God decided to afford you a chance to achieve eternal spirit-soul salvation. Rather than transforming you into non self-aware, Othereal Holy G'Host Body Spirit, God wants you back home as Mental Consciousness Cells, as Humangels. Achieving that is difficult and so you must assist her in making it happen. Surely you must have realized by now you're in a real life or death struggle in either helping God or hindering her in saving you as eternal Mind Cells."

~~~~~~

PRAY!
Help God help you!
IIIIIIIIIIIIIIIIIIIIIIIIIIIIIIIIIIIIIIIIIIII
(CHAPTER 22)
Life

"Living is what "life" is all about - not death, and certainly not evil, since evil won't be around much longer and life will forever move only in moral ways. As with the pre-tested Adam and Eve prototypes, mankind will no longer think of itself as naked. He and she won't be. The concept of sensual nakedness, to include all memories of sex and immorality, will be deleted, to include even the knowledge of evil as a concept. There will be no need of such in Heaven, where only pure God Consciousness will live as Wisdom, Intellect, Logic, Love, and *Grace* as the Essence of all Mental Acuity and Activity.

"Let's make this abundantly clear. There is only One Life; God's; and so there's no such thing as "death of life." 'Life' is energy of God that exists forever. Some aspects of it are simply on loan for use by a variety of her creatures in the material world. For example, there are people, tigers, squirrels, fish, sheep, etc; but there is no such thing as a dead person - a dead tiger, fish, sheep, or a dead anything else. 'Death' is non-existent. It only represents consciousness removed from an entity that no longer can contain it and it can be put to more productive use elsewhere or reincarnated into a new form.

"Things that once held life may, for God's good reasons, at some point, no longer hold such energy, but the 'energy' is not dead. Yes, a particular "vessel" that once held it may be empty and no longer viable, but the life energy it had from God still lives. God will use it elsewhere, transforming it according to her needs. SHE may use it for reincarnation into the same species. SHE may put a tree's essence back into a new tree, or human essence back into a new human or into a tree or other non self-aware life if it did not live up to moral maturity, having had many chances. Losing one's self consciousness would amount to death of an individual spirit, but the energy of that life is not lost and the soul can be recycled.

"Of course, any life in Heaven keeps its "Self" forever because that is how God would have it. In your "book to be," you will state that the author is 'on the verge of dying.' You are not familiar with that context yet, but allow me to add to your thought, please: 'He was on the verge of dying'... into a better life. People can die into a better or worse life, depending on how they are living their current life. Their Mental Consciousness can be raised to equal God in Moral Essence, or consciousness can go the opposite way and be lowered to the point of non-existence. In actuality every hybrid is on the verge of dying. Life is short in the material world.

"'Let the dead bury the dead,' Jesus said, referring to those who believe in death. He knew He would live forever in the form that his Creator had chosen for him. He knew that his followers also would live forever, if they would understand the lessons He tried to teach, and if they would live according to those moral principles.

"For example, if you were willing to risk temporarily losing your life in its current form, to save an innocent person, or persons; you would be showing a true knowledge of what God and her Children are all about, because that is exactly what Jesus did. He died to save any of you worthy enough to be saved by God's Grace. Some of your readers may not be so worthy at the moment, but that could change as long as your vessel contains the life spirit God has loaned it, and your tiny soul can participate in renewing that spirit by overcoming id/ego. Like Jesus though, you must be innocent enough to <u>not</u> kill anyone else, just to stay alive in your world. That is quite tough for those who don't care to take the chance of believing it. But, taking that chance could immediately gain a person heaven and the opportunity of angel apprenticeship, as long as they essentially are moral beings within the framework of Grace otherwise, and it's likely they would be.

"The Son of God died a physical death in order to save the spirit-souls of the sons and daughters of mankind, those unborn children who could be adjudged morally worthy <u>if</u> properly taught those lessons that Christ wanted to pass to them through their parents and society. Society, as Egod, is failing miserably in that regard. Some parents still are succeeding; many others not.

"Good parents would try to teach their children how to weigh the true value of the so-called "goods and services," of the material world when compared to eternity. Parents helping to save their children by teaching them moral goodness could, in turn, be saved through Grace as purified versions of themselves, but in perfect Othereal forms that never expire.

"So, my friend, I would ask every parent now reading your book: "Have you allowed Jesus Christ to save your children, by teaching them such lessons and by showing them how to live with their soul article of God 'life' temporarily granted them? Can you show them you have allowed Jesus Christ to save your current self of spirit-soul for eternity? If not; God's "value tester," Satan, knows "why not?" All COG know that Egod is distracting parents with toys for adults who cannot or will not allow themselves the moral maturity to help save their children. That is so obvious that Satan-testing is not required."

Eno paused momentarily to take a call, excusing himself to Deepy who took the opportunity to drink some guava java and eat a couple of doughnuts that CHIP had left for him. A minute later, he was lost in that sweet taste when he heard his friend say, "Mankind goes to war too easily – always has, but God can forgive people who kill to save the innocent, unless SHE knows them to have killer character traits or ulterior motives. However, when those protectors of "the innocent," do kill; they themselves no longer are innocent and so must constantly call on God for protection from their own mental anguish. SHE may give it, depending on what their karma dictates. It could dictate post traumatic stress disorder (PTSD), a physical wound, or their own untimely loss of life. God is merciful, but eventually most people will go as karma dictates, which could include finding peace within.

"Warriors who believe they are morally on the right side must answer for the hard decision they make in judging who is innocent – and innocent or guilty of what? Sometimes it is not so obvious, especially with politicians involved and they always are, when it comes to war. They can incur brutal karmic debt also. Even if Hitler, for example, never personally killed anyone, it is obvious millions of people suffered and died because of him and those unwilling to stop him. So-called "leaders" and their minions also will pay a heavy price for unnecessary suffering and death during their days of vain glory. Supporters of such people are guilty of moral ignorance and will have much to suffer to attain eternity. Most of them will never see or understand the words of your book in this lifetime, my deep friend, which really could mean never.

"Those persons who send other humans to fight and possibly kill or die for a particular "cause," had better know on the issue of war, they will be as liable to God for any moral injustice as those protector warriors who are acting under their orders. You can fool yourself in this regard – politicians - and too many of you will, as you disregard all moral intelligence. Good people have been sent into war for another country's "oil," or to enrich the military-industrial complex, or to get some politicians reelected, as well as other nefarious reasons, such as becoming or remaining a dictator.

"Cynically enough, Egod has justified the idea of war as part of the business model of some advanced nations. Some nation's leaders support that, as part of their business of selling weaponry to other countries. It is all for protection against "bad guys," they say, often with the aloofness of their own "bad guise." Mankind (as Egod) speaks loudly with big money at stake and quite willingly provides tools for 'making war' to sell to all potentially warring factions. The weaponry and economy must go rolling along, and killing is allowed, so long as "freedom" is being preserved for the living profiteers of business, such as investors, politicians, and other assorted "elite." Then too there are those flag-waving nationalists and others who agree war should be waged, just as long as they don't have to fight it. Still, they can suffer too if family or friends are lost, but that may be the only reason they care.

"A war against a virus pandemic can also bring out the same selfish feelings of people who only learn to care when they, or someone they love, are directly affected. Until then many might consider all the deaths and suffering just a "hoax," because they are ignorant fools of Egod. What will the hoax of hell do for them? Will they consider the eternal bleakness a hoax, as they experience suffering of the type that made them scoff at; ridicule and attack others?

"The ultimate sticking point with the rationale of killing for "good reason" is that God said 'Don't kill' and SHE likely intended an exclamation point after that commandment. SHE did not add, "unless necessary," because that would require your judgment and not hers. SHE knows killing is not necessary because SHE will provide better and eternal life for those who follow her commandment. Your karma in fact might dictate that you are the one who should be killed. If so, you will have paid a debt, but God will take you into her life if you give yours for the sake of not killing. Obviously you would not know that, unless you know it now through understanding. Of course you should try to save your own life, but not by killing. It takes real wisdom to understand eternal life is the only "real" life.

"Er, excuse me, Eno, but isn't it okay to kill if you are trying to save the life of someone you love?"

"Believe it or not, the answer is always 'no' to killing. Of course you should try to protect people from being harmed, and even to the extent of trying to wound a "would-be killer" if need be. God will never stipulate that willful killing is okay under certain circumstances. It never is. However, inadvertent killing while trying to save someone who needs protection is forgivable.

"God's judgment is that killing is not necessary, unless SHE guides the Karmic circumstances that dictate a "life for a life." SHE puts her life into her vessels for her needs. SHE also knows SHE has a better life awaiting those who value moral intelligence and live that way. The point is, your life is not your body, which is only a vessel for your life and while you may like it, ultimately it is God's for her purposes. What's necessary is when your 'life' is set free by your body's demise, it returns to its Creator in a Spiritual, Othereal form and possibly forever, **IF** moral enough, or to gain Grace for another incarnation at least.

"Giving up one's life for God's sake, rather than taking someone else's life, means giving up your temporary life energy for eternal life energy. That type of martyrdom for the sake of a loving God, and understanding her laws, earns immortal life. Blind allegiance to political leaders seldom is morally right. Have the courage of your own convictions. Conscientious objectors should be allowed to live in peace without having to kill or run away. There is a world filled with such objectors. It's called Heaven. If you had rather go to war than to Heaven, go to war.

"How many wars could be avoided if each politician or so-called leader had to search out and personally kill those whom he or she wanted dead? It seems obvious that someone would have killed Hitler, long before he could personally have killed all those people he is responsible for having killed. As always, God would judge whether anyone had a moral right to stop Hitler that way if he or she had no other recourse, such as capturing him for trial. But, know this: God sometimes requires large-scale death events for karmic reasons. The world does need a cleansing from time to time, even though many of the spirit-souls, who get caught up in such as that, do get a quick judgment and new beginning according to what they deserve. God will use certain evil leaders to accomplish wide-spread death at times, to include pandemics, but such leaders and those complicit with them will pay an extreme price, possibly to include a final death of self awareness.

"We COG are not here to disparage your war dead or anyone who facilitates such deaths, because they already have been judged. Anyone who makes the decision to kill had better pray they are - to the best of their ability - making it through 'moral intelligence' supplied by God. You might think you can make your case to her that you killed on behalf of moral justice, but SHE would already know what you have yet to discover; that your subthoughts are on file in her Assembler.

"Figure it out ahead of time if you can; and for the really immature or careless among you, it could help to know that life is not a game on some electronic screen. Your remote-controlled distance from killing anyone does not make you less guilty of their deaths; nor does sitting in a cushy office having given the execution orders. You will answer for it to God in the most personal and profound way possible, so you had best know through prayerful guidance you are doing justice to morality.

"Jesus Christ says: '... *he that loses his life for my sake shall find it.*' [Bible: Matthew 10-39] His 'sake' is the same as God's - that of morality. Notice He did not say "he who dies," since he knows life can be 'lost' to a particular 'vessel,' while being retained to an eternal one. And because you can lose life and 'find' it at the same time, there is no death; and your new vessel would be for eternity if you lost your old one for the sake of morality as taught by Jesus Christ."

"... CHIP?"

"Yes, Deepy?"

"Put me through to Eno as soon as you can, please."

"Go ahead."

"Eno, can you hear me?"

"Clearly, my friend."

"Sorry about that. A sudden urge just drew me back to the ship when I thought about it. A quin was here to help me, thanks to CHIP, and thank you for your patience."

"Not a problem my friend – I'm back aboard ship as well. I will let you know the time and place of our next meeting. Meanwhile, take time for your taste buds or whatever you can do for yourself. Take a break in other words. 'Chill out,' as some of your friends might say."

"Uh, okay, Commander, if you say so; will do. Thanks." Wow, Deepy thought, Eno sure stays up to date on human dialect.

~~~~~~~~~~~~~~~~~~~~

Meow?

"Well now, let me think ... hmmm – cheesecake sounds good – yeah, that's what I'll have please, CHIP... a double helping if you don't mind, and a bowl of guava. Thank you kindly." Deepy and Eno had been talking for a few minutes when Deepy realized he also could be eating. It had, after all, been three hours since breakfast, with a 'tiny' teaching session after that.

"Just a cup of my usual, CHIP... and tell Fets I'd like to see him in my office in fifteen minutes to get his views of this morning's procedure. Thank you."

"Procedure? - this morning - without me?" Deepy paused, "I thought I was always on call for that, as a full-time volunteer."

"You were teaching. Besides, I meant to tell you, we're trying a cat. Partly your idea, as you may recall?"

"A cat - my idea? I Don't remember, but come to think of it, I seem to recall dreaming about a cat recently. Gee, I wonder how he did... or she did... She – He? ... Whatever."

"I'll let you know how 'she' did. Are you going to be available for lunch, say ... about one?"

"Sure, I can be here. Will she be here too? I guess we're going to have to meet sooner or later."

"She might be able to make it. We'll see." Eno picked up the space juice "gulp" container as he called it. When the quin set it down, he said "Thank you," and gulped the living spirit within. "See you then, my deep friend."

Chitchat Cat

"Hi," Deepy said.

"Well, hello there, yourself," Cisy replied, as she nodded to the quin who hurried on down the corridor.

"Thank you again," Deepy teleped to the departing quin.

Cisy had been strolling past Deepy's door as the quin opened it and came out. Cisy peeked around Deepy, into his room. "CHIP told me Eno was back aboard. You two were out together, weren't you?"

"So, you're the cat, er, I mean, yes, and we're supposed to meet for lunch at one. Perhaps you'd care to join us?"

"I'd love to. You don't suppose he would mind, do you? Maybe you'd better check with him first."

Deepy waited for the CHIP connection, as he and Cisy stood on opposite sides of the doorway, her trying to see around him ... him casually moving slightly to keep her from doing so, just because her curiosity annoyed him.

"Eno?"

"Yes, Deep?"

"I caught a certain, young cat snooping outside my door. Okay if she joins us for lunch?"

"Sure, happy to have her. Capton Nai and Dr. Nafets will be there too. One o'clock, then."

"All right, sir – we'll see you then. Thanks, Eno."

"Snooping, you say, as if I'm Snoop Catty-Cat."

"Huh? Eno knows I was joking. So, why don't you just come back by at twelve forty-five? I'd invite you in for a soda or something now, but I'm beat and really need a nap. I hope you don't mind."

"Of course I don't mind. What kind of pussycat do you think I am anyway, to come into the room of a dog I barely know? And speaking of 'barely,'" she looked him up and down rather sternly for just a moment.

"Er, I was just going to take a shower... I mean after my nap. I forgot; I'm sorry."

Cisy smiled and winked coquettishly. "I'll see you back here then."

"Roger that," he winked and smiled at her and then watched as she sauntered away, off into the distance, about six feet.

"I stay here," she said, giving him a double wink this time as she disappeared into her room. "Huh?" he thought, "Most people would say if they are neighbors. But then, she's a cat. Cute little thing too," although he told himself there was no way he had just been flirting with a feline.

He checked with CHIP for a wake-up and "quin" call, but then lay there thinking about so many things; he finally gave up trying to sleep. When he did get up he headed straight for his shower, hoping it would help him shake off his grogginess. Odd that he had been a little bummed out by the way Cisy had looked him over. He felt lewd. Thinking of Cisy, he could hear her turn on her water next door. "What the heck, why not?" he thought.

"Blue Cisy."

"Good meow morning."

"Hi neighbor, guess who? 'Meow morning?' Do you always answer your phone that way?"

"Only in the mornings."

"Well, yeah." Deepy looked at the wall for the time. "Yep, it's five minutes 'til noon. Still a meow morning, I reckon. You'll have to forgive me; I'm about half asleep but I gave up on the nap. I'm just about to step into the shower to wash the groggies away."

"Me too," Cisy told him, "but not for that reason."

"Really, I can't imagine a cat taking a shower for any reason. I thought cats hated water."

"Well now – you know I may be cat on the outside, but the 'me' inside loves being clean. The idea of licking myself all over is not so appealing."

"I hear you... say listen, you in the shower yet?"

"Yea, verily. Just stepped in. Why?"

"I'm going to serenade you."

"What?" Cisy laughed, "That's pretty funny."

"Just stay tuned," Deepy told her, "'cause here comes, "The Shower Song;" you ready?"

After surmising that Cisy must have thought the question rhetorical, Deepy opened his mouth and heard...

"I sure hope so" at about that same moment.

"All right then - here we go, ready or not," he told her, while wondering what she must be thinking. "Music Maestro, please," Deepy thought - hoping CHIP would read his intentions. [CHIP's Headband always provides music if Deepy tries to sing.]

I like to be... happy and free,
A singing star with no company;
But you're welcome to sing along
With my soap-sudsy shower song

It takes a measure of timing
To sync a bar of soap with a song,
So lather up now and sing right along
With that wonderful waterfall

Sour notes don't have to float
Just let 'em go down the drain
And who needs a fancy refrain
Just to sing in the rain?

A hook on a line
That sticks in your mind,
Will cause you to sing-along,
With a simple all-wet, hard to forget
Soap-sudsy shower song

Splash out a rhythmic melody,
Then toss in some rhyme, like
"Can't you see...
I love you; Do you love me?
Arkan-saw! ... Did Tenne-see?"
Somehow it all makes sense to me,
So come on and sing along
With my simple all-wet, hard to forget
Soap-sudsy shower song.

A hook on a line
That sticks in your mind,
Will cause you to sing-along,
With my simple all-wet, hard to forget,
Soap-sudsy shower song;
So lather up now and sing right along
With that wonderful waterfall,
And my simple all-wet, hard to forget

Soap-sudsy shower song.
My simple all-wet, hard to forget
Soap-sudsy shower song.

~~~~~~~~~~~~~~~~~~~~~~~~~~~

"I like your outfit."

"Thank you." Deepy was wearing blue shorts and an orange tee shirt with green lettering, which read, "Deep Creep," on one side but Cisy couldn't see what was on the other.

"CHIP's trying to be more like me, and this is what he came up with - pretty pathetic, eh? But, I must say you're looking cat-egorically terrific. Those ruffles suit you – CHIP tells me you're married."

"Thanks, you're sweet and funny even when you're not trying." She laughed when Deepy looked at her askance.

"If you knew I was married, why did you call me up to serenade me?"

"I didn't plan to sing. I just called to chat for a minute and it wasn't exactly a romantic ballad. I sing "The Shower Song" a lot. But I'm sorry I burned your ears."

"I'm not going to tell you again that I enjoyed it, and I want you to write the words down for me. Anyway, you're just fishing for compliments now. Yes, I am married, let's see what's on the other side," Cisy said, as she pranced around Deepy. "One Hot Dog!" she read from his T-shirt. "Wow," she said, "You must relish that. CHIP must think you're hot stuff."

"I'm married too," he told her, then said, "I caught your little joke and it was funny. You might not think CHIP thinks that, if you knew CHIP like maybe I think I know CHIP. Like I say, he's my wardrobe designer, but I suspect he thinks I'm a "show off" type of hot dog."

"Anyway, you're much cuter than he is," Cisy commented.

"Huh? ... Cuter than CHIP?"

Cisy chuckled, "Than my husband."

"I wonder how he'd take that. Oh, damn... er, excuse me... I mean I see what you mean. You were speaking of this dog body. Yeah, I agree most dogs are cute. Most of 'em make good friends too. Although, I must say," Deepy prattled on, "that I've always preferred cats, myself."

"I suppose I might be flattered, but wouldn't you know I like dogs better. Perhaps we should ask CHIP to switch our bodies for us."

"Except, I'm not sure I'd be happy as a female. Do you like being a girl?"

"I understand they can reverse sex organs fairly easily around here," Cisy continued with her train of thought.

"What? That's outrageous. Why would they want to?"

"I'm just teasing you," Cisy laughed.

She has a nice laugh, Deepy sub-thought, grinning back at her, "... acts coquettish too, or "cocattish" maybe..." He loved making word play.

"By the way, I guess we've never actually been formally introduced. I'm Cisy LePurr." She stuck out a paw.

Deepy gently touched it with one of his. "Yes, I'm sorry we didn't get to meet earlier, but I understand you were busy. Anyway, I'm... ahem, er... – D. P. Dog, PhD."

"Really? Well, consider me impressed," Cisy told him.

"Yes, well... PhD, in my case stands for part hound dog. Cisy grinned at him and asked him what D. P. stood for.

"Dog Project," Deepy told her, "as a matter of fact. Has a certain "ring" to it, don't you think? But I'm wondering why you're not called Ceepy, instead of Sissy. And do you really spell your name like it sounds?"

"Yes, I think it's spelled the way it sounds, but it's different." she added.

"What do you mean?" Deepy wondered, "Only got one "s" in the middle or something?"

"Yes, it only has one, but it also starts with a 'C'; I spell it C-i-s-y," Cisy laughed.

"Yep, I'd say that's different," Deepy told her. "I like it; it's kind of classy, I suppose, but why that spelling – just to be different?"

"CHIP determined it because of something that caused him to say I was a 'fraidy cat,' - a sissy and he was going to name me that. I said okay as long as it's spelled C-i-s-y. CHIP said he meant he was going to name me "Fraidy." I said, 'Fraidy' sounds like a guy's name, so it will be C-i-s-y."

"Well, I'd say you're no s-i-s-s-y if you stood up to the CHIPster that way. I like it. It suits you. You do have a certain – how shall I say it? - 'Look' about you... classy, like I said."

"Thank you; that's sweet. I am a copy though... seems I'm a clone of some pet owners in Houston, Texas. CHIP gave me some other name choices, like "Copy" and "Fax," after he made his little joke. I told him I would stick with Cisy."

"Really? No kidding?" Deepy was half listening, hung up on another thought. "That's used to be my home town."

"Fax? ... Copy?" Cisy inquired with a hint of a smile.

"Houston, silly... you know what I mean. I was born in Texas, and migrated around there some, but was raised mostly in Arkansas."

"The dog calls me 'silly,' and we just met. OK, I confess."

Deepy thought of asking her to whom her human spirit belonged, but they strode through the doors to the virtual reality room just then and entered Deepy's Diner, each taking a chair at a table with Eno, and the Captons – one a physical doctor, one a Psyentist. Seems everybody around the place was some sort of doctor, minus the seeming "professional aloofness*" shared by so many hybrid types, although he understood why they wouldn't care to be buddy-buddy with their patients. Everyone greeted everyone; smiley faces all around. *{many "experts" think people are not giving them the respect they think they have earned through years of study and practice. Folks are asking too many questions; expressing too many predetermined opinions, perhaps imagined from too much blasphemous Internet information!}

"We just need a few more minutes to finish up some mission-related conversation, if you two don't mind ignoring us that long." Eno said, while smiling at his cute little friends.

"We'll carry on. It will give us time to order and continue getting acquainted," Cisy replied, returning his smile.

She turned to Deepy. "God" - she teleped, "That's who my human spirit and soul belong to. At least, that's the prayer I purr the most... if SHE will have me. And, yes, I love being a girl, although I think of myself as a woman," she continued on the private line CHIP provided.

Deepy was startled at her ability to read his sub-thoughts, many of which even got by him. But then, he was lost again in that smile and those eyes. He had a dopey grin on his face when he asked, "What would you like?"

"I beg your pardon."

"To eat?"

"Oh, yes - of course. Sometimes I can read sub-thoughts, but then again, the obvious can slip right by me - just a small salad. It hasn't been that long since I had breakfast. Thank you."

"I can't picture a cat eating a salad, but I can see for myself, I guess. On the other hand, a dog eating... oh, heck we'll eat most anything," he said, thinking of all he did eat.

It took Deepy about half a minute to figure out what he wanted. Oddly enough, and he commented on this to Cisy, he wasn't for some reason, feeling all that hungry. Unusual for him, he added. She just smiled. He ordered for both of them.

"So tell me," they both began at the same time... and then laughed together. Deepy nodded to Cisy to go ahead.

"I was just wondering about your morning. I'm a little envious. He's never taken me to his special place before."

Deepy looked at her quizzically. Paused a moment, then said, "But you only just got here Friday. And that reminds me, how in the world did you get a wardrobe so quickly... and such a pretty one at that?" he flattered.

"You're sweet. I placed an advance order," she laughed, "and one of the other ships brought it from Phobos."

"Phobos? That's one of the Mars' moons."

"CHIP tells me it's really a control satellite for them. They apparently have a base under the surface. Much of it is a shell type of structure - like here, as engineered by them."

"You just got here, and already you know this kind of stuff."

"Maybe we should become a team and confide in each other."

"Umm," he was about to think of an answer for that, but was distracted by the aroma of hot food being stuck under his nose. "Umm," he repeated, "that sure looks and smells yummy for the tummy."

"And that's what you call not being very hungry?" Cisy teased with a wink.

"That is a "dog-sized" helping," he agreed. "Here, try some of this shrimp," he offered, "I can never get enough of it myself."

Eno was looking at him. CHIP tuned everyone in.

"I hope you two won't think us rude and will excuse us. We need to go back to my office for a staff consultation."

Capton Nai bent in their direction. "Enjoy your meal," he told them. Fets gave them a friendly smile and nod.

"I wonder if all this official consultation has anything to do with me." Cisy commented, as they watched the three depart.

"Meaning?"

"Oh, I'm sure I'm just being self-centered. We had a little incident this morning in the E-R that's all. It didn't amount to much. It was really an accident, and I wasn't hurt."

"Hurt? My goodness, what happened?"

"Our guest threw me across the room."

"Oh My God! - And this woman was a cat lover?"

"Man. Yes, as a matter of fact. He didn't realize what he was holding. He made that very clear afterward. He was extremely upset. That's why he did it. Then he was more upset about doing it, as soon as he realized I was a cat - am a cat."

"And you weren't hurt? Your cat sense-of-balance save you, or what?" Deepy was curious and serious.

"Somehow a Marsian managed to catch me. It happened so quickly, I was shocked."

"But you weren't afraid to go back to the man?"

"Oh, no - he came across the room and got me; he was so sorry. I felt sorry for him too. He was able to calm down a lot though, and I feel like I made a difference. I really do. I never got so much attention in my life... except from my husband... or when I'm occasionally serenaded by strange, but cute, dogs," she nodded at him. "But, anyway... tell me about your morning."

"Well, it wasn't as exciting as yours, but very enlightening. Talk-talk-talk, but I enjoy being out with Eno. Here try this shrimp." Deepy pawed the plate across to Cisy, who double-pawed one of the butterfly shrimp into her bowl, and pushed the plate back. "Ah so, flied buttafly slimpp," she said as she took a bite, adding "Hmm, that is good," after a moment's chewing.

She swallowed and then said, "Sorry 'bout the accent. Don't know what got into me. I'm Persian, though, so maybe I should speak with an accent, but I was just being silly... again. I already admitted to being guilty as charged on that account."

"Tell me about it; I can certainly relate. 'Silly' can be a good release mechanism. I use it all the time."

"Ah, Dr. D. P. Dog, your reputation precedes you." Cisy paused, "Now... you tell me."

"Huh...?"

"About your morning with Eno."

"Oh – well, obviously you know where we are?"

"Of course - you don't think they're keeping me prisoner here, do you? I was out and about for a little while with Dr. Fets and Capton Nai. They just showed me around the complex a little. We're inside Mars."

"Well, I guess if you believe that, you'll believe anything else I might tell you."

"What? Of course you know. Come on now."

"Of course I do." He smiled, "Without a doubt, and why not; after all, we got here in a TranShip." He then told her about his morning with Eno; the beautiful scenery and the deep message about the "LOG," as Eno called it – meaning the Life Of God, and how there is only One Life, but shared with all living things.

That evening, Deepy and Cisy continued their getting-acquainted chat over dinner. They seemed delighted in one another's company.

~~~~~~~~~~~~~~~~~~~~~~~~~

Chapter 23
Deep Dreamer

Deepy was at it again. He tossed and turned. And no wonder – he somehow had become CHIP. Eno, the creator, had made them into one being, saying CHIP wanted personality and Deepy should be more "mindful." CHIP needed spirit so that he could relate to people better, and Deepy needed a bigger Soul nexus so that he could think more deeply.

They both begged him not to do it, "But I'm the creator," Eno had said, "and creators must create. That's what we do. It's our job."

"But, I gotta be me... to give it a try... to do it or die," Deepy wailed.

"Don't do this, boss, I'm begging you," CHIP chirped. "I have to go it alone... to do it my way. If you mix me up with him, you'll just bring me down to his level."

"No, no, you don't understand, either of you. Together you'll both be better. You each have what the other one needs. You'll see. And besides, I guarantee if you don't like it after six months, I'll return your money, no questions asked. That's a better deal than the competition can offer.

"Trust me. If you buy Egod's baloney, you'll be getting shortchanged. I know whereof I speak. Now take hand in paw while I perform this wedding ceremony."

CHIP fainted – short-circuited, actually. The whole idea was just too much for him. It blew his mind.

"Don't worry about him," Eno told Deepy. "He'll be all right. He's not real anyway. Not like you. You'll really be in control when I get through here. You'll be perfect. There won't be anything you can't do, except of course, you can't be me. You'll never be me. Do you understand? I and I alone am the One Creator of all life." Eno laughed diabolically and then snorted.

"Now, be a good doggie and put on this helmet and take CHIP's hand in your paw, so I can make you a CHIP off the old blockhead," Eno chuckled, apparently quite tickled with himself.

"I won't do it!" Deepy yelped.

"Oh, you'll do it. You'll do it all right. I have my ways, Mr. Hot Shot doggie boy."

Somewhere, Larray whimpered in his sleep, and the deed was done. "I now pronounce you CHIPanoid and doganoid, and officially pairanoid, Eno laughed at his witticism. "Get it? – 'pair' anoid."

CHIP and Deepy were one. In someone's sleep, "Cheepy" was born. Then, Deepy slipped a little deeper into his nightmare. Some awful sound was coming from a jukebox – no, that was no jukebox.

"…Mama was a CHIP… Daddy was a Deepy," Eno sang.

"You've sold my soul!" Cheepy chirped. "You've stolen my spirit," he barked. "You had no right."

"Oh, I had a right, all right. I had a right. You seem to always forget who the Creator is and who's the created. I know you've always secretly wanted to be me. You didn't really think you could hide yourself from me, did you, from the very one, and the only one who created you? You may have called me Boss, but you never really meant it before. Now, I've given you the love you need to see me with new eyes – big brown, doggie eyes. Maybe now you can learn to appreciate me. Love me! Do you hear? Love me! That's an order, son."

"Dear God," Cheepy sighed.

"You finally got that right. Just don't forget it."

"I feel cheapened, used, degraded, and dogmatic," Cheepy moaned.

"You feel cheapened?" another part of him said. "I feel quirky, crystallized and also dogmatic. It's horrible, but I do feel like proselytizing for Jesus," he carried on, drooling all the while.

"Oh well," Eno said, "I'm sure you'll both be very happy together."

Cheepy walked up the church steps. It was a beautiful, sunny day, and it matched his disposition. His "marriage" seemed to be working out after all. He felt he was melding into one new being, with a witty new personality, but most of all he appreciated his wonderfully loving new character. He had felt a lot of warm fuzzy feelings toward the world in general lately. He laughed out loud. "I'm glad," he thought, "that Eno decided to meld the two of us into this cute dog body. People everywhere just seem to automatically fall in love with me. How sweet it is."

He was feeling thoughtful. He knew, in fact, that he was just about the perfect mix of mind and body and it allowed him to be almost pure "thoughtful-feeling" all the time now, gracious to everyone and thing, even trying to dodge ants on the ground. He was not a destroyer.

The only thing missing, Eno had said, was a dose of femininity, separate but equal, he had said, and that would be supplied momentarily within this church, in another, more formal and elaborate ceremony, as Dr. Eno Mai would unite Cheepy the male with Cisy the female, in holy matrimony. Some Yin and Yang were about to bond, completing a duality of polar essences in one entity.

"Oh dog of wonder… dog of light… " he sang under his breath as he toddled up the two remaining steps and entered the church. A computer-mind with the spirit, soul, and shape of a very special dog waddled down the aisle toward the podium where Eno stood with a beautiful woman named CeCe, in the form of a cat. "Gorgeous," Cheepy thought, knowing she also was seeing both his Larray James Othereal Spirit and material forms.

Eno motioned for him to continue coming forward. Shel had appeared beside Eno and was now introducing him to the congregation. Smiling at Cheepy, she finished her introduction "… our loving pastor, Dr. Eno Mai."

Eno thanked her as the crowd took their seats and Shel just seemed to dissolve into Eno. "I will have a few words in a moment about what we, your selected Psyence leaders, were able to accomplish this past week, and then we will talk about what we and those volunteers among you will undertake on your behalf next week. And, of course, we will be asking for as many volunteers as we can get to help us. But, before that, as you know, I have a most special ceremony to perform – a consecration of wedding vows between a couple, dear to my heart." Eno glanced at Cisy, and now Cheepy who had joined them next to the pulpit.

"However," he said, "it gives me great pleasure to first introduce the groom-to-be… a most favored friend of mine who will sing a song for us. His bride to be, whom you've already met, will join him. Eno then noticed that Cheepy was wearing a tux with satin stripes down each side. On one of the stripes was a subtle stitching which read "Uni," and as Cheepy turned to face the audience, Eno noticed the other stripe read "form."

"I give you, in gracious duet," Eno announced, "… Deepy… er, "Cheepy," – "Deepy-Cheepy-CHIP" – whatever," Eno swept his arm around to indicate his dog-shaped friend, and accomplished the same move with his other arm to his right side, as he announced "… and Cisy LePurr, soon to be Ms. Cheepy CHIP… or whatever."

"Er… Eno!" Cisy tried to whisper.

"Excuse me," Eno told his audience, as he leaned over so Cisy actually could whisper in his ear.

"Correction," he said, raising up a moment later, "Make that 'soon to be Ms. Cheepy 'LePurr' CHIP, and I do believe they are going to sing something appropriate now," he added, looking at Cheepy.

"Love is a Many Splintered Thing," the groom-to-be told everyone. There were several scattered "Amen's" from the congregation.

"Splendored!" Cisy corrected to the audience. *"Love is a Many 'Splendored' Thing."* Again, there were more "Amen's along with some laughter and applause.

"Was just joking," Cheepy muttered, winking at Cisy.

Two beaming bodies of light approached each other to meet at the front of the altar, behind the railing, as Deepy's dream trailed off into that light. He snoozed silently and peacefully, and deeper than he had in a long time.

/////////////////////\\\\\\\\\\\\\\\\\\\
Let Mercy and Grace define you,
along with Wisdom, Intelligence, Logic, and Love.

IIIIIIIIIIIIIIIIIIIII
Reprieve

Eleven o'clock at night… the phone was ringing as CeCe unlocked her door. She was on the verge of collapsing, which she did, on the sofa as Sal went over and picked up the phone. CeCe was dizzy from grief and tiredness. Thank God, Sal had been with her through all this. She knew she could not have made the hour drive from the hospital after watching Larray's life slip away. She didn't know how her daughter managed to stay on the road. She was exhausted too, after their combined vigil at his bedside – a vigil that ended after two weeks of hope and prayer. Little hope – the doctor had wanted to be honest about it, but lots of prayer just the same '… *thy will be done, Lord'*. Apparently, God had willed that Larray was ready to move on. She knew God must have other plans for her husband of almost thirty-five years.

There was a cloth of some kind over the face of Larry R. James and he vaguely wondered why, because he could barely breathe. His back was hurting. He struggled to lift himself upright from the hard surface he was laying on but could not. He groaned. He heard someone gasp, "Dear God," and then heard glass shattering. Air! He needed air. He thought maybe he was dreaming again. The cloth suddenly moved off his face.

Now, swooning on the couch, CeCe wondered what was causing her daughter to sob hysterically, while turning around to smile at her at the same time. Sal hung up the phone, went and sat beside her mother, grabbed, hugged her and said, almost incoherently "... We're going back, Mom. Dad's alive. Almost right after we left." Sal struggled to bring herself under control. CeCe appeared to have fainted. Sal brought her water from the kitchen, and splashed some in her face and then scolded her to drink the remainder.

After what seemed like an eternity to Sal, who was thinking of the drive back, CeCe was smiling, through tears, at her precious daughter; "their" daughter. Larray was back. "Thank you, God."

"We're going back, Mom," Sal told her. "Do you need to go to the bathroom first? Are you hungry? Dad's alive," she giggled. They hugged each other. CeCe got up to go to the bathroom. Sal followed her to the door, talking all the way to it and then finally through it.

"Doctor Blake said that Dad was resting comfortably in stable but critical condition; that we could just sleep and come over in the morning – it was up to us." Sal was questioning her first impulse now, and thinking of her mother, as she finally turned around to give her some privacy. "Maybe that's what we should do. What do you think? The nurse said our recliners were still in place for us to sleep some if we go now. But it's so late, and Dad will probably be asleep. I want to see him now. Don't you? I know you do. Doctor Blake said Dad's not heavily sedated or anything and he's out of the coma, thank God. I can drive. I'm going to make some instant coffee. You want some?"

"Yes, sweetie, thank you."

"Thank God, Dad will get to see his twin grand babies before long – Wren and Wron"

"I still don't know where you came up with those names, dear, but I'm getting used to them. I think your dad will like them."

"Like I told you, they just popped into my head for no apparent reason, and Blain liked them. Wonder what Dad will think? At least I get to tell him now. I need to call Blain, again," Sal mumbled as she closed the bathroom door and headed to the kitchen. Her mother was still crying, but smiling now too.

Larray appeared to be sleeping when they entered the room. The nurse who was checking his oxygen whispered something to him. CeCe saw him raise his head slightly and turn their way, but she could barely see his raised face from the doorway. When they got up close, he actually smiled and spoke. "I had the strangest dream," were his first words as they approached his bed. "I heard someone say "He's gone." That's not part of the dream. I know that, even though I can't remember the dream right now." He had to stop talking. His lovely wife and almost duplicate daughter seemed to be taking turns planting kisses on his face from both sides. He had no desire to talk. He figured there was time. Besides, he was too busy thanking God for this special moment with people he dearly loved. He knew he had been raised from 'gone' to back again, and now had a pretty good feeling he would be around a while longer.

[Nothing quite like good karma]

IIIIIIIIIIIIIIIIIIIIIIIIII

-On Reflection-

"Where are they now?" BB wondered.

"Home, making plans," CHIP told his best buddy. "Dr. Larry Ray James is on his way to a full recovery. The doctors say the tumor appears to have just melted away. Sal tells her parents they both look ten years younger. CeCe says that's just from thinking about their upcoming second honeymoon. Actually, Larray is remembering the first one as if it were yesterday and he tells Sal if she thinks they look younger now, 'just wait until after their third honeymoon.' And by now he has forgotten all about that supernal dream he had of aliens and UFOs. Of course we will flood him with memories when the time is right. Right now though, they just need some time to themselves."

~~~~~~~~~~~~~~~~~~~~~
~Fifteen Years Later~
(2012)

"Are you sure about that?" It was a familiar voice. It had been awhile since Larray had heard it, but as soon as he did the previous year, the memories flooded back, and "Deepy" and CHIP began to write. Now, here it was again, on a bright September day.

"Hey, what say? How are you? How's everybody? How are Deepy-- and CHIP and Cisy? You gotta admit that was a funny dream I had about those three becoming one. I just finished writing about it. Am I sure about what?"

Eno chuckled, "We're all fine, thanks. But, I see you just wrote "The End". Are you sure about that?

"What do you mean?"

"You're a Christian."

It sounded like a question. "Of course."

"Of course, and that means you're going to be around forever – writing, reading, living, breathing, listening to music, making music, wondering at the rain on the roof, the snow falling, the chaotic storms that come and go, but never causing concern anymore. You will be there until there turns to here, and then you will be here with God in her Heavenly home forever. So relax, take a break. Go fishing or something.

And, instead of writing 'The End," would you consider a "Transc*ending*" instead - for a new beginning?"

"Of course, but you just said I will be here until it turns to there, so I'm trying to figure out when that might happen. Can you give me a hint, maybe?"

"Not right away – in terms of years. But I am glad that during your continued bouts of sickness, you finally realized what I meant when I said you would have perfect health upon your return Home."

Larray relaxed..."Yes, thank you. I'm sorry. I certainly didn't mean to imply that I'm not looking forward to my return "Home." I truly am and feel so blessed you shared that information with me. I hope I didn't sound like I wasn't ready. I'm ready whenever God is ready for me, but it's good to know I have some time left for fishing here."

"By all means, take a fishing break." Eno reassured him, and then added, "You know though there will be a new beginning for you and many other hybrids. This time you made it! You will be stepping into Gaia's Garden when you depart this life, and from there – eternity is yours."

"I pray my whole family will be with me."

"Keep on praying, since I'm not allowed to comment on that. Telling your future is a reward for what you did for us."

Larray heard a chirpy voice in the background. "Tell Larray it's a small step for man, but a giant leap for a hybrid doggy-man."

"There you go again, CHIP. Did anybody ever tell you and BB you're really good characters. I like your odd humor, some of which you may have picked up from me."

This time, Larray could hear Deepy laughing from somewhere. It was Larray's own laugh. He knew Eno and CHIP had created a "doganoid Deepy" and a "catanoid Cisy," replete with that part of Larray's and CeCe's spirits with which Deepy and Cisy originally were endowed and he knew they also were granted that same tiny soul nexus each had with CHIP and BB.

He knew the ship Assembler would regenerate them into other TranShip classrooms of tiny spirit souls preparing for service with the Lord in Garden Gaia, while they also would serve in their roles of "comforters" to guest humans, although Eno said those would be fewer guests now.

"Tell everybody 'hi' for me, and I want to thank you all again; and thanks for helping me with my writing, CHIPster."

"We thank you likewise," Eno said, "for the part you played."

"Amen," was the retort from the Ship crew, and it came in a jumble of voices, some of which Larray recognized.

"Oh, Eno – one more thing, while I'm thinking about it – Could a hybrid human ever become a Trangel?"

"I'm glad you asked, because I have something to tell you and I can do that in part by answering your question. As you know, Trangels were Mind Cells that survived intact from the instant of God's Big Bang birth. There were many, including Jesus Christ who briefly was in your hybrid world, but not of it. Jesus appeared in pure Human form with his Christ Soul Mate, thereby making him/her a Trangel cohabiting a fused Spirit form. But, the answer to your question is 'yes,' as far as their scope of potential is involved. Nothing is impossible to God.

"What I wanted to tell you is that Jesus Christ took the opportunity to do what COG did with Perfect Humans during that earlier Garden era in which COG Co-Created Humangels within the fused spirit bodies of those Humans. Essentially the COG were taking back much of the Mental and Spirit Essence that belonged to God prior to her consequential Big Bang. The news is that Jesus, along with his Christ Soul Mate, contributed to God's Child, "Junior," by also Co-Creating their own Human Trangel while on Earth.

"The Co-Created Spirit body was perfect as a clone of the fused Spirit body of Jesus. God then beamed a pure Soul into the body as it gelled forth into the material world. The Soul for the new Angel Co-Creation was of Trangel Essence. Combined into one form, they were a full adult replica mix of Yin and Yang; and virtually another Trangel in the material world but not <u>of</u> it. This "twin" of dual polarities was born in time to serve as a special friend to her Lord God Co-Creator. Also, SHe could switch polarities, even in the material realm, and serve as either a male or female friend, which SHe did, while somewhat disguising herself in either case, so as to not look too much like Jesus. But, SHe did look like a male and female version of herself, enough to be designated "twin." In fact, you, my deep friend, met both the Yin and Yang versions of this replicated Trangel."

"No, come on – really? - I must be dreaming again. – This is "mind-blowing," and I'm only just now hearing about it; that I actually met a Trangel that Jesus and Christ Co-Created. Would you care to tell me their names?"

"I was only recently given permission to tell you this, in time for your book. CHIP will tell you their names later; they have been christened anew since their material service to the Lord God. For now, you and CHIP have a lot more work to do on that book than you realize, so don't take too long a fishing break.

"We must say, 'bye' at the moment, but never forget God loves you, just as SHE does all her tiny hybrids."

Larray looked out the window in time to see a TranShip shimmer, and disappear. He sort of wished he was onboard. But he knew there would be time for that too. Thank God for 'time,' he thought, thinking of CHIP. "Thank God for God. Thanks, Eno, Shel, CHIP and BB; I love you guys."

Book of John, Chapter 16, Verses 13 - 15: (Jesus said...)
'Howbeit when he, the Spirit of truth, is come, he will guide you into all truth; for he shall not speak of himself; but whatsoever he shall hear, that shall he speak: and he will shew you things to come.' 'He shall glorify me: for he shall receive of mine, and shall shew it unto you.' 'All things that the Father hath are mine: therefore said I, that he shall take of mine, and shall shew it unto you.'

CHATS and NOTES

"As one obverse replica to another, I can understand the Commander wanting to give Larray a respite before we hit him with the big news."

"As a polar opposite original facsimile," BB told CHIP, "I agree. You know, as his temporary O'Soul, I did spend as much time with that human dog as you did. He really was the right man for the job. But yeah, Lord Eno wanted Larray to put the "Deepy dog" character to rest while he and CeCe enjoy their latest honeymoon vacation, which will be intimately loving in a gracious, thoughtful manner. But regarding that new information, our Lord Commander will let us know how much of it Larray can include in his work - just as soon as God lets him know. Just thinking about it all now, it seems like only yesterday this whole process was set in motion."

"And you seem never to tire of making "timely" references, since our "time" discussion for Deepy's book, even though everything to us seems as if it happened only yesterday."

"Only we don't have any yesterdays."

CHIP laughed, "Yeah – quite right!" he replied to his best bud, who was now reminiscing...

"Let's see, as I recall, it was toward the end of the biblical *Book of John*, that "a certain party" was formally introduced into the biblical picture; but I especially recall the comments about him in Chapter 21, Verses 20 through 24, as Jesus was leaving a seashore supper scene with his disciples:"

20; Then Peter, turning about, seeth the disciple whom Jesus loved following; which also leaned on his breast at supper and said, Lord, which is he that betrayeth thee?

21; Peter seeing him saith to Jesus, Lord, and what shall this man do?

22; Jesus saith unto him, If I will that he tarry till I come, what is that to thee? Follow thou me.

23; Then went this saying abroad among the brethren, that that disciple should not die; yet Jesus said not unto him, He shall not die; but, If I will that he tarry till I come, what is that to thee?

23; This is the disciple which testifieth of these things, and wrote these things: and we know that his testimony is true.

"I am looking forward to the expression on Larray's face when he finds out a certain acquaintance actually is the replica Angel, co-Created by the Christ/Jesus Mind within the fused Spirit Body of Jesus, and allowed to materialize, and 'tarry,' rather than proceed directly to Heaven. Deepy, er... Larray is likely to figure out who SHe is, but we will give his memory a jolt if we get the go-ahead, and then of course he will have some re-writing to do."

"It seems we spend a lot of time re-writing. Irradiative wave communication can at times be unduly influenced by shall we say "weather conditions," just to keep it simple. Anyway, while our certain Trangel only had a cameo role in our setting, her Spirit-Soul of course will again play his/her acquiescent parts to perfection when the time comes, in the same gracious way SHe* did last time, in the role of the mystery 'disciple' Jesus is said to have loved. *(reminder: "SHe" is the personal pronoun of COG and Humangels)

"Since their Creator left the area, they have had responsibility and authority over this realm as Sam Antha - the Jesus/Christ-replicated twin Self, who was christened anew as the twi-polar, Trangel Acting Commander of TranShip 1. Even now, they await that time when they again assist their Trangel Co-Creators upon their return to this realm for Earth's Garden Gaia.

"Sam Antha will never forget how wonderful his/her Mentor-Creator was during those sad, biblical days. Even those few Humangel disciples, who materialized for the first visit of Jesus Christ, needed much patience to manipulate that special hybrid redemptive period. Even then, dealing with the knowledge of what awaited his/her Co-Creator showed the Sam Antha Trangel to have all the godly Grace and Character Essence Christ Jesus could expect from her lineage."

"Soon, the four of them, plus TranShip-Two Commander Satan Nasat and TranShip III Commander Shel Eno, will play major roles in the end result of the hybrid world, with Garden Gaia now just a matter of a brief time away, relatively speaking.

"A big aspect of the story though is that Sam Antha, by her previous biblical name was just as often seen as female, but when SHe appeared in male form, her name was not as Peter said, 'this man.' He knew the man's name, but he had petty envy of 'this man,' and Peter also could not tolerate "that woman" twin who oftentimes appeared. Even though he was disdainful at times, Peter often did recognize each of them by their given "polar gender" names.

"*'The Secret Gospel of Thomas'* has something to say on the subject of this Jesus Christ "Replica." Larray is supposed to include some of that *'Secret Gospel'* in his book, but doesn't know it just yet.

CHIP and BB (also replica-related)

IIIIIIIIIIIIIIIIIIIIIIIIIIIIIIIIIIIIIIIIIIIIII

Post Scriptures

[*Holy Bible*, slight variations of the *King James Version*]
[*Book of Matthew*, Chapter 14, Verses 51 and 52]

Jesus said '... Have you understood all these things? ...' 'Yes, Lord.'

'Then he said... Therefore every scribe which is instructed regarding the kingdom of heaven is like a man that is a householder, who brings forth out of his treasure things new and old.'

IIIIIIIIIIIIIIIIIIIIII

[Mark, Chapter 4, Verses 14 and 15]

'The sower sows the word.'... *'And these are they <u>by the way side</u>,* where the word is sown; but when they have heard, Satan, comes immediately, and takes away the word that was sown in their hearts.**[CHIP note: "Way side" represents those not on the sought-after path. 'Hearts' are brain-ego physically related and emotional, or not steadfast as are spirit-souls coupled together as mind.]

[Mark, Chapter 4, Verse 19]

'And the cares of this world, and the deceitfulness of riches, and the lusts of other things entering in, choke the word, and it becomes of no value.'

[That's the devil, Egod's world – all hybrid made]

[Mark, Chapter 4, Verse 22]

'For there is nothing hidden nor kept secret which shall not be revealed.'

[CHIP note: My Lord God Commander says the biblical translations throughout this work are well within the Spirit of God's Virtues and the Virtues of God's Spirit.]

'God loved the world enough to allow one of her pure Children to be born as a human being, to die and then rise from

death to show that eternal life can be attained through God's Grace - by spirit-soul mates capable of understanding.'

[Adapted from the *Holy Bible, Book of John, Chap. 3, Verse 16*]

IIIIIIIIIIIIIIII
After Words

CHIPs always want the last word, but of course God will have it, as another effort to communicate with you.

Yes, this is a "wordy" book that treats words in a very respectful manner. But, there are plenty of egodly words in circulation, as you know, and they should be viewed for what they are. Let's look at one particular useful word as we make our way to communion.

"Semantics:" the study of meanings; the historical and psychological study and the classification of changes in the signification of words or forms viewed as factors in linguistic development. {Example: the change from animated 'trees' to the word 'humanimals'}

"Generative semantics:" a description of a language emphasizing a semantic deep structure that is logical in form, that provides syntactic structure, and that is related to surface structure by transformations.

Those definitions offer some clues and flexibility, as do many words and definitions, if you seek to see or to hear in a certain way. Notice in the word, 'semantics,' we could select six other words, as it is written, or of course restructure the letters for other meanings. On the surface though, we have the words: man, ant, mantic,* anti, antics and tics. That makes seven words, including the original, for the price of one, and all without rearranging just nine letters. *[of or relating to the faculty of divination: PROPHETIC]

Within the definitions above, we have the words to restructure meaning: 'classification' - 'of changes' - 'of words or forms.' We also have 'generative' - 'deep structure' - 'logical in form' - 'related to surface structure by transformations.' That could almost be a definition for Humangels.

What about "syntax": A connected or orderly system; harmonious arrangement of parts or elements? It almost sounds as if we are talking about God as 'The Word.'

We referred to the preceding words or word groups as 'offering some clues,' but to what? - "A doctrine and educational discipline intended to improve habits of response of human beings to their environment and one another especially by training in the more critical use of words and other symbols." Well now, that is the definition of 'general semantics.' We use words to think, so why not try to think more deeply about the words we use, especially now?

God gives meaning to everything. God may also define words according to their essence. Unfortunately, humans have not done a good job of that in the case of man and woman, who have equal essence in God's Mind ... equal, but opposite. The Godly translation from essence to definitions is often lost in the material world of id/ego.

Words do not necessarily represent essence in pure form. Essence is essence. Yin and Yang are polar opposites. Call yourselves what you will, it does not change your essence. If you are one 'gender,' but refer to yourself as the opposite gender, that would seem odd now based on your definitions of words, but it should not necessarily have any sexual connotation at all, such as meaning you are to be labeled 'unnatural.' Oftentimes Egod gives impure or unclear meaning to words, without consideration of godly essence of moral purity. The point here is that some words are meant to be defined by essence, and then referenced according to God's WILL, so they would not defy or deny such essence. Listen now. How can some idea that already exists be affected by new information? New *'understanding'* is the answer.

We will say it yet again: God loves you. You are a product of God, no matter how much you allow Egod to misuse and abuse you. And God needs you to be perfect, even while SHE recognizes you must accomplish a certain genesis effort toward that goal, in order for her Grace to assist you to the finish line, in what has become a race against time for this generation.

'And the light shone in darkness; and the darkness* did not, or could not, or would not, understand.' *[ignorance]

[CHIP rendition of *John, Chapter 1-Verse 5*]

IIIIIIIIIIIII

Enote

If you were Egod, what would you do to overcome the essence of goodness within this work, and its positive, godly influence in the lives of humans? First you would try the usual: ignore the work as long as possible – then find "experts" to deny its validity as necessary. You might also seek information that would diminish the messenger somehow in the eyes of his/her readers.

Egod should save himself the trouble of trying to divert attention to the messenger, because he cannot save himself from the messages of this book – not even if only a few dozen people ever were to read it, or no one does. As to pointing out the flaws of its imperfect scribe, he would be the first to tell you there are many. And he is humbly grateful to be allowed to serve in the role of messenger, or scribe, if you believe God can dictate her WILL through imagination. The human co-author has prayed many times that this is a divinely inspired work... so that the true "Author" is God, doing the best SHE can through the imperfect medium of a hybrid human spirit-mind.

But this imperfect entity does aspire to become perfect, even as God is. Then again, you share the same Parents, who dare that you also be perfect. SHE would not expect the impossible. Therefore it is logical that you have received more than one chance to serve God in this material world. Perhaps your acquiescence to God's WILL – through Christ - will lead you home, relatively soon. Thanks to God's Grace, this one lifetime could be the next-to-last material one for you, if you overcome your id/ego entity. That means Garden Gaia would be your next stop. That will become heaven on Earth and you will proceed from there to eternity.

If you have the capacity to understand the imperfectly enunciated concepts and ideals presented in this book, you are among the truly blessed, but only if you also have the moral capacity to change on behalf of God. Moral capacity is required. Change for God is required. You receive God's help in doing this, through her own Moral basis. If you have the intellectual capacity to understand this work, but do not attain the gift of moral enlightenment to change for good, then effectively you have chosen Egod.

If need be, start your walk anew down God's path. Don't give up your desire to be perfect, since this may be your last opportunity for a "stay of Grace." Continue to pray for guidance in gaining Wisdom, Intellect, Logic, Love and your own grace towards God. Always remember, you have the power to change your future – not now – but then, then again; then, then, and then, but before it's too late. It would be good to know you did it 'then.'

The good to be found within the pages of this work comes from the Parents, of course. Any ego remnants come from God's imperfect messenger. But it is still your responsibility to discern for yourselves what you will take from this offering.

Now, it is up to you to continue writing your own book of eternal life. Commune with your Creator to make it so.

Your confidante,
Eno Mai

/////////////\\\\\\\\\\\\\\

(Deep Note)

This work tries to reflect the combined Yin/Yang within us. It is not fiction ... nor is it nonfiction. It strives for a balance between those two, while recognizing even the "fictional" aspect (the dog) could be made *actual* if God wanted that. Of course, some people believe religion is fiction anyway. It is what it is, and for you to reconcile for yourself. Luck will have nothing to say.

The Essence of the book is true, even though "played out" in the author's chosen setting. But it is only an outline. Christ will provide the whole truth ... and relatively soon. God has a logical answer for every question we might raise and when Christ comes, Jesus will tell everything to those who incarnate during his time. That is his promise. You don't want to miss that, so start work on your godly imagination now; grow it and maintain it.

God is the Word ... meaning the progenitor of thought. Most all the words in this book are in God's modern dictionary for good reason. God wants her words to serve her whenever SHE needs them, whether from the original form of their etymology; today's definition; or even as pseudonyms or affectations. The words of this book are meant to glorify God, through her own *Grace* toward us.

For many spirit-souls, life in this world has been very much like hell. But, should the rest of us just say 'they' had it coming; it's their karmic fate? Is that the type of grace that God would want from us? The law of karma bereaves God, even if SHE logically knows it is pure justice and so it often is autonomously carried out by her Assembler. At the same time, SHE would appreciate all the help that we can give each other to ease our suffering; and we all do suffer in ways of our making. In our prayers, we ask for God's mercy. God is merciful. As a key aspect of her mercy, God also is our Teacher and we have much to learn. SHE is trying to teach us how to practice grace through Wisdom, Intellect, Logic, and Love.

We must always be gracious to one another. As of now, we are not fortunate enough to occupy a perfect Humangel form, but we can help make that change. When we are with other people, in person or thought, let's recognize them as potentially acceptable to God, just as we are. Notice that while the outline of their human form is basically the same as ours, they might be purer in spirit-soul than we are at the moment, especially if we believe we are more gifted or more fortunate. Do not see them as old, young, ugly, pretty, fat, thin, green, yellow, red, or gray, for example. If we can achieve the power to see the countenance of their inner being, we may consider ourselves blessed. Their spirit-soul conceivably could shine some light on us. Let's see them as we would see ourselves, as one with God some day.

It should bereave us that life on our planet could be a living hell for anyone. It is necessary that we condemn Egod, who is very real in our lives and who also would condemn us to hell, if we do not help a moral God save us. The density of this world distorts our thinking and memory, but we can pray that we all become as little children to be born again into perfect health.

It did not escape notice during the writing of this book that we seem to have a God of great irony. But, we do have a last chance. There is a majestic and glorious "T's" worth of difference between immorality and immortality. That 'T' is a cross and it stands for 'transformation.' With God's help, through Jesus Christ, we can be transformed for eternal life.

Larray "Deepy" James
//////////////\\\\\\\\\\\\\\

PRAYER IS QUITE SOOTHING REALLY;
WHEN APPLIED WITH SINCERE REVERENCE!
GO TO SLEEP PEACEFULLY WITH ONE OR MORE.

CHAPTER 24
Satan's ~~Apology~~ Analogy

"Your Honor, the prosecution has one other witness, but I would point out that the "defense" has decided not to cross examine your Son, who will now take the oath and the stand."

Having said that, the prosecutor disappeared, startling everyone paying attention. Within seconds, while murmurings still hung in the air, a man appeared where SHe had been standing. He spoke: "Placing my left hand on the *Bible* and raising my right hand, "I do solemnly swear to tell the truth, the whole truth and nothing but the truth, so help me, God?"

"Thank you. Take the stand, please."

"Objection, your Honor, the "defense" did not know the Yang Essence of the prosecutor herself is the Son who would be called to testify. We were expecting another Son. We would like to withdraw our refusal of cross examination."

"Denied! You have maligned this Son forever and He graciously has held his peace, according to my Will. Anyway, you know we have more than one Child. At one time, we even thought of adopting you. Though, I must say, that's hard to imagine now. Please, go ahead, Son, and speak your piece. You have earned it."

"Thank you, Dad, Mom… ahem… your 'Honor.' Since neither the prosecution nor defense has any questions, I am here to offer an apology to hybrid humankind. I will keep it brief."

"Objection – we do have questions!"

"Counselor, how conveniently you forget you were just overruled. Now, you will please respect the witness, as I ordered. Continue, Son."

"Make no mistake; we Children logically are disappointed by the ways and means of Egod. He insults both your WILL and Grace. It is through this summary proceeding that we are trying to impart a much vaster knowledge to hybrid humans regarding their unique species and situation. In that regard I would start by filling in some background as to how both the species and situation developed.

"'Eve Illness' (eve-ill) is a result of God's perfect design of the body's instinctual id which automatically tries to protect the body, of which the brain is a vital part. The id and ego (or personal god aspect) have become partners wielding influence on the hybrid brain, causing it to interfere with the tiny soul. Individual id/egos and society as Egod have convinced nearly every individual spirit that I - Satan - one of God's sons - is trying to deceive them by tempting people to do the wrong thing.

"Now: addressing our wider, hybrid audience; if you have read the *"Deepy Dog"* book about Egod, then you know the id is an organism intended by God to act as a protective/immune system to guard the Human entity from dangers both inside and outside its body. It also carries out some other autonomous functions of the physical entity. Id also is programmed to update id-self to act instinctively to dangers and opportunities in its environment by whatever means work to keep its host functioning autonomously.

"The word 'environment' includes the body's interior, in which full COG Mental Cells took charge of humanimals so that COG cohabiting them could Co-Create a Spiritual replica of the total Human form for God's Heavenly use. That was during the so-called Perfect Human generation. The id was aware of that presence within the so-called "Third Eye," or pineal gland, but COG Mind could not be "hacked" by id, whereas its tiny homing soul could be unduly influenced when COG stepped away during humanimal mating cycles. That Perfect Humangel generation ended long ago. The id/ego later was able to take control of the hybrid generation that is the current human species.

"The hybrid generation began with Adam and Eve. It had essentially the same goal of creating Humangels for God's use in the Otherealm. But, rather than having indwelling COG, hybrids would need Otherealm Over-Souls to guide their 'tiny' essence of former homing souls to achieve what full COG had done in the past. The id interfered with the tiny O'Soul process from the outset of all hybrid gardens and for that same reason very few such gardens are yielding moral fruit on a majority basis.

"Regarding Larray James' efforts working with COG on your behalf to co-create the book in which this court is a vital part, I would just say "job well done," especially considering how difficult it can be to explain new concepts that sometimes are expanding old concepts already cemented into one's thinking. In this case it almost would seem impossible, so of course along the way some readers just gave up even wanting to understand. That's unfortunate, but perhaps they will change their minds at some point. Perhaps some will conjure the patience and fortitude to give the work a second or even a third try. God will take note of that determination.

"Here is what humans must realize: if they work with God, they loosen id's hold on their brains and thereby strengthen their tiny souls. The id can only _id_entify ego brains that primarily communicate with the world as an autonomous entity unrelated to God Mind. That being the case, the id's electrochemical schema can be taken advantage of by a tiny soul that keeps God in mind on an almost constant basis. That also allows the O'Soul to become more involved. Such consistent moral thinking can affect some brain neurotransmitters in creating and maintaining moral influences. Scientific details would be too involved for most readers; so we will leave it at that.

"The id lives in fear of godly thinking. The brain/ego can be said to be in an id state whenever it does not feel the presence of God within its subconscious mind. People just do not know how imperative it is to keep God in mind, even subconsciously through their tiny soul. In a God or moral state of mind, the id makes itself scarce. Id learned that was necessary during its time in perfect Human Gardens. Sadly, these days the majority of people live under id's influence on a relatively permanent basis, rendering them the mortal "indiv_id_uals" they think they are. Id/ego takes credit for their _id_entity through id's own protective mechanism. Effectually id/ego is saying, "I am my own creator," and therefore autonomous, with no need of answering to a higher authority. All hail the conquering 'id entity' with its masterful brain.

"The id never interfered with COG who cohabited Humans. COG never had ungodly thoughts. Without COG protection though, the tiny soul must develop a morally inclined subconscious mind, capable of calling its COG Over-Soul into the mix. Moral thinking on a fairly constant basis would cause the id to purposely let go of the indiv*id*ual hyb*rid* of which it is a ruling aspect. This endeavor will take resolve and practice to become routine or habitual. However, you can become morally intelligent this way, and intelligent enough to want to be this way eternally.

"Meditation that consists of godly, moral thoughts interspersed with silence can cause the id to lose track of its prey. If the tiny soul continues a ritual of prayer and meditation on a regular basis, along with moral living and thinking, it can replace the 'id entity;' and the soul then becomes who you are. You then can respond to the moral urgings of your conscience more readily, even though the fight might be far from over because id never quits its programmed ways, especially since the ego brain often summons it to sensual pleasures without moral thinking.

"These are the ways and means a tiny soul has of ridding itself of id's control. The tiny soul must at first play a 'cat and mouse' game to lose its egocentric hybrid self by taking on the mantle of its godly self. Then the soul can become (enhance) God through much repetition of a new and steady moral ritual. If you don't practice 'moral intelligence,' id forces the ego aspect of the brain to serve the whole fused body organism in a co-protective role with id. That shuts out the tiny soul's efforts to clone or co-create a viable inner self, meaning a spectral pattern of Othereal Spirit which develops inside each person according to the strength of its core character essence. It forms within the whole of the body as an unfused spirit that one might sound similar to a nuclear or subcutaneous polymeric membrane. It is a spirit copy of your total physical form, to include the brain with stored loving and moral memories only and no others.

"If the spirit is a morally influenced form, it will have a certain amount of potential to grow as an angel when it leaves the physical realm for the Othereal or heavenly one. Or, with very little moral fiber, the shape can become a ghost-like specter, instead of a potential angel. In any case, it cannot be measured in the physical world, even if it sometimes can be seen momentarily. Many ghosts reincarnate eventually – God willing. If they go to hell, they can remain there indefinitely. Those without enough loving, moral essence just evaporate, as they are of no use to God.

"One DNA turning point in the forbearance of hybrids toward moral thinking came at the time of the *"Old Rugged Cross,*"* which my brother/sister volunteered to bear. Since then, many sincere Christians have been trying to spread the word regarding the gracious offering Jesus Christ made on our Parents behalf, so that tiny souls might be saved. However, because of id/ego and Egod, that word 'might' has become a mighty big hurdle and one that most people are not clearing in the only way possible - through moral values, ultimately those aligned with Christian teachings. *(hymn)

"Now, I feel yet again obliged to tell our audience - including the defense team across the aisle - please understand your 'tiny' minds can neutralize that id/ego beast within you. In fact, some of you should use your souls now, otherwise you may not succeed in navigating – not my opinions – but my observations, as they are about to be unleashed on this pre-trial hearing. Many of you, however, will recognize this for the 'id/ego' test it is. Others of you will make snap judgments, followed by quick decisions that put you in even more harm from ego.

"Oh yes, you will be thinking hard, but will those thoughts be deep enough to include our most gracious Parents? This could be a final chance to earn some much-needed Grace. But, wouldn't you know - we have saved one of the most divisive issues of Egod's trial for elaboration here – his "politics." 'Politics' theoretically should be an honorable profession, but in practice it rarely seems to be. Yes, many public office holders going into their profession have had mostly honorable intentions until they realize how much they like the presumed power, prestige, financial security, and the opportunities for even more income if they are willing to make their own rules. Once all that is realized, they know they must above everything else get reelected, and many will do whatever it takes, but they should take the expression of "selling one's soul" much more literally. Instead, they often become bogged down in the reality of political "slag." Of course in your society, many of you, including current and future politicians, have waded in 'slag' for most of your lives."

"Your Honor, excuse me, but might we get a definition of 'slag,' as your Son intends it?"

"If I may, your Honor… I advise the counselor to please think of it as self-indulgent excrement. That is the polite term, but really in your vernacular it's "bull shit," or phony utterances for mostly immoral and/or self-aggrandizement purposes. Please excuse me for not being more precise, but if I may continue now, it is most unfortunate that the hubris of politicians, as major players for Egod, usually means ungodly, selfish actions aimed at primarily benefiting that individual, regardless of the consequences to the public good. I hope I am now making myself understood in your language."

"No need to get testy… it was a pertinent question."

"And now it has been answered. I will remind the both of you to address the Court and not one another. Please continue with your testimony, Son."

"Thank you. Let me just preface these further remarks by saying that most of you in the audience will not like what I have to say but most of you will hear me out, since we have come this far. If anyone has opted out along our journey, that does not present a problem for me or anyone else on this side of the aisle. We do empathize though, because we love all tiny souls and pray they co-create moral spirits with their Over-Souls.

"Now, regarding all the prior testimony, as well as the entire book test, I would ask - are those episodic adventures of a good dog among "aliens" just more scary religious fantasy from a so-called "Jesus Freak" or, are we essentially speaking truth to those who have empowered themselves with id/ego – to all of you? Actually, the book represents the religious concept of an omnipotent God – scary to some – a promise to others; but do give thanks if you find yourself afraid of your own ignorance and/or denial of God. Please get over it right away and in the right way. You can do that by praying about it on a regular basis.

"Politics is one of the most important aspects of the story of Egod, but please understand that what I say here is a moral and not a political dissertation. In either case though it would be wrong to ignore the importance of politics in your lives or the obviously terminable life of your planet, graciously on loan to you and the politicians to whom you have entrusted it. Politicians and their consort of selected or appointed advisors unfortunately, as a whole, are the more gross aspect of Egod as a societal entity because it is their duty to "manage" society in a responsible way and they fail all too often by serving themselves above all else.

"Some politicians are psychological terrorists who use lies and slag on a continual basis, targeted at an audience they know will be the most willing to accept it, because they harbor similar brain sets of greed, bitterness, and hate. Thank God the majority is not included in each of those id/ego categories. However, all too many persons make up a "base" of haters primarily for what Larray calls the Gangsters of Powertics, or 'GOP' – a once respected "Grand Old Party" now dumbed down to a base of low intellect and "free-wheeling" egos, willing to lie, cheat, steal and in some cases to kill or allow people to die unnecessarily. Some of them even allow the idiocy and hatred of white cops to go about the subtle business of culling, by killing, most any other skin color. Hateful, idiotic thinking is a pandemic, but not forever. The grossly infected will evaporate prior to Garden Gaia.

"The bias on behalf of a bleeding-heart moralist named Jesus Christ might seem interminable to some of you – but many fewer now than those first sitting down with the book's co-author who prayerfully professed to speak for our Parents through his work. COG partnered with this co-author in order to show you just who you really are. Make no mistake; God does know you – even below the depth of your own sub-thinking, which you often refuse to recognize. Catch yourself at it and refute it when it is evil. Change it through prayer and morality with your soul in charge!

"This moral assessment of humankind at this stage is not aimed at political philosophies, per se. It focuses rather on the nothing short of ferociously disingenuous or otherwise evil tactics – even strategies - used to underwrite and carry out one's personal ambitions and beliefs by some, not all, so-called public servants. It would be much better for them and you if they would but serve God first in order to serve best. They couldn't care less.

"For examples of immorality, I will focus primarily on the nation that prides itself the most, as regards virtually everything. As one of God's most blessed nations, it has far too long given itself over to taking credit for those blessings, offering little room for godly morals in its politics, other than superficially. Politicians care only to appease superstitious or otherwise foolishly-regarded constituents, whom they depend on for votes even as those politicians are the bigger fools, and have a supreme karmic judgment coming their way. They don't have sense to know that.

"Ascribed-to political beliefs in the so-called 'good ol' USA,' usually divide at the line that would specify which governmental duties come under the heading of the oft-maligned big, federal, "Constitutionally-chartered" United States – or, which governing responsibilities could and should be assumed at a local or individual "State mandated" level. Political games and maneuvering are carried out within the scope of those two "divides," with 'divides' the operative word in their tug of uncivil war. Very little progress is made in actually governing, since at least one of the two main political parties would rather play politics with an eye on the next elections. They generally are inferior when it comes to moral intelligence, and so being at a loss for Wisdom, Intellect, Logic, Love, and grace, they are incapable of good governance. That is why they are anti big-government. Most GOP Presidents have proven that, as well as so many Republican governors and legislators elected by slag-infused voters.

"What many citizens don't realize, but most politicians do, is there also exists a voter division level based on emotions, as reflected in the attitudes of brain-washed reactionaries - as contrasted with voters more apt to make thought-related, cerebral efforts to understand pertinent issues and situations and the actual character of their politicians. Yes, there is a moral divide, with godly attributes mainly in the morally intelligent minds of democrats in the USA - that "God-blessed nation" on which we now are concentrating, as it has been a leader for human rights for so long. How long can this now 'house-divided' system continue to stand and function as a democracy, as one nation – under God? Every non-democracy in the world is using cyber warfare directly against U-S citizens through social media. Greed-driven news and entertainment platforms also contribute to this war.

"Republicans long ago chose emotional voters in order to play to as many divisive issues as they could, by using spite, hatred, jealousies, envies, bigotries, fears, etcetera, against them. You heard that right; they deceive their constituents with lies and promises. They usually will stop at nothing to win their elections. Ethics is of little or no consequence to most Republican politicians. Obviously they would protest such a notion until they are red in the face, but that still won't make them honorable. I reiterate: we are not talking politics now, but rather moral intelligence. Of course we know those dullards likely will never approach any of this with an open, moral mind. Most are incapable of attaining moral essence and of course they refuse to see themselves as Egod.

"The more thoughtful type voters however don't always seem able to discern the honorable from the dishonorable among the field of competition, and so the political landscape is a quagmire at best, and with a growing number of would-be voters just preferring to distance themselves from the muck and slime – sadly essentially giving up on their system. So many politicians are viewed as slick, slimy, foxy, crafty, cunning and plain dishonest, and in that regard they fully represent the "anti-Christ" attitude of folly reflecting mankind's underlying evil.

"Some independent would-be voters are even being intimidated by the emotional, non-thinking, down-with-big-government politicians who are that way because of their own inability to govern intelligently. Egod has them under lock and key. Sadly for everyone, they are easy prey for the propaganda of bought brainwashing that tells them big government is everything that's wrong with "their" country. Big-Money advertising allows that message to be driven into some pretty thick skulls that eventually can learn to parrot their puppeteers and spread the hate of those same messages that are dredged through virtually every election cycle, ad nauseam.

"To somewhat re-phrase the situation: on one side of the dividing line you have reflexive non-thinking emotions purposely contrived by politicians and activated through psychological propaganda; while in the opposing lineup there are higher-IQ, political think-tank types along with some pseudo-psychologists attempting to play the voters more subtly, even as virtually every would-be voter is trying to get a handle on the truth, which is being spun in all directions. Of course some politicians tell the straight-up truth, but most politics smell of the bowels of swamp creatures. Unplug the id/ego drain; clean out the immoral swamp scum and refill it with moral intelligence.

"These political party divisions are purposely condoned and cordoned off by each set of politicians as "their" people. The voters who can be "psyched" through 'feelings' get a particular brand of "slam-bang, sock 'em in the jaw, kick 'em in the ass" politics, to which they best can relate. This is the brain-washed "re-Republican party," or fringe radical fake-patriotic, America-can-do-no-wrong, gut-instinct, flag-waving, gun-toting, in-your-face, self-righteous "heart of America," consumer/voters who are courted by those politicos most polished in the art of slag-slinging, because it is how they were raised and it's the good ol' God-fearing, love-it-or-leave-it American way – by God! This is the crude, rude, louder-than-you-are party and therefore must be right to go to the trouble of having - or in some cases faking - such emotional, self-righteous but non-Christian values that are not in the least manner 'by God.'"

"You're depressing the hell out of me," said a voice from the defendant's table.

"People must repress hell in the first place, so that it does not depress them because of their own stupidity."

"ORDER IN THE COURT!" Gentlemen, I know I won't have to tell you again to contain yourselves."

"Your Honor, I apologize. Hopefully though, I'm not being too subtle with anyone whose ways simply are just irrationally and ungraciously out-of-order with you on a more permanent basis. It's just that so many id/ego self-gods are think-alike voters because of brain-washing Bot* designs that confuse them through the filth of politics to the extent they just identify with the simplest, loudest and most hateful party. They can relate to such raw attitude as a result of their feeling mistreated by a system they have been led to believe is going to somehow work for them, judging from the lies told every election cycle.

*(Social networking bots are sets of algorithms that take on the duties of repetitive sets of instructions in order to establish a service or connection among social networking users.)

The real system in control is the one manipulating them as they just continue taking the word of some sham artist with whom they would identify because of whatever emotion they can be made to feel if you squeeze them hard enough where it hurts - meaning in whatever hateful prejudice they favor the most. A "white-skin pity party" is quite often the favorite grievance of follow-the-hater cults.

"These emotionally-inflamed partisans are told over and over they are right and the other side is just plain pro-big-government, aka job-killing, baby-killing, anti-gun and anti-American wrong; and having heard it for years, if not decades, they believe it. And their politicians know spiteful voters want to believe that and most any other indecent slag they can invent against the liberal "socialists" whose hearts really do bleed for those very hateful voters and the democracy they are ripping to shreds. The Gangsters of Powertics appear not to care they are creating the potential for a monstrous backlash that could unleash hell between their side and "the other side," even possibly extending into war in the wider world. Ignorance has no boundaries. WILL and Grace have moral boundaries set by God.

"Violence could happen between parties of any affiliation if one party is being taught all genres of hatred. Hatred is the backbone of radical Islamic terrorists who are not true Islamists at all – but rather just idiotic, propaganda-believing killers – much like white-supremacist racists – many of whom claim to be Christians. Let me just say, your honor, if ever you are ready for another Armageddon, you have many volunteers to light the fuse. If you do let that happen, maybe you can blast the stink from this world, the way you once had to wash it clean with oceans of water pouring from the skies. And as outraged as I seem to be, all of you should know a perfect God has no temper. SHE merely does what SHE knows needs to be done.

"That more morally brighter, political "other side" meanwhile knows with little doubt that so-called "Big Money" has bought the USA's political system in the country where everything is for sale, including souls – even so-called evangelical, truth-dodging souls who would like to set the world on fire for their own God-awful reasons. We Children, as you know, stand ready to help you destroy this world out of love, to allow you yet another beginning. On the other hand, we know you are capable of much more love and graciousness than anyone and so we pray an Apocalyptic, but painful, change will work in place of a fiery Armageddon that destroys pretty much everything.

"Back to politics: the wisest voters are a pragmatic bunch and quite okay with big-but-efficient government. They need the stability for their stock market investments. The 'Stock Market' itself might be in favor of greedy big businesses that would prefer to regulate themselves – if at all - in the hope of increasing their wealth. It would seem any number of greedy hybrids have no compunction in destroying the planet as they pursue their money god. In the meantime, it is being used by some oligarchs as their personal playground. Short-sighted "rich-at-any-cost" greed mongers don't see their immediate futures endangered and they refuse to think much beyond their own grandchildren, if they would go that far.

"Even so, it is the big business, greed-monger side that ironically supports the *"basket of deplorables,*"* - who *"cling to their bibles and guns.*"* These gun-toting voters do not and cannot seem to realize their politicians and oligarchs are hypocrites and treasonous to God by ignoring the loving, moral ways Jesus Christ tried to teach, such as *'Turn the other cheek;' 'You are your brother's keeper;'* and *'Blessed is the peace maker, because his is the kingdom of God.'* But some politicians and greedy business types encourage an ignorant public, easily persuaded by sales pitches or propaganda. *{two separate comments a couple of American politicians may regret having said; respectively Hillary Clinton and Barack Obama}

"Does not-following the afore-cited Jesus Christ moral teachings make you irredeemable? It very well might, if some of you so-called evangelical "leaders" believe you are wiser than Jesus and possibly depending on whether your evangelical politicians are willing to hoax/coax you along for the votes. What does your id/ego brain have to say? (Every hybrid has one.) Perhaps it is telling you that Satan and his brother, Jesus, just don't know what the Heaven or hell they are talking about?

"Fret not, "real Americans;" sooner or later another would-be dictator will tell you what you are supposed to *think* – if you *feel* you are not hearing the truth now. While you wait, pray that God's WILL and Grace finally will speak to you in a way SHE would have it. Despite your feelings, God will speak in the only way SHE does and that is morally, even if it comes down to your eternal demise through denial and ignorance of her Essence.

"Now if you believe a house divided can still stand, take another hard look at the sectarian violence around the world, or just continue with the vitriol your self-worshipping, self-righteous politicians have fomented for their own personal gains, through the financial support of their puppeteers. Those self-serving egos have nothing truly righteous to say about Jesus Christ* unless it gets them votes.

"We are tired of preaching to you, but none of us COG is tired of trying to teach what God requires of you. Of course, many of you are tired of hearing *her* story, still unaware of how much gratitude you owe a God who cares enough to put us through all this for the sake of your under-developed spirit-souls.

"'Moral intelligence' is what this discourse is all about. That's it, and teaching about morality must include teaching about its evil opposite also, and that has been, and still is, my job. The tone of this dialogue also is required for – how would Jesus put it: '*Vipers like you.*'

"We COG, along with our hybrid human author, thank you for caring enough to listen to a Son of God preach to you on the virtues of his noble, loving, gracious Parents – even that Son whom most of you were led to misjudge and scapegoat and who now is placing the blame for your sins right back where it belongs – in your laps. Most of you are innocent in your belief that I am guilty of evil. I, and my mate, will continue to forgive you, but that will not relieve you of any karmic debt owed our Parents.

"Now, I would just like to say our Parents always know exactly where we COG stand on every issue – and that is with them. I am not here looking for vindication – from whom? There is no one apart from God. My Parents have no reason to love me any less than all their Children and Humangels.

"I and my mate Nasat, along with our brother and sister, Jesus and Christ, and all other Mental Cells of God are at home in that Otherealm of the Holy G'host - that peaceful, loving, and trusting Holy Spirit, which subconsciously "lives" as the very foundation of the Parent's Child, affectionately known as Junior. So, I would say to those faithful servants of God within this temporary material abode, I am not asking that you change your ministries on my account. Belittle and judge me as always, if you truly believe it serves your calling. I am as secure as any Child of God could be. Do what you think is best for God, in the long run; and as always, you will be guided through your sincere prayers and faith, so that all things work to God's benefit and glory.

"Thank you, your Honor, for this opportunity to serve once again in my job of bringing evil to the forefront, so that prayerfully it finally may enlighten some people enough to re-COGnize you. That 'evil' still is no less than the whole of mankind's phony self-made god - derived from the old serpent brain survival function of id - coupled with the extremely misguided brain function known as ego, which together created their societal monster "Egod," as a material icon to replace you. As Jesus Christ once said, '*... they know not what they do,*' and yet because of our diligent efforts to guide them, they no longer will be excused of their sins of ignorance and denial, except through fervent seeking of your Grace through enlightenment. That of course will require humility on their part, and so sadly again, many are being called but few will be chosen.

"Still, you are to be praised your Honor, that this ego beast is exposed and I am happy to have my say on your behalf. I am, always have been, and will forever remain a Son and Daughter of God – a Trangel, hosted by Junior's Holy Spirit within your Heavenly Home. I truly honor and thank you, Father and Mother. I also thank my mate, Nasat, and our loyal Apprentice Assistants as well;

<u>AMEN</u>."

IIIIIIIIIIIIIIIIIIIIIIIIIII

CHAPTER 25
<u>Rest</u> <u>Assured</u>

"And I thank you, our good and faithful Child, for your loyal, loving, gracious, logical, wise and intelligent service, as always.

"Now... I find the defendants temporarily guilty as charged, and continue their sentences to life on Earth, or in purgatory or hell, awaiting permanent judgments, and since that won't be long; I will simply suspend these proceedings until then.

"Still, we have two more items, one procedural and one for my deep, judicious, prosecutorial daughter, Nasat, who is back now in place of her mate: My dear, I am now assigning Satan to your staff until the time of Garden Gaia, to continue his work as your assistant, as your time has come again. You may take this gavel as a souvenir and hold it for me until that day of final reckoning. I know you will do as well as your mate has done in discerning those hybrid humans who need great scrutiny regarding their accountability to me. Of course most of them will accuse you of being the enemy just as they always accused Satan.

"Someday the eyes of good hybrids will be fully opened to the fact that you and your mate truly are my Children and as perfect as all the others. In the interim, do some more good on my account.

"Now then if you would, Daughter, take this note and read its statement into the records, please."

"Certainly your Honor; I do thank you for the personal assignment and I know my mate will appreciate the relief. This note indicates You are of One Mind, as always, and so your joint statement will be noted into the records, as I now read aloud to the court, your "Hybrid Trial" Epistle, dated December 18, 2012:

"To Whom It May Concern... our beloved Son and Daughter, Jesus Christ, will soon return to their Earthly mission. Of course, their Spirit-Soul's successor Trangel, Sam Antha, has tarried on the scene both in and out of material form, while awaiting her Co-Creators' return. Jesus and Christ will make their presence felt somewhat later. They will appear to hybrids as perfectly Human also, just as soon as I allow for Garden Gaia, sometime in the not too distant future, while giving time for a relatively small number of spirit-souls to take note of this gravest situation on Earth, and change themselves before it's too late."

"Your Epistle is so noted for your records, your Honor."

"Thank you, Nasat Satan."

"Objection, your Honor!"

"How many objections do we now have for this trial, Daughter - approximately?"

"We have roughly, nine-hundred trillion, three hundred, forty-six billion, four-hundred million, your Honor."

"What? That's crazy your Honor."

"That's the number of times that Earth's hybrid humans have objected to, or denigrated, God in one form or another, since Adam and Eve. Now then, counselor, what are you objecting to this time? I already know, but you want it in the record."

"That date, your Honor… your epistle is untimely now, as the year 2012 is long past – so why not record the most current date in your record?"

"You seem to have lost track of the time, which by now you should know doesn't exist for me. There is no such thing as 'now' in my world. Even where you exist, now always becomes 'then,' before it is ever recognized, and yet for me and my Children, now is forever unlimited by time.

"Of course, I live in every one of your so-called years, to include 'now, then, and always.' Spiritually I'm always in every aspect of my world and all parcels of the time I have given you. But I must say my Children are becoming pessimistic that most of you can be saved forever. That 2012 date has always represented a turning point for hybrids. It is when we took you into our final phase of an upgrade program to save your tiny souls. It will always remain the time the "Grace Era" began its final phase."

"Well, I mean 'come on' – how could you really be God and not give people a fair warning? The hybrid trial has gotten virtually no publicity. We have seen to that, and you don't seem to care. So, what I'm saying is - it seems you're being disingenuous."

"This trial and that date are not connected in the manner some might choose to believe. People have been warned all their lives about the end of this world at a time of my choosing. You have stood there and essentially called me a liar, so obviously you have no fear of me and underestimate me as usual. That is going to change and fairly soon, following what I consider a short reprieve. But, you are right; most people will not choose to understand this work until they reside in purgatory or hell, where it is mandatory reading, along with any updates, just as all written, moral works are subject to changes by me. They serve as appAngel lessons and part of our continued teaching.

"Now then - when my Lord Child Spirit-Soul known as Jesus Christ does appear in Earth's realm again, you will realize the '2012' date marked mankind's calendar in a way similar to when Earth's time went from "BC" to "AD." That 2012 date marks the beginning of the end of time as a material world marker for me. It starts the last phase of the 'Grace Era' in which I shall pick my final fruit for replanting in Garden

Gaia, as part of my eternity. Now – do you have anything else for me? You are fast running out of time."

"What do you consider a 'short' reprieve and a reprieve from what?"

"That would be a reprieve from another interim judgment day, and perhaps the permanent death for a lot of people still living then, or a quick turn-around reincarnation. Time is relative to eternity and therefore a 'short' amount of time could be one year for some or quite a few more for others, but it all means relatively soon for your momentary part of my world.

"That of course means that many of you will believe as always that God is giving her Self a way out of taking decisive action at a specific time. You just don't seem to get that I am always active in this aspect of my world. It would seem that those who reach their personal death markers are the only ones who know that; as they stand before me for judgment. It would be a huge miscalculation for you to assume anything about your fate. Whatever the amount of time turns out to be for each spirit-soul, it will be as I see fit, but rest assured when that time does come, there won't be any long-term mistaking it for exactly what it is. Now, I know you have something else for this court before we recess."

"Yes, I do your Honor, even though it appears you now are anxious to close this proceeding. We on this side of the aisle have held ourselves in check rather admirably I would say, considering all the so-called slag the prosecutor put before you. Now, you would also have us believe that Satan is a good guy after letting us think the opposite for so long."

"I let you think what you want to think. I have always done that. You certainly are proving that right now."

"Even Jesus condemned Satan and now you would hold us accountable. Quoting the book of Mark, Chapter Four, verses 14: *'The sower sows the word,'* and 15: *'And these are they by the way side, where the word is sown; but when they have heard, Satan comes immediately, and takes away the word that was sown in their hearts.'*"

"You are wrong as usual. While Jesus did seem to scorn his brother at times, it was only because biblical writers were misled regarding Satan and at times purposely so in remarks attributed to Jesus. Jesus only pointed out that Satan would be doing the job I assigned him... namely tempting people, to show who would fail their tests of grace and WILL power. Those by the 'way side' are not directly on the *'Word'* path, and having the word sown in their hearts or emotions is not the same as having and *'keeping the Word in the mind of their tiny soul.'* Those who don't keep *"The Word"* in mind are easily led to temptation. That's why they remain by the wayside where the word is sown. Just imagine, if you can, how many hybrids will remain at the wayside of the 'Word' presented in this very trial. Some of you here might study this id/ego test long enough to take it to heart before you turn around and dismiss it out of hand.

"That biblical verse you quoted says people "do hear the word," but then give in to sinful temptations, while electing to excuse themselves by blaming Satan as a scapegoat and as their way out of responsibility. You have heard the *"Word"* here before me and from Satan himself. It is up to you what you do about it, but of course I know already and it saddens me greatly.

"You also may recall that Jesus told his disciples: *'Unto to you it is given to know the mysteries of the kingdom of God; but to others in parables; [that seeing they might not see, and hearing they might not understand.']* You do not understand and likely do not know why *'Mark'* used the name of Satan; while *'Luke'* referred to the "devil" in repeating that parable you quoted. By now you should know the devil is society, and it would seem you did not hear a word that our Child, Satan, just told you only moments ago – forcefully and without subtle parables. Do not contend with me, little one, as you remain *'by the wayside'* even now.

"You, yourself, representing Egod, have stood before us here to proclaim you will do everything you can to keep the words of this interim trial from becoming widely known. People need to deal with their weaknesses and therefore these will continue to be pointed out to them and you quite specifically, allowing you to know without doubt just when and where you are lacking Wisdom, Intelligence, Logic, Love and a hybrid version of grace. Why do you suppose the *"Lord's Prayer,"* directed to God, renders the phrase: *'lead us not into temptation, but deliver us from evil'*? That's because it is a well known fact that Satan does tempt people on my behalf, but I sometimes answer that prayer and ask him not to, as I do know the sincerity of all who pray.

"His brother, Jesus, has his own job to do, as does my Son, Satan, whose role now will be taken by his mate, as He deserves a break from dealing with all mankind's evil. He also must prepare himself for the hell that awaits so many of you, and in which He will play a key role. All my Children, both Sons and Daughters, have responsibilities and while some are more heralded than others, each one stands just as glorified before me as any of his or her brothers and sisters."

"Yeah, well, we just want to go on record as saying we still don't believe you really are God and we never will, no matter what you say or do. We are too logical and sophisticated for any of that. And NO, I will not mince words with an alien who is said to be the very definition of the "Word" and the big 'O' Originator of everything that is. Talk about stupidity. But I will say this: as aliens from another world, you really have come up with a master plan for taking over this planet, so I give you credit for that bit of cleverness anyway. You actually thought you could fool us by making us appear as idiots who somehow should be ashamed of ourselves for producing the goods and services and jobs needed and appreciated by our people. And frankly we think this trial was way too critical of republicans. Why not just admit you are a far-left socialist – a 'bleeding-heart' liberal with an agenda to take more taxes from the rich to give to the poor and downtrodden? You would never qualify to be on any Wall Street firm's Board of Directors.

"Anyway, the prosecution has been very subtle at times in trying to paint us all as stupid, especially in trying to lead us away from the truth that you really are a bunch of aliens even though you would propose to make that idea a laughing matter and point of absurdity regarding our intelligence.

"Well, we are not fooled by any of this and if there is a hell, we would suggest you go straight there now! That's all, and that is being nice. You should see us when we really get mad, which we will - just as soon as we see your first space ships. You have been warned. We are not fools. We are republican patriots and evangelicals and proud of it. And by the way – when will you ever "appear" to us from behind your cloaking curtain, "Oh mighty Wizard of Alien Weirdness?"

"If ever you were to see me in your present condition, it would mean your instant annihilation, but I will see each of you again when your time comes to personally appear in my chambers. Counselor, you and everyone else on either side of any aisle or issue have always been "on record" with me, so none of that disparagement was really necessary. You just wanted to be on record with your base followers and now you are. Anything else before you announce your candidacy for President?"

"No!"

"You are forgetting something very important."

"Really? - Just a moment please while I consult with my colleagues."

"Time still is of the essence, but not for much longer."

"You are right, and it seems your Son took so much of it, I forgot He had some earth-shaking news to reveal, which He also apparently forgot."

"He is perfect. You are far from it. He knew I was going to re-call to the stand, another daughter/son – that one who has hosted this whole procedure via TelepVision within her TranShip. He and She are still under oath, and so again we welcome to our forum, Eno and Shel Mai. They have something quite pertinent to reveal. Please proceed."

"Thank you, Mother and Father. I have some news I received a short time ago from Satan, and now I ask your blessing in revealing it to the world."

"You of course have that. Please continue."

"It is in regard to the tinys onboard this craft and others within the fleet, as well as those inside Mars and elsewhere. They do in fact contain advanced DNA/RNA that will cure those allowed to reincarnate in Garden Gaia. Hybrid humankind's id/ego problems will be rectified. That will clear the way for those final incarnations to thrive in a new era of perfect Humans who, along with their COG guardians, will produce Humangels for God Jr's Heaven.

"I trust everyone who knows GOD also knows SHE could have made this happen at virtually any time, but SHE knew hybrid humans needed a good dose of the reality they brought about. Granted that hybrids were not to blame for the whole Eden situation, but when they chose evil over good, God already knew they would need and benefit from suffering of their own making. They also would benefit from humility of God's making, so their spirit-soul mates would be accepting of her moral laws, which SHE must have for their eternity. Of course, anyone who doesn't begin now to live morally may not be admitted into Gaia. At any rate, they must prove themselves psychologically moral before their physical and spiritual dichotomy is removed and their genetic structure is modified to delete id/ego.

"Included in our primary news is that Marsian Humangel brothers and sisters helped us attain the DNA/RNA mixture we will use to cure hybrids, and for this we owe them a deep gratitude. A combined genetic formula consisting of polar neutral Marsian humanimal stock and an Earthite variety gave us the breakthrough we needed to "unwed" hybrid id from ego. This formula will be used for humans who serve in Garden Gaia and who deserve to attain God Jr's Heaven for eternity. It also will serve some tiny souls who reincarnate before then.

"If one chooses to think this is a Marsian or otherwise alien plot to take over "what?" - then one should be feeling pretty foolish if they have any wisdom at all. If not, one's chance for salvation is outweighed by one's dimwittedness.

"Thanks to all of you who should be thanked, and God will personally tell you at some point who you are and why you have our gratitude. In the meantime, I thank you for your patience in reading our hybrid/dog friend's long and wondrous tale, assisted as he was by a couple of CHIP mates.

"Jesus Christ also shall personally thank you in Gaia, as you render gratitude to him and her; and you may warrant a "no problem" from Nasat Satan at some point as well. By then, you and your Humangel Mate will have the WILL and Grace to say thanks, even though SHe considers no apology necessary.

"All God's Children, of the Trangel or Humangel variety, want me to assure you that God eventually will render some of you as our brothers and sisters. Now, with a closing bow of acknowledgment to my Parents, I conclude our revelations."

"Thank you. This Court is now declared in recess – but not for long – relatively speaking."

"ALL RISE!"

(Court reporter's note: None of the defendants rose, nor did their followers.) [It is unlikely they will ever 'rise' to moral essence.]

IIIIIIIIIIIIII
(Shel Note)

This work is not complete... God has someone else in mind to finish it. <u>You!</u>

Why would you need to finish this work? Because it is a book of each of your lives, not deaths - <u>IF</u> you all agree to share the 'One life' of God, so graciously offered. Finish this temporary work as best you can. Perhaps you will find the foregoing prelude to the rest of your life to be food for thought, and prayerfully nourishing, as you seek growth for life everlasting.

With God, there is no such thing as "false hope" – instead there is prayer, so don't ever give up. With God, anything is possible. Jesus Christ is living proof. Yes, this work requires a lot from you because to whom much is given much is required.

Pray that God will help you. SHE WILL. The One who created us will always be with you, so long as you ask. Think of the original message of salvation that Christ brought you and pray that God recognizes and remembers you as her Child someday. Praise God, in the name of Jesus Christ and Christ Jesus. Amen.

Oh, one more thing - that certain Humangel of whom my CHIP friends spoke – Christ Jesus created him/her to serve as her body which Christ and Antha will cohabit within the combined fused form of Jesus/Sam upon their return to Earth. It stands to reason, since Sam Antha is their perfect vessel. SHe has remained mostly in your solar system but will not show herself until the Gaia time comes. That's when Jesus and Christ will join Sam and Antha.

SHe will not arrive until after the Earth-cleansing process has begun - preferably by mankind, but if necessary through as many natural acts of God as it takes. May our Father/Mother have mercy on you, through her Grace? That is my prayer. Please pray that you become one with us.

Truly, and forever as SHE wills,

Shel

\\\\\\\\\\\\\\\\V//////////////
[PRAY WHENEVER YOU CAN.]
{WE PRAY IT WILL BE OFTEN.}

Author - author

The human author of this work is Julian Harkett, but he simply goes by 'Hark.' He prefers anonymity and has no aspiration to be in anyone's spotlight. He knows that "who" anyone "is," is defined by God, and only has meaning as it regards that person's relationship with God.

Hark agreed to provide this information under the "small a" author heading in order to point out again that this narrative is about each of us, as potential Children of God. The word 'potential' should mean positive/negative polarity, but in this case it means we have some very serious problems standing between God and us. Those problems go by our individual names. They separate us from God to the extent that we allow ourselves to identify with the egos wrapped up in those names, rather than with our Creator.

Hark prays it is obvious this book was not written for material gains. The book is a message he prays will be 'discovered' when God deems the time is right! Any material profit would be used by his heirs for good purposes. Primarily the only profit that counts will come each time a spirit-soul is saved for eternity. We pray it happens exponentially, as time truly is of the essence, because when lived in godly ways, just a tiny bit of it can translate into eternity. There is no bigger reward than that or any bigger loss for those who don't survive this material trial.

Hark hopes the messages of this work are delivered in ways that most of you can fathom. He knows that not everyone will understand all of it in just one reading. Many won't bother trying, while still others will say it is all fiction. Of course, there always will be anti-Christian and other extremists who like to confuse good with evil, in order to rationalize their own views so they might go on living with themselves. God gave mankind the knowledge of good and evil in the garden of Eden, therefore we each must take responsibility for our choices. Ignorance and denial won't serve as excuses or reasons. For God, they never did.

As hybrids, we all have much in common and in no wise does Hark consider that he is much different from anyone else. However, he does admit to being ill – by God's standard of moral perfection. That does not depress him though because he is a Christian – no, not a self-righteous supposed superior

"Evangelical" – but simply a Christian. You're either a Christian or you're not. You don't need any adjectives that separate you from other Christians. 'Christian' (i.e. Moral) essence is the only true Essence of God.

Hark gratefully accepts God's Gracious Gift of her Son's life as payment for his own karmic sin debt. God and her Child made that sacrifice, which no wise mind would refuse. All that is required in return is to make one's best effort at living wisely, intelligently, logically, lovingly, and graciously toward everyone else, especially with God in mind.

Hark also believes in saying "thank you, God; thank you Jesus Christ and all Children and Angels," and in his words: "Thank you, God, for your *Grace*. My own small portion thereof allows me to pray on your behalf for my fellow human beings. I pray you make each of us morally intelligent through your *Grace* and mercy – for our renewed and forever life with you. Amen."

Lina: (soul mate, writing on behalf of Hark, her Yang Spirit)

('Thy WILL be done, Lord')
{WITH MERCY AND GRACE}
Amen!

{Eno's Update}

As far as COG are concerned, the days of the hybrid era now are numbered to a relatively short period. How much time God considers as 'relative' is up to her, but as of a certain date in 2012, the "Grace" era began a countdown to God's Garden Gaia, which will open as an event designated as year "Zero." Year "0" will remain year zero for one-thousand years as it will mark the beginning of 'non-time' or eternity for those hybrids who survive from that day onward when time will no longer be referenced.

This final time period before 'Year Zero' is set aside as "exclusionary time," or a time in which people will decide to exclude themselves from God's life for eternity. They will do this by not making their most genuine effort at living moral lives from the moment they are intellectually capable of understanding the messages of this work. You should also know that ignorance of moral messages offers no excuse for immorality.

Of course we could have called this period "Inclusionary Time," but since the numbers will be greater in the excluded category, this is in "Memoriam." We pray you will change the category name to include yourself. God would include you, but if you do not choose her at some point during this exclusionary time period, this also will be your demise.

Every year since that 2012 date, hundreds of thousands of angelic tinys have incarnated into the Earth's population. All such tinys will stay here or return for the Gaia era of Jesus Christ. He/She (SHe) will not reveal herself to mankind prior to year Zero and the grand opening of Hearth's new Garden.

[The Apostle Peter wrote, *"Prophecy never had its origin in the will of man, but men spoke from God as they were carried along by the Holy Spirit" (2 Peter 1:21)*] {Judge this work as you will; but please know the author is not claiming to be a prophet.}

Jesus Christ will have more "truth-telling" later, so abide with God if you would ever know the full and perfect truth. Meanwhile, we hope you can appreciate this abbreviated version of God's oldest orthodoxy: <u>MORALITY</u>.

IIIIIIIIIIIII

{Prayer space for you}
Don't take it for granted;
Your life could end at any moment.

IIIIIIIIIIIIIIIIII

YOU ARE HERE – Y...

<u>AT</u> a fork in the road, with your life's biggest decision awaiting. You have godly directions now, but do you have the will and grace for eternal life and the wisdom to say "Thank you, God?"

It is time for you to write the rest of your story, but will you now include God as your Co-Author? SHE must be included as never before, if you would become a chapter in her "LOG* Book" forever. For just a moment longer, you hold the power of the quest: *'to be or not to be'*. *{Life Of God}

Keep in mind you are alive for a reason - even if your life is miserable. Live it morally and you could be happy knowing you are fulfilling a karmic fate and will soon move on with a cleaner soul slate; perhaps eventually to be worthy of salvation through God's Grace.

Your moral impurity is like a cancer to God. Therefore it must die or be cured. Since you are the host of that cancer you will die with it, unless you work with God to be cured.

Here is what it takes to cure you: Accept the tenets of this work as truth; Treasure a loving, peaceful life enough to want it forever, after you leave this material world. Live and love that life now as best you can.

You can live the tenets of this book through wisdom, intelligence, logic, love, and grace, all of which God will help you attain, so that you deserve eternity for the moral way you live now. It can be simple to understand, but as difficult to practice as you are willing to make it.

IIIIIIIIIIIIIIIIIIIIIIIII

In his book, "*Dark Nature* - A Natural History of Evil,*'" Lyall Watson notes that regarding one's genetic make-up, there exists a strange human behavior pattern referred to as 'spite.' He writes, '*... It is possible for me to help my brother indirectly by harming an unrelated competitor.*' He continues, '*I gain nothing myself. In fact, I might even lose, but go ahead anyway, perhaps in the hope of helping my brother.*' As a biologist, Watson then switches the question of such a peculiar behavior to how it might relate to animals, '*... The question is, could we expect an animal to harm itself merely in order to harm another more? And the answer seems to be, certainly.*' '*... An animal can increase its inclusive fitness by being nice to close relatives, indifferent to distant relatives, and antagonistic to strangers.*' Watson goes on to say, '*... If such antagonism takes little time or effort, if it costs the animal nothing, we can expect it to do a lot of it. But if the behavior is difficult or expensive, we can also expect him to be less quick to act, more deliberately and indiscriminately spiteful.*'

Watson also adds: '*... There is a lot of spite about, some of it perhaps just selfish in the sense that it does present some selective advantage to the actor, who succeeds as a result in gaining more food, more space, greater status or increased reproductive opportunity.*' *(copyright 1995 by Lyall Watson, published by Harper Collins)

Considering what Watson wrote, you might wish to consider the question: "Are some hybrids still just spiteful humanimals operating only with a brain and spirit energy, but without a tiny soul that can outreach to an Over-Soul, guardian Angel? Does anyone come to mind? Pray for them."

In closing this work, and irrespective of what is happening in the world at this moment, we leave you with two possibilities to consider: Antarctica could soon reveal some profound truths; but it may not, even though it holds some. Secondly; when Jesus returns, SHe might be Christ Jesus, rather than Jesus Christ or he/she could alternate his/her Yin/Yang polarities. They are indivisibly-dual polarities – not genders. He/She could alternate their one twi-polar self, without much, if any, change of their outward appearance. Think about that. You can if you have read this book; and you will know them as the Heavenly Trangel they are. They then will reward and entrust you with many more truths than this book holds.

(Romans 8:1, 3, 4, 5 and 6:
There is... no condemnation to them which are in Christ Jesus, who walk not after the flesh, but after the Spirit.* *[or spirit-soul]
3. For what the [Moral] law could not do, in that it was weak through the flesh, God sending her own Son in the likeness of sinful flesh ... condemned sin in the flesh; 4. ...That the righteousness of the law might be fulfilled in us, who walk not after the flesh, but after the Spirit. 5. For they that are after the flesh do mind the things of the flesh; but they that are after the Spirit the things of the Spirit. 6. ...For to be carnally minded is death; but to be spiritually minded is life and peace.)

//////////\\\\\\\\\\\\

{EPILOGUE}

APOCRYPHAL* GOSPEL TRUTH
"The Secret Gospel of Thomas"
*(Early Christian writings not included in the *Bible's New Testament*)

Most readers of religious literature need no introduction to the best-selling author – Elaine Pagels, who won the National Book Award, and the National Book Critics Circle Award for her work, "*The Gnostic Gospels.*" Ms. Pagels also is known for her books: "*Adam, Eve, and the Serpent*;" "*The Origin of Satan*;" and "*Beyond Belief*" (The Secret Gospel of Thomas), as well as other titles.

It was in Egypt in 1945 that about fifty early Christian writings were discovered; to include the writings of an author who either was the "Jesus Disciple" named Thomas or had very close ties with him.

We wish to quote Professor Pagels from her offering of the "Thomas" writings; and then expound a bit more on our own book's meaning and how we might interpret a few of the sayings of Jesus, offered in "*The Gospel of Thomas.*"

Many such early Christian texts are considered "sacred" in the eyes of some believers. Thus, we would share with you a most insightful view from Ms. Pagels' own personal thoughts about orthodox Christianity in general and then offer a few of the disclosed 'sayings' of Jesus, as offered by Thomas, who is portrayed by some Christians as possibly the Jesus disciple with the Greek nickname of "Didymos," meaning the "Twin."

On page 184 of her book, '*Beyond Belief*,' Ms. Pagels quotes sociologist Peter Berger as saying – in part – '*… Christianity has survived for thousands of years as each generation relives, reinvents, and transforms what it received.*'

In the paragraph to follow that partial quote, Ms. Pagels writes:

'*This act of choice* (to relive, reinvent or transform) *then leads us back to the problem that orthodoxy was invented to solve: How can we tell truth from lies? What is genuine and thus connects us with one another and with reality, and what is hollow, self-serving, or evil? Anyone who has seen foolishness, sentimentality, delusion, and murderous rage disguised as God's truth knows that there is no easy answer to the problem that the ancients called discernment of spirits. Orthodoxy tends to distrust our capacity to make such discriminations and insists on making them for us. Given the notorious human capacity for self-deception, we can, to an extent, thank the church for this. Many of us, wishing to be spared hard work, gladly accept what tradition teaches.'*

I will conclude quoting Ms. Pagels with her statement: *'But the fact that we have no simple answer does not mean that we can evade the question.'* – That question being 'How can we tell truth from lies?' – Other than taking the easy way out of allowing someone else (as in orthodoxy) to decide their minds are better and more guided by God than our own?

We offer our own interpretations (to follow) of a number of the "Jesus" sayings from the Apocryphal* *Secret Gospel of Thomas*. There's a catch of course; that being that one must read and understand the concepts in this book, in order to have proper context. God bless you if you make the effort. Too many won't.

However it must first be noted that just because we share a tiny bit of Ms. Pagels *"Beyond Belief"* (highly recommended) commentary with you, it does not mean she agrees with anything else we have written in this book. She did not get a chance to read this total work prior to publication, and therefore can let us know if she wishes to be excluded from it and we of course will oblige.

{Even if you have read our particular take on the matter of religion, some of the Jesus sayings in *'The Secret Gospel of Thomas'* will seem cryptic to you. Having read our book though, we hope you can put these sayings into a meaningful context as relates to our text. If you have not as yet read this book and are not sure you will read it, you won't have some much needed information for understanding this section. If your curiosity is not piqued by reading what follows, then you really _need_ to read what comes beforehand, to re-set your frame of reference. Even so, we will point the way for others, by putting our interpretation in parentheses, as follows...}

Jesus Saying # 11: *'This heaven* (material existence) *will pass away, and the one above it* (minor heaven, aka purgatory) *will pass away. The dead are not alive, and the living will not die.* (Time is no more. It is a moot, unneeded concept. What existed in *'time'* is no longer of consequence and those dead souls will never again be alive – no more reincarnations. Those alive in the "God Junior Brainchild" of Heaven are alive for eternity.) *During the days when you ate what is dead, you made it alive.* (It was alive in its role of keeping you alive as a physical entity) *When you are in the light* (Spiritual Heaven) *what will you do?* (The only sustenance you will need will come from God's Mental WILL and Grace) *On the day when you were one, you became two.* (Upon your body's passing, your integrated spirit-soul separated from your physical self) *But when you become two,* (as a spiritual entity of Yin/Yang twi-polar opposites) *what will you do?* (You will be one entity of a negative and a positive polar force. You could be an indivisibly-dual angel serving God as one of her eternally conscious Mental Cells and therefore polar-switchable at her discretion to suit her needs. What you do depends on how well your spirit developed.)

Jesus Saying #13: (Jesus said to his disciples,) *"Compare me to someone and tell me whom I am like."* (…Thomas said to him, *"Master, my mouth is utterly unable to say what you are like."* (Jesus said,) *"I am not your master. Because you have drunk, you have become intoxicated from the bubbling spring that I have tended."* (The preceding was stated in parable form because of the other disciples listening. But Jesus took Thomas aside and told him that He, Jesus, was {tending} "taking care of" the Christ Soul {bubbling spring} from which Thomas had drunk, meaning Thomas had become enlightened because he "was Co-Created" from within the body of Jesus. He also told Thomas that God had given him a Soul Mate {a Master} of his own, but he should only call her forth into physical form when he was sure no one was watching. They then should practice calling each other forward. In other words they should practice switching polarities, but only when they were certain no one could observe them, even though they looked identical.)

Jesus Saying #14: (Jesus said) *If you fast, you will bring sin upon yourselves. If you pray you will be condemned. If you give alms, you will harm your spirits.* (This saying speaks to hypocrites and implies that such ceremonies will not matter; as though everything already is decided by God, especially as far as so-called *evangelicals* are concerned. Even so, God won't take away hope. SHE would rather they become sincere. If you're Christian, you don't need a label, as if you are superior to regular Christians or even Jesus him/her Self – {for shame}.)

Jesus Saying #15: *When you see one who was not born of woman, bow down and worship. That one is your father.* {COG co-Creator} (Neither Jesus nor Thomas, the Twin, was born of woman, but rather each was Co-Created by God's two opposing polar forces. Jesus Christ was born during the 'Big Bang' event. Thomas was Co-Created through the Mind/Body of the Jesus Christ Trangel, within the material world. Jesus and Christ "begat" Thomas as an inner COG Self-Replica of the fused outer spirit of Jesus. Both Thomas and his twin looked identical and quite similar to Jesus.)

(When the Spirit-Soul "pairing" was complete within the body of Jesus, the replicated twin Spirit named Thomas stepped out of the body and into the world, to be rewarded by God with a Perfect Yin Soul Mate *(Master)* of his own. They later would be christened anew in Heaven as Sam Antha, but since then have returned many times to the COG Outpost in and around the material world of Earth.) {Read this book in order to understand these interpretations. With prayer as guidance, many of you will find the ability.}

Jesus Saying #16: *"Perhaps some people think that I have come to cast peace upon the World. They do not know that I have come to cast strife upon the earth: fire, sword, war. For there will be five in a house: there will be three against two and two against three, father against son and son against father, and they will stand solitary."* (Standing solitary means neither side will compromise.) (Jesus made it clear that He hated this world. He hated it for what mankind as Egod is doing to mankind. He hated it for the ignorance and denial of his Parent's love and guidance. This author hates the world for the same reasons. We now have all the strife that Jesus brought with him at that time; so He had known we would be living with it until He returns for Garden Gaia, at which time He will bring peace to the world. That should be our constant prayer, with thanks giving.)

Jesus made his empathetic position for people quite clear in his *"Saying # 28: "I took my stand in the midst of the world, and in flesh I appeared to them. I found them all drunk* (an adverb in this case meaning uncaring) *and I did not find any of them thirsty.* (Seeking enlightenment) *My soul ached for the children of humanity, because they are blind in their hearts and do not see, for they came into the world empty, and they also seek to depart from the world empty. But meanwhile they are drunk.*

When they shake off their wine, {their unwillingness to understand} then they will repent.")

God has pure Children {Trangels and Angels} – who are cloncs of God's Moral Essence, such as the one known as Jesus Christ. Each 'one,' however also is two, consisting of polar opposite, liquid crystal energies in the Otherealm or electro-magnetic energies in the material realm. Thomas and his Soul Mate were one entity who became indivisibly-dual polar Essences upon arrival in Heaven. Normally a Humangel would depart with the COG who created it; however Jesus (with Christ as his Soul Mate) told Thomas and his Soul Mate to tarry in the material realm until He returned, which He did soon after her/his crucifixion. Thomas and his mate then went to Heaven briefly. They soon returned to Earth to await the next coming of Jesus Christ, who departed when they arrived to 'tarry' again as Christ had requested.

The "Entity" of Christ Jesus and his twin Spirit-Soul always will be the only Trangels begotten into the garden world as "passer-by" messengers sent to save us with the enlightenment of God's WILL and Grace operating within the physical realm. The pure Children Of God (COG) are here to save those who would recognize them, to be saved by them. It will soon be time to show themselves to those who have 'eyes to see,' with the enlightenment of WILL and Grace}. Otherwise, our Angelic sisters and brothers might be treated in ignorant fashion by those who would number among the forever dead by trying to harm our Heavenly benefactors.)

Jesus Saying #19: Blessed is the one who came into being before coming into being. (An Entity conceived within God Mind, before God gave birth to it {separated it from her main Self} as its own indivisibly-dual Mental Cell, with a twi-polar likeness to God's own polar opposite Minds of Mental energies. Thomas – the twin - was one such Entity, as was Jesus Christ. Other COG Mental Cells or Souls also were Spiritual entities, many of whom God made manifest in her physical world so that they would replicate their Spiritual forms and Mental forces inside material "cocoons," and then return those cloned forms as Spiritual Entities to her Heavenly abode as Mental Children Of God, in order to complete her "Brainchild" known as Junior.)

'... *For there are five trees in Paradise for you; they do not change, summer or winter, and their leaves do not fall. Whoever knows them will not taste death.* (Those five trees are:

1. Mother {Yin or negative Polar Mind};
2. Father {Yang or positive Polar Mind};
3. The Holy G'host {an annihilated but living Fundament of liquid crystal, that is the Heavenly God-Host for God's middle Child – consisting of indivisibly-dual Cells. Jesus called Junior's foundation "Living Waters."};
4. Self-aware Souls {Trangel and Humangel Mental Energy Cells}; and...
5. God Junior {the Conjunction of all indivisible, twi-polar Mental couplings or Cells of God's Brainchild} (Not tasting death means as an eternal Humangel Child Of God, you will never have any memory of existing in the hybrid material world. The totality of all your happiness will be held only in Heaven, even if some of it originated in the material world).

Jesus Saying #22: (Jesus saw some babies nursing, and said to his disciples) {*'These nursing babies are like those who enter the Kingdom.'*} (They said,) {*'Then shall we enter the Kingdom as babies?'*} (Jesus said,) {*'When you make the two into one, and when you make the inner like the outer and the outer like the inner, and the upper like the lower, and when you make male and female into a single one, so that the male will not be male, nor the female be female, when you make eyes in place of an eye, a hand in place of a hand, a foot in place of a foot, an image in place of an image, then you will enter [the Kingdom}.* (Translation: The 'two into one' means a firm coupling between the tiny Yin or Yang soul/O'Soul and the polar opposite brain, so that together they use the fused spirit body as a cocoon for structuring an angel spirit {e.g. primary cell membrane – outer to inner and inner to outer – chemical to electrical} replicating all required aspects of the physical organism as a spirit body, just as COG did with perfect Humans in Gardens prior to the imperfect hybrid generations.

In the perfect generation prior to hybrids, COG begat replicas of themselves within Human sanctuaries. Such Co-Created mature Angel Spirits of COG Mind could depart the body upon completion to transcend into Heaven with its COG Host, adding to the Spiritual Essence of the God Junior Entity.

Hybrid humans however, must be judged after each lifetime as regards their continuing status, whether into reincarnation or appAngel apprenticeship that could lead to the permanent, Heaven-proper home of God Jr. Too many spirits however are too weak for such a transition and must receive counseling in a more ghostly shade closer to the material world, perhaps with a chance of reincarnating for better results.){During the Perfect Human era, replicated Spirit-Souls could do as their Co-Creator wished. That also was the case with the Perfect Humangel that Jesus Christ Co-Created. Thomas, however, was meant to be an integral aspect of the Christian era and so was given a Soul of his own, as chosen by God.}

This book outlines details of the most likely hybrid transitions]

Jesus Saying #37: (His disciples said,) *"When will you appear to us and when shall we see you?"* (Jesus said) *"When you strip off your clothes without being ashamed, and put them under your feet like little children and trample them, then [you] will see the son of the living one and you will not be afraid."* (In other words you will no longer have sexual desires, but your thoughts will concentrate on your Creator. Adam and Eve were afraid to have the Lord God see them naked because they felt lewd after physical fornication, and so they hid from him when He called to them in the garden of Eden. They knew He would see them for the unfaithful souls they were. "Lust," as "evil," had entered the minds of the hybrid couple and they were afraid. Since then, sexual lust has been the main deterrent to moral thinking and it is much worse now than ever it has been. Unfortunately, it is not the only evil exposed as the moral ignorance of the self-righteous id/ego.)

The foregoing interpretations of several *'Jesus Sayings'* from the apocryphal *"Gospel of Thomas"* are just examples of how one can rationally think for oneself – with God's guidance of course.

Hopefully you can take the guidance given to this author and conceive of even more 'Wise, Intelligent, Logical, Loving, and Gracious alternative possibilities as to how God lives in her realm, with all parts of her Self; perfecting and keeping as many of her self-aware aspects as is possible, with her Co-Creative help.

Jesus Saying #29: *'If the flesh came into being because of spirit, that is a marvel, but if spirit came into being because of body, that is a marvel of marvels. Yet I marvel how this great wealth* (of spirits) *has come to dwell in this poverty* (of hybrid bodies). (Jesus is reflecting this way for the purpose of underscoring the amazing opportunity hybrid humans have been granted by God. He emphasizes that flesh came into being because of spirit, as every bit of materiality and all else comes from spirit, even if "densely" fused into matter. And yet He seemed to marvel that God would entrust tiny spirit souls to such a poor species as hybrid humans. Even so, He understands her love and Grace for them, even if they refuse to love her , or can't love her through ignorance and denial.)

'Jesus Saying #114: *Simon Peter said… Make Mary leave us, for females are not worthy of life. Jesus said, 'Look, I shall guide her to make her male, so that she too may become a living spirit resembling you males. For every female who makes herself male will enter the Kingdom of heaven.* (Yes, and the converse also is true for Humangels when it comes to polarity {gender} switching, but Jesus would not provide such detail in that time of "superior" males (Yang polarity) being in a switch mode to (Yin polarity) females." [Explained in this book]

Indivisibly-dual Mental Cells, aka Children Of God, are known <u>not</u> as 'gender,' but rather as positive and negative polar opposites and switchable at God's discretion from inner to outer or conversely.) [*Noteworthy*: Thomas and his Soul Mate would later change their names to Sam Antha, after being confirmed in Heaven as Trangel clones; and since their godly nuptials and christening they have transformed between the material realm and the Otherealm many times. And, by the way, both did appear at separate times as 'the disciple that Jesus loved.']

{Now, let's pause our story on a musical note}

If you know God's within you
In a soul kin to Jesus
Sing Glory Hallelujah,
Mighty fine and Amen!
Mighty – mighty fine… and Amen!

If you want the soul that's in you,
To be born again with Jesus,
Be sure the life you're living's

Right with Christ,

Praise God in all her glory
Celebrate her story,
Sing Glory Hallelujah,
Mighty fine and Amen!
Just sing it out – Hallelujah!
Mighty-mighty fine and Amen!

If you know God's within you
In a soul kin to Jesus
Sing Glory Hallelujah,
Mighty fine and Amen!
Mighty – mighty fine… and Amen!

Praise God in all her glory
Celebrate her story,
Sing Glory Hallelujah,
Mighty fine and Amen!
Just sing it out – Hallelujah!
Mighty-mighty fine and Amen!

(Instrumental bridge)

If you want the soul that's in you,
To be born again with Jesus,
Be sure the life you're living's
Right with Christ

Make it a true thanks-giving
To the one who saved you
Thru the Loving Grace of her son
Just shout it out – Hallelujah!
Thru the Loving Grace of her son

If you know God's within you
In a soul kin to Jesus
Sing Glory Hallelujah,
Mighty fine and amen!

Praise God in all her glory
Celebrate her story,
Sing Glory Hallelujah,
Mighty fine and Amen!
Mighty, mighty fine and Amen!
Just shout it out – Hallelujah!
Mighty- mighty fine and Amen!

(Original songs written by Thomas E. Alford:
"Your Old Love Game;" "The Downhill Bar;"
"The Shower Song;" and "Amen.")

We pray you continue to pray.

Pray like there's no tomorrow!

INSERT PRAYER – GET GOD AND CHANGE!

Pray there is no "ending" for you
and those you love, and those they love.
Pray for a transc**END**ence into Heaven.

IIIIIIIIIIIIIIIIIIIIIIIII

TURN THE PAGE.
IF YOU'RE NOT THERE,
NOTHING IS!

'I'm not here to judge you.

I'm here to judge me; so

that I might be better prepared for

God's judgment someday.'

(The author)

NOTICE

And disclaimer:
THIS BOOK TEXT IS OFFERED UNDER A VARIETY OF TITLES AND COVERS.

www.ingramcontent.com/pod-product-compliance
Lightning Source LLC
Chambersburg PA
CBHW050905100426
42737CB00048B/3000